The King's School, Worcester

From 1541 into the 21st Century

Edited by Danny Payne

The King's School, Worcester: From 1541 into the 21st Century
Edited by Danny Payne

© 2015 The King's School, Worcester

First Edition 2015
Published by The King's School, Worcester
5 College Green, Worcester, United Kingdom WR1 2LL

A CIP catalogue record for this book is available from the British Library
ISBN: 978-09523-507-8-1

All rights reserved. No parts of this publication may be reproduced, stored in a retrieval system, or transmitted in any form or by any means without the prior consent of the copyright owner.

Printed and bound by CPI Group (UK) Ltd, Croydon, CR0 4YY.

In addition to material from individual contributors, the Editor has drawn on information provided by Caroline Roslington, Donald Howell and Galen Bartholomew, on research undertaken by James Bartholomew, and on existing histories of The King's School, Worcester:

A History of the King's School Worcester	(1936)	Alec Macdonald, MA
King's School Worcester 1541 - 1971	(1972)	Michael Craze, TD, MA
College Hall Worcester	(1981)	Michael Craze, TD, MA
The King's School, Worcester - and a history of its site	(1994, 1998)	Edited by Caroline Roslington
100 Years of the Cadet Corps	(2009)	Edited by Caroline Roslington
The King's School Worcester Boat Club Anecdotes and Memoirs	(2012)	Edited by Carol Bawden

A full list of contributors can be found on page 270 with references and select bibliography on page 274.

All proceeds from the sale of this book will be donated to The King's School Worcester Development Trust, Registered Charity Number 527530, for 'The Anniversary Appeal' for the Enduring Bursary Fund, which aims to provide funding for free places for forty King's Scholars in time for the school's 500th Anniversary in 2041, in line with the Statutes with with King Henry VIII refounded The King's School in 1541.

www.ksw.org.uk

The King's School, Worcester: a company limited by guarantee. Registered in England: Company Number 4776324.
Registered Office: 5 College Green, Worcester WR1 2LL. Registered Charity Number 1098236.

τὰ μὲν διδακτὰ μανθάνω,

τὰ δ'εὑρετὰ ζητῶ,

τὰ δ'εὐκτὰ παρὰ θεῶν ᾐτησάμην.

I learn what may be taught,
I seek what may be sought,
My other wants I dare
to ask from heaven in prayer.

School motto, taken from Sophocles

Contents

	Foreword	1
1	**The origins of The King's School, Worcester**	4
	Music at King's	10
2	**King's under the Tudors and Stuarts**	18
	College Hall	20
	Edgar Tower	31
3	**The 18th and 19th centuries**	34
	KSW Boat Club	42
	The Vigornian	46
4	**Bolland and the birth of the modern school**	48
	The buildings of College Green	56
5	**Chappel and Creighton - conflict and change**	74
	Cadets at Kings	78
	The Chappel Memorial Reading Room	90
	From Worcester Castle to the Creighton Memorial Gardens	94
	The King's School evacuation of the Second World War	100
6	**Post-war King's - rebuilding and development**	104
	Winslow Building	108
	Old Chapel	111
	Annett Building	118
	Wolfson Building	124
	Old Vigornian Club	134
7	**Junior Schools**	140
8	**King's at the end of the second millennium**	158
	The John Moore Theatre and Drama at King's	163
	A century of sport at King's	172
9	**Taking King's into the 21st century**	180
	School Archive	184
	Foundation Development Office	188
	School House - a new Library for King's	192
	The Art School	196
	Michael Baker Boathouse	204
	King's School Worcester Development Trust	210
	The Keyes Building - sports and performing arts centre	215

	Appendices	226
1	King Henry VIII's 1541-42 Statutes founding The King's School	226
2	Chronology of King's School events	229
3	Names and badges - the identity of the school	234
4	Headmasters and their deputies	236
5	The Houses at King's	238
6	Junior School Heads	240
7	School motto	240
8	School songs	241
9	School prizes	242
10	Heads of School	243
11	Sports Captains	244
12	Presidents of the Old Vigornian Club	248
13	Barnabas Group	249
14	2014 staff photos	250
15	The archaeology of The King's School	252
16	A photographic miscellany	263
	Index	266
	Acknowledgements	269
	Contributors	270
	Picture Credits	272
	References and **Bibliography**	274

Foreword

Simply to pass beneath the arch of Edgar Tower is to gain a sense both of the historic context of The King's School and its enormously privileged location. Re-founded in 1541 but the inheritor of buildings which are considerably older, the Foundation has at its heart scholarly traditions which were initially rooted in the monastic community which flourished here alongside one of England's great cathedrals. As evening light strikes the cathedral stone and College Hall is illuminated by sunshine there is a powerful sense of the long history of education at King's which this book celebrates, and of the Christian tradition which underpins it and which has been continuously upheld on this site since the seventh century.

To spend time at King's is to become imbued in its long history, whether attending concerts in College Hall beneath the Majestas or gathering in the Cathedral for assemblies or acts of worship. The surroundings of College Green, their tranquillity occasionally interrupted by the sounds of choristers playing cricket or climbing trees, are formed of buildings largely residential in character which give little immediate hint out of term of what is now their educational purpose. Visitors during the school day, however, gain an immediate sense of a vibrant and purposeful community where long traditions of scholarship continue to flourish.

From College Green it is also hard to appreciate the full extent of the senior school site, which has undergone a transformation in recent years and now, in the Michael Baker Boathouse and The Keyes Building, has two fine examples of modern architecture to set alongside the foundation's ancient beginnings. With the opening of its new centre for sports and the performing arts, named after my distinguished predecessor Tim Keyes, King's has again expanded its facilities and provided a stunning setting in

Matthew Armstrong, September 2015

which the next generation of actors and sportsmen and women can develop their talents.

Academic pursuits too have benefited from the site's development, with the conversion of School House at the heart of the school to provide a beautiful library and more recent work in Castle House to ensure that musical facilities are also state-of-the-art. New additions are also in evidence both at King's St Alban's, with its beautiful pre-prep facility, and at King's Hawford where the new Bartholomew Barn will provide a fitting setting for the productions of the future.

The inspirational surroundings in which those fortunate to attend King's live and work of course contribute to the feel of the school, but it is the pupils themselves who make it. 475 years on from its re-foundation the curriculum at King's has changed, and I fear that but rarely does the modern Headmaster's work involve the application of Latin 'polish' to his pupils in the mode described in the original statutes published as the first appendix in this book; but we hope that those who attend the schools of the Foundation still emerge 'proficient in learning' in the way envisaged all those years ago.

Certainly, although what is studied has been utterly transformed, the goals which underlie education here have not. It remains our hope that those who study here will develop a passionate interest in academic pursuits, and that this enthusiasm will continue to be nurtured and fed long after they leave the school. This love of learning must of course be combined with appropriate preparation for the modern world, and the blend of ancient and modern in our environment means that teachers at King's are wonderfully positioned to provide this.

Pastoral care of the highest quality remains central to our vision. Although no longer a boarding school, King's holds dear

Number 9 College Green, the Headmaster's house, 2015

to its heart the all-round care which makes such an important contribution to our pupils' development. The continuation of the house system in the senior school is enormously important in all of this, as is the supportive atmosphere of the Fourth Forms. This in turn builds upon the warm and welcoming atmosphere of our two junior schools, King's Hawford and King's St Alban's, where so much good work in building the confidence of our pupils is done.

Alongside its academic standing King's fully merits its reputation for excellence in activities beyond the curriculum. A glance at the successful sportsmen and women, musicians, actors and artists among our alumni is enough to furnish evidence of historical excellence in these areas, and they continue to thrive thanks in part to new facilities and in part to the dedication of the staff who support them. The vision of a wide-ranging education, combined with academic excellence and a strong interest in at least one extra-curricular sphere, is of huge importance to us here.

Crucial too is the spiritual development of our pupils, and their preparation for the roles they will play in the wider community. Our mission statement talks of preparing them to lead 'confident, fulfilled and unselfish lives', and the vibrancy of this vision today is encapsulated in the myriad charity events and in the engagement of King's in support of the local community. We relish our position at the heart of this city, and those who attend the school are keen to make their contribution to it.

My hope is that, for those who attended the school, this history will bring back many happy memories. I hope it will also provide an insight into the exciting future which King's looks to with confidence. For the book's existence we are indebted to the sterling work of its editor, Danny Payne, and Galen Bartholomew, long-serving Bursar and guardian of the school's heritage. His vision, together with that of Tim Keyes, set this project on its way; I hope that, like me, you will enjoy exploring the riches of this book and share my delight in the richness of the school's past. I hope too that it will encourage readers to visit and experience the warmth of King's today as we continue the educational work begun so long ago on College Green.

Matthew Armstrong

Matthew Armstrong
Headmaster of The King's School, Worcester
September 2015

1: The origins of The King's School, Worcester

James Bartholomew and Danny Payne

Education at St Mary's Priory, Worcester

Introduction: A new school?

On 7th December 1541, by means of a deed of appointment, King Henry VIII appointed John Pether Schoolmaster of the Cathedral Church of Worcester. This deed states that the Cathedral Collegiate Church was "newly by us erected and established"; as such, in the Letters Patent of 1542 and the Cathedral Statutes, Henry VIII purports to found the Cathedral Foundation and its associated school as new establishments.

The founding documents notwithstanding, the Cathedral Foundation was not a new establishment, but a re-foundation. Worcester's ancient Benedictine Priory had been dissolved on the King's orders. Prior Henry Holbeche, with his thirty-three monks, had surrendered the Priory to the Crown on 16th January 1540. In the 'new' Foundation, Holbeche was installed as the first Dean, with five former monks among the Canons and nine among the minor Canons, living in former monastic residences on College Green.

The extent to which the cathedral school can likewise be regarded as a successor to previous institutions is disputed. A.F. Leach (1913) argues that the seat of public education in Worcester was the city grammar school, and that the secular education available at the Priory was sporadic, its school being suppressed in 1504. Conversely, M.R. Craze (1972) concludes that, in light of the evidence of tuition provided by the monastery's almonry from the fourteenth century until the Dissolution, the 'almonry school' warrants recognition as a significant educational establishment and a precursor to The King's School.

Monastic education

The original cathedral church at Worcester, dedicated to St. Peter, was founded circa 680 AD. It is thought that, in common with the practice in other parts of England, the cathedral would have included a school of some description. There is limited information about such schools, although one is known to have existed at Canterbury, which is claimed to be the original school on which The King's School, Canterbury was founded.

St. Oswald was consecrated as Bishop of Worcester in 961, serving until his death in 992 despite his additional appointment as Archbishop of York in 972. Born into an ecclesiastical family of Danish heritage, Oswald had been sent by his uncle Oda, Archbishop of Canterbury, to study at the ancient and distinguished Benedictine monastery at Fleury in France. Oswald became a leading figure in the English Benedictine reform, which saw churches staffed by secular clergy – clergy

Conjectural painting showing St Mary's Priory circa 1500 by Dr Pat Hughes
- notice the campanile (bell tower to left of main church tower), the dormitories (between the cloisters and the river) and the Guesten Hall (behind the Chapter House). The Almonry (position of Number 15 College Green) was home to a small school in the years around 1500.

not bound by any monastic rule, and permitted to have families – converted into monasteries under the Rule of St. Benedict. During the reign of King Edgar (959–975), forty new monasteries were founded in England, including the monastery at Worcester.

Oswald converted a new cathedral church, dedicated to St. Mary, into a Benedictine monastery during the years leading up to 969, when the nearby church of St. Peter was handed to the monks at this new St. Mary's Priory. One or more senior monks would have educated their junior brethren, mostly young adults, according to the Rule of St. Benedict. Such education would have covered the grammar and scripture required for the Mass, with some tuition in singing and music. This education would not have been available to those outside the monastic community, as members of the public were not permitted within the monastic precincts except to hear Mass.

In the following century, St. Wulstan succeeded as Bishop, serving from 1062 to 1095. Born in Warwickshire and educated at the Benedictine monasteries of Evesham and Peterborough, Wulstan joined the Worcester monastery as a secular clerk. He was not ordained until 1038, at the age of thirty, but then progressed through the ecclesiastical ranks at Worcester: Craze lists his offices as childmaster, precentor, sacristan, and prior, before his accession as Bishop.

As Bishop, Wulstan rebuilt the Cathedral and enlarged the monastery considerably, the number of monks increasing from twelve to fifty. Wulstan was also heavily involved in secular affairs: he campaigned vigorously against the slave trade, succeeding in suppressing the transport of slaves from Bristol. Craze notes that Harold Godwinson sought his counsel. Wulstan's stature was sufficient for him to retain his office through the Norman Conquest: by the time of his death he was the only remaining pre-Conquest bishop in England.

Wulstan's career is well documented by the chroniclers William of Malmesbury, whose source was a now lost biography by Wulstan's own chaplain and chancellor Coleman, and Florence of Worcester, a monk at Wulstan's Priory. Florence styled Wulstan *'magister et custos infantium'* (Master and Keeper of the Children); William of Malmesbury used the term *'puerorum custos'* (Keeper of the Boys).

Leach notably argues that Wulstan's role as an educator is exaggerated: he would have taught monastery boys the Benedictine Rule, but would not have taught classics. Leach places secular education at a putative secular school, although such a school is not attested by documentary evidence until the thirteenth century. Craze, however, notes Wulstan's considerable secular learning, a clerk long before he took holy orders, and argues that Wulstan's teaching would have matched his broad erudition. To Craze, the offices described by the chroniclers indicate that Wulstan taught not merely religious education but, according to William of Malmesbury, *'litteras et ecclesiastica officia'* (letters and church services): 'letters' in Medieval Latin may refer to Latin grammar, or to secular learning in a broader sense.

In 1265, Bishop Cantilupe endowed four chaplains, including one as Master of the Charnel-house chapel, with the instruction *'quod omnes scolas exerceant'* (that they all undertake schooling). Leach reads this as an order to attend a school, and since this school was evidently not on home ground because the chaplains had to go to it, Leach cites it as evidence of an extant city school. Craze interprets it simply as an instruction to teach, whether at a school or not. In either case, the priory undertook to provide secular education for the city.

Boys of the Chapel

After the thirteenth century, the Priory continued to make provision for boys. In the fourteenth century, the establishment of the Lady Chapel, where prayers and services were sung for the Virgin Mary, created a need for singing boys. The Lady Chapel maintained a distinct account roll, in which a 'Clerk of the Chapel' appears in the 1392–3 account, and two 'Boys of the Chapel' appear in 1394–5, each receiving two yards of cloth for vestments. In the same year, the clerk John Ylleway was paid 2s.9d., in addition to his clerk's salary of £1.6s.8d., for instructing the boys of the chapel: Worcester's first recorded choirmaster. Thereafter, the Chapel consistently maintained clerks and boys, at most four of each at a time. In 1486 John Hampton was appointed 'Organist and Instructor of the Choristers of the Chapel of the Blessed Mary'. According to Craze, Hampton took charge of eight boys; Leach set the number at ten or twelve. This arrangement continued until the Dissolution, with Daniel Boys succeeding Hampton in 1522.

However, these boys were choirboys, not schoolboys. The Priory church continued to support choristers, but by the fourteenth century, education in a broader sense had been taken up by two Worcester schools: the Priory's almonry school, and the city grammar school.

The city grammar school

Definite documentary evidence for a public grammar school in the city appears in 1291, when Bishop Giffard settled a dispute between the schoolmaster and the Rector of St. Nicholas' Church regarding the ownership of candle wax. It is likely to have been run by secular clergy not associated with the monastery. The school was based within the city of Worcester, whereas the priory stood outside the city wall.

This grammar school subsequently received the patronage of the Guild of the Holy Trinity of St. Nicholas' Parish, and moved to the Guild Hall. The Guild was reformed by a 1547 statute of King Edward VI, which noted that the Guild's 'free school' based in the Guild Hall had been in abeyance for the previous four or five years. The Cathedral Grammar School founded by Henry VIII, it seems, superseded all previous arrangements for schooling in Worcester.

The 1547 statute re-established the city grammar school, which was granted Royal Charters in 1561 and 1843. Following a further Royal Warrant in 1869, this school became known as the Worcester Royal Grammar School. Later chapters of this book chart the changing relationship between the two schools.

The almonry school

The Almoner was a chaplain responsible for the distribution of alms to the poor; the almonry was the chamber where these alms were distributed. The almonry at Worcester, believed to have been built circa 1320, stood on the site of 15 College Green.

Craze cites the decree *De Mandato Prioris* (Of the Prior's Maundy), undated but placed by Leach "some time in the second quarter of the fourteenth century" (although an estimate "circa 1290" also appears in Leach and is quoted by Craze), as the earliest evidence of an almonry school at Worcester. The Prior was to maintain thirteen paupers during Lent, of whom three were to be clerks (scholars) nominated by the *'magister scolarum'* (Master of the Scholars). They each received a loaf of bread and a gallon of ale per day. The schoolmaster was to receive the same, and if he was teaching, he was to receive a sum from the almoner to give to a scholar of his choice, in exchange for teaching relatives of the monks and other alms boys.

Almonry accounts survive from the year 1341–2 onwards. The almonry chaplain consistently received an annual payment, initially £1, raised in 1356 to £1.16s., and in 1380 to £2.13s.4d. In 1381 an extra payment for the almonry chaplain was recorded and then struck out: "and to the same man for teaching the poor boys", 6s.8d. Craze suggests that there were always poor boys taught by the chaplain, and that teaching was among the duties covered by the chaplain's regular salary, and therefore did not warrant extra payment.

In 1397 the almonry paid John Ekynton 5s. in expenses for tunic cloth, "for instruction of the existing poor boys in the almonry". Thereafter, 'boys', 'clerks' or 'scholars' appear consistently in the accounts. Craze notes a payment for a bed for boys in 1487, indicating that some of the almonry boys were boarders. They were certainly fed: in the 1498–9 account they had a whole ox, cheese, butter, eatables and other necessities. Based on a payment to the Prior for the almonry boys' Easter Communion, Craze surmises that the boys numbered ten or fifteen.

Also in the 1498–9 account, Hugh Cratford makes his first appearance, paid £1 as *magister scolarum*. In 1501 a charter of Prior Thomas Mildenhall appointed Cratford "teacher of our monks, commonly known as the schoolmaster, for the full term of his life … the said Hugh Cratford shall instruct and teach, or cause to be instructed and taught, our monks and the boys of our almonry in grammar and logic humanely, well and faithfully" (translation by Craze). Cratford's income, drawn from three different Priory accounts, totalled £4 plus board and lodging, of which the almonry contributed £2.13s.4d.

The Bishop's Charter: the end of the almonry school?

A charter of Bishop de Gigli and Archdeacon Thomas Alcock, dated 9th June 1504, appears to cancel this arrangement abruptly. Hugh Cratford was transferred to be master of the city grammar school, "inhibiting all men of whatsoever rank from presuming to teach grammar learning publicly in our said city of Worcester to the prejudice of the said Hugh, on pain of excommunication" (translation by Craze). Leach concluded that this inhibition was aimed at the priory, intended to remove the monastic rival to the city school, and that it terminated the almonry school.

However, Cratford remained on the Priory payroll. He received his schoolmaster's £2.13s.4d. from the Almonry for the 1504–5 year. Thereafter, some accounts have been lost, but Cratford was paid as an ecclesiastical magistrate in 1506–7 and acted as a Bishop's court notary in 1511, and in 1514–5 was paid £1 by the cellarer. C.F. Roslington (1998) notes that this £1 matches Cratford's salary as *magister scolarum* in 1498; Craze and Roslington argue that, although Cratford ceased to teach novice monks, he continued to teach almonry boys.

An unnamed *'magister scolarum pro conventu'* received £1 from the almoner in 1520–1 and 1521–2; the cellarer paid 5s. to 'the Schole master', plus expenses for gown cloth, for a quarter in 1525, and £1 to 'the Scholemaster' in 1529. Leach, believing that the almonry school had been terminated by the 1504 charter, suggests that the annual £1 payment was for almonry boys to be sent to the city grammar school. Craze rejects this suggestion, arguing instead that this payment was for a schoolmaster at the almonry, probably still Hugh Cratford. Craze and Roslington contend that the 1504 charter did not apply to the almonry school, because the Priory was outside the bounds of the city of Worcester. Cratford was able to retain his life tenure at the almonry school alongside his new exclusive right to teach in the city.

In the *Valor Ecclesiasticus* of 1535, Thomas Cromwell's nationwide survey of monastic property, Worcester Priory's return included expenses for bread and beer for "fourteen poor scholars of the almonry". Craze argues that these poor scholars and the forty King's Scholars of Henry VIII's foundation can be regarded with absolute continuity. The location of Henry VIII's school is unknown until 1561, when it moved into College Hall: it was very probably situated in the almonry.

Reformation and Refoundation: The King's School

The Refoundation of Worcester Cathedral

The Reformation in England, which commenced during the reign of King Henry VIII and continued during the following century, is well documented elsewhere. This book will not attempt to recount that story beyond the establishment of the Cathedral Foundation and its associated school.

Henry VIII is widely considered to have been among the most highly educated monarchs in English history, and he certainly placed a high value on education; much of the proceeds from the dissolution of monasteries and religious houses was intended for use in the establishment of schools. The King's School in Worcester would certainly have been a beneficiary of this passion for learning.

Portrait of King Henry VIII by Joos van Cleve, c. 1535

Worcester's Benedictine monastery surrendered to the Crown and was dissolved in 1540. Two years later, the Cathedral Church was refounded by Letters Patent; a further patent endowed it with all its former possessions, as well as the churches which had belonged to the monasteries at Evesham and Pershore.

The Priory church was already a cathedral, as the seat of the Bishop of Worcester. The Cathedral's governing statutes, drawn up in 1541 under the supervision of Archbishop Cranmer, were given at Worcester in 1544. They established a secular (non-monastic) Chapter, comprising Canons presided over by a Dean. The same pattern was followed in the reconstitution of the suppressed cathedral monasteries at Canterbury, Carlisle, Durham, Ely, Norwich, Rochester and Winchester, and in the conversion into cathedrals of the suppressed monasteries at Bristol, Chester, Gloucester, Osney (Oxford) and Peterborough. These cathedrals, together known as the 'New Foundations', were brought into line with the nine 'Old Foundation' English cathedrals already possessing secular constitutions – Chichester, Exeter, Hereford, Lichfield, Lincoln, St. Paul's, Salisbury, Wells and York.

The Cathedral Foundation would henceforth comprise 105 members, a significant increase from the forty to fifty monks of the monastic community. The Letters Patent specified endowments for a Dean, ten Canons (Prebendaries), ten minor Canons, a Deacon and Sub-deacon, eight singing men, an organist or teacher of choristers, ten choristers (boys), two schoolmasters, forty scholars, twelve university exhibitioners and ten bedesmen.

Despite the upheaval of the Reformation, Worcester Cathedral maintained considerable continuity. The former Prior, Henry Holbeche, was appointed Dean. Five of the ten Canons were former monks, as were nine of the ten minor Canons. The monastic library remained untouched, with 390 books preserved, of which around 350 still exist. Later, more radical changes would be introduced by Protestants in the name of the young King Edward VI; it was reportedly during this time that the vandalism of the cathedral, and the defacing of the 'Majestas' in College Hall took place.

The Cathedral Grammar School

The nine 'Old Foundation' cathedrals each had an associated school. These schools were to be continued, often with an increased endowment awarded to them. The 'New Foundation' cathedrals, as former monasteries, did not have public grammar schools, although in each case a school was available to boys in the city. Winchester and Oxford were deemed by the King to be adequately provided for, with significant, long-established schools nearby, but he sought to provide a grammar school for each of the other reconstituted cathedrals, including the seven 'King's Schools': Canterbury, Chester, Ely, Gloucester, Peterborough, Rochester and Worcester.

As at other Cathedral Foundations, the cathedral statutes established and endowed a public grammar school for Worcester Cathedral, providing for a Schoolmaster, an Usher and forty King's Scholars "to be taught both grammar and lodgicke in the Greke and Laten tongue". These scholars were not to be confused with Cathedral Choristers, who were provided for separately. The King's Scholars would have their school fees paid by the Dean and Chapter, at a total of £66.8s.4d. per year. We can therefore deduce that the earliest school fees would have been £1.5s.5½d. per pupil per year.

The main door to College Hall, from College Green, installed in the southern wall by 1348

The salaries of the Schoolmaster and Usher, also provided by the Cathedral, were set at £30 together, and allocated as £20 and £10 respectively, including an allowance for clothing and the provision of wood, barley and wheat; the level of these salaries underwent only minor alterations during the following three centuries, so that a generous wage in the sixteenth century (certainly higher than those of many contemporary headmasters) had become a comparatively paltry sum by the time of the Ecclesiastical Commissioners Act of 1866 (see Chapter 3).

Under the Cathedral statutes, the Schoolmaster and the Usher were to be appointed by the Dean and Chapter (after the first appointment, made by the King himself). The Schoolmaster, also to be known as the Head Master or Chief Teacher, was required to be "learned in Latin and Greek, of good character and pious life"; the Usher had to meet all the same requirements except proficiency in Greek. The Usher was also to be known as the Lower Master or Second Teacher; over centuries, the post evolved into that of the modern Second Master. The rules for pupils' behaviour, the pattern of the school day, the curriculum and the requisite prayers and services were also set out in the statutes.

Although Worcester's Letters Patent are dated 24th January 1542, the year of the school's establishment is traditionally cited as 1541. The statutes were dated in the thirty-third year of the reign of Henry VIII, which corresponds to 1541, the regnal year running from 22nd April 1541 to 21st April 1542. The traditional date may be read as referring to the deed appointing John Pether Headmaster, dated 7th December 1541, seven weeks ahead of the school's formal establishment.

The deed of appointment of John Pether as Schoolmaster of the soon-to-be-established school, 7th December 1541

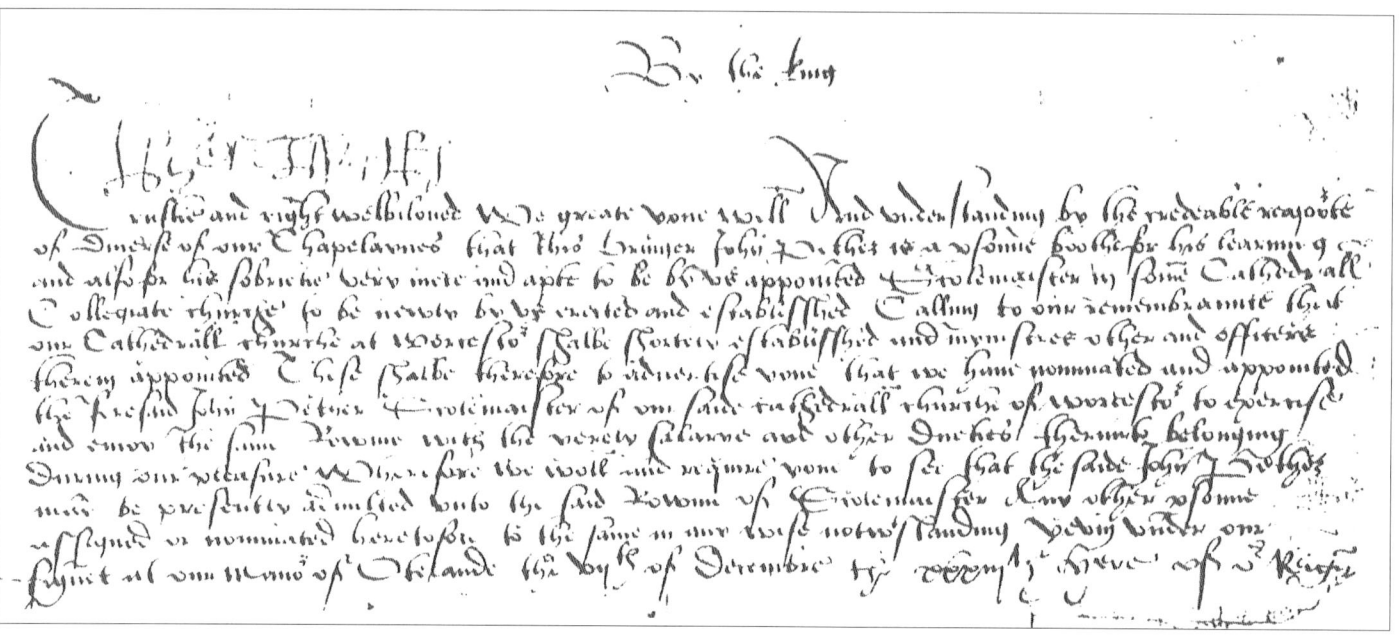

By the King

Trustie and right welbiloved We greate youe well And understanding by the credeable reaporte of diverse of our Chapelaynes that this Bringer John Pether is a personne boothe for his learning and also for his sobrietie very mete and apte to be by us appointed Scolemaister in some Cathedrall Collegiate churche to be newly by us erected and established Calling to our remembraunce that our Cathedrall churche at Worcester shall be shortely establisshed and mynistres other and officers therein appointed. These shall be therefore to advertise youe that we have nomiated and appointed the aforesaid John Pether Scolemaister of our saide cathedrall churche of Worcester to exercise and enjoy the same Rowme with the yerely salarye and other dueties therunto belonging during our pleasure. Wherefore we woll and require youe to see that the saide John Pether may be presently admitted unto the said Rowme of Scolemaister. Any other personne assigned or nominated heretofore to the same in any wise notwithstanding. Yevin under our signet at our Manor of Otelande the viith of Decembre the xxxiiird yere of our Reign.

The King's School

John Pether was appointed Schoolmaster for the Cathedral Church of Worcester by royal deed. Pether was to deliver the deed to Sir Richard Riche, Chancellor of the Court of Augmentations, which managed the property of dissolved religious houses. In the deed, the King deemed Pether "a personne boothe for his learning and also for his sobrietie very mete and apte to be by us appointed Scolemaister". Leach identified John Pether as an Oxford graduate (B.A. 1537, M.A. 1537) who resigned a fellowship at Exeter College, Oxford on 6th March 1542 to take up his post at Worcester. To Leach, this appointment of a fellow of a prestigious college indicated the status intended by the King for his new school, equal to that of Eton and Winchester, and with double the schoolmaster's salary.

The first Usher was Walter Graver (or 'Graner'), who had graduated from Cambridge University in 1536. Graver did not stay with the school for long, and was succeeded in 1545 by Richard Allen, churchwarden of St. Michael's-in-Bedwardine, a church then adjacent to the Cathedral, since demolished.

While the statutes detail a host of regulations for the school, a key piece of information seems to have been omitted: there is no reference to the premises to be provided for teaching, although the Common Table, described below, would certainly have been intended to be held in the former monastic refectory, College Hall. We know that the school 'moved' to College Hall in 1561 (see Chapter 2), but there is no record of the provision of a schoolroom for the first twenty years of the school's operation. It is possible that teaching resumed in the almonry, although the 'Carnary Chapel', to which the school was removed during 1637-1642 might also have been used; other possibilities include a chapel within the cathedral church, the Schoolmaster's own house or even the central rooms of Edgar Tower.

Of the forty or more statutes which established the Cathedral Foundation and the Cathedral Grammar School, four relate specifically to the school (numbers 26, 32, 39 and 40), one to the cathedral choristers (number 25) and a further three refer to the Schoolmasters within the context of the Foundation (number 29 which describes the Common Table, number 30 which provides an allowance for clothing, and number 31 which details the salaries due). The full text of Statutes 25, 26, 32, 39 and 40 can be found in Appendix 1.

Under Statute 26, the Dean and Chapter would provide funding for "forty boys, poor and destitute of the help of friends, of native genius as far as may be and apt to learn". The Dean would nominate the scholars, after assessment by the Dean and the

Schoolmaster in respect of their ability to read and write and to understand "the first rudiments of grammar". As a condition of entry, boys had to be able to recite from memory, in English, the Lord's Prayer, the Angelus, the Apostles' Creed and the Ten Commandments. The pupils were to be aged between nine and fifteen years, except former Cathedral choristers, who could remain beyond the age of fifteen.

The school would teach the boys, these forty plus any additional local boys whose parents could meet the fees, for four or at most five years, until they had learned to speak and write in Latin and to understand the grammar.

However, if any boy should be found "to be of remarkable slowness and stupidity or a character to which learning is abhorrent", he would be expelled by the Dean "lest like a drone he should devour the bee's honey", and another boy nominated in his place. The Dean and Chapter also had the right to depose either the Schoolmaster or the Usher "if they are idle or negligent or found unfit to teach", after three warnings. Each master would be required to swear an oath on appointment to fulfil his duties.

A Common Table was to be established, at which the Dean and Chapter, other members of the Cathedral Foundation and the choristers would dine each day with the schoolmasters and pupils. According to Leach, the Common Table was never established, and its absence was noted by Queen Elizabeth's Visitors in 1569.

Each pupil was allocated 2 ½ yards of cloth, at 3s 4d a yard, to be made into suitable outer garments to be worn for church services; the school (masters and pupils) was required to be present in the quire on feast days, and to attend the celebration of Mass in the Cathedral during at least the elevation of the host and the singing of the *Agnus Dei*. The King also stipulated that a service to mark his death must be observed, and that this should continue for perpetuity on the anniversary of his death.

The King allocated £40 per year, for two years, for the restoration of the buildings used by the Cathedral and the school which he deemed to be "in a state of ruin, waste, unkempt and hideous".

Twelve scholarships for Oxford and Cambridge universities were to be established (six at each university), for suitable school leavers, with the provision that the scholarships could be allocated elsewhere if no suitable King's boy could be found to fill a place. The scholarships would be awarded by the Dean.

The school's name

The school attached to Worcester Cathedral was not established with a definite title, and was to be known by a number of names during the centuries which followed (for a full list, see Appendix 3). The names have all followed common themes, generally featuring the words King's, Grammar, and Cathedral. Under William Bolland's 'New Scheme' of 1884 (see Chapter 4), the name 'Worcester Cathedral Grammar School' was formally used. Bolland's successor, William Chappel, adopted the name 'Worcester Cathedral King's School' (see Chapter 5), but this was not a legal change. The title 'The King's School, Worcester' was not legally adopted until the school was incorporated as a limited company in 2003.

For the purpose of clarity, unless otherwise indicated, 'The Grammar School' will refer to Worcester Royal Grammar School (currently known as 'RGS Worcester'). This book will henceforth refer to its school as 'King's' or 'The King's School'.

The school curriculum

Specific prayers had to be said every morning before school, led by the Usher at 6.00 am (the Schoolmaster was not required to start work until 7.00 am), including the reading of Psalm 21; every evening at 5.00 pm, just before pupils were dismissed from school, further specified prayers were said, and Psalm 134 was to be read. The school day would end after evening prayers; however, the boys would return from 6.00 pm until 7.00 pm when they "shall do their repetition and render to their fellow pupils... whatever they have learnt through the day" - an early form of 'prep' or homework.

Pupils were to be divided into six classes; the First Class, Second Class and Third Class were taught by the Usher, the Fourth Form, Fifth Form and Sixth Form were taught by the Schoolmaster.

Generally, therefore, the school taught boys between the modern Year 5 and Year 10. The modern Years 5 and 6 would normally be in a primary or junior school, and at King's in 2015 Years 7 and 8 were known as the Fourth Forms (Lower Fourth and Upper Fourth respectively), while Years 9 and 10 were known as the Removes (Lower Remove and Upper Remove respectively).

In the First Class (mostly ages 9 - 10) boys had to learn rudimentary English, construction of spoken sentences and translation of simple phrases from English to Latin.

In the Second Class (ages 10 - 11) the genders of nouns and inflections of verbs were taught, in Latin. The boys were to read Cato's verses, Aesop's Fables and some Familiar Colloquies.

Boys in the Third Class (ages 11 - 12) were to read Terence's Comedies and Mantuanus' Eclogues; they were taught irregular Latin nouns and verbs "so that no noun or verb can be found anywhere which they do not know how to inflect in every detail".

Those in the Fourth Form (ages 12 - 13), by now under the Schoolmaster's tuition, would be taught Latin syntax and "be practised in the stories of poets, and familiar letters of learned men and the like".

Fifth Formers (ages 13 - 14) were to learn the "Figures of Latin Oratory" and the rules for making verses. They were also to be taught to translate the works of "the chastest Poets and the best Historians".

In their final year the Sixth Form (mostly ages 14 - 15) would learn Erasmus' *'On Copia of Words and Ideas'* and should be able to speak Latin fluently and be capable of arguing ideas intelligently. Reading matter would include works by Horace and Cicero.

Every other day the Usher and the Schoolmaster would each devise a short sentence in Latin for their classes to translate; the Schoolmaster was required to visit each class several times per week to "diligently test the abilities of the scholars, and ascertain their progress in learning". The Schoolmaster would determine when a boy was ready to move up from one class to the next, and would allow such moves three times each year.

The King's statutes imposed two other key rules for the schoolboys to obey: firstly that breaks, when given, should be spent participating in sport together, and that all games should be "of a gentlemanly appearance and free of all lowness"; secondly that the boys, whether in lessons or not, were permitted to speak no other language than Latin or Greek while at school.

Music at The King's School

James Bartholomew

The King's School can trace its earliest musical heritage to the Cathedral choir. In the Cathedral accounts, choristers first appear in 1394–95, alongside John Ylleway, a clerk paid as their tutor. The Cathedral first appointed an organist, Richard Greene, in 1467; his successors John Hampton in 1486 and Daniel Boys in 1522 were styled 'Organist and Instructor of the Choristers of the Chapel of the Blessed Mary', charged with instructing the choristers in plainsong and music theory. The Cathedral Organist retains this dual role as Master of the Choristers.

On the Refoundation in 1541, the Cathedral statutes provided separately for choristers and scholars. The choristers trained at a choir school, a separate institution from The King's School: they were not automatically King's Scholars, but when of age they were usually admitted to receive their general education in College Hall. A Chapter Act of 1639 clarified that a chorister "may be a King's Scholler". The statutes permitted former choristers to remain at school for an extra year beyond the standard leaving age of 15, in consideration of their time as choristers.

Little is known about the musical activities of the other scholars. The curriculum was devoted to classical languages and literature: music, if played at all, would have been extra-curricular. Attendance at High Mass in the Cathedral, and at services on feast days, was mandatory for the scholars under the statutes; this was their musical education.

Thomas Tomkins and the Civil War

The fortunes of The King's School and the Cathedral, inextricably linked, ebbed and flowed in synchrony. The school's golden age under Henry Bright and Henry Moule coincided with that of Thomas Tomkins at the Cathedral. Appointed Organist and Master of the Choristers in 1596, Tomkins was among the most distinguished composers of sacred and secular music of his time. Also organist of the Chapel Royal, and appointed Composer of the King's Music in 1628 (the appointment was revoked), Tomkins supervised the installation of an organ in the Cathedral, completed in 1614; Henry Bright (Master 1589–1627) was among the donors who funded it. Some King's boys certainly played the organ, including Tomkins' son Nathaniel, subsequently a Cathedral prebendary and a noteworthy musician in his own right, and Richard Davis (chorister 1638, King's Scholar 1641), Cathedral Organist 1664–86.

John Toy (Master 1644–46, 1660–63) is reckoned by Craze (1972) to have been a chorister under Tomkins, and was schooled by Bright and Moule. As an adult, Toy sang under Tomkins again, as Cathedral Gospeller. Toy penned a warm and musically literate verse tribute To Master Thomas Tomkins, Bachelor of Musicke, within his narrative poem Worcester's Elegie and Eulogie. Their partnership would have enriched the musical life of The King's School, but for the iniquities of the Civil War.

In 1642 the Parliamentarians had occupied Worcester, vandalising the Cathedral and damaging the organ. They returned in 1646 to silence the school and the music. The Cathedral Foundation were ousted, including John Toy; the school broke down in 1650. Cathedral services ceased, the choir was disbanded, and the organ dismantled. Tomkins remained at 9 College Green, composing music that would not be heard in the Cathedral. An ardent royalist, who had composed several anthems for the coronation of Charles I, on the King's execution in 1649 Tomkins composed his Sad Pavan for these Distracted Times. He died in 1656, not living to see the restorations in 1660–61 of the monarchy, of John Toy as schoolmaster, and of the Cathedral music under his nephew Giles Tomkins, who installed a replacement organ.

The Restoration Era

Giles Tomkins was dismissed in 1662; John Toy died in 1663. The Cathedral and the school, despite their difficulties, continued to produce musicians. William Davis (chorister 1684, King's Scholar 1686), son of Richard Davis OV the Cathedral Organist, was paid to play the Cathedral organ as a schoolboy; subsequently a lay clerk, and Master of the Choristers 1721–45, his life and his considerable compositional output are elucidated by David Newsholme OV in his doctoral thesis The Life and Works of William Davis (2013). John Hoddinott (chorister 1700, King's Scholar 1701–06), also a boy organist, was expelled as a lay clerk for loose living in 1713, but returned as Cathedral Organist 1724–31.

The Three Choirs Festival traces its origins to informal music meetings with personnel drawn from the Cathedrals of Worcester, Gloucester and Hereford, and is believed to have been established as an annual gathering, rotating between the three cities, by 1715. Every Festival meeting involved the school's choristers; those in Worcester used College Hall as a venue, and Thomas Miles (Master 1733–68) served as one of Worcester's two Stewards responsible for the Festival's administration. John Hoddinott was the first Old Vigornian to direct a Festival (Worcester 1725); he was to be followed by Hugh Blair (Worcester 1893, 1896) and Adrian Partington (Gloucester 2010, 2013, 2016). Countless other Vigornians have participated in both musical and administrative capacities in the world's oldest non-competitive classical music festival.

Early evidence of music at King's

By 1800, the school was offering musical tuition: according to William Smart's Worcester Guide (1799), "Music, Drawing, the French, Spanish and Italian Languages, and other fashionable accomplishments are taught by proper masters". This claim is echoed in John Britton's entry on Worcestershire in Beauties of England and Wales (Vol. 15, 1814). Thoughts of music as a curriculum subject are anachronistic: the "proper masters" were probably external visiting tutors, the antecedents of today's peripatetic teachers. Roslington (1998) cautions that these claims have the air of marketing material, and may portray the school generously. However, Maria Hackett in The Gentleman's Magazine (Vol. 124, 1818), reviewing provisions for choristers' education at Cathedral foundations, found no fault with the Cathedral or the school, noting their good record in producing distinguished musicians.

The Cathedral choir was then directed ably by Charles Clarke (Organist and Master of the Choristers 1813–44), a Worcester chorister and organ prodigy, appointed organist of Durham Cathedral aged 15 and of Worcester Cathedral aged 17. The King's School, most unusually, was then also directed by a precocious musician. William James Porter (Headmaster 1813–20), son of Canterbury Cathedral organist Samuel Porter, had composed two anthems while still a King's Scholar at Canterbury, and continued to compose sacred music thereafter. Porter's successor Allen Wheeler (Headmaster 1820–37) served concurrently as Precentor, responsible for the delivery of Cathedral services. Music, while not on the curriculum, cannot have been absent from school life.

The Cathedral Choristers

Until 1835 the choristers' status at the school remained unchanged since 1541: "They do not belong as a matter of course to the College School, but by the kindness of the Dean and Chapter they are almost invariably admitted upon the Foundation, and form a part of the forty boys called King's Scholars" (The Gentleman's Magazine, 1818). In 1835, guided by Headmaster and Precentor Allen Wheeler, the Dean and Chapter decreed that choristers were all to be King's Scholars throughout their time in the choir.

Members of the Cathedral Choir lead the singing, King's Day 2007

It seems that the combined demands of choir and school caused timetabling issues: in 1851 the Dean and Chapter ordered that the choristers be tutored by a separate master. A distinct Choir School therefore operated from 1852 until the choristers' reintegration into The King's School in 1860. In 1882 the choristers were again removed to a Choir School, under the direction of Rev. Herbert Hall Woodward, a Minor Canon and subsequently Precentor, notable as a composer of anthems. Under P.F. Davis (Headmaster of the Choir School 1923–43) the school expanded in to a full preparatory school, admitting non-choristers; in 1943 the Choir School amalgamated with King's (see Chapter 7).

The Cathedral Choir and The King's School, whether in unison or in harmony, combined to provide Worcester Cathedral with five Assistant Organists: Alfred James Caldicott (chorister 1851, King's Scholar 1858), Professor of Harmony at the Royal College of Music and the Guildhall School of Music, and a prolific composer of light vocal music; Henry Holloway (left KSW 1881), organist at St. Stephen's Church, Bournemouth, and composer of two symphonies; Hugh Blair (left KSW 1882), organist at Worcester Cathedral and Holy Trinity Church, Marylebone; Alexander Brent-Smith (chorister 1900–03, KSW 1904–07); and later Adrian Partington (School House 1966-76). In 1897 Hugh Blair was succeeded as Cathedral Organist by Sir Ivor Atkins, who in 53 years tutored generations of choristers including Brent-Smith, Atkins' Assistant Organist until 1912, then Director of Music at Lancing College; and Claude Brown (chorister 1915–18, The Hostel 1918). Brown, accompanist for many School Concerts in the 1920s while articled to Atkins in the Cathedral, was subsequently Director of Music at the Diocesan College, Cape Town, and director of Cape Town's Melodic Choir.

Under the amalgamation agreement finalised in 1944, choristers up to the age of 13 would rehearse for an hour each day, six days per week, outside school hours. They would sing at Sunday services and at evensong. The former Choir School evolved into a junior school, moving to the present King's St. Alban's site in 1952. Today, the choristers attend King's St. Alban's until age 11, and the senior school thereafter. They rehearse under the Cathedral organist before and after school, and on Sundays; they sing four weekday evensongs, and Eucharist and evensong on Sundays.

The Cathedral Voluntary Choir (established in 1874) and the Cathedral Girls' Choir (established in 2006) also deliver Cathedral services. Their chorister membership is partly, though not exclusively, drawn from the King's pupil body.

The Musical Society, 1879

William Bolland (Headmaster 1879–96) oversaw fundamental reforms to The King's School (see Chapter 4). Among his first innovations was the establishment of a Musical Society, under the direction of Rev. Edward Vine Hall, the Cathedral Precentor – and therefore no stranger to the choristers, who formed the treble line for the new choir. The Musical Society delivered the first School Concert in College Hall on 17th December 1879. Percival Quarterman who played the violin at King's until leaving in 1882, was subsequently a composer and conductor in South Africa. The school song, *Floreat Schola Vigorniensis*, was a setting by Vine Hall of Latin lyrics composed by Bolland. Vine Hall's composition has not survived, but in 2013 Peter Shepherd (Bright House 2002–13) composed a new setting for Bolland's lyrics (see Appendix 8).

Precentor Vine Hall retired in 1890. Dr Herbert Wareing, organist of King's Norton Church and a composer, took charge of the school music until 1896, when the newly arrived William Chappel (Headmaster 1896–1919) appointed George Smith OV, a Cathedral lay clerk. Smith's appointment was very much on a part-time basis: in 1910 the Masters for Music, French and Drawing taught a combined total of ten hours per week.

Nonetheless, the energetic Smith achieved much: besides the School Choir, he established and directed a Glee Club, providing light music for school concerts. The School Orchestra, which had lapsed, was revived as a joint undertaking between pupils and Old Vigornians, first performing in June 1903 under the direction of Rev. Charles Powell, the Minor Canon in charge of the Voluntary Choir. *The Vigornian* of June 1903, which thanks *"Mr. Elgar, who lent a piano for the occasion"*, can be forgiven for using the terms 'orchestra' and 'band' interchangeably: the orchestra comprised three first violins, two second violins, cello, oboe and piano. Smith's pupils secured three choral scholarships and an organ scholarship at Cambridge between 1913 and 1915; Sam Strong (Castle House 1906–14), baritone, returned as Geography master and Housemaster of Castle House.

Edgar Day, 1921

Cuthbert Creighton (Headmaster 1919–36, 1940–42) sought to expand the school's performing arts. In 1921 the Musical Society merged into an Entertainment Society which also encompassed drama, and Edgar Day, the Cathedral's Assistant Organist, took charge of music. The school's particular association with the Cathedral Assistant Organist was to prove long-lasting: Harry Bramma was to serve concurrently as Director of Music, and Messrs. Paul Trepte, Adrian Partington OV, Raymond Johnston and Daniel Phillips all provided valuable organ tuition and classroom work; Christopher Allsop continues to do so.

Able to provide teaching hours that George Smith could not, Edgar Day "had Choir and Orchestra willingly working for him without any sort of fuss" (Craze, 1972). The strength of the School Choir and the ambition of Day's choral repertoire are illustrated by the Brahms Requiem performed in April 1929 – with piano accompaniment, indicating the variable quality of the orchestra at this time. October 1925 saw the début of a jazz quartet led by School Secretary, lay clerk and bandleader H.E. Nicholls. Throughout the 1920s, Nicholls and three masters (Messrs. Edgar Day, A.D. Franklin and G.K. Tattersall) provided light relief in school concerts as a humorous quartet. A peripatetic music teacher emerges in *The Vigornian* of July 1929: Mrs. Winifred Hill, violinist, invites string players to rehearse for the School Orchestra on Sundays, including those who are not her own pupils.

The school's evacuation to Criccieth in 1939–40 necessarily caused the suspension of all musical ensembles except the Officer Training Corps band, which rehearsed on the promenade and led the O.T.C. contingent on marches. To supplement the musical life at Criccieth, and then at Worcester, masters Alec Macdonald OV and Paul Longland OV hosted evening 'gramophone concerts'.

On the arrival of Ronald Kittermaster (Headmaster 1942–59) and his wife Meriel, Mrs Kittermaster expanded the tradition of music appreciation, continuing the gramophone concerts as a Sunday evening Music Society, and organising celebrity concerts in College Hall. The Kittermasters moved into 14 College Green in 1946, releasing the top floor of their house for music practice. Upon the merger with the Choir School in 1943, King's gained a cohort of musically gifted boys with an extremely strong musical grounding. Andrew Hambling (Choir School/School House 1937–48) secured a Cambridge choral scholarship, and taught at Haileybury College for 38 years.

Reginald West, 1951

Kittermaster appointed the first Director of Music in 1951: Reginald West, previously Organist and Master of the Choristers at St Patrick's Cathedral, Armagh. Edgar Day remained Assistant Organist.

Prominent among West's pupils was John Langdon (The Hostel 1952–61), who proceeded to the organ scholarship at King's College, Cambridge – returning to the tutelage of Sir David Willcocks, his choirmaster at Worcester Cathedral, Director of Music at King's College from 1957 – and lectured on Harmony and Counterpoint at the Royal Conservatoire of Scotland for 46 years.

In 1965 the three 'Fishermen's Cottages' on Severn Street (now adjoining the John Moore Theatre) were converted into the department's first fully-fledged Music School, with a large classroom and seven practice rooms, an instrument store-room and a record library.

Harry Bramma, 1964

Reginald West was to remain on the music department staff until 1969, but in 1964 he passed the Directorship to his Assistant Director,

Concert in College Hall, 2014

Harry Bramma, who continued as Assistant Organist at the Cathedral. After fifty years as Assistant Organist, Edgar Day had retired in 1962; his successor, Christopher Robinson, taught music part-time at King's; on Robinson's promotion to Organist the following year, Harry Bramma had been appointed to both assistant posts. The King's School benefitted greatly from the partnership of Robinson and Bramma, not least in gaining a generation of choristers who developed into outstanding musicians.

In *The Vigornian* of December 1967, David Annett (Headmaster 1959–79), himself an amateur organist, and Harry Bramma noted a "great increase" in the number of boys learning the organ, and announced their intention to install an organ in the gallery of College Hall. The two-manual instrument, with pipework salvaged from the defunct Holy Trinity Church, was installed by Nicholson & Co and completed in June 1969. It proved to be a valuable asset, providing accompaniment for assemblies and a tuitional instrument for the school's organ students. In May 1966, Stephen Cleobury, Nicholas Cleobury and Roger Parkes had jointly delivered an organ recital in the Cathedral at the behest of the Festival Choral Society; they were the first of Bramma's ten Oxbridge organ scholars, whose scholarships and subsequent musical careers are detailed in the panel (right). To these should be added Jonathan Darlington (The Hostel 1964–74), Music Director of the Duisburg Philharmonic Orchestra and Vancouver Opera. Given the sum musical impact of his charges, Harry Bramma's educational legacy is remarkable.

Internal music competitions were introduced in 1970: the Middle School Music Competition (latterly the Fourth Form Music Competition) and the House Music Competition. An external adjudicator assesses solo performers before presiding over the song contest, with forms and houses competing en masse in exuberant fashion. Prize-winning soloists and ensembles return for an evening concert.

Established in the Autumn Term 1973, the Keys Society gave its first concert, arranged by Jonathan Darlington, in February 1974. The society's patron Ivor Keys, Professor of Music at Birmingham University and a school governor, delivered a lecture-recital in November 1974, and another in 1983 for the Society's fiftieth concert. The society delivered five concerts per year, co-ordinated and performed by pupils, who also rehearse and direct the society's chamber choir. With School Concerts programming ensemble items, Keys Society Concerts provide the primary performing outlet for solo musicians. The Society

Bramma's Organ Scholars

Stephen Cleobury (Choir House 1958–67)
Award: 1966, St. John's College, Cambridge
Career: Director of Music, King's College, Cambridge;
Conductor, BBC Singers;
President, RCO

Nicholas Cleobury (Choir House 1958–68)
Award: 1967, Worcester College, Oxford
Career: Director, Mid-Wales Opera;
Conductor, Britten Sinfonia, Oxford Bach Choir

Roger Parkes (Chappel House 1960–68)
Award: 1967, Corpus Christi, Cambridge
Career: Music master, Shrewsbury School

Christopher Tolley (School House 1961–69)
Award: 1968, New College, Oxford
Career: Director of Chapel Music, Winchester College;
Conductor, The Exon Singers

Stephen Darlington (Chappel House 1960–70)
Award: 1970, Christ Church, Oxford
Career: Director of Music, Christ Church, Oxford;
President, RCO

Andrew Millington (Creighton House 1968–70)
Award: 1970, Downing College, Cambridge
Career: Director of Music, Exeter Cathedral;
Director of Music, Exeter Philharmonic Choir

Adrian Leang (The Hostel 1964–73)
Award: 1973, Christ's College, Cambridge
Career: Director of Music, Berlin International School

John Penny (Bright House 1966–73)
Award: 1973, Pembroke College, Oxford
Career: Director of Music, Woodbridge School

Adrian Partington (School House 1966–76)
Award: 1977, King's College, Cambridge
Career: Director of Music, Gloucester Cathedral;
Director, BBC National Chorus of Wales

Geoffrey Webber (Choir House 1972–77)
Award: 1977, New College, Oxford
Career: Director of Music, Gonville & Caius College, Cambridge

received valuable guidance, until 1976 from composer Roger Hemingway, then on the school staff, and thereafter from Keith Bridges, Housemaster of The Hostel and a Cathedral lay clerk.

Popular music also found a voice in this era. In the 1960s, Derek Griffiths, Bill Pidgeon, Peter Webster and Nick Chance performed as *The Mavericks*, the band appearing at school parties and at the 'Beat Meet' of the Worcester schools' joint Sixth Form Club. The Undercroft of College Hall, fitted by the school Works Group as a Sixth Form social club, opened in 1971; equipped with a stereo unit, the club hosted monthly dances. College Hall hosted its first rock concert in 1976, featuring the band *Fine*. For *Fine* keyboardist Geoffrey Webber (Choir House 1972–77), this represented a departure from the norm: an organist and choirmaster, and, since 1989, Director of Music at Gonville & Caius College, Cambridge, Webber's academic work focused on the music of the seventeenth century.

Creighton House Choir in the House Song Competition, 2007

The King's School, Worcester *From 1541 into the 21st Century*

Musical Theatre

Music does not exist in isolation, but takes its place in the broader performing arts. The strong King's traditions of music and drama, and more recently of dance, are united in musical theatre – often to spectacular effect.

The lineage of musical theatre at King's descends from the 1967 production of *The Pirates of Penzance*, which featured Nicholas Cleobury (Choir House 1958–68) as the Pirate King and Andrew Reekes (Choir House 1964–69) as the Sergeant of Police. The biennial Gilbert & Sullivan opera became a calendar fixture: *Pirates* was followed by *The Yeomen of the Guard* (1969), *The Mikado* (1971), *Iolanthe* (1973), *H.M.S. Pinafore* (1975), *Patience* (1977) and *Ruddigore* (1979). In the years before co-education, these productions were collaborative efforts with the girls of The Alice Ottley School. Musicals were co-directed by a musician – Harry Bramma or Michael Young – and a dramatist – Peter Diamond or Martin Fagg, often supported by Mrs Sarah Knight. The incomparable Gilbert & Sullivan enthusiast P.C. Thompson directed *Ruddigore* (1979) and *The Pirates of Penzance* (1984).

The school had never been confined to Gilbert & Sullivan – in 1972, Harry Bramma had staged Britten's *Noye's Fludde* with the middle school – but the repertoire expanded in the 1980s. Brian Griffiths made his directorial debut with *The Bartered Bride* (1981); in 1983 an Old Vic-trained actor, Stephan Le Marchand, arrived to teach English. Alongside Peter Diamond and Malcolm Drummond, they would take the dramatic arts in new directions. *Mystery and Merriment* (1984) was performed in the Cathedral in 1984 to mark

Cabaret (1990)

the 900th anniversary of St Wulstan's cathedral; this remarkable rendition of Biblical narratives, written by Peter Diamond in the style of a medieval mystery play, featured music composed by Adrian Partington and Nick Owen (Chappel House 1975–85). Both *The Boy Friend* (1983) and

Les Miserables School Edition (2012)

Mystery and Merriment starred Alison Nott (College House 1981–83), later known as Bella Merlin: an actor, director and musician, Professor of Acting and Directing at the University of California, Riverside.

School musicals had hitherto been staged in College Hall – a majestic venue, but one ill-suited to the acoustic and technical requirements of musical theatre. The completion of the Theatre (now the John Moore Theatre) in 1987 provided a first-rate facility for the performing arts.

Appointed Director of Music in 1989, David Brookshaw first collaborated with Diamond, Griffiths and Le Marchand in *Cabaret* (1990). This was a bold statement of progressivism and co-education, deemed *"efficient, moving and provocative"*, with *"pace, imagination and style"* by *The Vigornian*. David's son Alastair Brookshaw (Chappel House 1993-98) was later to appear in *Cabaret* on the West End, having cut his teeth with notable school performances in *Guys and Dolls* (1996) and *The Boy Friend* (1998).

The dual musical and dramatic skills required for musical theatre – and the value of such productions for honing both skill sets – is illustrated by the parallel yet contrasting paths of two performers in *Joseph and the Technicolor Dreamcoat*, the Removes and Fourth Form production of 1999. David Newsholme (Oswald House 1993–2003) and Ben Humphrey (Creighton House 1993–2004) were both former choristers. Newsholme, the future organist, musicologist and choirmaster, starred as Joseph; Humphrey was later to star as Valjean in the magnificent *Les Miserables* of 2004, en route to the Bristol Old Vic; an actor, dramatologist and director, in 2009 he was appointed Director of Youth Theatre at Worcester's Swan Theatre. The versatile voice of George Watson (Creighton House 2002–07) – Javert in *Les Miserables School Edition* (2003), a deadpan butler in *Me and My Girl* (2006) and Judd Fry in *Oklahoma* (2007) – has subsequently gained him spoken and sung recording work alongside his primary career in animation.

The 24-year partnership of Stephan Le Marchand and David Brookshaw received much support from Sarah Le Marchand; from Simon Atkins, who as Head of Drama from 1998 directed several musicals; from choreographer Trudie Marskell; and from Chris Crosswell, who succeeded David Thurlby as Theatre Technician in 2001 and consistently provided set design and stage management of a quality unimaginable for most amateur theatrical companies.

Simon Taranczuk, with directors Jules Price-Hutchinson and Lorraine Guy, continued the musical tradition in 2015 with Rodgers & Hammerstein's *The Sound of Music*, in which Maria and Captain von Trapp together reflect that *"Nothing comes of nothing: nothing ever could"*. This is certainly true of musical theatre. A fifty-year succession of increasingly ambitious and successful productions testifies to the dedicated efforts of generations of staff and pupils alike.

More on Drama at King's and the John Moore Theatre can be found in Chapter 8.

Malcolm Drummond, 1976

Harry Bramma was appointed Organist of Southwark Cathedral in 1976. In his place the Cathedral appointed Paul Trepte as Assistant Organist, and David Annett appointed as full-time Director of Music Malcolm Drummond, formerly Assistant Director of Music at Christ's Hospital. In 1977 the Music School moved into larger premises in the basement of School House.

Andrew Milne (Headmaster 1979–83) was a keen musician: an accomplished cellist and a jazz trombonist, he had co-founded the Milne-MacDonald Big Band, which appeared in College Hall in January 1983 with Humphrey Lyttelton on the trumpet. The school's choral tradition was already impressive; Milne and Drummond sought to foster an orchestral tradition to match. Improvements in the number and calibre of instrumentalists enabled the establishment of ensembles for strings and woodwind.

On his arrival, Drummond had taken charge of the Wind Band himself; in 1981 Adrian Partington returned to Worcester as the Cathedral's Assistant Organist, also teaching at King's and directing the Wind Band. Robin Thurlby arrived in 1980 in the new post of Head of Strings; in his 24 years at King's he was to combine his classroom teaching and his violin tuition to particular effect at King's St. Alban's, securing a strong supply of string players for the higher school. He also directed the Chamber Orchestra, established in the Autumn Term 1981. The new Chamber Orchestra and the Cathedral Choir embarked on a joint tour of Belgium in 1982, the Music Department's first overseas tour.

Musicians of Drummond's era include Nicholas Kok (Wulstan House 1975–81), Principal Conductor of Sinfonia ViVa and a frequent conductor of English National Opera; Jonathan Nott (Bright House 1971–81), Principal Conductor of the Bamberg Symphony Orchestra and Music Director of the Tokyo Symphony Orchestra; and John Harris (School House 1987–89), organist, composer, Artistic Co-Director and Chief Executive of the Scottish contemporary music ensemble Red Note.

Malcolm Drummond leading a rehearsal in the Music School (School House), late 1980s

David Brookshaw, 1989

David Brookshaw was appointed Director of Music in 1989, after nine years as Director of Music at Glenalmond College. Malcolm Drummond remained on the staff until 1993.

Under David Brookshaw's genial leadership, music tours became a regular calendar fixture. The Chamber Choir embarked on a joint tour with the art department to Prague in 1996; concert tours thereafter proceeded to Tuscany (1998), Barcelona (1999), Torremolinos (2001 and 2002), Lisbon (2004), Seville (2006), Prague (2008) and the Côte d'Azur (2011). From 2002, the annual concert at St. Clement's Church provided a trial run for tour repertoire. Despite the occasional mishap – a Seville organ console memorably caught fire at Christopher Allsop's hands in 2006 – these tours proved enjoyable and set high standards of musicianship, providing rare opportunities to perform to appreciative foreign audiences in a range of sacred and secular venues.

The Grand Piano delivered, by crane, to the Elgar Room, 2003

1997 saw the formation of a virtuoso close harmony group, *The Magnificent Seven*. Three of its members, Alastair Brookshaw (Chappel House 1993–98), Robert Webb (Chappel House 1991–98) and Allan Clayton (The Hostel 1991–99), proceeded to Cambridge with choral scholarships; Brookshaw established a West End career in musical theatre; Clayton, an inaugural Sir Elton John Scholar at the Royal Academy of Music, has gained international recognition as an operatic and concert tenor.

The Magnificent Seven, 1997

With the School House basement earmarked for the new School Library, Castle House, entirely refitted after the termination of boarding, became the new Music School in 2003. Castle House had considerable musical pedigree: it had served as Edward Elgar's home during the Worcester Three Choirs Festivals of the early twentieth century. In his honour, the Music School's centrepiece on the first floor was named the Elgar Room. Castle House provided purpose-designed practice rooms with acoustically beneficial irregular angles, classrooms, a recording room, and a computer suite with keyboards linked to specialist composition software. The Music School was opened in July 2003 by Stephen Cleobury OV, Director of Music at King's College, Cambridge; the accompanying gala Keys Concert was the last for Keith Bridges, after forty years at King's, for David Newsholme (Oswald House 1993–2003), then director of the Keys Choir, since 2011 Assistant Organist at Canterbury Cathedral and Musical Director of the Canterbury Singers, and for Alan Uren (Choir House 1996–2003) and

The Elgar Room, Castle House, 2015

Adrian Uren (Chappel House 1996–2003), then respectively Leader and Principal Horn of the National Youth Orchestra.

Robin Thurlby retired in 2004; Graham Gunter, Head of Strings, has since continued Mr Thurlby's work with string players, directing the Chamber Orchestra and from 2014 also directing First Orchestra. Vanessa Gunter had joined the Music Department in 1993 as the first woodwind specialist on the school staff, directing the Jazz Group and the Wind Band.

David Brookshaw's alumni include William Carslake (Chappel House 1983–93), composer of the Peckham Mass and conductor of the London Charity Orchestra; Thomas Blunt (Kittermaster House 1985–95), Erste Kapellmeister at Konzert Theater Bern; Shulah Oliver (Kittermaster House 1993–2000), prize-winning violinist and violist; and Peter Holder (Bright House 1997–2008), Sub-Organist at St Paul's Cathedral and Pidem Organ Fellow at the Royal Academy of Music. Peter Shepherd (Bright House 2002–13) composed the Christmas Carol *'There was a boy'* for David Brookshaw's final Carol Service in 2012, before proceeding to an organ scholarship at Merton College, Oxford.

Simon Taranczuk, 2013

After 24 years as Director of Music, David Brookshaw retired in 2013. His successor, Simon Taranczuk, was formerly Director of Music at The King's School, Rochester and Director of Chapel Music at Marlborough College.

Simon Taranczuk introduced masterclasses, harpsichordist Virginia Black being the first of a series of distinguished external tutors to provide tuition for a select group of senior musicians. A termly Informal Concert in College Hall provided performance opportunities for musicians yet to graduate to the elite Keys Society Concerts; Young Performers' Concerts continued for Fourth Formers. In 2014, the School Choir twice recorded for BBC Radio 4 sitcom *The Archers*. The latest incarnation of the school jazz band, the King's Swingers, formed in 2014. The Michael Baker Boathouse accommodated a further innovation: the Open Mic Night, an informal evening geared towards guitarists and singer-songwriters.

The King's musical scene has broadened considerably in scope since the Musical Society of 1879, and indeed since the Cathedral choir of the 1390s, but music retains its place at the heart of school life.

Above: Cathedral Choristers, 2015
Below: Britten's Noyes Fludde, *College Hall, 2010*

Recording for The Archers, *2014*

2: King's under the Tudors and Stuarts

James Bartholomew and Danny Payne

Henry VIII's King's School

There is little evidence of what daily life was like for pupils at The King's School in its early years, and certainly nothing to suggest that the school day was not carried on in accordance with King Henry VIII's instructions.

Forty scholars were duly appointed, although the word "poor" in the Statutes to describe suitable boys may not have been interpreted in the modern sense: the purpose of public schools in Tudor England was not to educate children (boys) of the wealthiest families, who would likely be tutored privately at home, or to educate the children of the poorest, working families who would have no need for Latin, Greek or classical literature, but rather to prepare the sons of those whom we would term 'middle class' - lawyers, merchants and doctors, for example - for possible admission to university, at either Oxford or Cambridge, or for ordination in the Church.

Indeed, early pupils at King's included Robert Wylde, whose father Thomas Wylde was among Worcester's wealthiest merchants and who purchased the Commandery, a former religious house and hospital, at the time of the dissolution and converted it into a grand private home.

The Statutes included provision for twelve university scholarships, six for Oxford and six for Cambridge, to support the further learning of King's Scholars, at the expense of the Cathedral Foundation. The Cathedral's records show that these twelve scholarships were awarded as early as 1543; one of the first university scholars or 'exhibitioners' was Roger Colborne, who would become the second Master of The King's School, although not a former pupil himself as the initial scholarships were awarded to those outside the school which was too young at that time to have *alumni*, from around 1553. Perhaps owing to a lower than anticipated income for the Crown from seized monastic lands, Henry VIII took away some of the properties of the new cathedral foundations in 1545 but also released them from the obligation to meet the cost of the university scholarships.

The forty King's Scholars, plus the ten choristers, would have been joined by other 'fee-paying' boys - according to Craze (1972) surnames on early school roles suggest families from villages around the county sent their boys to the school, which, with the city grammar school in abeyance in the 1540s, was the pre-eminent school in the city.

The school day would certainly have been gruelling, especially for the youngest pupils aged only nine years, with prayers and psalms from 6.00 am until the day ended with an hour of scrutiny by the Master after the last lesson finished at 6.00 pm, working by candlelight in an imposing, cold hall. Lessons would involve learning Latin grammar by rote and translation between Latin and English, with study of classical works of literature for older boys, in preparation for debating and argument at university. Severe punishments were handed down for breaches of the school rules, including cutting the hands of boys who dared to speak any words of English during the school day, even during breaks, or for failing to report any other boy doing so. Breaks were taken in the cathedral cloisters, with even the youngest expected to behave in a gentlemanly manner at all times.

The second of the school's teachers, the Usher, responsible to the Master for teaching the three younger forms, was a position initially held by Walter Graner (or Graver) from 1542, and later by Richard Allen, from 1545 until around 1550 (the exact date is uncertain) when Humphrey Harwood was appointed.

The impact of Henry VIII's successors

It is, perhaps, of some interest that while the Cathedral Foundation had undergone fairly limited upheaval during the Henrican Reformation, the Cathedral and its new school would suffer greater turbulence during the religious strife of Henry's successors, King Edward VI, Queen Mary I and Queen Elizabeth I.

As King Henry had stipulated, his death on 31 January 1547 (the official date given, although his death was kept secret for a few days during political wranglings) was duly marked by a service in Worcester Cathedral, with the anniversary held as a time of prayer for the departed King's soul for at least the next 120

Portrait of King Henry VIII by Hans Holbein the Younger, c. 1537

Portrait of Thomas Cranmer by Gerlach Flicke, 1545

years. The death of Henry VIII in 1547 left a young boy, barely old enough to be taught at The King's School, as the new King, under the protectorship of his uncle, Edward Seymour, the Earl of Hertford.

During the brief reign of Edward VI (1547-1553), significant physical damage was done to shrines and icons in the Cathedral Church, much of it attributed to Bishop Hooper, Bishop of Gloucester and Worcester during this time. The damage included the destruction of the Majestas in College Hall, which would later be rendered over and decorated with shields including a royal coat of arms before a state visit to Worcester by Queen Elizabeth I in 1575. Parts of the Cathedral's substanitial estate of property was taken by the Crown and assigned elsewhere, often to private individuals, but this did not affect the school.

The national progress of the Reformation continued under Edward Seymour's Protectorship, with laws passed which drew England ever further from the Roman Church, which itself had issued 'Six Articles' confirming Catholic rites and ceremonies. A law was passed in 1549 allowing English clergy to marry, and among the one in six ordained ministers to take advantage of this change was Rev. Humphrey Harwood, Usher from around 1550; Harwood would have been forced to stand down when the law was rescinded shortly after Queen Mary's accession to the throne in 1553.

The School Master, John Pether is understood to have fled to the continent on the accession of Queen Mary, having been a firm Protestant. According to Craze (1972), there is some confusion between the historical records of three men, John Pether, John Pedder and John Peter, any one of whom could be the Oxford graduate who duly served as the first Master of The King's School from 1542 until around 1553; any of these men could be the exile who returned from Germany shortly after Queen Mary's death in 1558 and would serve as Dean of Worcester Cathedral from 1559 until his death in 1571. The Dean's epitaph, written by Arthur Lake (Dean 1608-16), describes him as the fifth Dean of the Cathedral "but first to preach the true faith restored by Queen Elizabeth". It would certainly seem most appropriate for the story of the first Master of The King's School to have ended in this way, and would have cemented beyond doubt the relationship between the school and the Cathedral.

Graham Sutherland's tapestry, 'Christ in Majesty', Coventry Cathedral - the artwork is a conjectural depiction of how College Hall's Majestas might have appeared before vandalism in the late 1540s

Certainly, the departure of both the Master and the Usher would have been disruptive for the school, at a time of national disquiet; the new Queen was determined to restore England to Catholicism during her short but violent reign. One of many casualties (or 'martyrs' depending on personal viewpoint) was former Archbishop and protagonist of the Reformation Thomas Cranmer, who was the likely author of the Letters Patent which founded the Cathedral and The King's School in Worcester, on behalf of King Henry VIII.

As mentioned above, Roger Colborne was appointed Master following Pether's departure, most likely in 1553; other than his scholarship to Oxford University where he graduated from Christ Church, little is known about this man. A record of his estate, cited by Craze (1972), shows that he lived a meagre life, probably in a single room, with very few possessions. He was certainly a scholar and would have to have been a member of the clergy in order to hold the position of Master. He died in his early forties in 1558 or 1559.

When the Cathedral accounts resumed in 1557 after a break of seven years, the name of the School Master was Thomas Bradshaw. Bradshaw, an Oxford graduate, was in his thirties when he took up his post at The King's School.

College Hall

Galen Bartholomew and Danny Payne

College Hall - former monastic refectory and home of the Cathedral Grammar School from 1561

The original, magnificent College Hall, a 'Scheduled Ancient Monument', was mainly built between 1076 and 1099, above an 'undercroft' which is thought to be Norman in origin. Built on the instructions of Bishop Wulstan as the monks' refectory, or dining room, for the monastic cathedral church which would replace Bishop Oswald's earlier, smaller church, College Hall is the largest remaining monastic refectory in England after Westminster Hall, and internally measures 124ft in length.

One of the most striking features of the building is the sculpture of 'Christ in Majesty', known as the 'Majestas', located in the east wall of the hall, built in 1140.

Also built around 1140 was the southern 'slype' - a covered, communicating passage in a medieval cathedral, of which Worcester had three. This passageway connected a gateway in the southern wall of College Hall with the south-eastern corner of the cloister. As it runs below the dais platform of the refectory, the slype is low but has an impressive porch, with five moulded orders, framing the entrance, which became the 'front door' to the cloister.

The cellar, or undercroft, runs under most of the hall, to a depth of 7ft below ground level and to 3ft above ground. The overall size of the cellar is approximately 50ft wide by 115ft in length, with walls of around five and half feet thick. The space was lit by windows (probably twelve or fourteen) above ground level in the southern wall; all but eight of these windows were obscured by later works, and those remaining are now covered with doors or wooden boards.

The refectory included a pulpit, located in the second window from the east end of the hall in the north wall, from which a monk would read scriptures to the dining monks, novices and servants. A narrow staircase within the wall leads to the ledge of this window, but the pulpit and lectern have gone. Senior monks would have eaten near to the east end of the hall, with lesser members of the community towards the western end; the large, Gothic arched windows in both the north and south elevations bear witness to this arrangement - the two windows on each side nearest the west end of the hall have lower heads, reflecting the lower significance of this end of the building. The kitchens would be have located at the western end of the building.

Rebuilding work from the level of the string course, below the windows, was carried out between 1356 and 1386, replacing the original, much lower, Norman roof. The original windows would have been much smaller and built in the Norman, rounded design; the replacement windows followed the Gothic style typical of the period. The large door, in the south wall of the hall, used as the main entrance today, had been installed by the start of the Black Death in 1348; this would have been the 'back door' for the monks, who used a new 'front door' in the north wall to enter from the cloister, also installed around the same time. The window in the east wall, above the Majestas, dates to around 1372; from the outside it can be seen that this was originally a Gothic window, but is now a square - it is likely that this alteration was made following the re-roofing of the hall in the fifteenth century, when a tie beam was added below the original window arch.

The dissolution of the Benedictine monastery at Worcester caused much destruction of the monastic buildings; the northern wall of College Hall forms part of the cathedral cloisters, and it may be for this reason that the hall was spared from demolition. The Reformation did take a toll on College Hall, however, with the grievous defacing of the 'Majestas' during the reign of Edward VI, between 1547 and 1553.

When The King's School was established it was likely to have been housed in one of the former monastic buildings, quite probably within the almonry, located on the site of Number 15 College Green, in which the Priory's school had been based previously. Statute Number 29 of the Cathedral College, written in Latin on the orders of the King, decreed that:

"In order that those who meet together and praise God together in the choir may also eat together and praise God together at the table, we will and ordain that the minor canons and all other ministers in the choir, and the grammar boys' masters and all other inferior ministers in our church, and the boys learning music and grammar, shall, if possible, eat and dine together at the same time in a Common Hall."

The school's third Headmaster, Thomas Bradshaw, sought to move the school of 40 boys into a larger teaching room, so as to allow the school to grow. The opportunity arose when the 'Common Hall' in which all those living in the former monastic buildings ate, fell out of use - the inclusion of the words "if possible" in Statute 29 having allowed for this; the school moved into College Hall in 1561. This did, indeed, enable the school to grow - during Henry Bright's time as Headmaster, 1589 - 1627,

The Majestas - 'Christ in Majesty'

Dating back to 1140, the striking figure of Christ in Majesty, seated on his throne with one hand raised in blessing and the other holding a book, as described in Revelation, measures 8 feet by 12 feet, was sculpted in stone in the eastern wall of College Hall. The figure of Christ was surrounded by images of the four Gospel writers - Matthew, Mark, Luke and John - depicted as a Winged Man, a Winged Lion, a Winged Calf and a Winged Eagle respectively.

Late in the fourteenth century, the four niches were added, each holding the statue of a saint; the identity of each saint is unknown, although it seems likely that St Oswald and St Wulstan, with their particular personal significance to the Priory, would have been included.

It is understood that the sculpture was the inspiration for Graham Sutherland's tapestry in Coventry Cathedral.

During the reign of Edward VI, significant damage was caused to the Majestas - the statue of Christ was defaced, the relief flattened to the wall, and the smaller statues removed. Shortly afterwards, the wall was rendered and the Majestas hidden; a coat of arms painted on the wall was described by Richard Symonds in 1642, thought to be one of a number including a royal coat of arms.

During work carried out to replace the stage in the hall, the remains of the Majestas were discovered in August 1872. Maurice Day, Headmaster, sought consent from the Dean and Chapter for the plaster to be removed, which was done by workmen using chisels, resulting in the 'feathered' appearance of the sculpture today.

College Hall before restoration (c. 1884)

*College Hall transformed by the restoration work completed in 1887.
This photograph is reproduced from the June 1888 issue of 'The Vigornian', the first photograph to be published in the magazine;
the caption reads 'WORCESTER CATHEDRAL GRAMMAR SCHOOL. THE GREAT HALL. - EAST VIEW.'*

the number of pupils grew to 200. By the time of the Headship of Maurice Day in the 1870s, four separate classes would be taught at the same time in different parts of the hall, with an art class on the stage; the Headmaster would hammer with a mallet when the noise level became too great!

In 1636, the Dean and Chapter decided that College Hall should be split, with the eastern end converted into a library for the Cathedral and the western end separated as a prebendary house. The school was moved in January 1637 and rehoused in the small Charnel Chapel (or Carnary Chapel). The Mayor and Corporation and Citizens of Worcester presented a Petition to Parliament in 1642, alleging a number of grievances against the Dean and Chapter, including the removal of the school from College Hall; in 1642 the school returned to College Hall.

The school's use of College Hall was again interrupted in 1651 during the Battle of Worcester, when the building was used as an infirmary for injured Scots troops who had been defending the 'Faithful City' for Charles II. Records in the Cathedral Library show that pitch and rosin were purchased to perfume the hall before the school returned at a cost of two shillings.

John Griffin, Head Master 1777-1813, was given permission by the Chapter to form a separate house at the western end of College Hall in 1799, including a parlour and rooms above. A wall was built to partition the hall, and the gallery above divided into two rooms. Griffin did not live in this house, but the rental income would have been of benefit to the school.

In 1884, under William Bolland's 'New Scheme' (see Chapter 4), the Worcester Cathedral Grammar School became theoretically separate from the Cathedral. The school, which was still effectively controlled by the Cathedral's Chapter, agreed to take on sole ownership of College Hall from the Dean and Chapter, and carried out significant restoration of the building with funds from the Ecclesiastical Commission, including a new roof, wooden panelling and a new vaulted wooden ceiling; the architect, Ewan Christian, claimed that the new groined ceiling, supported by carved bosses, would emulate the ceiling as it would have been some 500 years earlier. The bricks which covered the west window during the building of the separate house for John Griffin were removed. The present gallery, widened and built faced in English oak, was installed, with a book room below. College Hall was reopened by Earl Beauchamp, Lord-Lieutenant and one of four lay Governors, on 3rd October 1887.

Soon after the restoration, the Dean and Chapter decided to take back ownership of College Hall. It took three years for the Charity Commissioners to agree that this was in the best interests of the school, but on 23rd June 1901, ownership of College Hall was transferred back to the Dean and Chapter, with

The Pipe Organ

Rt Hon Edward Heath MP playing the pipe organ in College Hall with Basil Edwards and Harry Bramma, Director of Music, 1969.

Donations to an A.D. Franklin Memorial Fund and proceeds from organ recitals and other gifts, enabled the building of an organ for College Hall, designed by Stanley Lambert of Nicholson's, whose firm built the organ in June 1969, much to the pleasure of David Annett, Headmaster and Harry Bramma, Director of Music.

The organ has 884 pipes, many from the organ in Holy Trinity Church (demolished in 1969). The case, keyboards and soundboards were sourced from other instruments.

This fine asset for the school attracted wider attention, and (Sir) Edward Heath, who was staying with Peter Walker MP, came to play the new organ.

The pipe organ, photographed in 2015 - a larger, electronic organ was installed in front of the stage in the 2000s.

College Hall's clock, which has tormented public examination candidates since the 1920s, donated by Sir Ernest Bird, OV.

the provision that the school would continue to have use of the hall in exchange for "an annual acknowledgement"; The King's School continues to rent College Hall from the Cathedral today.

The New Scheme had allowed the size of the school to increase, and additional buildings were constructed and others around College Green were leased from the Cathedral, so that College Hall was no longer the only room in which lessons would be taught.

When Creighton became Headmaster in 1919, the school would start each day in College Hall, with a roll call, a New Testament reading, prayers and daily notices. This started the tradition of 'College Hall assemblies' which continue today, although the assemblies are now twice each week, and, because of the size of the school, roll call (now 'registration') is held before the assembly, with the Fourth Forms (Years 7 and 8) having separate gatherings elsewhere. During the 1920s, in the absence of a suitably sized gymnasium, College Hall was the setting for the House Boxing Cup and the P.T. Competition.

During Creighton's headship, the Victorian gas lighting was replaced with electric lighting.

A memorial board to those pupils and staff who fell in the Great War was installed in College Hall, donated along with the table and chair for the Headmaster and the clock by Sir Ernest Bird, OV. This was joined later by a similar memorial to the fallen of the Second World War. Other Honours Boards around the hall list the Headmasters of the school, including St Wulstan in 1040, and record the achievements of scholars.

During the evacuation of the school to Criccieth in 1939-40, the Government commandeered the school's premises, including College Hall. The hall was to be used as a centre of communications for the Air Ministry and was equipped with modern telecommunications equipment. It is a little known fact that, in the event of a Nazi invasion, the Government was to be removed to rural Worcestershire. While College Hall was to become the Communications Centre, Madresfield Court, the finest (though conveniently little-known) mansion in the county was to be allocated to the royal family, while the Prime

The western end of College Hall, set up for summer 2015 examinations, showing the gallery installed during the restoration by Ewan Christian in 1887

Minister was to be accommodated at Spetchley. Lady Morrison, a Governor of The King's School from 1996 until 2016, recounts the story that her uncle received an enormous consignment of tinned meat at the beginning of the war ready for the royal family; at the end of the war, civil servants arrived at Madresfield Court to reclaim the meat!

Above: Lord Hemmingford presenting prizes on Speech Day, 1960
Below: The entrance from College Green, 2013

School life returned to normal after the war, and College Hall has enjoyed a wide variety of uses. In addition to weekly assemblies, the space is used as an examination hall, for concerts, plays, lectures, and dances. The Old Vigornian Club shares an annual reunion dinner in College Hall, and the Parents' Committee holds a Christmas Ball each year. School Open Mornings show off the impressive hall to prospective pupils and their parents. For many years the school held the Speech Day events in College Hall, until 1970 when the format of the occasion was revised to create King's Day, held in the Cathedral; annual Remembrance Day services continue to be held in College Hall to the present day.

Every third year, Worcester Cathedral hosts the Three Choirs Festival, and College Hall has been a popular venue since the first Festival Ball was held in 1755. A Festival Concert in 1788 attracted a visit from George III and Queen Charlotte, who sat in a specially erected gallery with their daughters.

In 1970, A.L. Cubberley and a number of pupils were removing an 18th century partition wall in the undercroft when they uncovered two graves, one of which had been previously disturbed, the other being largely intact. Expert analysis established that this was the grave of a Christian man, aged between 25 and 30 years, buried in the sixth or seventh century.

During the 1970s an oil-fired boiler was installed to heat the hall, the wooden benches were replaced with more comfortable, stackable chairs, and the book room was replaced by a kitchen.

A new heating system, with new ceiling fans, was installed in 2002; contractors discovered three ancient pairs of compasses embedded in the ceiling. Anxious to avoid such instruments falling out and causing serious injury, they carried out a search which revealed a total of 29 sets, thought to date back to the early twentieth century.

A fifth roof was installed in the summer of 2012, to protect the building which, for many, is the very heart of The King's School and which continues to play a central role in the life of the school today.

View looking up from the undercroft, 1993

It is understood that the school first occupied College Hall from around 1560, the Hall having been designated as the room for the 'Common Table'; the Common Table fell out of use following a letter sent to the Archbishop of Canterbury, Cardinal Pole, by the Dean and Chapter in around 1557, in which they asked permission to restore the Cathedral church following damage caused under the former Bishop Hooper. The Bishop was rewarded for his destructive efforts at the Cathedral church through burning at the stake in Gloucester in 1555. Part of the Dean and Chapter's request was to "dispence with us to kepe our commyns" - to remove the requirements of the Common Table. This would have released College Hall for use as a schoolroom, large enough for teaching all of the forms with room for the school to grow - an opportunity seized upon by Bradshaw.

The location of the school between 1542 and 1560 is less certain: it was assumed by Roslington (1998), and others before her, that the school would have been based in the almonry (site of the present 15 College Green) as a continuation of the previous 'almonry school'. This is certainly possible, although other potential locations would include the Chapter House, the Charnel Chapel, to which the school was later removed in 1637, or a number of other Cathedral properties.

A further request in the letter to Cardinal Pole was to increase the number of Choristers from ten to fourteen and reduce the number of Scholars from forty to thirty-six, as the Dean and Chapter sought to focus the waning finances of the Cathedral towards the function of the church in preference to the school. This was certainly the basis of reforms implemented by Dean Seth Holland who was appointed in 1557.

Queen Elizabeth

The new Queen, whose reign officially began with her coronation in January 1559, made rapid progress in reversing the changes effected by her predecessor, restoring England as a leading Protestant nation.

For Bradshaw, this included the right of clergy to marry, and the Master married the daughter of a local dignitary and went on to raise four children; of Bradshaw's two sons, one became a well-known poet, author of *'The Shepherd's Starre'* in 1591, while the other applied for admission to the English College in Rome in 1599.

During the early years of Elizabeth's reign, the city grammar school began a revival, endowed with lands and monies by local dignataries including Thomas Wylde, whose son Robert is among the earliest known Old Vigornians.

Meanwhile, at The King's School, now certainly based in College Hall, John Cox had served as Usher from around 1554 when Humphrey Harwood had to step aside; in 1561, with the ban on married clergy lifted, Harwood returned, staying until 1575.

Miniature of Queen Elizabeth by Nicholas Hilliard, c. 1575

In August 1575, Worcester was graced with a visit from Queen Elizabeth I; the itinerary included a service in the Cathedral; it is thought that the plaster coating applied to the Majestas in College Hall, as well as that covering damage caused to the reredos in the chancel of Prince Arthur's tomb, the Queen's uncle, was made ready in preparation for this royal visitor. One of the Scholars, Christopher Fletcher, gave an oration in Latin, much to the Queen's apparent pleasure, as she entered the Cathedral accompanied by Nicholas Bullingham, Lord Bishop of Worcester and the Dean with members of the Chapter. Macdonald (1936) cites records from St Michael in Bedwardine to identify Christopher Fletcher who, he claims, was the first recorded Old Vigornian to enter the medical profession.

Another renowned Old Vigornian of around this time is Edward Kelly (1555-1595) who, shortly after leaving The King's School, was tried for necromancy. Kelly's reputation as a famous magician and alchemist led him to travel around European royal courts, including that of Queen Elizabeth.

In Queen Elizabeth's time, the school was briefly known as 'The Queen's Grammar School'. Craze (1972) notes this usage in Thomas Bradshaw's will: describing himself as "late scholemaster of the Queenes grammar school within the colledge of Worcester", Bradshaw made a bequest of 4d. for ink and paper to each of his "Queenes Schollers".

Bradshaw was succeeded as Master by Henry Maye in 1585. A Cambridge graduate, Maye had served as Bradshaw's Usher from 1575 to 1580; as a man in his late fifties his short tenure was understandable. Maye's Usher was the Old Vigornian Thomas Inglethorpe. Educated by Bradshaw and at Oxford, and married to Bradshaw's daughter Elizabeth, Ingmethorpe was subsequently Headmaster of Durham School, and then established his own school in Stainton, gaining recognition as a schoolmaster and Hebrew scholar.

Maye was followed as Master by Henry Bright in 1589.

Henry Bright, Master 1589 - 1627

Henry Bright was born in 1562, the son of a Worcester glove-maker. He studied at The King's School under Bradshaw, matriculating at Oxford University in 1580. During his seven years at Oxford (B.A. 1584, M.A. 1587), Bright acquired considerable learning in Greek, Latin and Hebrew. Two years later, Bright was appointed Master of The King's School, taking up the post in June 1589 at the age of 26.

Shortly before his appointment, Bright had married Maria Tovey. Their marriage was to be cut tragically short by Maria's death in 1596. Bright subsequently remarried to Joan, daughter of Rowland Berkeley MP, a wealthy local clothier and founder of the Spetchley estate. Their son, Robert, was born circa 1616 and educated at his father's school.

Serving with Henry Bright was another Old Vigornian of Bradshaw's era, Henry Moule. Moule had preogressed to Oxford in 1584, aged 16; he graduated in October 1589 and immediately returned to College Hall as Bright's Usher. Moule married Elizabeth Tovey, cousin of Bright's first wife, Maria; two of their sons were King's Scholars.

Under Bright's leadership the school's pupil numbers swelled to approximately 150, vindicating Bradshaw's desire to move the school into College Hall. Craze (1972) identified a total of 188 pupils who progressed from Bright's tutelage to Oxford or Cambridge, a remarkable feat at this time.

Bright's alumni include the poet and satirist Samuel Butler; Dr. Thomas Good, Master of Balliol College, Oxford; Sir John Vaughan, Chief Justice of the Common Pleas; and most notably Edward Winslow, one of the Pilgrim Fathers.

Henry Bright also held several clerical appointments, serving as a canon of Hereford Cathedral from 1607 and of Worcester Cathedral from 1618. Seventeenth century historians made plain Bright's considerable reputation as an educator and an eloquent preacher. Thomas Fuller's *Worthies of England* (1662) praised Bright, "placed by divine Providence in this city... that he might equally communicate the lustre of grammar learning to youth both of England and Wales". Anthony Wood, in *Fasti Oxonienses* (1690s), also reported Bright's "most excellent faculty in instructing youths in Latin, Greek and Hebrew, most of which were afterwards sent to the universities, where they proved eminent to emulation".

Perhaps best placed to assess Bright's merits was Dr. Joseph Hall. As Dean of Worcester since 1616, Hall had appointed Bright to the canonry; his tribute to Bright, inscribed on a memorial tablet in the sideiaisle of Worcester Cathedral (pictured right), may be translated as follows:

Henry Bright's memorial tablet, Worcester Cathedral

> *Stop, visitor and read.*
>
> *Mr. Henry Bright,*
> *The most celebrated schoolmaster,*
> *Who over the Royal School here founded, for 40 years in all,*
> *Presided with the highest distinction.*
>
> *No other man was more diligent or learned than he, or skillful*
> *At felicitously imparting Latin, Greek and Hebrew letters;*
> *As witness, both Universities, which he supplied amply*
> *with numerous learned youths.*
>
> *For as many years, furthermore, ordained in theology*
> *and for seven years a major Canon of this Church.*
> *Very frequently, here and elsewhere, he played the part of God's*
> *holy herald with great zeal and effect:*
> *A pious man, learned, of integrity and virtue*
> *deserving the best recognition of Church and State alike.*
>
> *Strained at last by his exhausting labours by day and by night,*
> *from the year 1562 to 1626[1],*
> *On 4th March sweetly rested in the Lord.*
>
> *(Translation by James Bartholomew.)*

Henry Bright's death on 4th March 1627 brought to an end a remarkable partnership of 38 years between Bright and Henry Moule, who succeeded as Master. Moule took as his Usher another Old Vigornian, Thomas Taylor. Such was the continuity of this era that, in the 55 years from 1589 to 1644, The King's School employed only three schoolmasters: Bright, Moule and Taylor.

Eviction, plague and civil war

Henry Moule had been appointed Usher as a fresh graduate, aged 21; he succeeded Bright as Master at nearly 60 and held the post for seventeen years, until his death in 1644, aged 76. Moule's 55 years at The King's School surely set the ultimate record for length of service. His great age, most unusual for a schoolmaster then as now, was remarked upon: in 1641 the Dean and Chapter affirmed, in reply to a city petition, that "special care is taken to provide a most able master"; Craze (1972) reads this as a response to a complaint at the Master's age and (probable) infirmity. Nonetheless, The King's School continued to grow. Bishop Thornborough reported in 1637 that the boys "are in number neere 200".

---

[1] At this time, New Year's Day was 25th March. This date is therefore recorded as 1626, but in modern reckoning it fell in 1627.

Moule's headship was marred by three significant events, all beyond the control of the Master: the eviction of the school from College Hall in 1636; an outbreak of plague in 1637; and the opening engagements of the English Civil War in 1642.

The first of these potentially disastrous events followed an inspection of the Cathedral property by Archbishop Laud in 1635. The Charnel House had been constructed in the thirteenth century, a vault for the mass re-internment of human remains excavated during construction work. In the Charnel Chapel above, masses were sung for the dead. The Charnel Chapel variously saw service as a schoolroom and a library; by 1635, long neglected, it was leased to Bishop Thornborough for use as a hay barn. The Archbishop ordered that the chapel be restored and returned "to the wonted use".

The Dean and Chapter seized on the opportunity to regain College Hall, which they used as a home for the cathedral library. At a Chapter meeting in October 1636 they decreed that the school be moved to the cramped, damp conditions of the Charnel Chapel. This aroused much protest. The Bishop, whose Palace was adjacent to the chapel, protested against the disturbance caused by the school boys, and noted the meagre size of the new schoolroom. With two King's Scholar grandsons, the Bishop had an interest in the school's welfare – but the Dean and Chapter argued that he was seeking to retrieve his hay barn. The scholars themselves complained about the smell which arose from the human remains which lay in the vault below the chapel.

During the forced relocation of the school, the City of Worcester was struck by plague in 1637. The severity of the plague led to the death of around one fifth of the city's population, about 1,500 people. Amid such devastation, the school could do little to campaign for its restoration to College Hall during this time. Eventually, after much argument, including the presentation of a petition to the House of Commons and the intervention of the powerful Wylde family, the Mayor and Town Clerk - all Old Vigornians - the school was permitted to return to College Hall in 1642.

The opening engagement of the English Civil War, at Powick Bridge outside Worcester in September 1642, was a decisive victory for the Royalists. However, the Parliamentary forces of the Earl of Essex occupied Worcester, vandalising the Cathedral and wreaking havoc in the city. After a month-long occupation, the Parliamentarians withdrew following the battle of Edgehill, and Worcester became a Royalist stronghold. Siege defences were constructed, which would have included fortifications around Worcester Castle and the ditch (Severn Street), and guards were posted at Edgar Tower and the castle gate. In June 1644 the King visited Worcester, and with his nephews Prince Rupert and Prince Maurice, would certainly have been seen by the King's School boys.

Dark days for The King's School

Henry Moule's successor as Master was another Old Vigornian, John Toy. A Worcester-born pupil of Bright and Moule, Toy was closely associated with the Cathedral Foundation. The Cathedral had granted John Toy an Exhibition to Oxford University in 1627, and appointed him a Minor Canon of the Cathedral in 1629, Gospeller in 1638 and Vicar of Stoke Prior in 1641. Toy's epitaph in the Cathedral (since lost) recorded that he was Master of the city grammar school before he succeeded to the King's School on Moule's death in 1644.

Also a published poet, Toy's teaching credentials are established by his authorship of two didactic works: *Grammatices Graecae Enchiridion in Usum Scholae Collegialis Wigorniae* ('A Handbook of Greek Grammar for Use at Worcester College School', published 1650), and a book of Latin verse for beginners, *Quisquiliae Poeticae, Tyrunculis in re metrica non inutiles* ('Poetic Trifles, not useless for young initiates in the matter of metre', published 1662). His tenure at The King's School was to be marred, and interrupted, by the Civil War.

Roslington (1998) cites the diary of Henry Townsend, resident of Worcester during the siege of 1646, when the Scots besieged the city on behalf of Parliament. Townsend records that Castle Hill was strongly fortified and that able-bodied citizens of Worcester, which would have included at least the older school boys, were assembled to defend the city with whatever tools were available to them, on pain of death. By May 1646 Oxford, the Royalist capital, surrendered; Worcester held on until July when supplies ran out and the city was occupied by Parliamentary troops.

The Dean and Chapter were known to have Royalist connections and Laudian religious views, unacceptable to the Parliamentary forces which now controlled Worcester. In 1646, those responsible for the Cathedral were ousted, their

During the seventeenth century, three former pupils of The King's School achieved prominence as statesmen. Their achievements shaped the political and legal landscape on both sides of the Atlantic Ocean.

EDWARD WINSLOW

Edward Winslow (1595–1655) was a leader among the Pilgrim Fathers who settled Plymouth Colony, Massachusetts, serving three terms as the colony's Governor.

Born in Droitwich, Edward Winslow was a King's Scholar under Henry Bright from 1606 to 1611, and was then apprenticed to a London printer and stationer. In 1617 he moved to Leiden, and joined the Separatist Church. He assisted in the printing of illicit Puritan literature, becoming a leading figure in the community of English religious exiles which resolved to set sail for the New World.

Edward Winslow, 1651

The Mayflower sailed from Plymouth on 6th September 1620. After an extremely arduous, stormy voyage, land was sighted at Cape Cod on 9th December.

Two days later the Mayflower Compact, Plymouth Colony's first governing document, was signed on board ship; Winslow was the third signatory. Facing malnourishment and extreme cold, half of the settlers did not survive their first New England winter, including Winslow's wife Elizabeth. Winslow remarried, the first marriage in Plymouth Colony.

Winslow proved his diplomatic abilities both with the Native Americans and with the English. His personal amity with Massasoit, chief of the Wampanoag tribe, secured peace and much-needed agricultural support. Winslow represented the colony as envoy in England several times, procuring funding and cattle. In 1635 he was imprisoned by Archbishop Laud for preaching and officiating in marriages despite not being ordained.

Having served as Governor of Plymouth Colony 1633–34, 1636–37 and 1644–45, Winslow returned to England in 1646, to represent the colony and to assist the Puritan Commonwealth as an administrator. Appointed by Lord Protector Cromwell as commissioner on a naval expedition against the Spanish colonies in the Caribbean, which failed to take Santo Domingo but captured Jamaica, Winslow died at sea in 1655.

Old Vigornians in high office

SIR JOHN VAUGHAN

Sir John Vaughan (1603–1674) was a politician and judge, who as Chief Justice of the Common Pleas ruled that a jury cannot be punished for its verdict.

Born into an ancient Cardiganshire family, Vaughan was another pupil of Henry Bright. He progressed to Christ Church, Oxford, and then to the Inner Temple. He prospered as a barrister, and represented Cardigan in the House of Commons from 1628 until expelled by the Parliamentarians in 1645. A moderate Royalist, Vaughan retreated from public life during the Civil War.

On the Restoration, Vaughan refused an offer of judicial appointment from the Earl of Clarendon, an old friend and chief minister to Charles II. Returning to the Commons in 1661, he instead distinguished himself as a leader of the 'country party' which opposed Clarendon, and secured Clarendon's impeachment in 1667. Samuel Pepys rated Vaughan the finest speaker in the Commons.

Appointed Chief Justice of the Common Pleas in 1668, Vaughan heard numerous property lawsuits arising from the Great Fire of London. Bushel's Case concerned a jury which, upon finding the Quaker William Penn (subsequently founder of Pennsylvania) not guilty of unlawful assembly contrary to the established facts, was fined and detained for contempt of court: Vaughan upheld the right of a jury to deliver a verdict according to its convictions. Penn subsequently founded Pennsylvania; 'jury nullification' – a jury's returning a verdict contrary to evidence, in order to nullify an outcome deemed unjust – remains a contentious issue in American criminal law.

LORD SOMERS

John, Lord Somers (1651–1716) was a jurist and statesman, whose leading role in the Glorious Revolution and the subsequent settlement shaped our constitutional monarchy.

John Somers is claimed as a pupil by The King's School, Worcester and Queen Mary's Grammar School, Walsall: it is believed that he attended both schools. He then proceeded to Trinity College, Oxford and the Middle Temple, and was called to the bar in 1676.

In 1688, the Seven Bishops were tried for seditious libel against James II. As junior defence counsel, Somers cited Sir John Vaughan's ruling in Thomas v Sorrell, securing the Bishops' acquittal. In secret, Somers was central to the planning of the Glorious Revolution to overthrow James II.

Elected MP for Worcester in 1689, Somers held that James II, by subverting the constitution and then by fleeing to France, had abdicated the throne; Parliament transferred the Crown to William and Mary. Somers framed the declaration which became the Bill of Rights 1689, limiting the power of the Crown and establishing the rights of Parliament.

Somers' advancement thereafter was rapid: Solicitor General in 1689, Attorney General in 1692, and head of the judiciary as Lord Keeper of the Great Seal 1693–97 and Lord Chancellor 1697–1700. As a leader of the Whig Junto, the dominant political force, Lord Somers' influence was supreme. Under political pressure, William III dismissed him in 1700. Nonetheless, he served on the committee which oversaw the Act of Union 1707, and regained office as Lord President of the Council 1708–10.

Beyond politics, Lord Somers served as President of the Royal Society, and published translations of Demosthenes and Plutarch.

Statue of Lord Somers,
St Stephen's Hall, Palace of Westminster, 2015

properties on College Green sequestered. John Toy and his Usher Thomas Hunt were likewise ousted, in favour of a more politically acceptable man. Dr John Hardinge was appointed as the new Schoolmaster and, according to the Parliamentary Commissioners' survey of 1649, took up residence at a large house to the south of College Green, described and pictured on page 54, which would continue as the Schoolmaster's House until it was demolished in 1866.

Much demolition and vandalism took place around the Cathedral precincts during this time, including demolition of the bell tower in 1647 and the use of the Cathedral for stabling horses, while the County Committee used the Deanery as its headquarters. With the demise of the Cathedral, The King's School also deteriorated and was eventually dissolved in 1650.

The following year, the army of Prince Charles (later Charles II), driving into England from Scotland, halted at the already fortified city of Worcester in August 1651. Before the Battle of Worcester, the troops constructed further defensive earthworks around Castle Hill (the present-day Creighton Memorial Gardens) and built Fort Royal, overlooking the gates through the city wall at Sidbury Gate and Edgar Tower.

The result of the Battle of Worcester, on 3rd September 1651, was a victory for the Parliamentary troops, at a cost of more than £80,000 of damage to the city, the death of 2,000 Scottish soldiers and with 10,000 Royalist supporters taken prisoner. The former school room, College Hall, had been pressed into action as a first aid post; many people died there and were subsequently laid out on College Green.

The Restoration and a new order

On 12th January 1653, an Inquisition of the Commission of Charitable Uses convened at The Talbot (now Ye Olde Talbot Hotel) in Sidbury, to establish the facts pertaining to payments for the abeyant school. The Inquisition found that the Parliamentary Commissioners of 1649 had arranged for the school to be funded by means of charges to the lessees of the confiscated Dean and Chapter properties. These charges had not all been paid, including the charges to fund the salaries of the Master and Usher. The Master, Dr Harding, had departed; the schoolmaster's house was let to another tenant.

Three weeks later, on 2nd February 1653, the Commissioners met again at the Talbot. They established a legal footing for the collection of the school's funds, and appointed Thomas Barfoote Headmaster, with Richard Hoare as Usher. The King's School reopened, with a new set of King's Scholars selected during the following few weeks.

The death of Cromwell in 1658 led to the demise of the Commonwealth; Prince Charles, who had escaped to France after the Battle of Worcester, returned and was crowned King Charles II in 1660; to mark the coronation, bells rang all day, with the sound of guns, trumpets and drums heard into the night, when bonfires were lit on College Green.

The Cathedral reverted to Anglicanism, with Dr Thomas Warmstry appointed as the new Dean. Townsend's diary recalls that Warmstry's arrival, with around a hundred horses, was greeted by a clergy band and the forty King's Scholars at the city gate (probably Edgar Tower).

More significantly for The King's School, John Toy was restored as Headmaster in 1660, after a fourteen-year absence from College Hall. Thomas Barfoote and Richard Hoare, the incumbent Parliamentary appointees as Master and Usher, were compensated for loss of office. Thomas Hunt resumed his role as Usher, but would remain for one year only, the first of nine men to hold the position of Usher between 1660 and the end of the century - their names are recorded in Appendix 4.

In 1662, Toy was joined by John Wright as Usher. Their partnership was cut short by John Toy's death in December 1663. Wright took charge of the school ad interim, while the Dean and Chapter deliberated for nearly a year over Toy's successor, appointing Thomas Stephens in November 1664.

The school's governing statutes were officially altered for the first time in 1666. King's Scholars no longer needed to be *'destitute of the help of friends'*; older boys were to be appointed as *'monitores'* to assist the Master in controlling the behaviour of pupils, especially at church services in the Cathedral. The Master required an M.A. and must be *'endowed with faculty of teaching'*. The first formal reference to fee-paying pupils was made: the Master was to *'instruct in piety and adorn with good learning those forty boys of our church and the choristers free, but receiving for the others who come to our school whatever he may agree with their friends'*. Various other minor amendments were made, including a formal salary of £20 and £10 for the Master and Usher respectively (which was the same as they had received before but comprising a range of smaller allowances).

Thomas Stephens, possibly dissatisfied with the new statutes, departed in 1667. He was succeeded by John Wright, the former Usher and interim Master. Wright's 28-year tenure left two significant legacies. The first was the institution of a Speech Day in 1672 - a trend for Restoration era public schools. The second represents the school's first benefaction.

John Meeke, King's Scholar 1613-17 and graduate of Magdalen Hall, Oxford, was known to have been planning to bequeath part of his estate to Magdalen Hall, to provide £100 per year in perpetuity to support at Oxford ten poor scholars from his former school. On Meeke's death in 1666, his will could not be found, and Magdalen Hall had to contend with a counter-claim to Meeke's estate, which was apportioned by the Commission of Charitable Uses in 1668. The first Meeke Scholars were probably elected circa 1670. Of the 60 pupils known to have progressed from Wright's tutelage to Oxford, 23 matriculated at Magdalen Hall, including three of Wright's sons. Access to the scholarships was challenged by the Royal Grammar School in the 1860s, but Meeke Scholarships continued to support Old Vigornians at Magdalen Hall and its successor Hertford College, Oxford into the twentieth century,

A Chapter Ordinance of November 1673 permitted the Dean to make monthly visits to ensure compliance with the statutes - the first instance of a school inspection régime. The following years saw further rules restricting the school, including fines for the Master and Usher for non-attendance at six o'clock morning prayers to supervise the behaviour of the boys.

According to the Dean's accounts, geography could be introduced into the school curriculum for the first time in 1687, following the purchase of a 'Terrestriall Globe' and a copy of Horne's *Geographia* - this would have seemed somewhat progressive at the time.

On his death in 1695, Wright was succeeded as Master by Benjamin Slater. The King's School had failed to regain the status or size it had enjoyed under Bright and Moule, but it had survived the seventeenth century against remarkable odds.

Edgar Tower

Originally the gateway to the monastery of St Mary, and known as St Mary's Gate, it is thought that the name 'Edgar Tower' was coined during one of the many restorations (probably in the eighteenth century) which have taken place, in which a stonemason cut the date 975 into the wall near the statue of the Saxon King Edgar - the date of his death - replacing a worn inscription. The name has been in use since.

Construction of the present monastic gatehouse started around 1320, with the main parts of the building completed by 1347. This clearly represented a significant enlargement of an older Norman gatehouse, as evidenced by the inner arches. Cathedral records show a payment made by the Cellarer of £42 18s 2d for 'a new tower' in 1347, understood to be St Mary's Gate. Sections of chevron ornament have been discovered, built into the internal walls, which might have been recycled from the previous Norman gatehouse. The building work was completed after a licence to add crenelations, or fortifications, was granted in 1368.

The monastery undertook a significant and costly series of building projects, of which Edgar Tower was one, in the seventy years from 1317. The other projects included the construction of the Guesten Hall, the Water Gate and an infirmary; rebuilding of

Edgar Tower, photographed in 2013

the refectory (see 'College Hall') and the cloister on their Norman foundations; remodelling of the Chapter House; installation of a grand west window and north porch in the monastic church (now the Cathedral) and the construction of the lower parts of the church tower.

Once completed, the gatehouse would have been a residential property of high status, with vaulted chambers in each of the turrets and a great hall above the gateway, which was used as a courthouse.

Following the dissolution of the monastery the tower was primarily used as lodgings, with two school masters in residence by 1660. In the first half of the nineteenth century the space was used as offices for the Chapter Clerk and Registrar, and in the 1860s the main rooms provided a temporary home for the books of the Cathedral library, during the Victorian restoration of the Cathedral.

Numerous renovation projects have been carried out on Edgar Tower, most significantly in the nineteenth century, but while much of the stonework and windows have been replaced, the huge wooden gates are original; until the latter part of the twentieth century, the residents of Number 1 College Green (the southern turret of Edgar Tower) were responsible for closing the gates each night at 10.00 pm.

The statuary, including the effigy of King Edgar, adorning the front (east elevation) of the tower were replaced in 1910-12.

Scaffolding protected Edgar Tower during major repair works between 1986 and 1991

Canon Wilson, acting Headmaster, gave a lecture to pupils in July 1912, describing the statues and the historically significant individuals represented, including St Oswald and St Wulstan, former Bishops of Worcester.

The King's School gained the use of Edgar Tower in the early part of the twentieth century, leasing the upper floors and the northern turret (Number 16 College Green) from the Dean and Chapter of the Cathedral in 1921.

The smaller room to the north of the building became a classroom, and has remained so ever since. It is widely thought to be among the oldest classrooms in Europe, and was used as an English classroom for many years, until the Classics department moved into Edgar Tower in 2011.

The main space at the front of the first floor was Miss Campbell's Art room from the 1920s until the first extension to the 1925 classrooms was completed in 1936, with the other rooms divided for use as Sixth Form studies and day boy accommodation. Graffiti inscribed into the stonework of some of the upper rooms date from as recently as the 1970s.

A large project was undertaken from 1968 to convert the main space on both sides of the tower, with the adjacent room to the south, into a new school library, replacing the 'Old Library' at number 4 College Green. The new library, with cantilevered wooden galleries providing valuable extra space for bookshelves, opened in 1971. Maureen Kings was the School Librarian until she retired in 1996; Mrs Kings was the well-loved custodian of the many books of the library, including the extensive Reference Room in the southern room, and, by 1990, even a computer!

As the photograph (left) shows, a new roof was installed and major repairs undertaken to the east and west faces of the building, during the five years from 1986. During this time Edgar Tower was protected from the elements by scaffolding and plastic sheeting.

The school inspection in 1999 made clear that, while the library was a great resource for the school, it was already falling behind the times and, with its location now on an extreme edge of the campus, was hardly central to school life. With Alison Scaiff, who ran the library from 1996 until her tragic death in 2002, plans were formed to move the library to a new location. Alison started the preparatory work by removing skip loads of old, outdated books from the library's stock, and, in doing so, made space for more computers and other resources. By the time Alison's successor, Pauline Baum, took over in 2002, plans for a move into a new library in School House were firmly in place. See 'School House - a new Library for King's' (Chapter 9) for a full account of the move from Edgar Tower to School House in 2006.

Once the library had vacated the space, the Art department returned briefly to Edgar Tower during 2007, while the new Art School was being developed from the former Porcelain Works' refectory on Severn Street.

In 2008, Caroline Roslington took over most of the tower's rooms - the large front room became her History classroom, while the School Archive was granted a permanent home with a display and exhibition space in the western room and a workroom and storage space in the former Reference Room and Librarian's office. Liz Allen-Back, who took over from Shenagh Griffiths as English teacher and Head of Key Skills, and the long-term occupant of the northern classroom, was the only other 'resident' in the tower.

After Caroline's retirement in 2011, Pauline Baum, in a move which returned her to Edgar Tower, took over the School Archive. The English classroom became available after Liz's retirement in 2012, and so the Classics department took over this and the former History classroom, along with the small office, and Edgar Tower is now home to both the School Archive and the Classics department.

For more on the School Archive, see Chapter 9.

According to an article in *Worcester News*, January 2014, a grant of £69,500 was awarded to the Dean and Chapter for further renovation of Edgar Tower; this was the start of a fund-raising campaign to repair the stonework on the north and south sides which had fallen into a poor state of repair, and aimed to raise £300,000. A number of Old Vigornians contributed to a scheme which offered names to be engraved in the new stonework in exchange for donations. Masonry work commenced in the summer of 2015.

Top: Miss Campbell's Art Room in Edgar Tower, late 1930s

Above: The Library in Edgar Tower, 1990s

Left: The original inner Norman arches, around which the later Gothic building was constructed

Below: The statuary on the east wall, including King Edgar, seated at the bottom of the central column, with St Oswald to his left and St Wulstan to his right, 2015

3: The 18th and 19th centuries

'The run of the Cloth' or 'A College Walk' by Maria Caroline Temple.
This early nineteenth century illustration shows a College Green with a number of recognisable features: the stables (before reconstruction in 1845) are to the left (south side of College Green) with Hostel House next door; the next building was demolished to extend Castle House which can be seen beyond. The original prebendal buildings, including the Tudor Schoolmaster's House can be seen in the south-west corner of the green, with the roof and gable of Number 12 on the far side of the Green. The east elevations of the prebendal houses are shown to the right of Number 12, with, from left to right on the north side of College Green, the Dean's house, part of the Guesten Hall and College House (Number 15, now called 'The Guesten'). The Dean's house obscures the view of College Hall; the house had been demolished by the 1840s.

A smaller King's School for the eighteenth century

After the upheaval of the Civil War and the reconstructions thereafter, College Green had begun to take on a form which would be recognisable today. Repair work in the Cathedral had enabled services to resume, although a full restoration would not be undertaken until the reign of Queen Victoria. The present Hostel House and Number 9 both date from the 1640s; the latter, built by Cathedral organist Thomas Tomkins, is presently the Headmaster's house. The Schoolmaster then lived at a house close to the present Number 7. Of course, College Hall, Edgar Tower and the Watergate were much older structures, providing a continuing visual link which must extend back at least 700 years.

The seventeenth and eighteenth centuries were perilous for schools. Many small grammar schools folded, in some cases due to financial irregularities on the part of their governing bodies. The King's School, Worcester had been revived following the closure of 1650-53 and managed to survive thereafter, with revised statutes and close governance by the Dean and Chapter, but by 1700 the school faced waning pupil numbers and a rapid turnover of Schoolmasters and Ushers.

John Wright's 28-year headship ended with his death in 1695; his successor, Benjamin Slater, died in turn in 1699. Slater's Usher, Robert Jones, was reprimanded for "neglect of the school" by the Dean and Chapter in 1701, and by December 1703 the Usher's post was declared vacant, Jones "having long since deserted the same". John Medens was appointed Master in 1700, transferring from the headship of Henley Grammar School, but resigned seven years later.

The pattern of short headships may have seemed set to continue, but it did not. Following the appointment of William Betterley in 1707, only five men held the headship during the following hundred years, allowing greater stability and so the chance for progress, albeit gradual, to be made.

The Dean and Chapter maintained a tight hold over the operation of the school, which certainly restricted the freedom of the Master and Usher over the school. In a measure to reduce the impact of short-term appointments, it was decided in 1703 that any future Master or Usher must agree to an initial probationary year before his appointment would be official.

The school would have been financially poorer by the eighteenth century: unlike many other schools whose endowments were land or property-based or shares of cathedral or church revenues, The King's School's statutes, revised just forty years earlier, still prescribed a fixed amount of money for salaries and running costs; inflationary effects on the value of money already left the school struggling for money.

It appears that it was customary during the eighteenth century for the Usher to resign whenever there was a change of Master. This might suggest that the Master was given a say over the man he wanted as his assistant, although the appointment remained within the gift of the Dean and Chapter until the nineteenth century, when responsibility for the appointment of all assistant masters was transferred to the Headmaster. Whatever the 'official' protocol, William Fellows resigned on the retirement of John Medens in 1707, and was replaced as Usher by Thomas Smith, who stayed for twelve years.

William Betterley, Schoolmaster 1707 - 1733

William Betterley, M.A. was born in London in 1682, educated St Paul's School, and graduated from Trinity College, Cambridge. Appointed at the age of 25, he moved into the recently renovated Schoolmaster's House with his wife Elizabeth. Three of the couple's eight children predeceased him.

One of the school's most prominent Old Vigornians is Dr. John Wall, a pupil of Betterley's and one of the founders of the Worcester Infirmary. Wall was also the first to suggest a link between foot and mouth disease in cattle and its human equivalent. According to MacDonald (1936), Wall's later research led to the establishment of Malvern as a health spa and the founding of Worcester Porcelain after his discovery of an alternative to china clay.

Betterley faced personal financial hardship, owing to the rising cost of living compared with his fixed salary: he took on the role of Cathedral Librarian in 1711 (a role which was then combined with the headship until the retirement of Maurice Day in 1869) and then added the post of Rector of Stoke Prior to add the stipend to his income. This combination of roles, with the mandatory post of Minor Canon, proved too much; Smith resigned as Usher in 1719 and it was agreed that these roles, and their conditions, could be shared between the Master and Usher.

Betterley secured excellent academic results, with 70 Oxford matriculations. He remained Master until his death in 1733.

Thomas Miles, Schoolmaster 1733 - 1767

Thomas Miles, M.A. was born in Biggleswade, Bedfordshire, and graduated from Clare College, Cambridge. Miles had served as Usher for Betterley from 1719 until 1730. He returned as Master in 1733 with his wife Mary, with whom he had two daughters between 1734 and 1740.

During Miles' tenure as Master, the treasurer's accounts reveal that the number of pupils fell below forty (the number of King's Scholarships) for the first time. This is perhaps remarkable, but not unusual: Repton School was reduced to just one boy by the end of the eighteenth century - King's was hardly in such dire straits.

The number of King's Scholar vacancies increased steadily from five in 1761 up to twenty in 1767.

One notable Old Vigornian under Miles was Samuel Foote, comic actor and dramatist. Foote's comedy earned him a reputation as 'the English Aristophanes' and his popularity after a thirty-year long career led to an unusual honour: Foote was buried in Westminster Abbey.

Like Betterley before him, Thomas Miles died before he retired, having spent 48 years in service to The King's School.

Thomas Goodinge, Head Master 1768 - 1776

Thomas Goodinge, B.A. was only 22 years old when appointed, in stark contrast, perhaps deliberately, to his long-serving predecessor. Goodinge, schooled at King's Gloucester and a graduate of Trinity College, Oxford, was the first to be appointed as 'Head Master'. Miles' last Usher, Pixall, retired when Miles died, and, owing to the small number of pupils, was not replaced for the next three years, with Goodinge permitted to draw both salaries until William Wormington was appointed in 1771.

The Dean and Chapter continued to make changes to the operation of the school throughout Goodinge's headship. In November 1768 the Chapter decided that a limit of 7s 6d would apply to the entrance fee charged to choristers admitted as King's Scholars, with an upper limit for 'others' set at one Guinea for entrance and a further two Guineas per year until admittance as King's Scholars. These charges would be in addition to any boarding fees charged by the Head Master. Attendance requirements for both the Scholars and the Masters were restated in 1769 and again in 1770; in 1771 it was decreed that the College Boys were to sit in designated seats to the north side of the Choir for Surplice Prayers every Sunday and Holy Day (this remained the case until 1917).

A further revision to the conditions of the school, which would surely have pleased the boys, was an amendment to school hours. The six o'clock start was replaced by a day running from 7.00 am until midday, with an hour allowed for breakfast, and from 2.00 pm until 6.00 pm; these were the summer hours - from Lady Day until Michaelmas Day - which were further reduced for the winter months - from Michaelmas Day until Lady Day - to an 8.00 am start and a 5.00 pm finish.

This eighteenth century painting of College Green shows the southern aspect of College Hall. In the middle-distance are three prebendal houses, the last of which to be demolished was, presumably, Number 11 College Green, which no longer exists.

To balance this, an order in April 1770 prohibited the boys playing in the Cathedral cloisters, the gardened area in front of the Deanery (that is, between College Hall and Number 15), or the Guesten Hall (which would be demolished in 1862). A ban on kicking a football anywhere on College Green had been introduced as early as 1708, leaving nowhere available for the boys to play.

The appointment of Wormington as Usher, or 'Undermaster', involved a complicated arrangement for the division of the salary previously held entirely by Goodinge. The Usher was only to be paid the 'extra' amount based on the number of boys in his charge - the Lower School - which led to disputes between the two men over when each boy should be promoted to the Upper School, at which point Goodinge would receive the 'extra' amount for that boy. In June 1775, Wormington made an official complaint against his superior, for this and for his timekeeping, and the two men came to blows after Goodinge made similar complaints about his assistant. The Dean and Chapter considered the matter and decided that both men were at fault in various ways, although it was stated that the supremacy of the Head Master was not to be questioned by the Usher. With reprimands issued to both men, it was apparent that one of them would have to go - Goodinge decided to resign and left The King's School in 1776, going on to recieve a Doctorate at Oxford before being appointed Head Master of Leeds Grammar School. In a break with recent tradition, Wormington stayed on until 1784, after which he became vicar of Norton.

John Bennett, Head Master 1777

John Bennett, B.A., 44-year old Head Master of Bromsgrove School, was appointed Head Master from New Year's Day of 1777, exactly two weeks after the resignation of Goodinge. According to the Treasurer's records, cited by Craze (1972), Bennett became ill, perhaps due to the stress of the move to Worcester, and resigned, presumably as a result of his ill-health, only half a year into his headship.

Craze laments Bennett's appointment, noting that his successor at Bromsgrove, John Best, a Worcester man and most likely an Old Vigornian, transformed Bromsgrove School during his twelve-year tenure as Head Master there. However, at the time he might have been considered too young for the headship of King's, if he had applied for the position, as the Dean and Chapter needed an older man with the authority to take charge of both the boys and the Usher.

John Griffin, Head Master 1777 - 1813

John Griffin, M.A. was an Old Vigornian, having been a King's Scholar from 1764 to 1768, before graduating from Worcester College, Oxford, in 1775. By contrast with his predecessor, Griffin was only 22 years old when he was appointed Head Master.

After only one year, Griffin achieved a remarkable change: he was permitted to rent a separate boarding house for King's Scholars, who had previously lived with him in the Schoolmaster's House. For the fee of 2s per annum, the Dean and Chapter allowed the school to use the upper storey of the Dean's coach house on College Green (now Number 4) as a dormitory. The lease commenced in 1778 and is likely to have continued until 1799, when work was carried out to provide accommodation within College Hall; there are no remaining signs of this conversion work, which included an extension and chimneys, following the restoration of College Hall in 1887.

Griffin's second notable accomplishment was the arrangement and cataloguing of the library, for which he received a vote of thanks, and twenty guineas, from the Chapter in 1780. His library catalogue remained in use until it was replaced by Maurice Day around ninety years later.

Wormington retired in 1784 and was replaced by John Harward who served with Griffin for twelve years.

In August 1788, Worcester Cathedral hosted a notable Three Choirs Festival, brought forward by a month to allow King George III to enjoy the festival with his family while he was in the area. The Royal Family attended an evening concert in College Hall, seated in a special gallery in the centre of the hall; the main musical performance was Dryden's *St Cecilia's Ode*, sung to a setting by Handel, whose *Messiah* had been performed in the Cathedral to an audience of 2,000, including the Royal Family, earlier that day.

A glowing commentary of the success of Griffin's headship can be found in The *Worcester Guide* of 1799, which carried a highly complimentary report by W. Smart which reads, *"Besides a regular preparation for the University, Music, Drawing, the French, Spanish and Italian Languages and other fashionable accomplishments are taught by proper masters."* It is possible that the source of the information for the report was an early form of marketing - the 'public perception' of the school rather than the actual state of the school. It is likely that the 'proper masters' referred to were brought in from outside and taught their subjects as paid 'extras', in the way that peripatetic music and drama teachers have operated at King's and elsewhere for many years. One reason for scepticism is the number of King's pupils going on to Oxford and Cambridge Universities; Craze (1972) observes that seven scholars were awarded places at Oxford University during the first three years of Griffin's headship, the same number as for the following decade with only four in the 1790s. This certainly casts doubt on the accuracy of *'regular preparation for the University'*.

The school's curriculum began to fall out of favour with the middle-classes of the later eighteenth century, having had only one subject, geography, added to Henry VIII's prescribed Tudor education of Latin grammar, public oration and study of classical texts. This led to a drop in the number of pupils, which had increased during the early years of Griffin's headship; pupil numbers would have fallen further following the decision of the Dean and Chapter in 1807 which insisted that all pupils must come from families who attended Anglican churches and must be baptised members of the Church of England

Griffin's tenure as Head Master is second only to Henry Bright's, falling one year short of Bright's 38 years. He had a total of six Ushers, having 'inherited' Wormington and 'bequeathed' Cornelius Copner to his successor, William Porter. Griffin died in office and was buried in June 1813 at Stoulton, a chapel in the parish of Kempsey at which he had officiated since 1787. Until the appointment of a successor for Griffin, Cornelius Copner, Usher, stood in as acting Head Master.

Early 19th Century: 'not particularly noteworthy'

Roslington (1998) comments that the history of The King's School (known at that time mainly as the Cathedral Grammar School) during the first half of the nineteenth century was *"not particularly noteworthy. It seems to have suffered from a succession of ineffectual headmasters, too insipid or too disciplinarian to make any impact."*

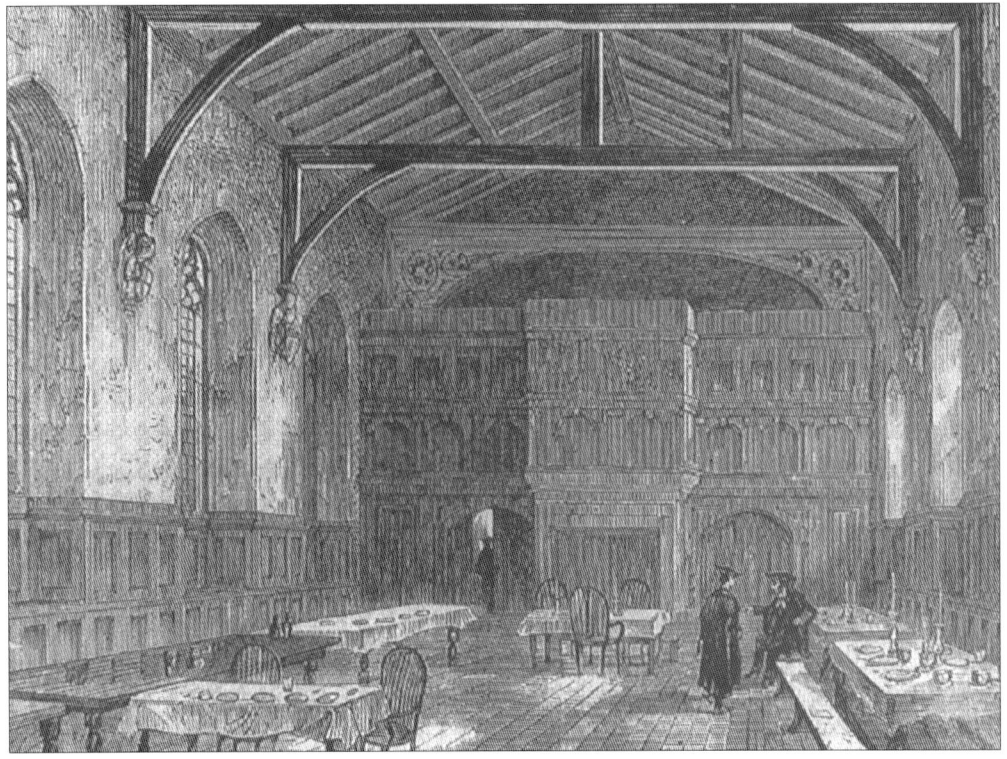

Early nineteenth century print showing the western end of College Hall. Although the scale might appear rather odd, interesting features to note include the roof and the large, enclosed gallery, both of which would be dramatically altered during the 1885 restoration. For a more detailed history of College Hall, see Chapter 1.

The first of these headmasters would have been William Porter, M.A., appointed to succeed John Griffin in 1814. Porter was followed by Allen Wheeler, B.D. in 1820.

The description, on the following page, of life as a pupil in the 1830s certainly seems rather bleak and it would appear that standards did certainly fall after John Griffin's headship, although Roslington may have been unfair in dismissing the succession of nineteenth century headmasters in such cutting terms.

William Porter, Head Master 1814 - 1820

It was not until March 1814 that the Dean and Chapter appointed Reverend William James Porter, M.A. as the new Head Master. However, Craze (1972) suggests that Porter, a Minor Canon and Librarian at Peterborough Cathedral, would have been teaching at the school for some weeks before his formal appointment, bringing Copner's interregnum to an end after around six months. It is for this reason that the date for Porter on the Headmasters' board in College Hall is incorrectly listed as 1813 (a similar irregularity exists for John Bennet, who is listed as serving in 1776, whereas his appointment was not until 1777). Porter was an accomplished musician and son of composer Samuel Porter.

An order was issued by the Dean and Chapter in 1814 insisting that *"the King's Scholars in future not be admitted until they are full 9 years of age according to the Statutes and are well grounded in their Grammar."* Porter is understood to have put a stop to Griffin's unofficial practice of admitting under-age scholars.

In 1815, the Dean and Chapter presented Porter with the vicarage of Himbleton, which he would hold for fifty years, although he is unlikely to have lived there. It is not known whether the reason for Porter's resignation in June 1820 was for musical, clerical or some other reason, but he left the school at the relatively young age of 45.

A fictional account

Ellen Price, born in Sidbury in 1814, had five brothers at The King's School, four of whom were choristers, during the 1820s and 1830s. In later life, as Mrs Henry Wood, she wrote three novels based on the Worcester of her childhood: *East Lynne* (1861), *The Channings* (1866) and *Mildred Arkell* (1868). The books, while technically 'fictional', are based on real people and the 'College School', which features prominently, is certainly The King's School of the 1820s.

The novels tell of a school in which discipline, when applied, was severe. *"Only in very flagrant cases was the extreme punishment of flogging resorted to by the present master. It had been more common with his predecessor. Of course its rarity made it all the more impressive when it did come."* Wood describes, preumably from anecdotes passed on by her brothers, the *"birch as big as a whole besom"* taken out by the master, the boy turning *"green and white"* while the school *"hushed itself into suspense"*.

Another account describes the Masters' fear of an examination announced by the Dean. *"The school was not in a state, in regard to proficiency, to bear an examination... In point of fact, the school had become notorious for its inefficiency... They could not spell; they knew nothing of English grammar, except what they could pick up through their acquaintance with Latin; they hardly knew a single event in English, French or modern history. What could be expected? For years and years, for many hours a day, these boys had been kept to work, always at the old routine work, Latin and Greek."*

Declining standards

It seems clear, if this account is to be believed - and it is widely held as accurate - that standards at the Cathedral Grammar School had slipped significantly from the time of Smart's report in the 1799 *Worcester Guide* (see above).

There was, evidently, little improvement during Wheeler's headship. Minutes of a meeting of the Dean and Chapter in November 1835 record a decision that canons would make surprise visits to the school, making a written record of the findings of each visit, *"for the purpose of enabling the Dean to ascertain the attendance of the Master and Scholars"*.

Allen Wheeler, Head Master 1820 - 1838

Reverend Allen Wheeler, B.D., aged 45 at the time of his appointment, was the younger brother of a King's Scholar and may have been an Old Vigornian himself. After taking up a

Minor Canonry in 1799, Wheeler took a B.D., established his own school in The Butts, Worcester, and became rector of Bredicot and then Broadwas.

Rev. Allen Wheeler, BD Head Master 1820-37

Among his first nineteen new scholars at King's were a number of former pupil's of Wheeler's own school, including his eldest son. Another new arrival was the new Usher, former King's Scholar Robert Sanders, still an undergraduate and aged only nineteen.

It was during Wheeler's headship that Thomas Eaton purchased the site of the former County Gaol and Worcester Castle buildings, including Castle Hill (see Appendix 15); the demolition of which took place during the 1820s would clear the way for the school to begin its expansion some sixty years later. The Dean and Chapter formally acquired the buildings on the southern and western sides of College Green from the Crown, having earlier disposed of some buildings and land in order to meet the taxation imposed during the Napoleonic Wars.

In his thirteenth year as Head Master, Wheeler received a gift from former pupils of a silver salver on which was an inscription praising Wheeler as *'an outstanding man, deservedly remarkable for the usefulness of his life and the integrity of his character'*. Seeing this as a sign of a forthcoming retirement, Sanders wrote to the Dean and Chapter in February 1833 asking them to consider him as Wheeler's successor. In fact it would be March 1838 before both Wheeler and Sanders would leave the school; Wheeler had been made rector of St Martin's and his former rectory of Broadwas was passed on to Sanders.

Octavius Fox, Head Master 1838 - 1852

Reverend Octavius Fox, M.A. was a graduate of Lincoln College, Oxford, who was appointed to succeed Wheeler in 1838.

Appointed with Fox was a new 'Second Master' (the first time this title is used for the Usher's role), Thomas Baxter, a King's Scholar from 1818-22 and son of an artist at the porcelain factory, was aged 28. Craze (1972) cites Canon James Went (King's Scholar 1858-62): *"This second master, Mr Thomas Baxter, was a fine musician and a good naturalist. his natural history lessons were the one redeeming feature of the school, and he gave many boys (myself included) a lifelong taste for geology and botany. Mr Baxter was hot-tempered but kind."* Baxter, who was not ordained and had not attended university, served under four Headmasters until shortly before his death in 1872; at a total of 34 years, Baxter's record is second only to Henry Moule's, whose length of service as Usher for 38 years is unlikely now to ever to be broken.

Two important reforms were introduced by Fox, confirmed by a Chapter Act of November 1838: a modernisation of school hours and the establishment of school prizes, which had first been introduced in 1832. For the first time since 1541, early morning and evening school would be abolished under a new timetable: school would run from 9.00 am until 12.30 pm and from 2.00 pm until 4.00 pm (with a 4.30 pm finish during the summer - defined as 26th March to 28th September). The Chapter awarded a total of £5 to be distributed as book prizes *'amongst the most deserving boys'*, with £2 to be used before the summer holiday

Rev. Octavius Fox, MA Head Master 1837-52

King's Remembered

Anonymous　　　　　　　　*Day Boy (1830s)*

Hardships had to be suffered by old boys, of which the present generation has had no experience. Would they think their task harder than it is now if they were expected to rise on dark wintry mornings so as to present themselves at the school door before daylight, and submit themselves to two hours' tasking before breakfast in the unwarmed old building open to the roof as it then was? There were no separate classrooms in those days, and no hot water pipes for raising the temperature above that which prevailed in the College Green outside.

What would the present scholars think of having to carry from home a bunch of brimstone matches, and two or three inches of dip candle - lucifers and wax lights and paraffin had not yet been invented - in order that they might see to improve their minds with Virgil or Xenophon before prayers in the dark mornings before Christmas?

The boys had no field or playground to resort to, for lack of which accommodations many a game of football in the sacred preceincts of the cloisters have I participated in, and many a game of fisticuffs have I witnessed in the same quadrangle.

The games in which the boys indulged themselves were of a rougher order then the refined cricket, or lawn tennis, or the 'football by rule' of the present day... 'Prisoner's base', 'hare and hounds', 'eggs and bacon' and rounders were more in vogue.

The idea of a master joining in the boys' sports had never at that time been entertained.

There was too, at that distant period, a never-dying feud, which I fancy has now died out, between the College School boys and the lads of St Peter's School - the 'Caws' and the 'Frogs'* as they designated each other - who engaged in regular battles on neutral ground in Edgar Street whenever an opportunity offered. Such engagements of course are now beneath the dignity of a College boy under the new scheme...

Published in *'The Vigornian'*, 1887. The author was recalling his time at the school in the 1830s.

* The King's School boys' name derives from the rooks who occupied the elm trees on College Green, while St Peter's School was on Frog Street (now Severn Street).

and the remaining £3 awarded at the 'November Audit'.

However, all was not well at the school and the boys were deemed by the Chapter to be out of control. The Chapter Act Book, in reponse to a report by the Treasurer, Canon Winnington Ingram, of June 1848, records three orders. First, the Head Master was to be asked to ensure that boys would be prevented from remaining in the school room (College Hall) after school hours and that he or the Second Master would undertake to lock the door and take the key home. Second, that the Head Master should pay more attention to the conduct of the boys so that the school would be more orderly. The third order expelled a pupil, William Boyd O'Malley, whose box of carpentry tools had been discovered in College Hall; the tools had evidently been use to cause significant damage to the school room.

The end came for Fox's headship, however, following the 1851 decision of the Chapter to separate the choristers from the school. A Master of the Choristers, Mr Thomas, was appointed with a salary of £20. The Chapter guaranteed Fox against financial losses as a result of losing these boys from his tuition but Fox tendered his resignation, serving only until a replacement Head Master could be found. Fox retired to the rectory of Doddenham, aged 41, in March 1852.

Stephen Denning, Head Master 1852 - 1856

The replacement Head Master was Reverend Stephen Poyntz Denning, M.A., who began his probationary year on 25th March 1852; a bachelor aged 24, Denning was ordained priest by the Bishop of Worcester and promptly married Frances Withington in June 1852.

Denning had inherited a school of only 50 boys, of which only four were older than 14, with none over the age of 16. He was swift to turn this around, welcoming 69 new boys during his brief tenure as Head Master. Denning was keen to reform the Henrican Statutes to allow him to take private pupils, to insist that the King's Scholars come from a social class acceptable to the parents of fee-paying pupils, and that a modern curriculum should be taught to all boys. Writing evidence for the Cathedral Commissioners in 1854, Denning was clear that the Dean and Chapter were supportive both of him and of his desire for reform. In 1856, Denning had been permitted to appoint a Third Master, William Helm; the Head Master would also have been content with his salary of £113 13s. 8d.

However, a number of personal tragedies befell Denning: his sister collapsed and died during a concert in College Hall in 1854; two years later, his ten-month old second daughter Matilda died, followed five days later by his first daughter Ella.

Denning submitted his resignation and was succeeded by his Third Master (and later, his brother-in-law), William Helm. Having taken some time to grieve, Denning accepted the

Rev. S P Denning, MA
Head Master 1852-56

headship of Bradford College in 1860, where he proved himself an excellent schoolmaster. Unfortunately, this was also a short-lived position, as Denning died of a stroke in January 1868.

William Helm, Head Master 1856 - 1859

Reverend William Henry Helm, B.A. lived with his sisters in the large house of his late father, former Mayor of Worcester Charles Augustus Helm, in College Yard. When he was promoted from Third Master to Head Master, he requested, and was granted, permission to have the boarders live in his own house and to rent out the Schoolmaster's house. Helm married Elizabeth Withington (sister-in-law of Denning) in December 1858.

Thirty-five new boys were admitted during Helm's headship to the enlarged school he had inherited from Denning. Among these boys was James Went (King's Scholar 1858-62) who, in a note cited by MacDonald (1936) described the entrance

Rev. W H Helm, BA
Head Master 1856-60

procedure. An examination by the Head Master in the Chapter House was followed by a test on Church Catechism by the Dean and Canon-in-Residence; the Dean nominated Went for a scholarship and he was told to start school the following day. Went described the composition of the school in 1858:

"The school consisted entirely of King's Scholars except five paying scholars, two older boys who were preparing for the universities, who took most of the time of the head master, two younger ones who were hoping they might get King's Scholarships, and one odd youth who boarded with the head master. The whole school consisted of forty-two boys, as there were vacancies among the King's Scholars. They bought their books from the second master [Thomas Baxter], whose perquisite it was to sell them."

Went described the Head Master as *"an old boy (and so dominated by the second master)"*, although he later acknowledged to MacDonald that this was schoolboy gossip and had little factual basis. *"His idea of teaching was to tell the boys to learn something. If they did not know it they got a severe caning on the hands."*

According to Went, arithmetic and algebra were taught by Baxter, while Helm directed their study of Euclid. Saturday mornings were used for religious instruction, with Baxter teaching catechism to the boys while Helm tutored the university hopefuls in Greek Testament. Sundays were used for prep, answering questions on Scripture history to be handed in on Mondays. The boys were responsible for organising their own games and had a four-oar boat on the river, although Went notes that it was not used during his time.

Helm's headship, and indeed his life, was cut tragically short when, following exertion while rowing on the river, he collapsed and died in June 1859. His wife later gave birth to their son, who was named in honour of his late father. William Henry Helm junior grew up to become a leading writer with several published titles and was Literary Editor of *The Morning Post*.

Thomas Baxter served as acting Head Master, while Mr Fowler, who had replaced Mr Thomas as Master of the Choristers in 1857, was brought in to cover Helm's teaching.

Maurice Day, Headmaster 1860 - 1879

The Dean and Chapter sought to bring some stability to the school after a turbulent decade. Reverend Maurice Day, M.A. was appointed with effect from 17th January 1860 and he served as Headmaster of The King's School for the next twenty years.

The King's School of modern times owes much gratitude to the work of Day: during his two decades he oversaw an increase in the number of boys at the school, the uncovering of the Majestas in College Hall, the establishment of the KSW Boat Club, and the publication of the inaugural issue of The Vigornian. Day also laid the groundwork for the New Scheme which would be championed by his successor, William Bolland (see Chapter 4).

Maurice Day was born in 1827 and was the son of the rector of Wickham Market, Suffolk. Day's career saw him progress from University College, Oxford in 1850 to teach at Sherborne School, Dorset, where he was married to Hannah Bertha Finch before being ordained deacon in 1852. In the same year, Day moved to the recently-opened Victoria College, Jersey, where he served as Professor of Classical Literature and established the school's first boarding house. Sadly, Hannah Day died of consumption in 1854. Day was ordained priest two years later before remarrying in St Helier. His new wife, Amelia Greaves Johnson, had their daughter Helen in 1858.

Two years later, the Day family moved to Worcester, where Maurice took on the headship at The King's School. His salary of £200 was less than the £250 he had received at Victoria College, but was accompanied by the Schoolmaster's House on College Green and use of the Dean's coach house for a nominal fee of 2s. per year. During the 1860s, the Days would have a further five children.

Flourishing numbers

One of Day's first actions was to recommend the disbanding of the Cathedral's school for Choristers, which was duly agreed by the Dean and Chapter, who paid £100 to The King's School for the Choristers' tuition and allowed for the employment of a Third Master, E.H. Love, to teach them. This added sixteen pupils to the school, who, with new boarders, three of whom followed Day from Jersey, enabled the school roll to swell to 79 boys by the summer term.

Further boarders from Victoria College followed during the next few years. The boarding fee was £80; Day would not allow boarders to be considered for King's Scholarships so as to ensure that the forty Scholars were local boys - a secondary reason would have been to preserve the fee income from boarding.

Unlike his predecessor, Day was a popular Headmaster, which must have contributed to his success in recruiting new pupils. According to James Went (King's Scholar 1858-62), *"Mr Day was much beloved by everyone"*. By 1872, the school had grown to 120 boys.

A model school

Between 1864 and 1867, The Endowed Schools Commisioners inspected most of the public schools in England and Wales. Craze (1972) cites the following report on The King's School by one of the Commissioners, James Bryce.

"Few schools in England have a school-room comparable to that at Worcester Cathedral... a superb thirteenth century hall... large enough to accommodate all the classes, the noise being moderated by the height of the room.

The Foundation serves the whole town, and the chief reason why it is used by the upper rather by the lower classes is to be sought in its educational character. The work of the school... was in most respects satisfactory. In the middle and lower parts of the school the classics were quite up to the average level of a large grammar school, in the higher parts they were much above that average."

The report went on to praise the pupils' ability to translate between English and French, the ability of the Fifth and Sixth Form to handle geometry and algebra, the overall standard of arithmetic in the younger classes, and the behaviour and general demeanour of the boys.

"The Worcester Cathedral School is in some respects a model of what a grammar school in a large provincial town ought to be. It is an instance of what is almost as rare as it is admirable, a really useful endowment, which has been put within the reach of the commercial class an education better than any they could or would have purchased for themselves. It teaches classics well, wothout neglecting mathematics and arithmetic."

This is a significant improvement on the accounts of the school during the 1820s, 1830s and 1840s, and clearly indicates that education at King's had taken a turn for the better; this improvement, which can be credited to Maurice Day, set the foundation for the continuing improvement and progress made during the following 150 years.

Beyond the schoolroom

Bryce was less positive in his assessment of the boys' access to sport and playing facilities. The playground was a sodden piece of uneven ground between the Cathedral and the river towpath. In 1873 and 1875 Day secured funding and permission from the Chapter to level and extend the lawn as far as the ruins of the monks' dormitories, surrounding it with wrought iron railings.

Boxing was a popular pastime, enjoyed by the Second Master's sons, Tom and Jim Baxter. Running battles between the feuding 'Cads' or 'Frogs' (boys from the factories or St Peter's School) and the 'Caws' (King's boys) took place throughout this time: see the anonymous report of a pupil from the 1830s on page 38.

Fives was often played by the boys, leading the Headmaster to raise funds for the building of a Fives Court in the playground in 1878. This was a well-used facility until the construction of School House provided a larger, more suitable playground for the school to the east of the building a decade later.

In an unusual act of co-operation between the Cathedral School and the public Grammar School, a short-lived Cadet Corps was established in 1865. Older boys, who had the strength to bear the weight of bayonets, were instructed by Sergeants from the Regulars or Volunteer Staff; the Corps was attached to the county's Second Battalion of the Rifle Volunteers and, according to Craze (1972), wore "a blue serge uniform and a round peakless cap, black leather cross-belt and waist-belt with a pouch and bayonet frog". This early Cadet Corps, which was disbanded in 1868, was a forerunner of the Officer Training Corps, which would be established some forty years later. For more on Cadets at King's, see Chapter 5.

A small field near to the Diglis Locks, unlevelled and without proper drainage or access, was leased by Day for the boys to play cricket and football. This was a meagre start to providing

Rev. M Day, MA (Headmaster 1860-1869)

playing fields for the school, but a foundation on which Bolland would be able to build.

Perhaps the most lasting addition to the life of the school was the establishment of the KSW Boat Club in 1877. The rather grand idea of a boat club would not be matched by any significant support from the Headmaster until William Chappel's time, since Day's successor was more keen on cricket than rowing; the first boathouse would not be provided until 1914. More about the KSW Boat Club and the development of rowing at King's can be found on the following pages.

University scholarships

A particularly contentious issue arose when the school's access to the Meeke Scholarships for Magdalen College, established by the will of John Meeke (OV 1613-17) in 1665, was challenged by the public Grammar School. The wording of the will referred to scholarships being awarded to 'the Free Grammar School of Worcester'. When Rev F J Eld became High Master of the Grammar School, he proposed that the boys of his school, and not of the Worcester Cathedral School, were the rightful beneficiaries. A war of words continued over a few years, with the eventual outcome that both schools were recognised as 'free' schools and 'grammar' schools, and so equal weight was given to applications from either school. It would be for this reason that Bolland would later insist that the name of the school should be changed to Worcester Cathedral Grammar School, including the word 'grammar'.

During the 1870s, the number of places gained by King's pupils at Oxford University increased. Unfortunately, the number of scholarships available decreased, owing to changes made by the University, at Magdalen Hall and Worcester College, which had previously been rather generous to the school. Dean Peel retired after the reopening of the Cathedral in 1874; he died the following year and bequeathed £1,500 to the school to provide a leaving scholarship at Oxford or Cambridge to be paid for from the interest.

The school's endowment

From the late 1840s, when the headmaster of the King's School Rochester filed a law suit against his Dean and Chapter for the extrication of his school from the Cathedral Foundation, much was made of the state of Cathedral schools, the influences of the Dean and Chapter of each Cathedral over its school, and the paltry value of scholarship awards, salaries and funding for facilities which, in many cases, had altered little, if at all, since the time of Henry VIII. The issues were further emphasised when the Ecclesiastical Commissioners took over responsibility for much of England's Cathedral estates in the 1850s.

In 1867, with the support of Maurice Day, a committee of the City Council of Worcester considered the matter of scholarships for King's Scholars, forwarding their resulting report to the Ecclesiastical Commissioners; the Commissioners replied that they were unconcerned. The City Council petitioned Parliament: *"That your honorable House will be pleased to take such measures as shall restore, for the purposes of education, that fair proportion of the present value of the endowments of Worcester Cathedral to which the school of such Cathedral is justly entitled."*

In 1869 the Endowed Schools Commission was granted the right to apply to the Ecclesiastical Commissioners for grants for Cathedral schools. The 1868 Public Schools Act had enabled Westminster School to receive £15,000 and an annual grant of £3,500 from the Ecclesiastical Commissioners; Alderman Edward Webb wrote to a member of the House of Lords in 1869 to request that Worcester's Cathedral School be treated in a similar manner. Webb also proposed such a motion at the City Council, seconded by Alderman T Rowley Hill, arguing that the Ecclesiastical Commissioners controlled three-quarters of the Cathedral's income but were using much of it to supplement the incomes of the most poorly paid clergy. Rowley Hill suggested that King Henry VIII had established the Cathedral Foundation with one sixth of its income set aside for the school: if the same proportion was available to the Worcester Cathedral School in 1869, it would provide forty King's Scholars with £40 per year and eight University Scholarships worth £100 each.

The Ecclesiastical Commissioners held an inquiry into the endowment provided for the Worcester Cathedral School. It was conducted by Walter Skirrow, who reported in 1887. The report was quoted in a letter of 1881 in the City's Chamber Order Book, cited by Craze (1972):

"The School should take its place not only as a high class Day School for the City, but also as an important Boarding School for the County of Worcester. With the exception of Bromsgrove Grammar School, which is very inadequately endowed, there is no First Grade Boarding School in Worcestershire nor any other foundation out of which one could be created under the Endowed Schools Act.

It is proposed that the School shall retain the character of a Grammar School, preparing Boys for the Ancient Universities. This cannot be done effectively without improving the Buildings and augmenting the Endowment.

It will be necessary to provide Class Rooms with special appliances for instruction on Natural Science. A considerable sum would have to be expended on the Establishment of suitable Boarding Houses and in the improvement of the Head Master's Residence if the Cathedral School is to be, what it is conceived it should be, one of the chief Boarding Schools of the District. In any case a proper Playground must be provided for the Scholars."

Skirrow proposed a grant of £7,000 from the Common Fund

KSW Boat Club

Megan Glenn

The KSW Boat Club was established in 1877 under the headship of Maurice Day. William Bolland became Headmaster in 1879 and brought with him the public school love of sport and competition. He favoured cricket, which led to a shaky start for the Boat Club as it struggled for numbers, but it battled through the late 1800s to become a strong social and competitive part of the school. William Chappel followed Bolland and shared his belief that sport produced 'well-rounded Christian gentlemen'. During the first decade of the twentieth century, he employed staff from Oxford and Cambridge universities to coach and develop the rowing programme at King's. Three important rules were introduced:

1. *A boat is a place for work, not for protracted conversations.*
2. *The stroke's authority is supreme in the boat.*
3. *Imaginary ills sometimes become very real when too much dilated upon.*

1st IV, 1912

At this time many of the boys went on to row at university with some returning to King's to coach in later years.

With dedicated coaches the sport continued to grow. The school IV trained every day after school and most mornings with its coach J.N. Allison, who understood that rowing was a sport that required plenty of hard work to get results. By this time, rowing had become the dominant sport and cricket was less popular. However, all funds for equipment had to be raised by the Boat Club as the school still had no budget for rowing, unlike other sports.

The first boathouse was bought in 1914 and was situated on the St John's bank of the River Severn. It was a barge purchased for £18 and was known as 'Noah's Ark' because of its appearance. The boys loved it and all agreed it was a valuable addition to the warm atmosphere at King's. *"Due to an 'unfortunate accident' in 1921 however, the barge had to be disposed of"* (Bawden 2012). In 1921, one of the masters, Sam Strong, started taking a keen interest in rowing. Moving rowing to the summer term enabled him to coach a competitive 1st IV to race at the prestigious Marlow Regatta. The school purchased two more fours, doubling the fleet of boats and allowing interest in the sport to grow.

A replacement boathouse was completed on Hylton Road in 1923. The rowers had been without a home for two years, and this second boathouse was even more appreciated than the first. It was a humble wooden structure similar to an army hut, but it served the school well until the 1950s.

By the thirties the feud between the cricketers and the oarsmen had finally ended. Rowing results were in decline but enthusiasm was high. At the 1936 Olympic Games in Berlin Peter Jackson (School House 1927-30) won a silver medal in the VIII. The Headmaster, Cuthbert Creighton, assembled the school in 1937 to listen to the commentary of the Boat Race and an Oxford victory.

The desire to row at the Henley Royal Regatta was sparked in the 1940s by Sam Strong. He arranged a trip for the oarsmen to go to the event to watch some of the world's elite oarsmen compete and also arranged for Peter Jackson to coach some sessions. The rowing world was modernising and in 1948, the Marlow Public Schools' Cup changed from fixed seat boats to sliding seats. For many King's oarsmen this was their first experience in such a boat. In 1949, a new

'Noah's Ark', 1914

coach, Bob Carlyle, joined the school and became a great influence.

In 1951, a King's IV made it to the final of the Marlow IVs race and won, bringing home the Henley Cup. Under the guidance of coaches Carlyle and Knight, the 1st IV won again in 1952, 1956, 1957 and 1958. The road to Henley Royal Regatta had begun. King's was now top of all the public schools rowing in IVs. This was also the decade in which Hugh Scurfield (Chappel House 1943-54) went on from King's to win the Silver Goblets at Henley. In 1958 the Boat Club purchased its first eight, beginning the transition into big boats.

In 1959, the Headmaster decided to replace the then dilapidated boathouse. He thought it would be better for the school if a new boathouse was built on the school campus, and a site was acquired next to the school gardens, at the end of Severn Street, only a few yards from the river bank. Designed by the Master in charge of Rowing, Richard Knight to house four eights and six fours, it was built by R.J.W. Bryer for £4,000, with most of the money raised by the Boat Club. The new boathouse was opened in 1960 by Mrs Scurfield and marked the start of another successful period for the Boat Club.

1st IV, 1955

The transition into bigger boats appeared to have paid off in 1960 when the Junior VIII won at Marlow. The next year they went on to race at the Henley Royal Regatta, the first entry for King's into the Princess Elizabeth Cup, getting knocked out in the third round. The following years saw further attempts at Henley, but to no avail. Richard Gabriel began coaching at King's in 1967 and was a great influence on the successes at the following year's National Championships. Under his watch, rowing became a more serious sport at King's with commitment expected six days a week. Tim Watson joined the coaching staff two years later and produced numerous charts to help to understand the new adjustable rigging systems.

This paid off in 1969 when the Boat Club won the National Schools Cup for Colt Eights in Pangbourne for the first time and had the most successful season for the club across all ages.

With a new boat in 1970, the First VIII won the First VIII's Cup at the National Schools Regatta, a victory that was repeated at the 1975 Regatta. In 1976, David Townsend (School House 1968-73) raced in the Men's Coxless IV at the Olympic Games in Montreal, taking twelfth place. Four years later, he achieved a Bronze medal at the Moscow Games in the same event. In the late seventies, following the gradual start of co-education at King's, girls were introduced to the Boat Club.

The Boat Club's first overseas trips included training and international racing against some of Europe's best crews in Ghent, Belgium. There were successes at local regattas in the early 1980s but none to rival the success at Marlow and Henley in the fifties and sixties. At the National Schools Regatta in 1983, Edmund Simpson and Peter Beaumont won Silver in the Championship pairs. A few years later, Peter Beaumont (Wulstan House 1981-83) raced in the Men's VIII at the 1988 Seoul Olympics, coming fourth.

In the nineties, specialist staff were employed who took rowing to new levels at King's. One key figure was Paul Sterckx who coached many girls' crews from 1996 to 2012. From 1995 to 1999 the same group of

Girls' VIII, 2001

Members of the KSW Boat Club, photographed in front of Richard Knight's Boathouse, 1996

girls won events at the National Schools Regtta and National Championships every year.

King's had a return to the glory years of First VIII's in 2001, when the Girls' VIII was chosen to represent England at the Home Countries Regatta, and in 2002 when the Girls VIII won the Championship VIIIs at the National Schools' Regatta. In 2004, the boys won the Championship Quad Sculls at the National Schools' Regatta. Zac Purchase (Oswald House 1997-2004) raced at the 2008 Beijing Olympic Games, winning Gold in the Men's Lightweight Double. Four years later, he raced again at the London Games, this time gaining a Silver medal in his event.

Fifty years after Richard Knight's boathouse had been completed, the Boat Club, with 140 active members, had once again outgrown its home.

In 2011, thanks to an extraordinary gift to the school from Michael Baker (Choir House 1948-55), a member of the 1955 1st IV, the boathouse was demolished to make way for the stunning Michael Baker Boathouse. During construction, the rowers were moved to a make-shift yard in the 'SPACE' car park. After surviving two winters in the yard, the rowers finally took possession of their new home with the same sense of pride and enthusiasm as their predecessors in 1923 must have done.

Since its opening in April 2012, the Michael Baker Boathouse has seen record numbers of rowers joining the KSW Boat Club. This enabled the Boat Club to achieve one of its goals, to give every pupil at King's the opportunity to try rowing, whether in games sessions or after school. Rowers continued to compete at regional and national events leading to the annual National Schools Regatta and the Henley Royal or Henley Women's Regattas.

Captains of Boats Reunion, May 2012

Megan Glenn, a native of New Zealand, arrived at King's in 2012; a passionate rower, she has been a KSWBC Coach and Boathouse Manager of the Michael Baker Boathouse since its opening.

In 2012, Carol Bawden produced a book 'The King's School Worcester Boat Club - Anecdotes and Memories' which provides a fuller history of the KSW Boat Club.

of the the Ecclesiastical Commisioners to provide an adequate endowment with a further £5,000 to improve school buildings and an additional £4,000 to be awarded from other sources.

These figures had not been officially disclosed to the Dean and Chapter, or to the Headmaster, when, in 1877, the Ecclesiastical Commissioners offered the school a grant of £3,000 and up to £4,000 for the improvement of school buildings, which would include much-needed renovation of the overcrowded and insanitary Schoolmaster's House. The Dean and Chapter were unable to accept this offer from the Ecclesiastical Commissioners, and the issue was left unresolved by the time of Day's retirement in 1879, although significant foundations for reform had been made.

College Hall

Although described in glowing terms by Bryce of the Endowed Schools Commission, College Hall had fallen into a rather sorry state. The western gallery was no longer usable and the window had been filled in with bricks. The roof was subject to urgent repairs in 1861, following damage resulting from ventilation holes being made. The eastern wall was still rendered and had against it a stepped platform for an orchestra, generally used by the art teacher, W P Bowen, for his classes.

The Headmaster's desk was in front of the platform, from where he taught pupils at desks in double rows facing in towards the centre of the room. The Third Master, R H Blair from 1861, had his desk against the north wall; his mathematics class faced him.

The eastern end of College Hall, set up for a school assembly, January 2015.
The striking 'Majestas' reredos was uncovered in 1872 when Maurice Day requested that the plaster covering be removed from the eastern wall.

The Second Master, still Thomas Baxter until his retirement in 1872, sat with his back to the sealed and curtained off door from College Green. Baxter was succeeded as Second Master by Alfred Beaven who left two years later to become headmaster of Preston Grammar School; Harman Ogle, a former pupil of Day's from Victoria College, served as Second Master for two years until his appointment as headmaster of Magdalen College School, Oxford, in 1876. Day's final Second Master would be Desmond Sampson.

The school had outgrown College Hall by 1872; Day appealed to the Dean and Chapter for additional classrooms. Unwilling to provide further accommodation elsewhere, the reponse was an instruction to remove the old orchestra platform and replace it with a full-width platform above the passageway between College Green and the cloisters; the rest of the floor would then be levelled to make the most of the available space. The work, carried out during the school holiday of July 1872, proved to have an enormous impact on College Hall. Not only was the platform now large enough to hold a full class, accessed by five wooden steps from the floor which was 15 feet longer, but the removal of the previous platform structure had exposed the string course of the eastern wall; the plasterwork was significantly damaged, so Day requested that the rendering be removed. This resulted in the remarkable rediscovery of the reredos showing Christ in Majesty, flanked by the empty niches on which the four evagelists would once have stood, and the inner framing of the window above (although the window would not be opened up until the restoration of 1885-87). The improvement to College Hall was dramatic, and led the Chapter to use the hall for the grand re-opening of the Cathedral in 1874 following its substantial Gothic restoration under Dean Peel, which had included reordering, repair, enlargement and the installation of a new ring of twelve bells.

Day's retirement

Day was offered the vicarage of Wichenford, which after twenty years as Headmaster, he accepted in August 1879. He handed to his successor a much-improved and enlarged school, with strong foundations laid for further development.

Day spent eleven years at Wichenford, where he taught his own son and a small number of other pupils. The parish played an annual cricket fixture against Worcester Cathedral School, as reported in *The Vigornian*, a magazine established by Day. Rev. Maurice Day died in March 1890.

The Vigornian

The Vigornian was first published in 1878 as *The Worcester Cathedral Grammar School Chronicle*. The first editorial cites the reasons for the publication as *"the desire not to be behind other Public Schools"* and to allow *"the management and direction of the boys' be practised, and afford opportunities for the expression of individual opinion and criticism on questions of general interest"*.

The magazine was published twice each year, until 1897, and then four times each year until the 1970s.

The earliest copy held in the School Archive is issue No. 4, Vol. 1, published in December 1880. Articles included 'A Tramp through the Isle of Wight' and 'Notes on the Architecture of Worcester Cathedral', alongside reports on Speech Day, the Library and Football.

Issue No. 12, November 1887 (pictured, right), reports on the school's return to College Hall after the three-year long restoration. The editorial reports *"The noble old Hall, endeared to so many by the recollections of happy days spent therein, cannot be said to have suffered in any way by the restoration, for, while every requisite improvement has been made, the striking features of the old building have in every case been carefully preserved."* The following issue includes a photograph of the refurbished hall (reproduced on page 22), the first photograph to be included in the magazine, which, at that time, was printed by 'Littlebury and Company' of Worcester. Issue No. 12 also features the first printed use of the school's Greek motto, from Sophocles.

These early editions bore a retail price of 6d, which was charged to parents' school bills. *The Vigornian* of June 1898 complained that "The time seems to have come when boys in the school merely take their copies of the 'Vigornian' as a matter of course and because it is charged on the bill, but when it comes to helping in any way to make it more interesting, they no more dream of contributing."

For many years *The Vigornian* was edited by teams of pupils, generally working with the oversight of one of the Masters.

The introduction to the Winter 1955 issue reported a concern about the purpose and readership of the magazine. *"Since the issue of the magazine in its new form the Editors have been what one might call Vigornian Conscious. They have endeavoured to present something better than their contemporaries. But have they succeeded? No, they have not! Admittedly they have eliminated the unnecessary entries such as School and Library Notes but their shrinking of the Vigornian has not altered its character in any way. What is wrong? For one thing the Editors are endeavouring to satisfy two parties at the same time; both the Old Boys and the School. It can serve one or the other but it cannot serve both. As things stand, the majority of O.V.'s receive the Vigornian merely to read the scanty O.V. news and to learn how the school is faring on the Sports field. The rest of the Magazine is designed for the interest of the present members of the school."*

At that time, the magazine's content was not unlike the current publication, with a list of staff, 'School Notes', reports on trips, sports and activities, and 'OV Notes'. Alongside this, however, were contributions from pupils, including stories and poetry. By the 1970s, the magazine had an entirely more 'avant garde' style, and included far fewer 'official' school reports and more creative writing, poetry, cartoons and other illustrations and even sheet music.

Peter Iddon (Staff 1980 - present) took over editorship of *The Vigornian* in 1983, and, during his first 30 years in charge of the magazine, it returned to a more formal record of school life, with reports on trips, activities, sports, drama, arrivals and departures to the Common Room, university places awarded and 'OV News'. The magazine was enlarged to allow for more detailed reports, and published annually, in December, covering the previous school year. Advertisements were included, to cover the increasing cost of producing the magazine, which, designed by John Roslington, Head of IT, from the 1980s until 2010, had become a large, full-colour publication.

In 2011, production of the re-branded *Vigornian* moved to the Design, Media and Reprographics department, where Danny Payne worked with Peter Iddon to update the design and review the content, to include a section for each of the Junior Schools, the Parents' Committee and Development Trust, and a larger Arts section to balance what had become a sport-heavy publication. A full list of support staff and Governors was also introduced. The timing was also considered, and, from 2012, the magazine, printed by 'Rotary Printers' of Stourport-on-Severn, was published in the summer and distributed on the last day of term. In 2014 the cost of printing each copy was around £3.00, with a print run of 5,500 copies, most of which were mailed to OVs, who renewed subscriptions in five or ten year blocks.

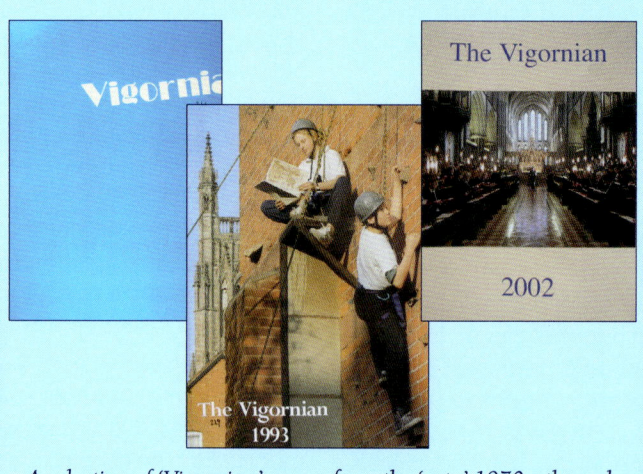

A selection of 'Vigornian' covers from the 'arty' 1970s, through the more formal designs of the 1990s and, right, the current style.

The Vigornian.

THE WORCESTER CATHEDRAL GRAMMAR SCHOOL CHRONICLE.

"τὰ μὲν διδακτὰ μανθάνω, τὰ δ'εὑρετὰ ζητῶ, τὰ δ'εὐκτὰ παρὰ θεῶν ᾐτησάμην."

No. 12. Vol. I.　　　　　NOVEMBER, 1887.　　　　　Price 6d.

Contents.

	Page
Editorial	175-176
The Illuminated Boat Procession	176
Re-opening of Worcester Cathedral Grammar School	177-183
The Cathedral School (a letter to the *Advertiser*)	183-185
Sermon on Education by Rev. E. Thring	185-187
Cricket	187-189
Athletic Sports	190
Rowing	190-191
On the Heights	191
School Officers	192
School News	192
Correspondence	193-194
Chess	194

Editorial.

AFTER nearly three years' exile, we have returned to our old quarters, not in the condition we left them, but beautified and embellished by the master-hand of the Architect. The noble old Hall, endeared to so many by the recollections of happy days spent therein, cannot be said to have suffered in any way by the restoration, for, while every requisite improvement has been made, the striking features of the old building have in every case been carefully preserved. It is not necessary for us here to enumerate the various additions and alterations that have been made, as a detailed account is given on a subsequent page; but, while congratulating the School on the possession of such a magnificent Hall, we feel that our thanks are due to all those who have been instrumental in bringing about the work of restoration, as well as to the contractors, for the admirable way in which that work has been executed. It was feared that the new roof and block-flooring would spoil the acoustic properties for which the room was famed; this fear, however, was entirely dispelled on the opening day, when they were put to the test. In our next number we hope to give an illustration of the Great Hall as now restored.

Though our Cricketers achieved no striking victory last season, great praise is due to them for the plucky stand they made against clubs far stronger than themselves. The new members, though by no means equal to those whose places they filled, did good service in the field, and the bowling was more satisfactory than we anticipated. The low scores show that there is still plenty of room for improvement in the batting, and this will only be attained by steady and regular practice all through the season. Equally

Vigornian No. 12, published in November 1887, which reported on the restoration of College Hall in an article entitled 'Re-opening of Worcester Cathedral Grammar School', and includes the first printed use of the school motto (see Appendix 7).

4: Bolland and the birth of the modern school

W E Bolland - Headmaster 1879-1896

William Ernest Bolland was born in New Zealand on 26th May 1847. His father, Reverend William Bolland, died three days later; his mother, Jane, stayed in New Zealand for two years before returning to England. At the age of 13, Bolland went to Tonbridge School, then on to Marlborough College when he was 16. At Marlborough, where Bolland encountered the philosophy of physical education expounded by Arnold, he was Head of School and editor of the school magazine, played in the cricket and football teams and was a member of the shooting team. On leaving school, Bolland was awarded an Open Scholarship to Merton College, Oxford, where he read 'Greats' (Classics).

In 1872, William Bolland married Margaret Hill, before moving to Bedford Grammar School, where he was a Master from 1874, becoming Second Master in 1875. While at Bedford Grammar School, where he was ordained in 1877, Bolland worked with Andrew Lang to publish *'Politics of Aristotle'* in 1879. Bolland was appointed Headmaster of Worcester's Cathedral School from September 1879, arriving with Margaret and their three sons and two daughters. While at Worcester, the couple had three further sons.

Early progress

On his arrival, Bolland was keen to develop the school according to the model of the new public schools, including Cheltenham College, Marlborough College and Malvern College (founded in 1841, 1843 and 1862 respectively); he found an immediate ally among the Governors in Canon Alfred Barry, a former Headmaster of Cheltenham College, at which he had built a gym, junior school and five boarding houses. Barry organised the enlargement of 10 College Green before moving in 1872, becoming the first Canon to live in the present-day Deanery.

Among Bolland's first ideas was to fully exploit College Hall, which could not be used after dusk; he proposed the installation of artificial lighting, which he discussed with Canon Barry and the Dean and Chapter, who decreed 'That the Schoolroom be lighted with Gas'. The cost of installation was met by subscriptions; three circular iron pendants with forty naked flames each were installed. An early result of this was that the first School Concert, arranged by the Precentor Vine Hall, charged by Bolland with the task of organising wider musical participation, took place in College Hall in December 1879.

The Headmaster quickly turned his attention to the school's meagre sports facilities. The rented playing field near the Diglis locks was far from ideal: it was remote and had no access road; there was no pavilion nor any means of providing one; the site had not been levelled and was liable to flooding. Bolland sought an alternative, and worked with Canon Barry to explore the Chapter Meadows, deciding on a large field next to the New Severn Bridge; the Dean and Chapter agreed that this could be rented instead of the Diglis field, and contributed £5 towards the cost of levelling the site; Bolland raised the remaining funds through charging admission to public events in College Hall. By 1882, the first school cricket match took place on what would later be extended into the New Road Cricket Ground.

In late 1880, the Schoolmaster's House, one of two buildings at 7 College Green, in which the Headmaster lived in poor conditions

Reverend William Ernest Bolland

with his family and the boarders, suffered an outbreak of 'diphtheric sore throats' leading to a temporary move to Powick while repairs were made. A month later, Bolland returned, but was the first victim of a similar outbreak the following spring. The boarders and Headmaster moved again, this time to a house in Malvern, travelling into school each morning. A survey of the Schoolmaster's House was undertaken, and it was determined that its drain-soaked foundations rendered it unfit for habitation. The Dean and Chapter agreed to demolish the old building, and the Headmaster established a new boarding house in St John's, at Cripplegate House near the new playing field, rented for £60 a year, until a replacement building could be developed at school.

The Choir School

The Cathedral's school for the Choristers, which operated between 1852 and 1860, when it was ended on the recommendation of Maurice Day, had evidently been missed, with parents of Choristers complaining that the boys were missing a great deal of school work, because the timetable of the Cathedral School (King's) made little allowance for them. Bolland agreed that there was a need for a special timetable for Choristers, and suggested to the Dean and Chapter that this would best be provided for in a separate school.

This proposal was accepted, following the appointment of H.H. Woodward as a Minor Canon in 1881, who was made Master of a 'School for Choristers', with an Assistant Master, Charles Shuttleworth, and the boys' musical training led by the Cathedral Organist under the charge of the Precentor. The sixteen Choristers were transferred from King's to the Choir School. After the first six months of operation, Woodward recommended that the school be given a building of its own;

the Dean and Chapter agreed, and 'Choir House' was formed, at Number 3 College Green, by the end of 1882. For further details of the formation and operation of the Choir School, see Chapter 7; for more information about Choir House (Numbers 3 and 4 College Green) see 'The buildings of College Green'.

The New Scheme

From 1869, under the Endowed Schools Act, public schools were offered 'New Schemes' to ensure adequate funding and provision of resources, often in exchange for changes to their Governance and curriculum. In February 1881 the Charity Commissioners published a draft New Scheme for the Cathedral School at Worcester, copied to the Dean and Chapter and local newspapers, requiring any objections to be made within two months.

In April, the 'Cathedral School Committee of the Worcester Town Council' produced a document calling for a grant of £20,000 as well as a site for a Headmaster's house, boarding houses, classrooms, other buildings and a playground. In response, the Charity Commission was willing to provide better terms, but wanted an estimate of the cost of alterations to Number 14 College Green (then the proposed site of the new Schoolmaster's House) to enable the building to accommodate classrooms, dormitories and a Headmaster's residence.

In November, the Dean and Chapter submitted plans for the work to convert Number 14 into a Headmaster's house, with a new building comprising four classrooms with a large dormitory above, to be built on the site of the ruined monks' dormitory, to the north of Number 14. The undercroft of College Hall would be used a 'play room' in lieu of a playground.

By March 1882, the Dean and Chapter had a letter from Bolland complaining about the state of the Schoolmaster's House with a report from his doctor and a report from the architect to the Charity Commissioners, Mr Perry, on the new plans. The task of repairing the Schoolmaster's House was to be delegated to the Treasurer, but in respect of the development plans, they resolved to partition College Hall so that it would serve as several classrooms and a large school room and to attempt, as part of the settlement with the Ecclesiastical Commission, to acquire the house adjacent to the Schoolmaster's House, at Number 7 College Green, to demolish both houses and build a new 'School House' on the site.

Progress in resolving the issues which had been delaying completion of the 'New Scheme' could now be made, with a revised offer from the Charity Commissioners received in June 1883. The Dean and Chapter requested that the number of King's Scholars remain at forty and that the lower age limit for pupils be reduced to eight rather than nine; the former request was refused but the latter accepted. A last-minute suggestion was made by Bolland that 'Grammar' be inserted into the name of the new school, to read 'Worcester Cathedral Grammar School', so as to avoid any repeat of the confusion over the Meeke Scholarships (see Chapter 3). The proposed endowment now stood at £15,000, with additional funds as required to complete the necessary works to school buildings.

The 'Cathedral School Committee of the Worcester Town Council', led by Alderman F. Dingle, also scrutinised the revised proposals, reporting pleasure in the increased financial support offered but concern that the Dean and Chapter were to remain sole governors of the school; the earlier proposals, in 1881, had included lay representatives on the governing body of the new school. After the scheme was almost de-railed by disagreement over the issue of governance, with the Town Council arguing strongly that the long-term success of the initiative depending on removing the Dean and Chapter as sole governors, several of the Canons conceded, and a Chapter Act was passed in February 1884, resolving that a lay element would be introduced into the governing body "Lay Members to consist of the Lord Lieutenant for the time being of the County of Worcester, the Mayor for the time being of the City of Worcester, one person to be Nominated by the Court of Quarter Sessions for the County of Worcester and one person to be Nominated by the Council of the City of Worcester." In response, the Cathedral School Committee agreed to withdraw all of their objections to the revised scheme, and requested that a £3,000 fund for Scholarships and Exhibitions be established; the leader of the Committee, Alderman Hill, donated the first £1,000.

One of the earliest school photos - Worcester Cathedral Grammar School, 1884; William Bolland, Headmaster, and Henry Clarke, Second Master, are standing at the back.

The Fives Courts, 1889

On 17th October 1884, the New Scheme was approved by Queen Victoria and came into force with immediate effect. The Worcester Cathedral Grammar School would be 'administered and governed wholly and exclusively 'in accordance with the terms of the New Scheme, meaning that King Henry VIII's Statutes were annulled. In his history of The King's School, Michael Craze recorded:

"Before that day its [the School's] land and buildings consisted only of "College Hall, with the site thereof" and "the dwellinghouse now or lately occupied as the official residence of the Head Master, with the site thereof". On and after that day there were added: a capital sum of £15,000 (five times what had been proposed in 1877); such a further capital sum as the architect to the Ecclesiastical Commissioners certified to be needed to put College Hall "into a state of complete structural repair"; 1 1/2 acres of the 3 1/4 acres of Castle Place, otherwise Castle Hill, in the possession of the Ecclesiastical Commissioners since the area was purchased from a private individual on 18 April 1867; and finally a right to purchase at £1,300 an acre any or all of the remaining 1 3/4 acres of the same area at any time within five years of 17 October 1884."

The final task to be carried out by the Dean and Chapter as sole governors of the school was to select the one and a half acres of Ecclesiastic land to be ceded to the school. Bolland wanted the plot of land nearest the river - where the Creighton Memorial Gardens would later be created (see Chapter 5) - however, the Canons were concerned to keep the pupils as far from the house at Number 10 as possible, so refused to permit this. An order was made on 2nd February 1885 to grant the land between the site of Number 7 College Green and the southern boundary of the property (there were, at that time, houses running along the length of Severn Street, where David Annett's 'New Block' would be built in the 1960s - see Chapter 6), extending as far back as Castle Place, where the playground quadrangle would later take shape.

The new Governing Body took over the administration of Worcester Cathedral Grammar School in October 1884, comprising the Dean as Chairman, with the four Canons of the Chapter (Wood, Butler, Melville and Knox Little); the Mayor of Worcester, W.B. Williamson and Earl Beauchamp, Lord Lieutenant of Worcestershire were ex-officio Governors; the Town Council elected Alderman F. Dingle as their representative, and the County Magistrates elected G.W. Hastings MP.

Although no longer a formal part of the Cathedral body, King's Scholars still attended a Roll Call in the Chapter House, although this was reduced from a monthly assembly to an annual event, given increaingly less emphasis at school, until brought back to promenance in the early years of the 21st century by Tim Keyes.

Bolland's School Song - 'Floreat Schola Vigorniensis'

William Bolland wrote a School Song, set to music by Precentor Vine Hall, Bolland's Master of Music and Warden of the Choir School, for Speech Day in 1884. The lyrics, written by Bolland in Latin, translate into English as:

> *"May Worcester School flourish,*
> *may the handmaid of the holy church flourish;*
> *may Worcester School flourish.*
> *A future giver of young to the ever faithful City*
> *and of safe defence for time to come,*
> *may Worcester School flourish."*

The first recorded use of the phrase 'Floreat Schola Vigorniensis' appears at the end of an 1871 article in the magazine of Victoria College, Jersey, written by former Second Master Harman Ogle; it may well have been used earlier than this.

The musical arrangement for the song was lost. However, in 2013, for the 110th Annual Reunion Dinner, at which the retirement of David Brookshaw, Director of Music, was celebrated, the song was performed, set to new music by Peter Shepherd (Bright House 2006-13), which can be found in Appendix 8.

School House

In anticipation of the approval of the revised scheme, the Headmaster, the Dean and all four Canons, met in March 1884, to draw up specifications for a new School House ready for the Ecclesiastical Commissioner's architect, Ewan Christian, famous for the National Portrait Gallery. The development was to include a private residence for the Headmaster, a dormitory for thirty boarders, three classrooms, one of which would also serve as school library, a science laboratory, a music room, a dining hall and kitchens to cater for 45 boys, and accommodation for a House Master.

The initial plans submitted by the architect were for an ornate and grandiose design in the contemporary Gothic style, and incorporated all of the desired elements within a single development. The new Governors would have to finance the project from the grant of £15,000, and at a cost in excess of the upper limit for the budget of £10,000, this building was too expensive. Simplified plans were submitted, which had two large buildings joined by an open corridor which would be flanked by study rooms, but even this could not be afforded. It was decided that the project should be split, with the most urgent aspects included in 'School House' - the boarding house, Headmaster's house, dining hall and kitchens, and a gymnasium (not included in initial discussions, but seen by Bolland as of increasing importance) - and the new classrooms and laboratories to be provided in a second phase, to be built at the site of Number 7 College Green. Much of the planned ornamental scroll-work, finials and chimneys were stripped away and the dominant material was to be red Ruabon brick, which, as it does not weather, would remain the same bold colour for the life of the building.

In the summer of 1886, work began on 'School House', with the architect employing Estcourt of Gloucester as the building contractor. Bolland, who was already familiar with boarding houses, went to visit a number of newly-built boarding houses at other schools, to ensure that his would be created to the most modern of standards. .

Unfortunately, the school lacked the funds to proceed with the second phase of the project, the building of a new classroom block, which would be delayed until 1899, or to purchase the remainder of the land offered under the New Scheme, which would later be purchased by Rev Cuthbert Creighton and transformed into gardens (see Chapter 5).

The restoration of College Hall

In 1885, while planning for School House was under way, architect Ewan Christian was able to make a start on the 'complete structural repair' of College Hall, as promised in the New Scheme. The restoration work was extensive (see Chapter 2) and included the opening of the west window, restoring of the east window, repairing of the doorways, removal and replacement of the gallery and timber panelling the walls up to the line of the windows. He employed Collins of Tewkesbury as the contractor to realise his increasingly ambitious plans for the building.

School House from the north-west, photographed in the Worcester Herald, 1889 - a view which had barely changed by 2015

Worcester Cathedral Grammar School, 1891
Bolland is seated at the centre of the second row, flanked by his four Assistant Masters.

The extent of the work was greater than could have been foreseen, and consequently the school was exiled from College Hall for far longer than could have been expected. Teaching took place in the four-storey house at Number 8 College Green from September 1885, which General Atlay and his daughter, tenants of the Ecclesiastical Commissioners, had vacated on the transfer of the property to the school the previous year. Speech Day could not be held in College Hall in 1884, 1885 or 1886, although a Prizegiving Ceremony took place in the Guildhall in December 1885. The Fifth and Sixth Form sat their Certificate examinations in the Chapter House.

The 'Re-opening of the Worcester Cathedral Grammar School' on 3rd October 1887 was a grand occasion. The Mayor, Walter Holland, processed with the Corporation from the Guildhall, joined at the Cathedral cloisters by the School Governors, onto the platform of College Hall. The Chairman of Governors, Dean Gott, presided over an audience including the Bishop of Worcester, Henry Philpott, the Headmaster and his four Assistant Masters, former Headmaster Maurice Day, and the Headmasters of Uppingham, Leicester, Bromsgrove, Bedford and Market Bosworth schools. Among those assembled was a small boy, the son of Canon Mandell Creighton, of Number 15 College Green; thirty years later, this boy, as Reverend Cuthbert Creighton, would preside over College Hall as Headmaster of Worcester Cathedral King's School.

The occasion warranted the composition of a new song, written by Canon Isaac Gregory Smith and set to music by Alfred Caldicott, OV. The full text can be found in Appendix 8; the first verse is as follows:

> *"Where Severn winds its stately course*
> *Beside the spreading meads,*
> *Where Wulstan's minster tall and grey*
> *Nor flood nor tempest heeds,*
> *Where stands the Faithful City, far*
> *Renowned in days gone by;*
> *God bless the old Cathedral School!*
> *With heart and voice we cry*
> *God bless our College School!"*

Bolland addressed the gathering, praising the restoration work and listing the school's recent successes, but used the occasion to highlight some of the outstanding needs of the school: the small stock of books in the library, the absence of a pavilion for the cricket pitch, the need for fives courts, a gymnasium and carpentry shop to surround the new playground, and, his personal wish for the school, its own swimming pool.

Bolland commented: *"We have waited for eight years in hope of a restored school and a new school house, if it had not been for hope, these would indeed have been weary years of waiting. With lighter hearts we can again invoke hope to cheer us up while our school is growing and spreading, until at no distant day it may, strong in numbers and reputation, take up a position worthy of its ancient foundation and history - worthy of the beautiful buildings which are its home."*

After this and other speeches, and a prize-giving ceremony, visitors were invited to tour the nearly-completed School House.

Education and examinations

Bolland entered Sixth Formers for the Higher Certificate offered by the Oxford and Cambridge Joint Board from 1882, and from 1885 entered the Fifth Form for the Lower Certificate (this continued until the School Certificate was introduced in 1911). To achieve a Lower Certificate, passes were required in five subjects, including one from each of three groups; the Higher Certificate required at least four passes. Results were good, with several First Classes achieved in the Lower Certificate, and occasional Distinctions awarded in the Higher Certificate. In 1888, the eleven members of the Fifth Form achieved 36 passes, with one pupil, H M Conacher, achieving First Class results in all his eight subjects - this gave King's the highest average number of First Class grades per pupil in England.

During Bolland's headship, the number of Assistant Masters was small, with usually only four employed at one time, and there was little change in the staff. The well-loved Henry Clarke, commonly known as 'Old Nick', had been appointed as Second Master in 1878, and took charge of the Third Form and senior mathematics; he was also the Master in charge of the King's Scholars. T S Dyball shared his great enthusiasm for ancient and modern literature with the boys. F Bond is described by Macdonald (1936) as 'athletic', suggesting that he was involved in physical education, although he does not clarify this. C D Locock was an expert at Chess, and wrote a treatise on the game. E D Jordan, an OV, started a carpentry workshop and was replaced by Mr Batchelor in the autumn of 1892 ; in the same term Richard Beach Hicks joined the teaching staff. Jordan had also been House Tutor in School House from 1888, a role in which he was succeeded by Thomas Rammell who joined the school in 1891 and took on responsibility for sport, with a particular interest in cricket. According to Canon Dimont, writing about his time as a boy at King's for Alec Macdonald's history of the school (see Chapter 5), normal practice was *"to have foreign languages taught by foreigners"* and four men took on this task during Bolland's reign: M. Ludecke, a Belgian, described by Dimont as *"a handsome but orgillous man, and we feared his aptness with the cane"*; a German, Herr Dieterle, who would regale the boys with stories about the Franco-Prussian War; and the much-loved Monsieur A J Froidefond, who would often be distracted by the boys into discussions of chemistry and French opera, about which he was enthusiastic; by the end of Bolland's headship, M. de Lemoelan was Languages Master.

A suggested amalgamation

King's had received approval for its New Scheme in 1884, but the Royal Grammar School had to wait until 1886 for even a preliminary draft scheme to be produced. In the period between the 1869 Endowed Schools Act and 1886, the school had moved from St Swithun's Street to a new campus on The Tything, and the school's academic standards, particularly in the sciences, had been improved under the headship of F J Eld, High Master since 1860. However, the proposed New Scheme for RGS was based on recommendations made by Bryce (who had recently written a hugely positive report on the Worcester Cathedral School - see Chapter 3) following his report on 'Queen Elizabeth's School' in 1866:

"Possibly it might be better, while allowing the Cathedral School [King's] *to retain its classical character and making it a great Boarding School for the County as well as a Day School for those Boys of the City whose Parents design them for the professions, to make the Queen Elizabeth's* [RGS] *the Commercial School of the Town and establish such a connection between it and the Cathedral School that boys who seek to enter the latter (meaning to leave at 14 or 15) should be advised rather to proceed to Queen Elizabeth's, while boys who distinguish themselves at Queen Elizabeth's might be passed on to the Cathedral School and have a chance of winning an Exhibition to the University."*

It is worth noting, however, that elsewhere in his report Bryce comments that, in a town with a population of 30,000, both schools were flourishing, and that Worcester had benefited from their "healthy rivalry".

A debate concerning amalgamation of the two schools was revived by the Worcester Chamber of Commerce in March 1887, with a Town Council Meeting discussing a motion from former Mayor F. Corbett and bank manager G. Abell in 1889. The argument in favour of amalgamation was broadly that the schools had, between them, around 120 pupils, that the Town had subscribed £2,000 towards the endowment for King's under the New Scheme of 1884 with little benefit to the Town, that King's had 'squandered' £11,500 on 'a headmaster's house', and that the fees at King's were too high.

Bolland held a meeting of parents in College Hall three weeks later, producing a petition against making changes to the 1884 New Scheme, which he circulated and sent to the Charity Commissioners. The response from Eld at RGS was to release an open letter condemning the proposed scheme for his school, emphasising the improved level of academic achievement at RGS, although he was thought to be in favour of some form of amalgamation. A flurry of letters to the newspaper followed, with each school defending its academic record, with much contributed in the defence of King's by Old Vigornians, and with RGS provocatively claiming itself to be a 'free' school, meaning 'free of ecclesiastical domination'.

A public conference was called, to be held at the Guildhall on 25th October 1889. Corbett and Abell proposed that the two schools' governing bodies would combine, and be augmented by additional members. A committee of fourteen members, including the headmasters and representatives of the governing bodies (although not the Dean and Chapter, who did not wish to be drawn in to the debate), gathered to establish a formal proposal for an amalgamation of the two schools. The size of the committee made it unworkable, so a sub-committee of six was established: Bolland and Eld, Corbett and Abell, H.Day and the Mayor, now R. Smith-Carrington (an Old Vigornian).

The sub-committee presented a report to the committee on 9th December, in which an amalgamated school was proposed, with a Junior Department for fifty boys aged 8 to 12 based at The Tything, for which the fee would be £6 per year, with a Middle Department for seventy-five boys aged 12 to 14 years, paying £9 a year, and a Senior Department for seventy-five boys aged 14 to 19, with fees of £12 a year, where the Middle and Senior Departments, divided into Grammar and Commercial classes, would be based at College Green. The new school would have endowments totalling £1,150 per year and a board of seventeen Governors.

Bolland had argued that this arrangement would not be in the educational interests of the boys, with timetabling and syllabus difficulties, nor would it be financially viable. Alongside the sub-committee's report, he presented his own minority report, in which he proposed a Commercial Department at The Tything, where RGS already had good scientific resources and a laboratory, for boys aged 11 to 15 and Classical and Modern Departments at College Green, but with their Science lessons taught at The Tything. All boys would be taught Latin at The Tything. Bolland suggested retaining his school's fee structure - £15 for boys over 12, £12 for boys under 12 in the Classical and Modern Departments at College Green and £12 and £8 fees for the Commercial Department. This would, he argued, result in a surplus which could be used for capital expenditure,

South-west corner of College Green, before 1882: the house on the left was the Tudor Schoolmaster's House, demolished in 1882; the four-storey Stuart house, built as a dwelling by John Wright, was used as classrooms until it was destroyed by fire in 1892 (these two houses formed the site of the present No. 7); the small house between this and No. 9 - at the right of the photograph - was built by Thomas Giles and demolished to make way for the School House drive in 1899. No. 9, built by Thomas Tomkins, remains largely unchanged and, since 1979, has been home to the Headmaster; this building was renovated in 2014.

would maintain a separation between first grade (Classical and Modern) and second grade (Commercial) education, and could be achieved without employing additional Masters, or causing significant disruption to the timetable or syllabus.

Both reports were put before a second public conference, called for 16th December in the Guildhall, at which the Mayor presided. The conference could not resolve the issue, and an official Inquiry took place in February 1890.

The purpose of the Inquiry had been to consider the objections to the proposed scheme for RGS, but Mr. Lefroy, conducting the Inquiry on behalf of the Charity Commission, was willing to consider the proposed amalgamation within his report. The cases and objections were made, before Lefroy made his decision: it would not be possible to merge the two schools, since one was a 'free' school (not bound to a particular religious denomination) and the other a 'denominational' school (Church of England), without the agreement of the Cathedral School, which would clearly not be forthcoming. He noted that, on the basis of national averages, the two schools should be able to accommodate 200 pupils, and so should be given room to expand. Lefroy also accepted the objections of Eld and his 'Six Masters' from RGS. His final recommendation was that amalgamation should not go ahead, but that there was not a need in the City for two schools offering a similar education, and that the 'Royal Free Grammar School' should provide a "practical, modern education at a low cost".

Lefroy's recommendation was officially summarised by the Government in the House of Commons in August 1890, and was the principle on which the revised New Scheme for the Royal Free Grammar School was based. The age range for RGS pupils was set at 8 to 16 year olds, but allowed the Headmaster to permit boys to stay on until the age of 18 at his discretion. The modern curriculum offered, and lower fees, enabled RGS to grow in pupil numbers more quickly than King's would, until the arrival of Ronald Kittermaster to King's in 1942.

Bolland's determination to argue his case in defence of his school is certain to have been critical in preserving King's as a separate school, with its own distinctive character. He could be rightly proud of this achievement.

Old Vigornians' Dinner

The level of interest among Old Vigornians in their former school had become apparent in the correspondence published in the newspapers during the debate about amalgamation with RGS. Bolland was keen to galvanise the body of former pupils and develop a regular network for the old boys, focussed on an 'O.V. Dinner'. The first such occasion took place on 30 December 1889, at the Bell Hotel in Broad Street organised by E.D. Jordan,

OV and later Bolland's first House Tutor in School House from 1886; Jordan had successfully organised a school excursion to London when Dean Gott, on his appointment as Dean had requested a holiday be granted to the whole school. Nineteen OVs attended the dinner, with Bolland invited as a guest. The success of the event formed the basis for the formation of the Old Vigornian Club in 1895. More on the Old Vigornian Club can be found in Chapter 6.

Physical Education and sport

Due to the unsuitability of the playing fields, Rugby Football was replaced as the main winter sport by Association Football, played on the school playground, from 1891, at Rammell's suggestion. Rammell took on the role of cricket coach, while E Poynton coached Hockey players. Around twenty of the older boys each year were trained as oarsmen by F Boon, with these members of the Boat Club (see Chapter 3) rowing in an annual regatta against local rivals Hereford Cathedral School. The fives courts were used regularly, as was the gymnasium at the top of School House.

A missed opportunity

On 2nd December 1892, the boys were woken at half past three in the morning to the news that College Hall was on fire. Fortunately, this was not the case, but the four-storey house remaining at Number 7, granted to the school in 1884 and used as classrooms, was indeed ablaze. *The Vigornian* of December 1892 described the event:

"The fire, when discovered, had got a good hold on the building, and the contents of the reading room only were rescued; it was soon impossible to approach the house on account of the falling walls, and one of the fellows was very nearly buried in their fall. There were several hoses at work, and about eight o'clock the fire was nearly extinguished. Everything was burnt except the books of the Sixth Form, which were in a part of the house that escaped the fire, and a valuable old staircase was lost... The loss of books and tools [the carpentry workshop was also in this house] *is a serious one, but we hope the destruction of the house may prove a blessing in disguise, if we can get the new classrooms erected, which we have so long wanted."*

Indeed, Bolland urged the Governors to proceed with plans to develop a new classroom block, as had formed part of the School House plans and had been designed already, using the insurance money from the destroyed house towards the costs, with the balance paid for by borrowing against the fees of two or three additional pupils. However, the City's representatives on the Governing Body were concerned about meeting the cost of the borrowing required, and asked Bolland to guarantee the additional pupils; of course, the Headmaster was unable to do that, although he argued that the new facilities would be certain to attract many more pupils to the school. Because of this reluctance to press ahead, the Governors missed an opportunity to develop the school, resulting in the loss of ten pupils over the following year, as makeshift classrooms were used instead.

The Governors rented a house at Number 6 College Green, vacant since the previous tenant of the Ecclesiastical Commission, Miss Davison, had died in 1885, and it was here that the 'emergency' classrooms were housed. This house would be purchased in 1900 by the Dean and Chapter, demolished and rebuilt as Castle House, and used by the school as a boarding house from 1902.

A new carpentry workshop was built on the playground, on a site which would later be used for Creighton's gymnasium (1929) and then the Wolfson Building (1973), paid for by fees for carpentry classes.

The new classroom building would have included a science laboratory, a facility which the school needed badly; before the restoration of College Hall, the gallery had been used for science experiments, often to the distraction of the rest of the school below. A solution was found in the building of the Victoria Institute in Foregate Street in 1894; the school was able to use a laboratory in this building, until it had one of its own. Members of the school had attended the ceremony at which the Duke of York, the future King George V, laid the foundation stone for the Victoria Institute; the Duke later visited the Cathedral and College Hall, where he is said to have been impressed by the school, and requested an additional week's holiday for the boys before making a well-received address.

The departure of William Bolland

In March 1896, Reverend Bolland was approached by Merton College with the offer of the vicarage of Embleton, Northumberland. After sixteen years, during which he oversaw the transformation of Worcester Cathedral Grammar School, and indeed the birth of the school which could develop into The King's School of today, Bolland was ready to move on. He accepted the position of Chaplain to Merton College, leaving the school at the end of the summer term. In order to allow for farewells and tributes to the Headmaster, Speech Day was moved from October to July.

In 1917, William and Margaret Bolland retired to Oxford, where the former Headmaster wrote an account of his old school in Worcester, which owed him its very existence, before his death in 1919.

The Headmaster's residence, within School House, 2015

The buildings of College Green

College Green, 1948

The buildings surrounding College Green, to the south of Worcester Cathedral, have undergone many changes during the past few centuries. With the exception of College Hall (see Chapter 2) and Edgar Tower (see below), the buildings used by The King's School today were mostly constructed, or significantly redeveloped, in the 18th and 19th centuries, with many of these (particularly numbers 3, 5 and 6 and 8) receiving radical reordering in the years following the end of boarding at King's. For the sake of clarity, the numbers used for the buildings in the following text, and the adjacent map, are those in use today - first established in 1876.

Number 1 (and Number 16) - Edgar Tower

Originally built as the gateway to the monastery in around 1346, Edgar Tower was named after the Saxon King Edgar, whose statue appears on the front of the building.

Number 1 College Green, the lower level of the south part of the gateway, is a private dwelling for one of the Cathedral's employees. Traditionally occupied by a Cathedral porter, it was the occupant of this house who was responsible for closing the monastic gates each night at 10.00 pm.

Number 16 College Green, the lower level of the north part of the gateway and the upper floors of the tower, will be known to generations of King's pupils. Leased from the Cathedral since 1921, the upper floors were used as dayboy accommodation and an art room, before conversion into the School Library in the 1960s. Today the main spaces have become a home to the School Archive and classrooms for Classics.

For more on the history of Edgar Tower see Chapter 2.

Numbers 2 and 3 College Green, c.1910

Number 2

The present house, dating from around 1715, occupies the same site as the residence of the Cathedral organist which was rumoured to have been used as a first aid station during the Battle of Worcester in 1651.

Number 2 was the home of the fictional Channing family, the subject of 'The Channings', published in 1866, by Mrs Henry Wood, a novelist who wrote about the experiences of her brothers who were pupils at The King's School in the 1830s.

In reality, the house was the residence for one of the Canons of the Cathedral until 1854, when it was let to private tenants. In recent times, the Cathedral has re-occupied the building and it is home to a member of the Chapter.

Western elevation of Edgar Tower, from College Green, 2012

Number 2 College Green (painted in pastel pink), 2013, from the Cathedral tower

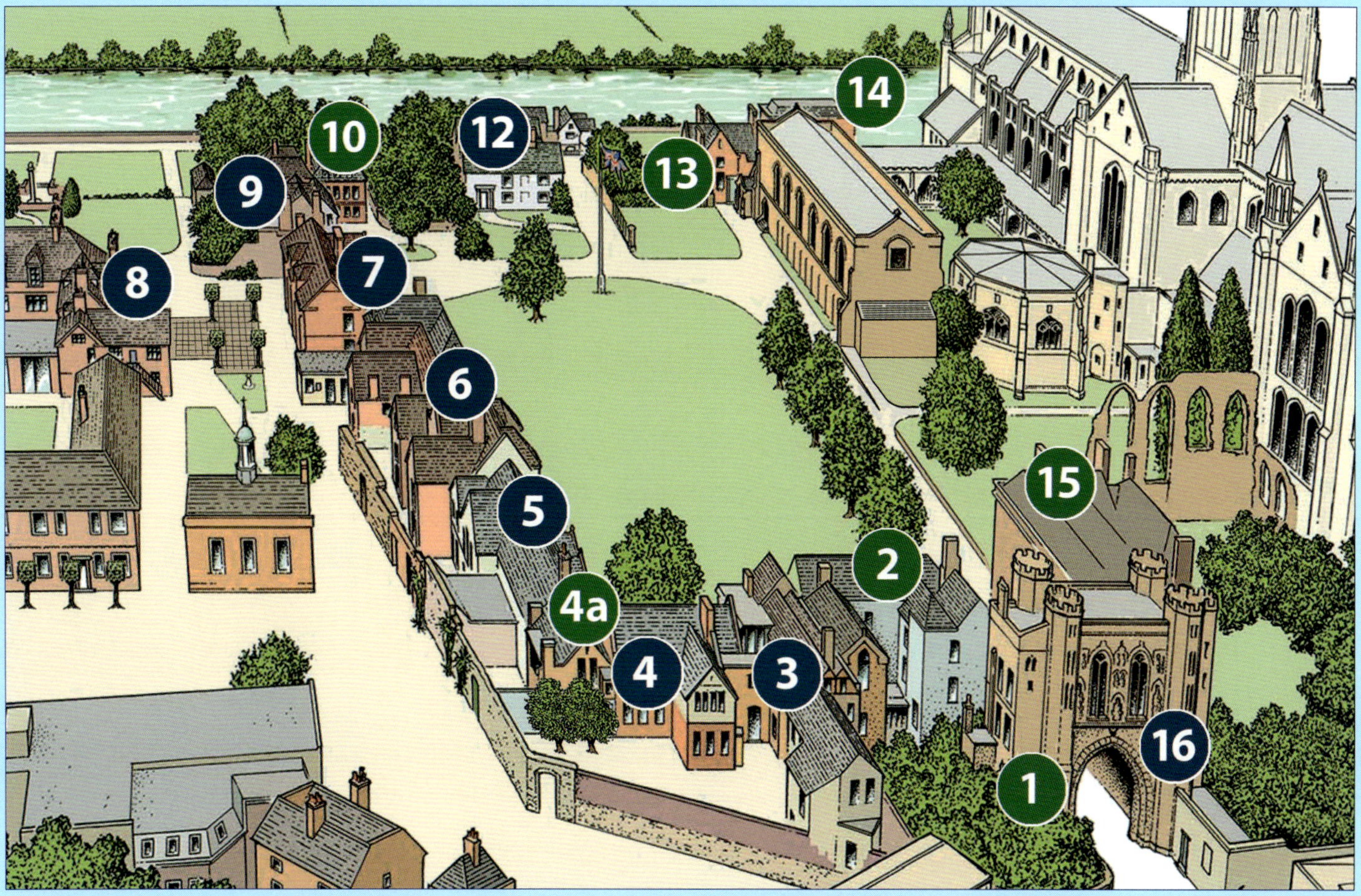

*Above: Graphical map of College Green, 2014
- blue numbers indicate buildings used by King's, green numbers indicate buildings used by the Dean and Chapter
Below: College Green as seen from the Cathedral tower, 2009*

Choir House in 2002, following completion of the re-ordering works, which included the addition of a glazed second floor extension above the extended main stairwell.

The rear courtyard of Choir House, 2001

Numbers 3 and 4 - Choir House

The present day Choir House, at Numbers 3 and 4 College Green, stands on the site of a 'singing school' in use as early as 1649. The current building was given to the Choir School as a place for the education of the Cathedral Choristers by the Dean and Chapter in 1882, when the Choir School moved from a room in Number 15. Precentor Woodward taught the choristers, aged between nine and eleven, at the Worcester Cathedral Choir School, which was separate from the Worcester Cathedral King's School.

The building underwent significant redevelopment in 1902, including the bringing forward of the front elevation and addition of a gable roof. In 1911 a large extension, dedicated as a memorial to Precentor Woodward, was added to the southern side of the main house, providing a dining room and day room on the ground floor with a large dormitory (known as 'the Barn') above. A statue of Woodward can be found in the first floor niche of the front of the building.

In 1927, Cuthbert Creighton persuaded the Dean and Chapter to expand the Choir School into a Preparatory School, accommodating non-choristers from the age of eight, avoiding having to take younger boys into The King's School.

In August 1943, the Choir School was amalgamated with The King's School by the Dean and Chapter, with the transfer of all of the school's assets (and significant liabilities) including the lease on the Choir House building.

Further information about the Choir School, including the amalgamation with King's and its move to St Alban's can be found in Chapter 7.

The first King's Housemaster was Paul Longland, who moved into Choir House in September 1943 with 35 boarders and 40 day boys, many of whom were under the age of ten. He was succeeded a year later by Lester Wilson.

Ian Brown's Choir House, 1988

Wilson moved, with the younger pupils, to St Alban's House, set up as a Junior School for King's in 1952. At this time, L M 'Bill' Bailey and his wife moved into Choir House from Tredennyke House in Barbourne, which they had been an independent Preparatory Department; with their 35 boarders now aged at least 13, the Baileys formed Choir House, which kept the name as a link with the previous occupants.

The number of boys in Choir House steadily increased. Bill Bailey retired in 1961 to be replaced by Peter Curle, who in turn was succeeded as Housemaster by Ian Brown in 1978. It was from the 1970s that Choir House began to take in dayboys alongside boarders, as the proportion of boarders to dayboys began to fall. Because of this, 'the Barn' was converted to provide more single study areas; carpets and curtains were also added.

Russ Mason became Housemaster in 1988, followed by Jonathan Martin in 1993. By the mid-nineties the number of boarders at King's had fallen sharply, and the decision was taken that Choir House would eventually close to boarders; from 1994, no new boarders were admitted. From September 1995, day girls were taken in to Choir House, which was then a combination of boys' boarding house and co-educational day house. The building was rather a jumble of rooms, with some of the former dormitories and studies used as classrooms for the increasingly large school. Marie Arthur took over from Jonathan Martin as House Tutor for the day pupils in 1998.

To allow for the conversion of The Hostel, which was to become the school's administrative centre when College House returned to the Dean and Chapter in 1999, boarders from The Hostel, with House Master Peter Iddon, moved into the boarding accommodation in Choir House, alongside the few remaining Choir House boarders. Boarding ceased completely in July 1999.

In 2000, a large re-ordering project commenced, converting the building into modern teaching accommodation. 'The Barn' became a large computer suite alongside classrooms for the English and Classics departments.

A new Health Centre, replacing the former Sanatorium which moved from Castle House, had been opened at the rear of the building a year previously. The old shower block, fire escapes and portacabin were removed, allowing a pleasant courtyard area to be created.

Among the most striking physical changes to the building was the addition of an award-winning glazed second floor extension with a modern, steel staircase and walkway, which opened up access to the smaller rooms at the top of the old house , to which the Classics department moved.

The 'new' Choir House was opened in January 2001, at an event attended by three Headmasters, David Annett, John Moore and Tim Keyes, and a number of local dignitaries.

The day houses, Chappel and Bright moved into Choir House in 2001, joined by Richard Davis' Kittermaster House in 2006. After Stephan Le Marchand stepped down as House Tutor of Chappel, he was succeeded by Sue Stone and the House relocated to School House in 2008. Creighton House, whose House Tutor was Lorraine Guy moved in to take its place. Shortly after the move into Choir House, Bob Stone stood down as House Tutor of Bright House, and was succeeded by Mark Poole; Chris Haywood took over from Mark in 2011.

A reorganisation of the English department classrooms in 2012 resulted from the move of the Classics department to Edgar Tower.

Above: Choir House in 1882
Below: Choir House, 1902, with new front and gable
Bottom: Three Headmasters (John Moore, Tim Keyes and David Annett) at the reopening of Choir House, 2001

Numbers 4 and 4a

A series of stables stood at the site of Number 4, originally used by the monastery. In 1778, The King's School used the upper level of the building as a temporary boarding house.

The stables were rebuilt in 1845 by the Cathedral architect, Mr Perkins; most of the building was leased by the school in 1908 and used as a Sixth Form room (the 'Old Library'), the remaining stable (far left of the photograph) acquired a year later and used as an Orderly Room and Armoury for the O.T.C.

By the 1980s, the 'Old Library', and the courtyard behind it, were connected to The Hostel, and used as studies for Hostel boys. The Orderly Room became a book store for the English department, whilst the Armoury remained with access from the rear of the building.

The Old Library was incorporated into The Hostel in 1999 to form 'Hostel House', which is Number 5 College Green. Number 4 is now the Woodward extension of Choir House and 4a is a flat above the book room and Armoury (accessed from Castle Court), used for Cathedral guests, accessed via a doorway in the front of the Choir House building.

Stables at number 4, around 1900, later to become the 'Old Library'

Number 5 - Hostel House

Hostel House stands in the middle of the row of buildings on the southern side of College Green, with grounds extending behind it to meet the old castle wall.

There is evidence that a building has stood on this site since Norman times and the current house was first constructed in the early 17th century, with additions to the rear of the building in the 1640s. The house was later described as 'a mansion house' owned by Rowland Crosby, a well-known preacher and Petty Canon of Worcester Cathedral.

The 17th century house received an elegant new frontage during the 18th century, resulting in the building which would look familiar to a visitor today.

The Hostel, with Reginald Castley (undated)

In 1900, William Chappel leased the house from the Cathedral to be used as a 'Masters' Hostel' for the unmarried masters to live in. The overcrowding in School House soon led to boarders being put up here as well, and the building was named 'The Hostel' in 1903 and opened as a boys' boarding house with Reginald Castley as the first Housemaster.

After a long tenure as Housemaster, Castley was followed in 1933 by A Franklin and then J Burnett. R Pedder was House Master in 1938-39 and again from 1945-58, with Paul Longland and Frank Thomas sharing the war years.

Richard Knight and Keith Bridges led The Hostel during a period of growth in the number of boys, between 1958 and 1990, during which time a number of studies of other smaller extensions were added in the courtyard between the house and the castle wall, and in the courtyard behind the Old Library, which itself became used as part of the boarding house.

The Sixth Form Reading Room, c. 1920, now the staff Common Room

Left: Hostel House, 2015
Above: The Hostel undergoing rennovation works, 1999
Below: The Hostel, with Keith Bridges, 1978

The last Housemaster of The Hostel was Peter Iddon, from 1990 until the end of boarding in July 1999. With the planned return of College House to the Dean and Chapter (see Chapter 9) due by the autumn of 1999, a plan was formed for the reorganisation of the properties used by the school. The staff Common Room, Headmaster's Office, secretariat and Bursary would move to Hostel House. To allow the necessary work to be carried out on the building, Peter Iddon moved, with his remaining few boarders, into Choir House in the summer of 1998, where he was responsible for the boarders of both houses (Marie Arthur having responsibility for Choir House's day pupils).

In readiness for the move of the Common Room and offices from Number 15 to Number 5, a significant reordering project, devised by Associated Architects, was carried out on Hostel House, removing old fire escapes and dormitory accommodation and incorporating the Old Library within the building. The renovated building was ready for occupation from September 1999.

The original house was now to become home to the School Office and Headmaster's Office (with the grand bay window) along with a large meeting room on the ground floor, with the Bursary above, which moved from 5 and 6 Castle Place, and also the Foundation Development Office (see Chapter 9) and the examinations office (later occupied by the Marketing Department). The former stables building is used as a spacious staff Common Room, with a workroom above, offices and other facilities. To the rear, in a wedge-shaped space between the rear of the stables Common Room, the side of the Armoury and the old castle wall, stands a modern Design, Media and Reprographics department. A pleasant and well kept courtyard stands behind Hostel House, which was much improved following the removal of a disused shower block when the Fives Courts were demolished in 2003. A later addition, in 2007, would be a visitors' reception, in a modern glass style extension, to the rear of the building.

Number 6 - Castle House

A 12th century house, most likely associated with the neighbouring castle, stood on the site of the current building, and was still present at the time of the registers which also recorded what is now Hostel House in 1649. By the nineteenth century, this older building had been largely demolished, although the western wall of the original house remains largely intact, and was replaced by the western part of the current Castle House. The western wall is regarded as a particularly fine piece of domestic Norman architecture, described in more detail in Appendix 15.

The King's School leased Castle House from the Dean and Chapter in 1901 for £63 per year, after £400 had been spent on rebuilding the house, and opened it as second boarding house (after School House) in April 1902. Thomas Rammell was to be the Housemaster, assisted by his sister, with seven boarders. By September the house had 23 boarders, and was already at full capacity. A further £400 was invested by the Dean and Chapter in enlarging the building, with an extension making up the eastern part of the current building (over the site of a stable block, used by the Dean and Chapter, between Castle House and Hostel House) with grand bay windows and incorporating the medieval western wall into the house (the former exterior face of the wall is now internal, exposing the inner face). This larger house was able to accommodate 30 boarders, and did so from 1906; the rent was increased to £90 per year.

On Rammell's retirement in 1929, Castle House was taken over by Sam Strong, himself a former Castle House boy.

Basil Eckersley MBE (Castle House 1930-37) recalled:

"Mr and Mrs Bentley, who took over when Strong gave up the housemastership in 1933, produced a marked improvement in our diet. Under Strong's bachelor regime our catering had been controlled from School House, which was of course considered sufficient explanation of our ills. Mrs Bentley thus achieved early acclaim as benefactress and friend. But even if the food had left something to be desired, we were in those days waited upon in a way which would astonish the present generation. There were maids in attendance at meal times, our beds were made for us and even our shoes were cleaned."

Arthur Bentley was succeeded as Housemaster by Stuart Sheppard in 1950, followed by Michael Points in 1965.

Points oversaw some relaxing of the harsh rules enforced by previous Housemasters, including the punishment of beating a boy for not collecting his shoes by breakfast time. Pupils were allowed to wear casual clothes on school premises and to return home more often during term time. Compulsory attendance at Cathedral services was made optional for boarders in the 1970s. Points also tried to curtail the practice of fagging and bullying, which were rife in the House, and denied the Head of House the right to use the cane, although retained this right himself for 'serious offences'. A small number of Sixth Form girl boarders joined Castle House in the 1970s, before the opening of College House.

Bob Allum, with his wife Sarah, took over Castle House in 1980, during the start of the decline in boarders' numbers. In 1985, when Bob Fleming became Housemaster, Castle became a house for Fourth Form boarders, and then, in 1993, a mixed junior boarding house, incorporating the Sanatorium and overseen by Claire Furber, School Nurse, with Junior School boarders from 1995 until the house closed in 1997.

Rear of Castle House, 2001 (above) and 2013 (below)

Kate Appleby's Creighton House occupied the lower floors of the largely unused building, once work was under way on conversion of the New Block into the Annett Building, until it moved to School House in 2002.

A major re-ordering project was undertaken on Castle House in 2002-03, including the demolition and reconstruction of offices and demolition of the changing rooms in the rear courtyard, and the removal of unsightly fire escapes from the rear elevation. Of all the boarding house conversions in the early 21st century, Castle House was the most problematic, due to the poor structural condition of the building; at one stage

Front of Castle House, showing the medieval western wall, 2001

during the works, the first, second and third floors were all removed, making it possible (from scaffolding) to stand in the eaves and look straight down on to the ground floor.

Castle House was to become the new Music School, allowing the lower floors of School House to be redeveloped. The new design included a number of individual practice rooms, shaped with odd angles to help their acoustics, and a large rehearsal space, named the Elgar Room, which was the room in which Edward Elgar played during Three Choirs Festivals. A grand piano had to be lifted into place, by crane, through a first floor window to complete the building. The new Music School was opened July 2003 by Stephen Cleobury (Choir House 1958-67), with a celebratory concert in College Hall.

For more on Music at King's, see Chapter 1.

The Second Master, by now Alistair Macnaughton, moved into a new office at the rear of Castle House, later home to Sue Hincks, Richard Chapman and then Jon Ricketts, the Senior Deputy Heads.

Castle House, front elevation, 2015

It would be Choir House, with Marie Arthur as House Tutor, which would use Castle House as a base, with a modern suite of rooms on the ground floor, but an impressive 'medieval' locker room. Monica Longley took over Choir House in 2003. In 2014, Choir House moved out to new rooms in the Annett Building, allowing additional space for music rehearsals, offices for the Academic Deputy and Second Deupty Heads and the addition of ICT facilities for music in the Elgar Room in 2015.

The 1899 Classroom building at Number 7 College Green, viewed from 'Library Square', 2013

Number 7 - 1899 Classrooms or 'Biology Block'

This building, described in the *Vigornian* of 1899 as *'Scholastic Gothic with Renaissance details'*, was constructed on the site of two houses: the former Schoolmaster's house, which had to be demolished because of its poor condition in 1882; the adjacent four-storey house (built on the site of the monastic brewery in the 1680s) had been home to General Atlay before being used as classrooms from 1885, burned down in 1892. The new classrooms had been designed as part of the development of new facilities provided for under the New Scheme of 1884, which led to the construction of the first phase, School House, in 1886; the projected costs of the second phase building, which eventually totalled £3,000 led the Governors to delay construction, even when the site became vacant after the fire of 1892. Architect Ewan Christian's vision was finally realised in 1899.

The building provided the school with its first science laboratory, a much-needed facility as the boys were having to use a laboratory at the Victoria Institute in Foregate Street; four new classrooms replaced the 'emergency' provision at Number 6; a reading room; an office for the Headmaster (although this was not used as such for long, becoming home to a school shop by the 1930s); and a changing room for day boys, which was replaced by an extension to the north of School House in 1920, when this room became a book store.

Further changes of use continued during the following decades, with the conversion of two classrooms into laboratories, allowing one for each of biology, chemistry and physics; after the opening of the Winslow Building in 1958 (see Chapter 6) the laboratories could be used exclusively for biology. With the Masters' Common Room having moved from Number 7 into School House, the Biology department had virtually sole use of the building, which now comprised five laboratories and a technician's prep room.

The only other occupant in the 1980s and 1990s was Tim Hickson, Second Master, who had retained an office in Number 7; his successor, Alistair Macnaughton moved into a new, prominent office to the rear of Castle House after his first year at King's (which can be seen to the right of Number 7 in the photograph above), when the conversion of Castle House was completed, shortly after his appointment in 2002.

Left: Physics laboratory, 'Wilson', 1948

Above: The same laboratory in 2005, now used for teaching Biology (the construction of offices to the rear of Castle House resulted in the reshaping of the window).

Below: Decorative gable bearing the coat of arms of the City of Worcester

Bottom: Illustration of the 'new classrooms' by Alfred Hill Parker

In the early 2000s, a programme of refurbishing the aging and outdated science laboratories began, both at Number 7 and in the Winslow Building. Completed over a number of years, the whole programme had been completed by 2008. The new laboratories were designed and installed by a specialist company. They are bright, light and colourful and allow for modern teaching styles to classes of all ages.

Number 8 - School House

School House was the easily the largest and most ambitious building project undertaken by The King's School until the development of The Keyes Building (see Chapter 9) between 2011 and 2014. Like this later project, the intention was to accommodate all the school's current needs in one development. In 1881, William Bolland identified a need for a new large boarding house, with kitchens, a dining room and dormitories, a replacement house for the Headmaster (following the demolition of the previous house in 1882) and a gymnasium, changing rooms, a library and a science laboratory.

School House was designed by architect Ewan Christian, the designer of the National Portrait Gallery and an enthusiast for the contemporary Gothic style, for the one and a half acre plot of land granted to the school by the New Scheme of 1884. His initial design was deemed too ornate and grandiose for the budget available, with two large buildings (more or less the present School House and Number 7) joined by an open corridor, resulting in a more simple scheme; even this reduced plan had to be abandoned, much to the disappointment of Bolland, as the cost was still too high. A further simplified design, which proposed School House as an initial phase, at a cost of £10,000 and a classroom building at Number 7 promised as a secondary development, was accepted, and building work commenced in the summer of 1886. The architect's passion for the Gothic remained clear in the final building - the scroll-work gables, chimney stacks, mullioned windows and pointed towers, although this was significantly scaled-back from the original plans, and the use of red Ruabon brick was a necessary compromise.

School House was completed in 1888, and included a Headmaster's house (at the southern end, with the grand porch), boarding accommodation for more than thirty boarders, a gymnasium on the top floor and a dining room on the ground floor with large kitchens in the basement level.

An increase in the number of boarders under the headship of William Chappel meant that the house had to be reconfigured,

The last fully 'boarding' School House photograph, June 1989
Marc Roberts, Housemaster, pictured with wife Julia and children Naomi and Joey, became Housemaster of Wulstan House later that year; Steve Bain took over School House, which quickly became a day house.

resulting in the conversion of the gym into a second large dormitory in 1897.

An extension was added to the north-east corner of the building in 1920, to provide changing rooms for day boys. When Creighton's gymnasium was built in 1929, the 1901 gym was converted into a carpentry workshop and provided space for day boy changing rooms, allowing this extension to be used as changing rooms for the School House boarders. Later, this wing of School House would be converted into a toilet block, with boys on the ground floor and girls upstairs, with an outdoor staircase leading to the upper level.

Until 1940, the Headmaster was also Housemaster for the boarders of School House. The first 'dedicated' Housemaster was Frank Thomas, succeeded by Ronald Kittermaster (who returned to the Headmaster's house from Number 14 in 1942), followed by Major Dan McTurk who was appointed by Kittermaster in 1946, Alan Stacey in 1962 and Marc Roberts in 1980.

Jonathan Raban (School House 1953-58), in his 1987 book

Eastern elevation of School House, 1889. Notice the single storey to the right which was enlarged in 1920. The foreground of this photograph is currently the position of the later extension to the 1925 Classrooms.

Western aspect of School House, 2015, with Numbers 9 and 7 College Green behind and the Cathedral tower in the background. The shared 'Scholastic Gothic' architecture of Numbers 7 and 8 is clear.

Coasting, recalls his time as a boarder in 'Major McTurk's' School House:

"On the dormitory windows there were bars, no curtains; the long uncarpeted room held twenty four narrow iron bedsteads spaced, by order, with an eighteen-inch gap. The doors had been removed from the lavatories. At 7.15 each morning they queued in naked lines for the cold showers, while the house monitor - another, older boy of seventeen or eighteen - stood by in a dressing gown, on guard."

By contrast, Donald Howell (School House 1953-61), remembers Dan McTurk as a *"kind, welcoming, firm and precise"* Housemaster and an inspiring teacher.

Alan Stacey, like Mike Points in Castle House, sought to de-regulate life in his boarding house, allowing the boys to enjoy greater freedoms, including the opportunity to leave school grounds, to go home for some weekends and, with permission, to allow 18 year olds to visit licensed premises.

When the dining room on the ground floor was no longer required as such, the room became used as a small assembly hall, known as 'Passey Hall' named in honour of the former cook. It was later the house room for Wulstan House and Marc Roberts' maths classroom.

The building underwent a major refurbishment as it approached its centenary year, with the number of boarders beginning to decline, and other buildings used to provide many of the original functions of School House - including the new dining hall and kitchens (1978), the Sports Hall (1971), and Number 9 College Green (1979). The lower floors were fitted out for use by the Music Department, which could move from the former Fishermen's Cottages on Severn Street, while the former boarding accommodation was converted into classrooms and House rooms for day houses - Wulstan House (in the former dining room) and Kittermaster House (in the former gymnasium) moved in and, in 1989, School House started to evolve into a day house, with Steve Bain as Housemaster (in 2014, Steve Bain remained the only Housemaster from this time to be in the same post, albeit now known as a House Tutor), occupying the middle floor. Religious Studies was taught in classrooms in the former

Ground floor of School House as 'Passey Hall', 1970s

Headmaster's house during the 1980s and 1990s, with History taught in the top floor classroom. School House was also the first proper home for the School Archive.

With development work around the site starting at the turn of the 21st century (see Chapter 9), School House had to accommodate Oswald House and Creighton House from 2001. Creighton later moved out, to be replaced with Chappel House in 2009; Kittermaster moved into Choir House in 2006, when Wulstan House relocated to the top floor of the building to make room for the new library on the lower floors.

Once the new Music School was opened in Castle House in 2003, the way was clear for another major redevelopment of School House, with the addition of the 'Long Gallery' to the eastern side of the building, and a new double height glass entrance to the north elevation altering the outward appearance of the house dramatically.

For a more detailed description of the Library development, please refer to 'School House - a new Library for King's' (Chapter 9).

The upper floors of School House became home to classrooms for Modern Foreign Languages (which had outgrown its own building), four day houses (School, Kittermaster, Oswald and Chappel) and the Learning Skills department; the Careers Department and the School Library, on the two lower floors, ensured that School House remained one of most-used, and most-loved, areas of the school.

Eastern elevation photographed in 2015; the addition of the Long Gallery in 2006 obscured much of the lower floors

Above: The McTurk Room, 2015
Below: An article published by Dan McTurk, displayed in the McTurk Room

Number 9 - Headmaster's House

The growing number of Assistant Masters, unmarried and unattached to boarding houses, led Cuthbert Creighton to lease Number 9 from the Dean and Chapter to provide accommodation for them and provide an office for the school secretary. In 1936, L.A. Wilding added the newly-formed 'Creighton's House'. In the following decades the building had a number of uses, including providing a common room for Mistresses - separate from the Masters - until the Masters' Common Room moved from Number 7 into School House.

With the return of Number 14 to the Dean and Chapter, and the former residence in School House already used as classrooms, a new house was needed for the Headmaster and his wife when David Annett retired. Number 9 was called into service for this purpose in 1979, and Andrew Milne moved in, with his wife Nicola and two daughters. Following Milne's tenure as Headmaster (see Chapter 6), Dr Moore occupied the house, with his wife Jill, from 1983. After Moore's retirement in 1998, Tim Keyes took over the house with his wife Mary Anne and their two sons, Sam and Bill. Headmasters often invited guests, including King's Day speakers, to stay in the house, and would host regular meetings of the Old Vigornian Club Committee there. Mary Anne held meetings of the Christian Union in the first floor sitting room, which looks out past the west side of School House towards the Annett Building and Michael Baker Boathouse. In September 2014, refurbishment work was undertaken on Number 9, after which Matthew Armstrong was the fourth Headmaster, with his wife Kate, to live here from January 2015.

The house was first built in the 1640s by Thomas Tomkins, Old Vigornian and Cathedral Organist. By 1800, the original building had been extended and refaced. Before the construction of the present Number 7, a house had stood to the left of Number 9, belonging to Thomas Chiles. It was demolished when work on the 1899 classrooms started to make way for a driveway for School House. Traces of this house can be seen on the side of Number 9. A grand gateway was built across this space, the first 'school gates'. New gates, in a modern style, were installed in this area in around a hundred years later.

Top: Rear of Number 9, 1993
Above: Numbers 9, 10 and 10a College Green, 2002
Below: School gates, early 20th century

Numbers 10 and 10a - The Deanery

The current house was built around 1700, with later extensions to the south (which now form 10a) around 1870. The house stands near the site of the former monastic bakehouse, which gave rise to the name 'The Ovens', often used to describe the house during the early part of its life.

The rear of the house is raised on a five-bay blind arcade of coursed stone, said to be part of the remains of the thirteenth century castle. The arches probably date back to the building of the terrace in the early eighteenth century.

The first recorded tenant of the Dean and Chapter was Elizabeth Marriott, around 1820, followed by Henry Grape, who sub-let the house to Frances Maria Kilvert until 1870. In 1870 the house was enlarged to accommodate Canon Alfred Barry, who borrowed money from 'Queen Anne's Bounty'; the work was carried out by the Cathedral architect, A E Perkins, and included the addition of a dining room, drawing room and bedrooms.

Number 10 has remained among the properties used by the Dean and Chapter, and nowadays is the Deanery. Number 10a, which sits between numbers 9 and 10, was the residence of the School Chaplain, Rev Michael Nott in the 1970s, before the Chaplain's house was established at 12a. The building is currently used as offices.

Numbers 10 and 10a College Green, 2015

Number 11

There is no longer a Number 11 College Green. The site of Number 11, between Numbers 10 and 12, forms part of the gardens of Number 12, to the south of that house. A number of buildings once stood on this plot, which were prebendary houses used by members of the Cathedral Chapter until the number of Canons in the Foundation was reduced by the Ecclesiastical Commissioners in the mid-nineteenth century; a watercolour reproduced on page 25 shows three Canons houses on this plot in the eighteenth century. A pretty garden wall now stands at the front of the site, hiding a sheer drop to the lower level of the gardens of Number 12.

Number 12 (and 12a)

The house known by members of the school as 'Number 12' dates from the late sixteenth or early seventeenth centuries, with earlier origins and later additions and alterations. The site had previously been the residence of the monastic shrine keeper (the tumbarius).

In 1844, the building was extended, with the addition of five bedrooms, a dining room, and several other rooms, at a cost of £750, designed by Harvey Eginton; the enlarged house, which then included a central open courtyard, around which the staircase climbed, became the home of Canon Ryle Wood. The house continued to be used by the Dean and Chapter until 1975, the last Cathedral occupants being Canon Eliot and Lady Alethea Eliot. Andrew Milne secured the use of the house for the school in 1979 with a 125-year lease.

The building was divided into numbers 12 and 12a. Number 12a became the residence of the School Chaplain in the era of boarding. The Chaplains at this time were Hammersley (1977), Gant (1984), Charles (1989) and Dorsett (1996).

During the early 1980s, following the introduction of Sixth Form girls a decade earlier, it was decided that a day house for girls would be set up to complement College House. Eliot House opened in number 12 in 1986, with Bob Allum as Housemaster. Eliot House was, however, short-lived and following the move to full co-education in 1991, the girls were integrated into the boys' day houses ready for September 1992, and Eliot House was closed.

The girls of Eliot House, with Bob Allum (Housemaster) and Rosemary Diamond (House Tutor), 1986

Number 12 became home to the History department, as well as Economics and some teaching rooms for English and Classics. The Careers library was situated in a former dormitory on the ground floor.

The building changed little since the 1990s, and remained the main home for History, where Peter Gwilliam, Head of Department, introduced 'Government and Politics' as a separate A Level course in 2009. In a similar way, Russ Mason introduced Business Studies to run alongside Economics in 1998. The re-opening of Choir House in 2001 saw the English department depart from Number 12, with the vacated rooms quickly occupied by History.

Brian Griffiths' Careers department moved into the lower floor of the new school library, which opened in School House in 2006; this space became a Chaplaincy, in which pupils could find calm, encouragement and religious support from Rev Mark Dorsett. The Chaplaincy was named 'The Selby Room' after the Rt Rev Peter Selby, Bishop of Worcester 1997-2007.

Above: Number 12 College Green, 2015
Right: Western elevation of numbers 14 and 13, in front of the western window of College Hall

Numbers 13 and 14

Currently the Cathedral's Music School, where the Cathedral Choristers are based, the house known as Number 14 stands on the site of the Sub-Prior's residence and, for the most part, was built in 1843 with an extension in 1847, although the southern section of the building is thought to date to around 1730, and there was significant rebuilding in 1904. The house has a connecting door into the Cathedral Cloisters.

After William Bolland had the Tudor Schoolmaster's House (at Number 7) condemned in 1882, it was intended that Number 14 would be rebuilt as a new Headmaster's boarding house; School House was built instead.

Canon Wilson lived at Number 13 until he became temporary Headmaster in 1908 (see Chapter 5) when he moved into School House. Canon Wilson later used Number 13 as a sanatorium during an outbreak of measles at the school.

After use by the Ministry of Works during the Second World War, Number 14 was leased by The King's School as the Headmaster's residence from 1945, when first occupied by Ronald Kittermaster, until 1979 when David Annett retired.

In 1950, following the appointment of David Willcocks as Cathedral Organist, the large house was divided, creating Number 13 as a separate residence, accessed via a front door to the west of the College Green entrance to College Hall.

David's wife, Romey Annett, took in a small number of girl boarders when girls were admitted to King's in 1971, prior to the establishment of College House at Number 15 in 1977.

Number 13 College Green, 1993. The gable end of Number 14 can be seen behind the house.

The College House girls, with John and Caroline Roslington, 1985

Number 15 - College House (The Guesten)

The present house was built in around 1745 over the sites of the almonry (see the 'almonry school', Chapter 1) and the original Deanery.

In 1851, the house became the residence of the 5th Stall Canon; a drawing room and bedrooms were added in 1869. It was later to become the Deanery, before the Dean moved to Number 10 in 1976 and the school acquired a lease for the building, which was renamed 'College House', at the suggestion of Richard Knight, Second Master.

The common room (officially the 'Masters' Common Room' until 1990) moved from School House, along with the Headmaster's office; the two suites of rooms faced each other from opposite sides of a grand lobby, behind an imposing black front door. To the rear of the lobby was an impressive staircase, which led up to the separate apartment which was to become home to a new girls' house, College House, for both day girls and boarders.

Little work was required to prepare Number 15 as accommodation for College House other than installation of additional showers; a small adjoining house, between Number 15 and Edgar Tower had previously been converted into a garage with an apartment above by Dean Kemp - the garage was turned back into a sitting room for the boarders, revealing a charming Victorian range in the process, and the flat integrated into College House. This part of the building, now known as 15A, is once again a separate residence.

John and Caroline Roslington opened College House in September 1977, with 21 girls. The number of girls entering the Sixth Form at King's rose steadily; by 1985 there were a total of 73 girls, both day and boarding, a large enough number to warrant the setting up of Eliot House, to look after some of the day girls, in 1986.

Such was the success of the introduction of girls to the school, the decision to convert to a fully co-educational school was made in 1989, and by the time John and Caroline left College House in 1992, girls had already been admitted into the Lower Fourth (Year 7).

Sarah Le Marchand, with husband Stephan, took over the reins of College House in September 1992, and the house continued until the end of boarding in July 1999, when, along with The Hostel (by that stage in temporary quarters in Choir House), College House closed.

The Dean and Chapter informed the school in 1993 that the Cathedral would want to take back Number 15 at the end of its lease in 1994. At a time when the school was growing under John Moore's headship, and with the new intake of girls in lower years, space was at a premium, and this announcement caused much concern. After careful negotiation by the Headmaster and Governors, the Dean agreed to extend the lease to 1999, to allow the school sufficient time to create the additional space needed within other buildings.

Once the re-ordering of Hostel House was completed, the staff common room and Headmaster's office moved into more modern, spacious accommodation on the other side of the Green, and College House was duly returned to the Dean and Chapter in 1999.

The Cathedral renamed Number 15 'The Guesten', after the Guesten Hall which once stood nearby - the ruined wall behind Number 15 is the last remnant of the ruins of this building which was demolished in 1861. The Guesten is let by the Dean and Chapter, and used as office space, including accommodation for the organisers of the Worcester Three Choirs Festival.

Above: College House, renamed 'The Guesten', photographed from the Cathedral Tower, 2012.

The house is impressive from ground level, in its Georgian splendour, but it is from above that the size of the building is revealed, with its numerous extensions. This photograph also shows the remaining ruined wall of Guesten Hall, which formerly stood on this site, and from which Number 15 takes its present name.

Right: College House, with its imposing, black front door (not for the use of pupils!), 1993

5: Chappel and Creighton - conflict and change

W H Chappel - Headmaster 1896 - 1918

Having narrowly missed the Headship of Malvern College in 1891, thirty-six year old William Haighton Chappel was elected from more than a hundred applicants to succeed Bolland in 1896. Described in an 1899 article in *The Worcester Herald* as "of tall, athletic figure, and with a face that tells of firmness and good temper", Chappel had previously taught at his alma mater, Marlborough College, having graduated with degrees in Classical Moderations, Literae Humaniores and Theology from Worcester College, Oxford. At Marlborough, Chappel had been a housemaster responsible for 45 boys until his marriage in 1890 and subsequent ordination as priest, by the Bishop of Salisbury, in 1891. He served as school chaplain and was an officer of Marlborough College's Cadet Corps during his last years before taking up his headship at King's, arriving with his wife Mary and their young daughters Dorothy, Marjorie and Gertrude.

The Worcester Herald reported that "Mr. Chappel distinguished himself at once by a firm grip of duty, genuine sympathy with all the interests of the school, and by the institution of prudent reforms, the fruit of experience at Marlborough. The rapid progress and admirable tone of the school speak sufficiently of his quality as Head."

There had certainly been rapid progress: Chappel had inherited from William Bolland a school of eleven boarders and sixty day boys; Chappel aimed to increase the size of the school to 100 boys in total, which was achieved in 1902 by increasing the number of boarders in School House to fifty. By the time of Chappel's retirement, the school taught around 200 boys.

Among his first changes, Chappel abolished half term holidays and brought afternoon school forward from 2.30 to 2.15 pm. The new Headmaster selected six Monitors from the Sixth Form, abandoning the practice of Sixth Formers automatically becoming Monitors.

Worcester Cathedral King's School

Chappel disliked the name Worcester Cathedral Grammar School, chiefly because of the proximity of the Royal Grammar School, so re-introduced the word *King's* into the school's name in place of *Grammar*. Chappel had also disliked the use of *Cathedral* in the name, as this might have suggested a choir school, although this was, perhaps diplomatically, retained. The name *Worcester Cathedral King's School* was adopted in 1896, with emphasis on *King's,* as in Ely and Canterbury, and this remained the unofficial title of the school until incorporation in 2003. As the school crest had traditionally been encircled by the Latin words 'Regia Schola Vigorniensis', the Headmaster argued that he was simply reviving the title. *The Vigornian* was, under Chappel's tenure as Headmaster, renamed *The Worcester Cathedral King's School Chronicle*.

Relations with the Cathedral Foundation

The New Scheme of 1884 (see Chapter 4) had left some bad feeling between the Dean and Chapter and the school. Chappel was the first Headmaster to be appointed under the new arrangements, following election by the Governors, chaired by the Dean; a number of Minor Canons protested at the induction of the Headmaster into the Cathedral's Foundation, but this was overruled by the Dean and Chapter, all five of whom were Governors of the school.

Reverend William Haighton Chappel

In January 1898, the Dean and Chapter attempted to recover ownership of College Hall, which had been surrendered for use of the use of the school in 1884. Negotiations continued until June 1901, at which time the conveyance was sealed and ownership of College Hall transferred back to the Dean and Chapter; the Chapter had responsibility for the structure of the building, and the necessary insurance and the school began to pay rent for its continued use.

The Dean and Chapter would not agree to enlarge the governing body, on which it had a majority of five to four, although a minor change in composition, proposed by Canon Shore, received Royal Assent in December 1900; an Oxford University Representative was included, in place of the Magistrates' Representative, alongside the Chairman of the County Council, in place of the Lord Lieutenant, and the Mayor and a city councillor making up the lay governors.

Inspectors from the Board of Education, established in 1899, visited King's for four days in May-June 1910. The report was as favourable as the ones carried out for the Cathedral Commissioners and Charity Commissioners had been, but although it did not recommend an increase in fees, the report made clear that the school could not "maintain its efficiency" with the fees and endowments provided. The Governors addressed the matter of endowment to the Dean and Chapter, who asked Canon Wilson to prepare a case for the Ecclesiastical Commission; an application was made for an increase in the endowment from the Cathedral of at least £400 a year, to be drawn from the Ecclesiastical Commissioners' Common Fund. This application was refused, with the reasoning that the New Scheme of 1884 meant that the school was technically no longer a part of the Cathedral establishment, coupled with a concern that agreeing to the increase would set a precedent for the other similar Cathedral schools. Canon Wilson worked hard to prepare an appeal, with the support of the Bishop, Dr Yeatman Biggs, who was a Commissioner himself. The Bishop postponed his holiday in November 1911 to plead the school's case personally.

The Bishop's argument was that the school was in grave financial difficulty and that the notion of the school no longer being part of the Cathedral establishment should be dismissed: the Dean and Chapter formed the majority of the governing body and owned most of the school's buildings. The appeal succeeded and a revised 'new scheme' was approved and received Royal Assent in August 1913, which provided the school with an additional £400 per year from the Common Fund on condition that the school continued to operate as a Church of England school.

Christianity at King's

As part of the continuing relationship between the school and the Cathedral, King's enjoyed use of the Lady Chapel in the Cathedral for services to celebrate Advent and Lent; King's Scholars and boarders had allocated seats in the Quire. Daily prayers were said each morning in College Hall.

In 1908, a new Dean was appointed, Dr William Moore Ede, who organised a series of 'Lectures for Men' on Sunday afternoons in College Hall, inviting some of the best-known speakers in the Church of England to talk and answer questions; the lectures were often followed by lively debates. Canon Chappel encouraged senior boys to attend, often asking probing questions during the following morning's 'Divinity Hour'.

Facilities

College Hall had recently been refurbished (see Chapter 4), and included the school's Museum of Natural History, maintained by Richard Beach Hicks. The hall was still the main teaching space for the school, with several lessons taking place alongside each other throughout the day.

School House had been opened in 1888, with dormitories, gymnasium and dining room as well as the Headmaster's residence; the house was altered, converting the gymnasium to a further dormitory, to provide additional space for the increasing number of boarders.

A new classroom building, at 7 College Green was completed in 1899, finishing Bolland's original plan for the School House development - the costs involved caused this building to have been left out until now and the final building cost a total of £3,000. The building included three classrooms, a science laboratory, reading room, a changing room for day boys, a masters' common room and an office for the Headmaster, and was opened by Dr J Perowne, Bishop of Worcester, on 26th October 1899.

In 1900, Chappel rented Number 5 College Green as a boarding house for unmarried masters, developing a sense of community between masters and pupils outside the classroom.

Chappel with School House, 1897

Canon J M Wilson

Acting Headmaster 1908

In 1908, after ten years of hard work, Chappel was advised by his doctor to take a sabbatical to rest. The Chappel's children, by now four girls and two boys, were sent to the Alice Ottley School, while they travelled in Europe before staying for a while in Cornwall.

Canon James Maurice Wilson, former Headmaster of Clifton College, a Canon of Worcester Cathedral since 1905 and resident of Number 14 College Green, agreed to stand in for Chappel. Wilson, despite being in his seventies, was highly energetic and well regarded. Wilson moved into School House with his wife; when a measles epidemic broke out, he used Number 14 as a sanatorium.

During his travels, Chappel wrote to Wilson, who read out the letters to the boys, as a reminder of their Headmaster. At the end of his four-month tenure as Acting Headmaster, the Sixth Form Room was opened in Wilson's honour, converted from the stables at Number 4 College Green (see Chapter 4).

A firm believer in the value of public schooling, Wilson helped to launch the Worcester Secondary School for Girls, later known as the Worcester Grammar School for Girls, in 1909. In 1915, he acquired 7,000 square yards of land which he donated to the city for the establishment of Fort Royal Park.

Canon Wilson's concern for WCKS was evident in his campaigning to secure a grant from the Common Fund of the Ecclesiastical Commissioners in the years from 1913 to 1917. Wilson had personally contributed £100 to the £400 cost of the Sixth Form Room in 1909. His interest in the school continued for more than twenty years, giving lectures to the boys on subjects ranging from the history of the Cathedral to astronomy, and the poetry of his favourite poet, T.E. Brown. The Canon and his wife entertained senior members of the school at their house and regularly offered accommodation to young boys travelling from great distances to sit the examination for King's Scholarships. Wilson's interest in monastic history led to his involvement in significant research for A.F. Leach's *'Early Education in Worcester 685 to 1700'* published by the Worcestershire Historical Society in 1913.

Canon Wilson retired in 1926 due to infirmity and failing eyesight, at the age of 90, and died in 1931.

The following year, 6 College Green, which had been used as three classrooms until the opening of the new building since the fire of 1892, was rebuilt and leased from the Dean and Chapter for the rental of £63 per year as a secondary boarding house, named Castle House, after the castle wall which ran alongside it, and opened the following year. Thomas Rammell, Second Master since the sudden death a year earlier of Henry Clarke, was appointed Housemaster, with his sister as housekeeper; he had seven boarders. Castle House quickly reached full capacity and was extended to accommodate thirty boarders from 1906 at the cost of £400; a new, longer lease was negotiated and the rental increased to £90 per year. Alongside this expansion, Number 5 was converted into a boys' boarding house and opened as 'The Hostel' in 1903, with accommodation for fifteen boarders and with Reginald Castley as Housemaster. The Hostel was extended and refurbished by the Dean and Chapter in 1907. At this time there were 130 pupils - seventy boarders but still only sixty day boys.

A new gymnasium was built in 1901, on the school playground, following a fund-raising campaign, with much of the apparatus donated in memory of OVs who had died in the Boer War. This building was later used for various purposes, including a day boys' changing room, carpentry workshop and art classroom, and was demolished to make way for the Weston Centre, part of The Keyes Building, in 2013. A further memorial to those lost in the South African War took the form of an Honour Roll in College Hall.

A new 'Sixth Form Room and Reference Library' was created from a converted stable at Number 4 acquired on a 99-year lease from the Dean and Chapter at a rental of £1 per year; this room, described by Chappel as "a centre of the disciplinary life of the school" was opened in honour of Canon Wilson, who refused the name 'The Wilson Room', in January 1909. The adjoining coach house and stable were acquired later that year, at a further rental of 10s per year, for use as an Armoury for the Officer Training Corps (O.T.C.). The remaining stables were assigned to the Choir School in 1910; the buildings were cleared and an extension to Number 3 was built, significantly enlarging the Choir School (see Chapter 7). The combination of these projects, with the extension of The Hostel, enabled a sympathetic collection of developments in the south-east corner of College Green, harmoniously linking Number 3 to Number 5, by architect Alfred Hill Parker of Foregate Street, who had recently completed the new building at 7 College Green.

The Houses

With the increased number of buildings serving as boarding houses, individual house identities, and specifically house colours, were established. Inter-house competitions, initially in Athletic Sports, Chess and Gymnastics, were introduced in 1904 and 1905. In these competitions, School House used sky blue, with day boys using yellow with The Hostel and Castle House together using red; from 1909, with more boarders in each house, Castle House retained red and The Hostel introduced green as its house colour.

Alfred Hill Parker's converted stables at 4 and 5 College Green, photographed in 2014

Chappel's staff

The number of Assistant Masters steadily increased, from just four under William Bolland - R Beach Hicks, F Boon, J Field and E Poynton, as well as Second Master Henry Clarke - with the appointment of a ninth Assistant Master following the inspection report of 1910.

Henry Clarke, Second Master, died suddenly in 1900, and was succeeded in this role by Thomas Rammell, who was Housemaster of Castle House. Reginald Castley was Housemaster of The Hostel from 1903. A House Tutor was employed to assist the Headmaster in running School House. Each House employed the services of a housekeeper. Chappel also engaged three part-time teachers, who provided a total of ten hours' tuition each week: George Smith OV taught music, Dr Solomon taught French, and the drawing and writing teacher was F Wells.

Sergeant Walter Fawke was Drill Sergeant with Captain Bede Fenton responsible for the O.T.C. from 1909; Captain Fenton was killed in action in July 1915.

Teaching and learning

Boys throughout the school were taught Latin, Greek and French, the Headmaster being particularly keen on teaching the discipline of Latin alongside a modern language which was seen as being of more immediate usefulness. Elementary Science was taught to all boys in the second form and above and offered to the Sixth Form if this was likely to be of use in their planned careers; older pupils were permitted to use the resources of the recently-opened Victoria Institute in Foregate Street. Boys were also tutored in mathematics, literature, music and carpentry. Sixth Form education was focussed on preparation for the universities (Oxford and Cambridge) and London matriculation, with the entire year group entered for the higher certificate of the Oxford and Cambridge Board examination each year, while the Fifth Form boys entered the lower certificate examination.

Financial problems

The increased endowment provided from the Ecclesiastical Commissioners' Common Fund of £400 per year averted financial disaster and the Board of Education's threat to withdraw their recognition of the school as 'efficient', but it was the minimum that Canon Wilson had applied for and far short of what he hoped to achieve. The outbreak of war in 1914 added further financial strain and an application to the Board of Education for a grant was considered, despite the natural resistance to this. However, the conditions of the grant required a change in the governing body - that a majority should be secular; the school would have to provide a substantial number of free places to boys from local elementary schools; that Church of England instruction should only be given on parental request; and that the Headmaster need not be a member of the Church of England - could not be accepted by Chappel or the governing body, for whom the school's relationship within the Cathedral Foundation was crucial. This left the school in financial difficulties which continued despite the Bishop having found an additional £200 a year for three years from 1917.

Canon Chappel had contributed personally to the finances of the school, providing an average of £100 each year during his headship, much of which was used to pay staff salaries and reduce the boarding fee burden to parents who could least afford it. The other housemasters, Castley and Rammell also helped to subsidise the boarding fees, sacrificing part of their own salaries of around £180.

Pupils' well-being

Chappel shared Bolland's conviction that physical activity, and competitive sport in particular, was important to the development of rounded Christian gentlemen. Thomas Rammell was placed in charge of a 'Games Committee' in 1897, which had responsibility for managing the finances for sports and appointing sports captains. Physical education continued to grow in importance, with the boys using the Worcester Gymnasium in Friar Street once a week in the four years after the loss of the top floor of School House in 1897 until the opening of the new gymnasium on the school playground in 1901. A Shield was offered in the first inter-house competition, Athletic Sports, in 1904, and won by School House. In 1905, a 3½ mile cross-country event was introduced into the athletics programme, 'The Ketch Run'. Games sessions after school continued in the autumn until late November.

A Scout Troop was established in 1908, formed by the newly-appointed master, H Reed. Forty boys joined, and the Troop was absorbed into the O.T.C. the following year (see below).

Interestingly, playing Chess was discouraged, as Chappel considered that an indoor game which involved severe mental exercise was inappropriate as a form of recreation, although the Library Committee introduced an individual inter-house Chess Tournament in 1904; Chappel was careful to avoid making excessive demands on the boys, with regulated prep according to age and a policy of 'no work before breakfast'. This is not to suggest that the Headmaster did not insist on steady work during school hours, and the school's performance in the Oxford and Cambridge examinations was considered to be creditable.

The design of the dormitories, along with the physical education programme, encouraged a healthier lifestyle than in many schools, and WCKS, as King's was then widely known, escaped the 1898 epidemic of influenza.

The Headmaster was keen to instil discipline in the pupils, preferring to encourage good work through the hope of reward rather than the fear of punishment. A boy's name was recorded in a register on completion of a piece of good work, with a half-day's holiday awarded for the school each time twelve names had been entered. Corporal punishment, only administered by the Headmaster himself, was reserved mainly for moral offences - including telling lies and disobedience. Minor punishments often involved translations or copy-book work, which would be educational as well as useful.

Scholarships

The 1884 New Scheme had provided for twenty King's Scholars, who would each receive a free education at the school, plus a salary of £5. Chappel saw limited value in this arrangement, so as part of his changes in 1900, the £100 was reallocated to the Headmaster for use at his discretion; Chappel used the funds to reduce the termly fees for boarding Scholars. Scholarship awards were made on the basis of an examination, which Chappel moved to November. Many awards were made to pupils from preparatory schools outside the city, with an upper age limit of fifteen.

University education was expensive at this time, with Oxford and Cambridge each charging £200 per year. Chappel was pleased to see additional scholarship schemes being made available during his time as Headmaster. In 1903, Canon Richard Cattley's will allowed reversion of a bequest to his housekeeper of £70 a year, which became two scholarships at either university in memory of his son D'Arcy Cattley, OV, from 1910. John Hughes, OV 1866-69, died in 1917 and left the Swan Inn at Whittington to be sold to finance a scholarship, stipulating that this should be for 'classical learning'.

Canon Chappel with his staff, 1918, including the first two female teachers, the Misses Campbell

Cadets at King's

James Bartholomew

Officer Training Corps, 1909

The War Office Committee on the Provision of Officers was commissioned by Richard Haldane, Secretary of State for War, to address a shortage of suitable officer candidates for the reserve forces. In 1907 the Committee issued a report recommending the introduction of an Officer Training Corps (O.T.C.) to provide standardised elementary military training. The O.T.C. was duly established in 1908, with a Senior Division for universities and a Junior Division for schools.

Serving on the War Office Committee was William Chappel. At Marlborough, Chappel had commanded the Volunteer Corps; at King's he had established a rifle club. However, he believed that the school, with 165 pupils, was too small to support an O.T.C. contingent.

According to the circular which Chappel sent to all parents on 12th May 1909, the boys themselves had petitioned him to reconsider. He announced that *"Mr. Fenton has undertaken the task of organizing the Corps as Commanding Officer"*, if he could secure at least fifty recruits. Eighty boys enlisted immediately.

Captain Bede Fenton

Bede Liddell Fenton had arrived as an assistant master in 1908 from Keble College, Oxford, where he had joined the O.T.C. Senior Division on its inception. He had taken charge of Chappel's rifle club, which merged into the O.T.C. After a month-long training course, Fenton was commissioned as a Second Lieutenant (later promoted to Captain), the first O.T.C. Commanding Officer. Chappel later recalled Fenton's "energy and wise initiative".

The O.T.C. was attached to the Worcestershire Regiment stationed at Norton Barracks, which provided Sgt.-Major Cooper to drill the cadets, and Trumpeter Latham to form a bugle band. The contingent attended its first O.T.C. camp at Aldershot in 1910; the cadets were visited by Lord Kitchener and reviewed by the Duke of Connaught. The band, which had first performed at Speech Day in 1909, won the band competition at Aldershot in 1912 and 1913.

All O.T.C. contingents gathered at Windsor on 3rd July 1911, for a Royal Review by King George V to mark his coronation. Among the 20,000 cadets on parade were eighty Vigornians, who had marched to Foregate Street station at 3 am, led by the band, in order to reach Windsor by breakfast. They returned, according to Craze (1972), *"feeling like veterans"*.

58 cadets were again at Aldershot in August 1914; on the outbreak of war, the camp was abandoned.

The Great War

The Great War took a heavy toll on The King's School. There were already 110 Old Vigornians serving in 1914; by 1918 there were 450. The O.T.C. expanded, although its rifles were given to the Worcestershire Regiment; in 1915 trenches were dug in the playground. A succession of Commanding Officers departed to join up, and were replaced.

Major Bede Fenton, who had left King's in 1912 for a headmastership in Johor (now in Malaysia) but had returned to enlist with the Dorset Regiment, was killed at the Somme in July 1916. An O.T.C. detachment formed a Guard of Honour for the funeral of Lt. George Nash (School House 1900–04) in 1915, his brother Lt. James Nash (School House 1903–12), Head of School and O.T.C. Corporal, having perished in the trenches two months previously; their younger brother Slade Nash (School House 1912-21) was still at school. The five Wilmot brothers all served; three did not return. The Headmaster's nephew, Lt. William Eldon Chappel (School House 1906–08) of the Royal Flying Corps, was killed in April 1917, aged 19. Among the 82 Vigornian casualties were three masters, all former O.T.C. officers: Major Fenton, Lt. Harry Smith, and 2.Lt. Henry Reed.

Amid the wreckage, Old Vigornians deployed their O.T.C. skills gallantly. They received 49 decorations in total, including 31 Military Crosses.

The Interbellum

The interwar period was rather happier. Capt. Arthur Bentley M.C. and Capt. Sam Strong (Castle House 1906–14), both Great War servicemen, were both highly regarded officers. O.T.C. Commanding Officer since 1922, Bentley ceded command to Strong in 1931. With Strong as Commanding Officer and Bentley as second-in-command, they continued until 1939; Bentley succeeded Strong as housemaster of Castle House in 1933.

David Bolland (School House 1932–37) fondly recalled Saturday morning O.T.C. parades, indoor and outdoor rifle practice on shooting ranges, Field Days in the Ombersley countryside,

Winners of the Chichester Cup, 1933. Sam Strong and Arthur Bentley are seated, centre.

J.T.C. Inspection, May 1945

and O.T.C. camps, even if the polishing of buttons and boots sometimes proved onerous. Cadets prepared for Certificate 'A', the benchmark of physical and technical proficiency. The school shooting VIII won the Chichester Cup in 1933.

The marching band lent its services to Worcester city for civic occasions, and competed successfully in camp competitions, under the leadership of Drum-Major John Reynolds (School House 1935–39). After Oxford, Col. Reynolds M.C. served with the Commandoes in the Italian Campaign and at the D-Day landings, and ended a distinguished military career as Commandant of the Worcestershire Army Cadet Force.

Criccieth, 1939–40

War intervened again in September 1939, when the school was evacuated to Criccieth. The boys became attached to the Local Defence Volunteers, providing nightly patrols and sentry duties. Field Days were taken in the Welsh hills; the O.T.C. band rehearsed on the sea-front.

Following the Dunkirk evacuation of 1940, Criccieth also hosted large numbers of evacuated soldiers. Unkempt, dispirited and in some cases shell-shocked, they provided a stark reminder of the realities of war.

The school returned to Worcester in September 1940.

Junior Training Corps, 1940

The O.T.C. Junior Division was reorganised as the Junior Training Corps (J.T.C.) in 1940. On the establishment of the Air Training Corps (A.T.C.) in 1941, The King's School and the Royal Grammar School jointly formed a flight unit, discontinued in 1946. The band was suspended until 1946. When the air-raid siren sounded, the school sheltered in the Undercroft of College Hall. The aircraft sighted overhead usually appeared more malign than the Spitfire of Michael Boddington (School House 1929–32), who performed aerobatics over the Cathedral in July 1941. Sqn.Ldr. Boddington D.F.C. D.F.M. had already destroyed seven enemy aircraft in the Battle of Britain, and subsequently commanded squadrons in North Africa and Italy.

For school leavers, Certificate 'A' enabled easier enlistment into the forces. Three O.T.C. men achieved particular distinction in the War and afterwards: Major-General Percival Napier White C.B. C.B.E. (School House 1917-19), O.T.C. Cadet Sergeant-Major, a wartime commander in the Middle East, later Assistant Chief of Staff at Supreme Headquarters Allied Powers Europe and Commandant of the Joint Services Staff College; Air Vice-Marshal John Embling C.B.E. D.S.O. (The Hostel 1926-31), an Oxford classical scholar, shot down over occupied France in 1942 and sheltered by the French Resistance, later Sector Commander of the Eastern Sector; and Air Commodore Bertie Wootten C.B.E. D.F.C. A.F.C. (School House 1933–36[1]), R.A.F. Liaison Officer to the Pentagon, Air Attaché to Venezuela and Aide-de-Camp to the Queen.

Forty-two Old Vigornians received decorations, all O.T.C. or J.T.C. alumni; 50 gave up their lives. Included in both tallies is Herbert Guimbeau (The Hostel 1941–43), who returned to France, received the Croix de Guerre, and was killed serving with the Free French Forces. Cyril Harvard (Castle House 1938–41) poignantly recalls his teammates of the 1940 rugby XV, of whom Jim Taafe, Michael Good and Peter Hulme did not survive. *"Sleep well, gentlemen."*

Combined Cadet Force, 1948

The King's School has never assumed a more militaristic character than in the post-War era. The Headmaster was Lt. Ronald Kittermaster of the Royal Field Artillery and the Army Educational Corps. The housemasters were servicemen. Lt.Col. S R Sheppard (Commanding Officer 1946–64) and his officers, Captains Dan McTurk, Bill Bailey, Wilfred Thomas and Bobbie Cash, all with distinguished War records, all accepted lower cadet ranks than they had held as combatants. The colourful Sgt.-Major Jim Barrett of the Irish Guards arrived as Staff Instructor in 1947.

---

[1] *Craze (1972) records Bertie Wootten as a member of Creighton House; as Creighton House was not established until September 1936, Craze must have meant 'the house of which Creighton was housemaster', i.e. School House.*

In 1948, the three services' cadet corps were amalgamated as the Combined Cadet Force (C.C.F.). C.C.F. was compulsory in all but name, with all boys facing the prospect of National Service on leaving school. Saturdays, following morning lessons in cadets uniform, were devoted to drills, marches, or a termly Field Day.

Some boys have fonder recollections than others. Jonathan Raban (School House 1953–58), famously unhappy at King's, nonetheless found an identity in the C.C.F., rising to the rank of Lance Corporal; in his travelogue *Coasting*, Raban vividly recalls a Field Day on Bromyard Down, leading a section in mock ground combat. Dick Bailey (Chappel House 1943–54) and Col. Richard McDonald (Day Boy 1946–54) both credit to the C.C.F. their decision to pursue army careers.

C.C.F. March past, in front of the Guildhall, High Street, 1948. The two leading officers are Lt.Col. Sheppard and Capt. McTurk.

The summer camps continued. At Pirbright in 1951, C.S.M. Neville Bulman (Chappel House 1944–51) commanded the Drill Squad to victory in the Drill Competition; at Castlemartin in 1955, under C.S.M. Peter Bulman (Chappel House 1948–55), the school's contingent was named the smartest on parade.

The shooting VIII finished third in Class 'A' of the Country Life Competition in 1952 and 1953. The school qualified for the National Rifle Association Schools Meeting at Bisley, where Michael Keating (Day Boy 1944-54) won the Sunday Times Challenge Trophy and Gold Medal in 1953.

Until 1956, as Tony Davis (Creighton House 1949–56) wryly observes, the C.C.F. offered a choice between the army, the army and the army. For older cadets, the choice broadened with the establishment of a Royal Air Force Section in May 1956 and a Royal Naval Section in September 1958. Under Tim Vivian, the Royal Naval Section, attached to H.M.S. Cambria at Cardiff, offered sail training and visits to submarine bases; the section did not survive Tim Vivian's retirement in 1971.

Royal Air Force Section, 1956

The R.A.F. section was founded by Wg.Cdr. Arthur Aldridge D.F.C., whose experiences as a torpedo bomber pilot are recounted in his memoir *The Last Torpedo Flyers*; Aldridge also served as C.C.F. Commanding Officer 1969–76. The R.A.F. section offered instruction in the Theory of Flight and Meteorology, and field visits to R.A.F. stations for flights in training aircraft. With a Flying Scholarship, outstanding cadets could receive flying or gliding instruction to private pilot's licence standard

Tim Garden (Creighton House 1952–62) joined the R.A.F. section on its inception, obtained his private pilot's licence on a Flying Scholarship at Wolverhampton, and participated in an International Air Cadet Exchange to the USA. Joining the R.A.F. from Oxford University (as had Aldridge), Air Marshal Professor The Lord Garden K.C.B. served as Assistant Chief of the Air Staff, Commandant of the Royal College of Defence Studies, Director of the Royal Institute of International Affairs at Chatham House, and Liberal Democrat defence spokesman in the House of Lords.

R.A.F. Section, commanded by Flt.Lt. Edward Reeves, at R.A.F. Abingdon, 1988

Aldridge was succeeded by David Hope, and then by Flt.Lt. Edward Reeves in 1984. The section was restricted to Fifth and Sixth Formers, with few reaching N.C.O. rank. The section expanded, with the ranking structure altered to grant senior cadets greater status and responsibilities. Many were awarded Flying Scholarships. Although officially allocated one flying session per year, the section made flying visits to R.A.F. stations as often as once per term.

Commanded by Flt.Lt. Daniel Orr from 2008, the R.A.F. section had sixty cadets and three officers. The section ran twice-yearly camps at R.A.F. stations, offering flying, shooting, night exercises and squadron visits. Cadets studied Parts I, II and III of the R.A.F. College Cranwell Syllabus. For senior cadets, Gliding Scholarships and the Air Cadet Pilot Scheme offered training for solo flight.

Army Section

After the abolition of National Service in 1963, the remit of C.C.F. changed, with compulsory preparation for National Service commissions no longer required. Under Commanding Officers Major Alan Stacey (1976–84) and Lt.Col. Stewart Davies (1984–2003), C.C.F. gradually evolved into an entirely voluntary activity. Stacey had done National Service; most C.C.F. officers by this time had not seen military service, but offered civilian skills such as camping, orienteering and canoeing. The acquisition of the Old Chapel near Crickhowell enabled camping expeditions in the Brecon Beacons.

Nonetheless, military training remained the core of the C.C.F. Cadets followed the Army Proficiency Certificate syllabus, training in drill, skill at arms, map and compass, fieldcraft and first aid. Drill parades took place on Fridays after school. Camps, expeditions and excursions combined the military and recreational aspects of the C.C.F.

For some, the C.C.F. still provided a pathway to a military career. Col. Mark Claydon O.B.E. (Wulstan House 1970–79) progressed from active command to Ministry of Defence strategic consultancy in the Middle East. Brigadier Christopher Claydon M.B.E. (Wulstan House 1977-82) toured Iraq and Sierra Leone as a helicopter pilot, later also serving the Ministry of Defence as a strategist. Col. Richard Westley O.B.E. M.C. (Wulstan House 1972–81) and Major Paul Bassett M.C. (Choir House 1976–86) both passed into Sandhurst; both were awarded the Military Cross on service in the Bosnian War. Lt.Col. Peter Jones O.B.E. (School House 1973–80) served in Bosnia and in both Gulf Wars, latterly as commander of The Pioneer Regiment. Capt. Oliver Doherty (Kittermaster House 1988–98) served with the Irish Guards in Iraq. Col. Westley and Major Matthew Westley M.B.E. (Choir House 1981–90) both commanded units in Afghanistan; Lt. Cameron Baldry (Choir House 1997–2004) undertook a six-month tour to Afghanistan as a private soldier, before Sandhurst and a commission with the Royal Engineers.

The fully co-educational status of the contingent was affirmed by the appointment of the first female Senior Cadet, C.S.M. Helen Jones (Kittermaster House 1999–2007). From 2009, the contingent was commanded by Sqn.Ldr. Nicole Essenhigh (College House 1984–86), a former King's cadet and a Territorial Army Officer.

Capt. Andrew Maund, Officer Commanding the Army Section from 2009, cites the C.C.F. Charter published by the Ministry of Defence: *"The broad function of the Combined Cadet Force is to provide a disciplined organization within a school so that boys and girls may develop powers of leadership by means of training to promote the qualities of responsibility, self-reliance, resourcefulness, endurance and perseverance, and a sense of service to the community".* Interviewed in 2009, Capt. Maund firmly believed that the C.C.F. continued to fulfil this remit to the benefit of its cadets.

In 2014, Wing Commander Essenhigh stood down as Contingent Commander and was succeeded by Sqn.Ldr. Ronan Head. The Army training sections were renamed 'Gheluvelt' and 'Badajoz' after battles in which the Worcestershire Regiment won full honours.

Army Contigent of the C.C.F. photographed in 1999

In 2009, Caroline Roslington produced 100 years of the Cadet Corps *from which many of the recollections included in this article are taken.*

Gearing up for war

In his time at Marlborough College, Chappel had served on the Select Committee of Head Masters and War Officials, and with the increasing tensions in Europe, and the likelihood of a conflict, he was keen that King's should follow the larger public schools in preparing the boys. A letter was sent to parents in 1909 advising that pupils would undertake elementary military training. A Chapter Act was passed in June 1909 to allow part of the school stables at 4 College Green to be used as an armoury, and an Officer Training Corps (O.T.C.) was formed, incorporating the existing Scouts and Rifle Club. The O.T.C. contingent officially began on 1st October 1909, and attended a Camp at Aldershot in the summer of 1910, where it received a visit from Lord Kitchener and was reviewed by the Duke of Connaught. The following year, in July 1911, eighty members of King's O.T.C. took part in a 20,000-strong parade at Windsor Great Park to mark the coronation of King George V.

The O.T.C. formalised the military drills which had taken place since the 1860s when the Cadet Corps was first introduced, and quickly became a significant part of the life of the school, and indeed in the city, with processions to mark public events. The Shooting Club was incorporated into the O.T.C. and placed highly in national competitions. The O.T.C. band provided services locally, and accompanied Territorial Army marches in Worcester.

The Great War - 1914-1918

King's men (and boys) in the War

The British forces included 110 Old Vigornians by the summer of 1914; by 1918 this had risen to 450. Chappel felt strongly that recruits were taken too young - boys could sign up at the age of 17 although they were placed in training camps until the age of 19 which was the youngest age at which they were allowed to fight; Chappel believed strongly that a further year in school, with the benefit of O.T.C. training would better prepare the boys for the war they were about to face.

Conscription was introduced in 1916, and a number of the masters were called up. Those boys with O.T.C. experience were allowed to remain in school until the age of eighteen and a half, rather than being enlisted at eighteen, because of the perceived value of their continued training and education. The O.T.C. encouraged pupils to sign up as soon as they were old enough.

The losses among OVs were heavy. Two masters and 82 former pupils died either in combat or as a result of injuries sustained; 49 of those serving in the war were decorated. Chappel read a eulogy to each King's casualty in College Hall, and issues of *The Vigornian* from this period were filled with obituaries.

O.T.C. Parade on College Green, 1913

College Green, March 1916

King's during the Great War

School life was significantly affected. The O.T.C. held training half-days - a practice which would continue with the C.C.F. until the 1980s. As the masters were called up, their positions were filled by older men and, for the first time, by women. Three boys from Belgium joined the school as refugees.

A number of elm trees around College Green had become old and diseased and were cut down, allowing the land to be cultivated as a kitchen garden. By 1918, when food rationing was introduced, farming squads had been established and grew crops in any available spaces around the school. An Agricultural Camp was compulsory during the summer holiday of 1918 for all aged 15 and above. The sale of vegetables, as well as helping the war effort, raised more than £40 towards the cost of building an additional fives court which would serve as a memorial.

Sporting fixtures were few and far between, although matches against Malvern College and Hereford Cathedral School were generally still played. Concerts were replaced with shows which sought to raise money for war charities.

It was at this time that the school started to use the upper rooms of Edgar Tower, a few years before a formal arrangement was made with the Dean and Chapter, whose lawyers had been based in the Tower. A private house, Natland on Battenhall Road, was operated as an additional, small boarding house from 1919, with Rev Robert Whittaker as housemaster.

Obituaries

Two obituaries of Old Vigornians who died in combat, published in *The Vigornian*, are reproduced below.

"**William Arnold Fergusson**, born September 22 1886, died 25 May 1915. One of the first members of Castle House, who represented the school on the river, at cricket and at football. He left the school to do farming in Canada. At the outbreak of the war he joined 7th Battalion of the Canadian contingent. He was promoted to sergeant after the first battle of Ypres.

On the day of his death all the officers in his battalion had been killed, yet he led his platoon capturing an enemy trench. A man had gone out of this trench to bind up a wounded comrade, but because of sniper fire he was forced to take cover in a shell hole. Sergeant Fergusson left the trench, and, despite warnings, tried to help the wounded man, but was shot and killed instantly."

"**John Gordon Eccles**, a captain in the Royal West Kents, was attached to the Royal Flying Corps. He was born on September 19th, 1888 and was killed on May 25th, 1917. He had entered the Fifth Form in May 1905. He left school in July 1907. He was a keen athlete, representing the school at cricket and football. After

Great War memorial board in College Hall, designed by architect Hope Bagenal, unveiled by William Chappel at the Reunion Dinner in June 1921

leaving in the Sixth Form he joined Lloyds Bank in Manchester and then worked in India. He returned to serve in the Royal West Kents in France in October 1915. He later joined the Flying Corps and on 25th May his machine received a direct hit from anti-aircraft fire and went down, out of control, behind enemy lines."

Centenary activities

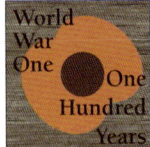

At the time of this book's publication, a national commemoration of the Great War was underway, marking one hundred years since the war which caused so much damage and led to such great loss of life. The School Archive organised a number of displays alongside a Twitter feed tweeting excerpts from the diaries of OVs who took part in the war and from newspaper accounts. Members of the school choir featured in a special episode of the BBC's *'The Archers'*, to mark the centenary of the outbreak of war on 4th August 2014.

Organised by the Foundation Development Office (see Chapter 9), the Old Vigornian Club commissioned a plaque to be installed at St George's Church in Ypres, Belgium at a special service of memorial in October 2014.

Retirement of William Chappel

As the Great War ended, and on the eve of his retirement, at the request of his successor Rev Creighton, Canon Chappel - made a Canon of the Cathedral in 1907 - sent out an appeal to parents and friends of the school for funds to create a fitting memorial to those lost in the war.

Chappel was well-loved by his pupils, to many of whom he was known as 'Daddy Chappel', and had worked hard during difficult times and expected the same standard of work and devotion from those around him. Chappel retired in 1918, leaving a school of which he could certainly be proud, having helped it to become regarded as one of the best small public schools in the country. At the school's Speech Day in 1918, Chappel announced that he would be joining the Bishop of Coventry, Dr Yeatman Biggs, who was moving from Worcester, who had invited him to be his Sub-Dean. Chappel died at the age of 62 in July 1922; simultaneous with his funeral in Coventry, a memorial service was held in Worcester Cathedral.

Canon and Mrs Chappel with School House, 1918

Cuthbert Creighton - Headmaster 1919-1936 and 1940-1942

Reverend Cuthbert Creighton would have been no stranger to the school at which he arrived as Headmaster in 1919, having grown up on College Green, living at Number 15 while his father, Mandell Creighton, was a Canon Residentiary at Worcester Cathedral, and having attended the re-opening of College Hall in 1887 as an eleven year old boy. Like his two immediate predecessors, Creighton was educated at Marlborough College, and even taught by William Chappel there, before taking a degree at Emmanuel College, Cambridge. Creighton went on to study modern languages abroad before taking a position at Uppingham, where he served for twenty years as a classical and modern languages master and a housemaster before his appointment as Headmaster at King's at the age of 42. Creighton was married to Margaret and had a three year old son, Tom. Later in 1919, a second son was born, Hugh, and the Creightons decided to purchase a family home, Tutnall, in Claines, three miles away.

The school had suffered during the last years under Canon Chappel, financially and as a result of the disruption to staffing and losses among Old Vigornians, although both physically and academically, King's was in good shape.

The Board of Education Grant

The school's ongoing financial woes, which had not been concluded by the time of Chappel's retirement, meant that it proved difficult to recruit new staff, and to retain existing ones, as the salaries offered were no longer adequate, and the National Teachers' Pensions Bill would not cover staff at public schools. While the new buildings, Number 7 College Green and School House, provided a good standard of accommodation, the school, which by now numbered around 200 boys, remained short of teaching space.

Reverend Cuthbert Creighton

Among his first decisions as Headmaster, Creighton had to increase the school fees, from £15 15s to £18 18s for tuition with the additional fee for boarding increased from £40 to £45. Creighton was reluctant to increase the fees any further than this in case of an adverse effect on pupil numbers.

Fortunately, at this time, the conditions for receiving a grant from the Board of Education were changed; it was no longer necessary for the majority of Governors to be from outside the Church of England, so the only change to the governing body required was that the Mayor of Worcester would be one of two members nominated by the City Council rather than an ex officio member. The other significant issue for King's had been the need to drop the requirement that the Headmaster be a member of the Church of England; with the Dean and Chapter now allowed to continue to form a majority of the governing body, this restriction seemed less problematic. In

The Fives Courts, initially two courts built in 1889 - a third was added in 1922 as a memorial to OVs lost in the Great War.
The Fives Courts, which had long been left unused, were demolished in 2003; the memorial plaque (inset) was installed on the castle wall.

The King's School, Worcester *From 1541 into the 21st Century*

1919, Creighton was able to convince the Governors that an application to the Board of Education would be the best way to secure the school's future, with assurances that the character of the school, with the freedom to determine its own educational schemes, would be safe.

The application was successful, and the result had a significant impact on the school's development in the early 1920s. The grant awarded was £1,346, with an additional £400 for the Advanced Course in Classics; when the new costs of supplying stationery and paying for a Secretary, a requirement of the Board of Education, the net benefit was an income of around £1,300 per year. This allowed Creighton to increase the salaries of his staff to a sensible level and to carry out repairs to school buildings. A further benefit was that teachers would now be eligible for the School Teachers Superannuation Scheme to pay their pensions. The school was required to offer free places to 10% of the annual intake - around five or six boys each year; this led Creighton to reflect in later years that the broadening of the school's social base was a positive measure and should be extended to all schools.

Memorials

In 1919, before taking over as Headmaster, Creighton approached Canon Chappel to launch an appeal for a War Memorial Fund, which he did on the eve of his retirement. A total of £2,000 provided a roll of honour board in College Hall, an additional fives court (see photograph on previous page), a memorial window in the Cathedral cloisters and scholarships for sons of OVs killed in the war. The roll of honour and memorial window were unveiled by Canon Chappel during a special two-day OV Reunion Festival in June 1921. In addition to this, Thomas Rammell paid for a new pavilion to be built at the playing field; school cricket had been a particular passion since his arrival in 1891 and he had been responsible for maintaining records of OVs involved in the war.

Creighton in College Hall

The Headmaster's desk, a carved table, donated along with a wooden chair and a clock for College Hall by Ernest Bird (OV 1889-94), was positioned in the centre of the platform in College Hall. The piano was to his left, on the south wall, and the Sixth Form sat to his right, facing south.

The school would assemble in College Hall each morning; Creighton rang a small bell to call for silence before school monitors would move down from the platform to take roll call, registering a form each. A hymn would follow, with a lesson and prayers, before the Headmaster would read any notices to the pupils. The bell would ring again to signal the end of the assembly, at which point conversations would resume and the boys were dismissed to their lessons.

In his book *'King's School Worcester 1541-1971'* Michael Craze (The Hostel, 1919-25) recorded his memory of Creighton on the day his wife died in 1923:

"Every human being acquires a private gallery of pictures from experience, recorded in a flash and indelibly imprinted on the memory. We have a picture of College Hall emptying unusually quietly on the most critical day of Mrs. Creighton's illness; a sympathetic backward glance at the headmaster took him in, kneeling now at the south end of his lonely desk in an agony of prayer. She died on Monday, 2 February. He still carried on, and allowed no public reference to his loss to be made."

The OV Reunion Weekend and Speech Day

In 1921, a special two-day festival for Old Vigornians had taken place to mark the unveiling of the various memorials to OVs killed in the Great War. This had meant moving the OV Dinner - held again in School House - from January to June, which Creighton preferred and persuaded the OV Club to keep the Reunion in the summer, as it could be combined with an OV v school cricket match and rowing event. In 1925, to coincide with the opening of the Chappel Memorial Reading Room and the new classrooms, Creighton moved Speech Day from October to June, creating a three-day long OV Reunion Weekend, with Speech Day on Friday 10th July, the OV Club Reunion Dinner on Saturday and a service in the Cathedral on Sunday. From 1930, Creighton introduced a rugby match between the school's 1st XV and an OV Club XV, followed by an evening concert in College Hall, at the end of the summer term.

David Annett, Headmaster, would separate the OV Reunion Weekend from Speech Day, with the creation of King's Day in 1970 as the last day before examination leave for the Fifth Form and Upper Sixth. The OV Reunion continued to operate over two or three days - a golf day was included on the Friday in more recent years - with the event later moved to the autumn but returned to the summer term, albeit the May Day Bank Holiday weekend early in the term, from 2010. In the 1980s, King's Day became the last day of the summer term, around 10th July.

Modernisation

After the war, the Dean and Chapter removed the railings around College Green and re-seeded the area as a lawn, planting lime trees on the northern side of the Green. The gas lamps remained until electrification in 1932, but College Hall, The Hostel, Castle House and School House switched to electrical lighting in 1922. A telephone was installed in the Porter's Lodge (1 College Green - the southern side of Edgar Tower) in February 1920, for which the Headmaster was required to pay an annual levy of £2; this was the first telephone to be installed south of the Cathedral. In 1921, King's leased the rest of Edgar Tower - the northern side of the lower floor and the entire upper floors; three classrooms for younger pupils were established, including an Art Room, where Miss Myfanwy Campbell, the first female teacher at King's (appointed in 1917), worked in the 1930s. Number 9 College Green was rented, as accommodation for the increasing number of unmarried masters and an office for the new School Secretary, H Nicholls.

Creighton established a Games Fund for improvements to the school's playing fields, and decided to exploit the new radio technology; in 1922, he organised a concert which was a combination of live music and wireless - unfortunately, the part of the programme during which music was to be heard through the wireless was unsuccessful, but it did certainly increase the level of interest in the technology.

In 1927, Creighton persuaded the Dean and Chapter to enlarge the Choir School into a full preparatory school, taking in non-choristers, so that King's would no longer have to accept younger boys. Pupils at the Choir School would be educated there until the age of thirteen, at which stage they would progress to King's or other schools.

Extending the school beyond College Green

Technically 'Number 8 College Green', School House had extended the reach of the school campus beyond the Cathedral

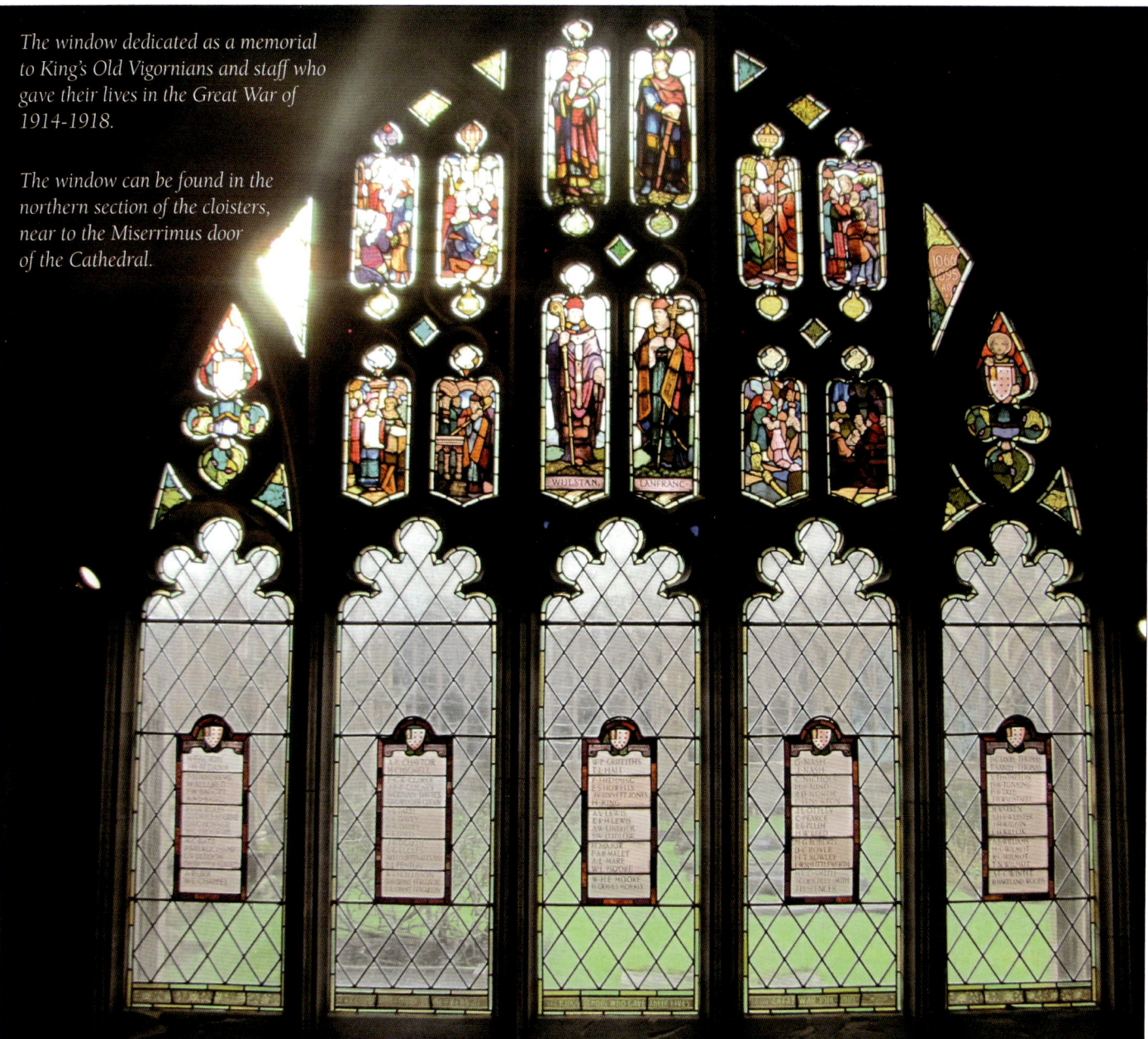

The window dedicated as a memorial to King's Old Vigornians and staff who gave their lives in the Great War of 1914-1918.

The window can be found in the northern section of the cloisters, near to the Miserrimus door of the Cathedral.

King's Remembered

D M Forrest — School House 1919-1922

I came to The King's School rather late, because I started at St. John's, Leatherhead, but when a scholarship was founded in memory of Dean Forrest (1890-1908), the first was offered to me - a notable piece of second generation nepotism.

Perhaps it is worth putting on record that School House was rather highbrow in my day, perhaps under Cuthbert Creighton's influence. At a time when most house plays usually consisted of trivial farces, School House staged J.M. Synge's 'Shadow of the Glenwith', parts played by Jack (later Sir Jack) Longland and Chartres (later Brigadier). I remember I was intensely moved by it.

To us of course the Canons did seem rather figures of fun, seen in the Cathedral Sunday by Sunday, or tottering about College Green, especially perhaps T.A. Lacey (eminent scholar and hymnologist) because of his extra vowel sounds when preaching the lessons - 'Arbraham, Eezark and Yacoob', etc.

One got his own back though. S. James was once drafted in to take Latin in one of the middle forms. 'Here's larks!' thought the chaps and started fooling around. What they didn't know was that the funny old character was an ex-headmaster of Malvern, and he got the lot sorted out in four minutes dead.

Another reminiscence of that time is trooping into the Cathedral in 1920 for the unveiling of the Worcestershire Regiment World War I Memorial. It was carried out by a very small, scarlet clad, white moustached figure - very much one's idea of 'Bobs' (Lord Roberts). This was General Sir George Higgison, the last man to receive his commission from the Duke of Wellington and as Wellington, then Colonel Wellesley, took a forward part in the 1790s in India, that carries us at only two hops way back to the 18th century.

First published in 'The King's School, Worcester and a history of its site', 1994.

precincts and into the site of Worcester Castle and the City Gaol, in the late 1880s. By the time of Creighton's headship, a collection of buildings had been built around the periphery of the enlarged site, including a pair of fives courts (1889) and Chappel's gymnasium (1901) surrounding a large playground.

Creighton developed a plan to create a lawned area between the rear of Number 7 and the northern end of School House, flanked by a new classroom block with a reading room facing the river and so screening the playground and bicycle racks from view as one approached School House from the Green.

In 1925, this vision was realised, with the completion of the new classrooms and the Chappel Memorial Reading Room. The classroom block contained four large, airy classrooms, and cost £2,500, paid for in part by the surplus in school funds provided by the 'Direct Grant', with the remaining £800 met by Creighton himself. The Chappel Memorial Reading Room quickly became an iconic building at the heart of the school campus. Both buildings were opened by Viscount Grey of Fallodon, at a special ceremony on Speech Day, 10th July 1925. The stone sundial from College Green, dated 1659, took pride of place in a new position at the centre of the lawn, known later as the Monitors' Lawn; the sundial would be repositioned in 2010 to make way for the creation of 'Library Square' next to the Monitor's Lawn (see Chapter 9).

Between 1925 and 1929, new changing rooms were built in the courtyards behind Castle House and The Hostel, and an extension was added to School House to provide changing rooms there. A new, larger gymnasium was built, designed and paid for by Creighton, adjacent to the 1901 gym, which was converted into changing rooms for the day boys and a carpentry workshop. This new gym made way for the Wolfson Building in the early 1970s, by which time a modern sports hall had been built on a newly-acquired site in Severn Street. Members of the school undertook to level the surface of the playground, making it more suitable for sports practices and O.T.C. parades.

The new classrooms allowed the tradition of teaching multiple classes at once in College Hall to end, and so the heavy desks brought in for College Hall in 1887 could be removed; new wooden benches were secured from Uppingham School, where they had been discarded on completion of that school's new hall. The gallery of College Hall was refurbished in natural oak, a leaving gift from Thomas Rammell in 1929, when he retired after 38 years at King's.

Creighton's wife, Margaret, had died in 1923; as a memorial to his late wife, Creighton purchased the disused allotments site, which stood between School House and the river, from the Ecclesiastical Commissioners, as the remainder of the site acquired by the Governors from the Dean and Chapter for the construction of School House. With the help of boys from School House, the ground was cleared, landscaped and planted, with a new fountain, the base of which was formed out of a cider press from Creighton's property at Claines, and a summer house, or loggia, which bore a plaque dedicating the gardens to Margaret. The Creighton Memorial Gardens were opened in 1931, and donated to the school.

King's Remembered

Michael Craze — *The Hostel and Day Boy 1919-1925*

Michael Craze published a well-respected history of The King's School in 1972 while he was Secretary of the Old Vigornian Club. Craze became a schoolmaster and taught at Bloxham and Felsted before retiring to Worcester, where he died in 1998.

The King's School in my time had about 200 boys of whom more than half were boarders. Its buildings were compact and few. The school had The Hostel and Castle House, owned by the Dean and Chapter. School House and the Classroom Block (now Biology) were owned by the school, which also owned the playground on whose southern side were a carpentry shop, gymnasium and miniature rifle range. In my time the Chappel Memorial Reading Room and the fives courts were added by subscription. The greatest lack was in science. In the classroom block, the master had one room for theory and one laboratory for Chemistry and Physics. Even so every boy below Sixth Form level was taught science. Downstairs there were two large classrooms and the smaller third room was the Masters' Common Room. In College Hall the Fourth Form under Castley had their classroom at the gallery end. Castley was in charge of the book room and at any point in his lessons a boy from outside would bring him an order, he would stop teaching, and service it. The Removes had their classroom at the other end of College Hall, below the platform. In Edgar Tower there were three rooms upstairs where the lower forms were taught. Only one was needed when the new classrooms were opened in 1925.

We did not feel cramped at all in space. The Cathedral and College Hall enlarged us and the two playing fields across the river were enlarged by the County Ground to which every cricketer with a Second XI blazer was always admitted free. The rowers for their part had the river and their own barge on the west side opposite Severn Street. They had to be able to swim, but only had the Corporation Bath in the Severn by Pitchcroft in which to learn the art.

Severn Street was out of bounds. Its eighteenth century fishermen's houses were the lowest of the low. Nevertheless, it was in these that food bargains could be secured because you could buy a penny-worth of broken biscuits from the bottom of the tin at 'God Bless You My Dear!' (that was the woman's greeting on your entering and leaving the shop). Better still you could buy a fresh hen's egg for a penny. Pocket money was sixpence a week.

I entered King's as a boarder in The Hostel, aged twelve and a half. As

Houses at the western end of Severn Street, 1920s, demolished to make way for construction of the Annett Building in the 1950s.

a King's Scholar, I processed with the Cathedral Choir at the Sunday 10.30 Matins and had the plum job of collecting from the Alice Ottley girls. As a boarder, I sang bass in Edgar Day's concert choir. A few days before my sixteenth birthday, I became Head of House and a School Monitor. As a School Monitor, I sat in a Canon's stall at the 4 pm Evensong and I carried a military sort of walking stick if I went down town. In the O.T.C., I was Corporal Craze and commanded the house platoon (which I may say came second in the House Platoon Competition). As a day boy, from September 1923, I abandoned the Corps. Those not in it were called 'civvies'. Not surprisingly my work in school suffered as my responsibilities and my ego expanded.

As a day boy in my last two years, I cycled the eight miles from Himbleton to College Green and back, six days a week. I was in the First XI and First XV both those years and the eight mile ride back after matches was often pretty exhausting. On rare occasions, I found a flat tyre in the morning and then I had to catch Polly, our pony, harness her and drive the dog-cart to school. All the Classical Upper Sixth lessons were in the Sixth Form Room (which became the Old Library). This had been a Canon's stable and there is still an iron ring in the outside wall on the right of the door. To this, Polly could be tethered until I drove her down to Sidbury Mews in the break. I claim to be the last pupil to have driven to The King's School in a horse and trap.

Michael Craze, with his book 'King's School, Worcester', 1972

I had made up my mind while still only eleven to be a schoolmaster when I grew up. I was therefore both a pupil and an inspector of the masters who taught me. A.D. Franklin laboured on our behalf in Latin, Greek and Ancient History and was both systematic and exacting. We translated Livy's Preface on paper and learnt the Latin by heart. He became a real friend of mine after I left. None of the men who taught me English were any good, but I did gain enormously from some other boys.

As a member of the school First XI, I was an opening bowler and a number eleven bat. Only at age 18 did I have a medical examination, when I discovered that I had little sight in my left eye! As a rugger player, I enjoyed most of the matches in mud and rain and the sight of G.K. Tattersall, our rugger master, going berserk when he played. My best game was chess. I won the individual cup twice and played top board against the College for the Blind.

I entered the school between the Armistice of November 1918 and the Versailles Peace Treaty of June 1919. College Green had its iron railings sent for scrap and the only 'green' had been the vegetables grown by the boys. The Officer Training Corps was hard at work preparing boys for Certificate A, the possession of which was the key to a later commission. The Corps paraded every Saturday at noon on the playground. Led by its drum and bugle band it marched up to Battenhall and back through Edgar Tower to the Armoury which was between the Choir School and the Sixth Form Room. What disturbed the Canons more was the Monday parade when Certificate A candidates, as part of their training, drilled a junior squad and a score of raucous voices filled the air at once. Band practices also woke babies and sent mothers frantic. Even so we learnt to throw our voices and I wish the clergy and lecturers could do as much today instead of demanding loudspeakers and microphones.

Any adolescent boy is always going to have troubles and disappointments as well as good days. No grown man should be bitter about what was done to him as a boy. I treasure a great deal that was good, including College Hall and the Cathedral.

Adapted from an account by Michael Craze, published in 'The King's School, Worcester and a history of its site', 1994.

Michael Craze claimed to be the last pupil to arrive at school by pony and trap in 1924/25. The iron ring in the wall of the former stables at 4/5 College Green, to which Craze's pony, Polly, was tethered, has been preserved, and is shown in this photograph taken in 2014.

The Chappel Memorial Reading Room

The Chappel Memorial Reading Room formed the central focal point of Cuthbert Creighton's plan to extend the school campus beyond College Green, creating a lawned quadrangle behind Castle House, flanked by a new classroom building. The reading room was to be named in honour of Canon William Chappel, Headmaster 1896-1918 who died in July 1922.

Having accepted the Board of Education Grant, the school's finances were in a better position than for many decades, which allowed Creighton to press ahead with the new classroom building and the impressive new reading room, which relieved pressure on teaching in College Hall to the level that only one form would be taught in the hall at any time.

The cost of the Chappel Memorial Reading Room was £1,425, most of which was provided by Old Vigornians, parents and friends. Significant contributions were made by Old Vigornians Samuel Southall, Col. A Webb, John Stallard, C W Dyson-Perrins and the Headmaster.

Worcester architects Messrs. Rowe and Heppel designed the building, following a Georgian style, with much of the detailing provided by J Smith, the Cathedral's Clerk of Works. R Haughton was responsible for the stone doorway with its carved coat of arms and motto.

The OV Club donated £50 to provide an ornate wooden desk for reading newspapers. A grandfather clock, which would later stand in the library in Edgar Tower and then the common room in Hostel House until its theft in 2013, was donated by the Graves-Morris brothers (OVs 1919-25). Classics master A D Franklin provided the motto surrounding the electric chandelier: 'Arte ego suppedito quam negat hora diem', which he translated as: *'The light that day denies, my cunning art supplies'.*

The quadrangle, open to the drive of School House, was completed by the repositioning of a sundial which had previously stood on College Green. The reading room, with the new adjacent new classroom building, was opened as part of the Speech Day ceremonies of 10th July 1925 by Viscount Grey

Opening of the Chappel Memorial Reading Room and the new classroom block, Speech Day 1925: Dean Moore Ede, Creighton, Lord Grey of Fallodon and Samuel Southall

of Fallodon - better known to many as Sir Edward Grey, Foreign Secretary from 1905 to 1916 and later British Ambassador to the USA, who famously commented on the outbreak of the Great War "The lamps are going out all over Europe. We shall not see them lit again in our life-time".

The reading room was used by members of the Sixth Form, until the opening of the new library in Edgar Tower in 1969. Since then the building has had a variety of uses, including as a social space for Sixth Formers in the 1970s, a choir practice room and a drama and dance studio.

Following the closure of Passey Hall when School House was refurbished in the 1980s, the building was renamed 'New Passey Hall'. However, the name was restored to 'Chappel Memorial Room' in the 1990s by Second Master Tim Hickson, effected by the simple use of two small blue signs.

At the suggestion of Keith Bridges (Chemistry and The Hostel 1963-2003), the cupola of this much-loved building was painted gold in 2002. Since 2003, the 'CMR' has been used as an annexe of the Music School in Castle House as a rehearsal space for choirs and orchestras.

Chappel Memorial Reading Room with the new classrooms of 1925. The sundial was relocated from College Green to serve as a focal point for the new qudrangle.

The Chappel Memorial Room, photographed in 2015

Detail from architectural drawings showing an intended gallery level and roof windows

Above: *Interior of the Chappel Memorial Reading Room, 1925*
Below: *The rather less formal use - Lower Sixth Common Room, 1970s*

Education at King's

As Creighton arrived at King's, the disruption of the war years was still evident, and this was reflected in the examination results of 1919 in which only two Higher Certificates and five School Certificates were awarded. Creighton was concerned to raise academic standards, and encouraged the masters to send boys to him with 'good copies' or 'bad copies' which he would read either smiling or frowning. The boys' academic performance would be compiled into a Form Order each term, allowing the boys, and their parents, to see where they ranked within the year group; the Headmaster would read these Form Orders in College Hall, using facial expressions to pass comment on the lists.

A number of new masters were appointed in Creighton's first years, with Captain A Birch Jones returning from the army to serve as School House Tutor and Fourth Form Master and D Walton teaching modern languages. F Salisbury ran Sixth Form Classics and shared his passions for archaeology, ceramics, chess, botany and rowing with the boys. Rev R Craze took over as School Chaplain. Creighton himself taught Sixth Form Divinity, teaching the New Testament in Greek. In 1920, Birch Jones left for the Home Civil Service and was replaced by Samuel Strong; Strong was Tutor to School House, took over rowing and worked to strengthen the O.T.C. alongside Captain Whittaker. Frank Thomas took charge of the recently-introduced sport of boxing and helped Creighton to return Rugby Football as the main winter sport. Edgar Day, assistant organist at the Cathedral, was employed to teach music and run the choir and orchestra, as Creighton was not satisfied with the small number of hours provided by George Smith. A Franklin, G Tattersall and Arthur Bentley joined the school during 1922, with Tattersall playing a key role in school sport.

The Board of Education, following the school's acceptance of the Direct Grant and therefore recognition within the state education system, recognised the Advanced Classics course in 1920, and the Modern Subjects course in 1926. The Classics course dominated the Sixth Form, drawing most King's Scholars, and was led by A Franklin from 1922, taught in the Sixth Form Room.

The School Certificate became established as the measure of academic ability, in place of minor examinations. Pupils needed to achieve a subject pass in each of three areas - Languages, English Subjects, and Mathematics and Science. In order to gain a Higher Certificate, at least one 'non-specialist subsidiary subject' pass was also required; to ensure the best chance of success, the Classical Sixth at King's studied English, Divinity and French alongside the core subjects of Latin, Greek and Ancient History.

Creighton's efforts proved successful; with largely static pupil numbers, the Certificate awards improved - in 1928 a record of nine Higher Certificates was achieved with 28 School Certificates awarded in 1933; by way of comparison, the Royal Grammar School, with three times the number of pupils, achieved a new record in 1936 of nine Higher Certificates and 47 School Certificates. During the 1920s and 1930s, Franklin's Classical Sixth achieved sixteen university entrance awards, five of whom were awarded first class honours degrees in Classics. There were also nine exhibitions and scholarships in Divinity, History and Modern Languages, including two Choral Scholarships, leading to seven first class degrees; one Old Vigornian was awarded a University Prize at Cambridge and three received University Prizes at Oxford.

Alec Macdonald, an OV who had served at school as librarian, museum curator and editor of *The Vigornian*, returned to King's in 1933 as a teacher of Modern Languages and with the brief to write a history of the school; at a previous school, Repton, Macdonald had written a school history, and Creighton was keen that King's should have one. Macdonald was considered to be a stimulating and inspiring teacher, who revived the Debating Society and began to produce plays, performed in College Hall, starting with the Trial Scene from Bernard Shaw's 'St Joan' in 1935 (for more on Drama at King's see Chapter 8).

During the Great War, the school's Scout Troop was absorbed into the O.T.C..The minimum age for joining the O.T.C. left a large number of boys without access to the range of activities available to O.T.C. members, so Creighton felt that there was a place for Scouts alongside the O.T.C. and so a new Troop was formed in 1930. A large number of boys applied to join, and the new master R C Pedder was appointed Scoutmaster and selected 36 boys to form four Patrols. Weekend camps often took place at the Headmaster's house in Claines, with the Pedder's family estate near Lake Windermere providing the setting for ten-day holiday camps in the summer.

Worcester Cathedral King's School, 1930

The Great Depression of the 1930s

The Direct Grant from the Board of Education had increased by £400 in 1926 to recognise the modern education offered alongside classics. However, as the Great Depression took its toll on the country, the Board of Education reduced the Grant from £9 per pupil to seven guineas, costing King's £30 a year from 1931. However, Ramsey MacDonald's new National Government had reduced all public sector salaries by 10% and extended this to teachers in Direct Grant schools, although this would not have saved the Government or the Board of Education any money; the school Governors were saving a significant sum as a result of this reduction in pay which was far greater than the loss of the £30 through the Grant reduction - this difference was saved in an account to be paid to the masters later.

An increase in the number of boarders had justified the founding of a fourth boarding house, for which Natland in Battenhall Road was purchased in 1918. For thirteen years, Rev R Whittaker ran the boarding house, but a decline in the number of pupils to 180 led to its sale in 1932, with the remaining boys placed into the other three houses.

In September 1934, the Government allowed half of the salary reduction to be reinstated and the Board of Education increased the allowance per pupil to £8. Unfortunately, the grant for the Advanced Courses of £800 was halved, with a further reduction of the amount for the Classical Course to just £300 and termination of the grant for the Modern Studies Course in 1935; both of these measures caused significant financial hardship for the school, for the first time since 1919, which had now reduced in size to 155 boys, as parents began to view the school fees as an extravagance at a time of such financial difficulties.

'A History of The King's School Worcester'

In 1936, Alec Macdonald published 'A History of The King's School Worcester', the first 'proper' history of the school. The book was almost completed at the time that Creighton announced his retirement. As a Postscript, Macdonald wrote:

"Not in increased numbers alone, nor in increased amenities, is that [Creighton's] service to be estimated. His generosity, his friendliness, his vigorous enthusiasm, his devotion to the school, are some of his qualities which neither boys nor masters will quickly forget. At the end of the present school year he hands on, to Mr L.A. Wilding, a school not only materially enriched and equipped, but also inspired with something of his own far-sighted courage to face the future that lies before it."

Natland, Battenhall Road, 2014, which was run as a boarding house from 1919 by Rev Robert Whittaker until the Great Depression forced its closure and sale in 1932.

By the 2000s, the house had been converted into twelve apartments.

Retirement of Creighton

Cuthbert Creighton retired as Headmaster in July 1936, after eighteen years at King's, during which he had been instrumental in driving the school forward, both in terms of education and the creation of a more pleasant school environment. The school had weathered the Great War under Chappel's headmastership and emerged from severe financial difficulties to become a well-respected, enlarged and enlightened school, well-equipped for the future.

His final duties included the OV Reunion Weekend and a sermon in the Cathedral. Creighton could rightly be proud of his achievements; in a leaving address he explained his educational philosophy, developed during his time at King's:

"Education consists in allowing a boy to develop naturally on the lines of his own God-given character and personality, and in providing him with a suitable environment in which to do so."

A final gift to the school from Creighton was the first of two extensions to the 1925 classrooms - a second extension was added in 1950; an Art Room and Geography classroom were added to the building, forming a corner onto the playground and alleviating the pressure on teaching space in Edgar Tower. The extension was completed in 1936.

From Worcester Castle to the Creighton Memorial Gardens

In 1069, shortly after the Norman Conquest, a motte and bailey castle was constructed on the east bank of the River Severn, on land adjacent to the Priory, including some land taken from Bishop Wulstan's monastery. The site encompasses the southern parts of College Green, the area now occupied by the school playground, School House and the school gardens, extending as far as Saxon ditch, which formed part of the city's defences, at Frog Lane (later, Severn Street). The position of the Worcester Castle, one of many housing a Norman garrison across England, would have been chosen deliberately to defend against attack from Wales - at that time, Worcester lay in the Welsh Marches, with the river serving as a border. The wooden castle was built on an artificial mound, known as a motte, constructed on the present-day site of the school gardens.

Part of the remaining castle wall, behind Castle House and Hostel House, 2014

Worcester Castle saw significant military activity, including the rebellion of the Lords of the Marshes in 1088, the civil wars between Stephen and Matilda, and the uprising against King John in 1216. King John's son, Henry III, returned the castle, and most of its grounds, to the monastery in 1217; the gateway to the bailey became the monastic gatehouse, leading to College Green.

The castle was sold to William de Beachamp, a local baron, who used the remaining buildings and land for the 'King's Prison', which was certainly in existence by 1221; a gaol stood on this site for 700 years, until stones from the castle were used in the construction of the prison in Salt Lane (later named Castle Street after the castle-like appearance of the prison).

In a 1613 report for the Bishop of Worcester, the site of Castle Hill, as the motte was known by then, was described as 'conteying about an acre and a quarter of land'. Two centuries later, this was divided from the gaol, and sold to a local bookseller, Thomas Eaton, who demolished the hill and sold the resulting gravel. The demolition began in 1823 but was not completed until 1846. Eaton's heirs sold the site back to the Dean and Chapter in 1867; the Cathedral used the land as allotments, until much of the site was passed to The King's School in the 1880s. The castle wall, which ran along Castle Place and behind the houses on the southern side of College Green, including the western wall of Castle House, has largely survived to the present day, and the name of the castle lives on both in Castle Place and Castle House.

School House, with a playground in front of it, was built in 1888, with additional buildings placed behind it during the next 40 years, including the Chappel Memorial Reading Room, the classrooms, later part of the 'Fourth Form Block', and the Fives Courts; during this time, the school site gradually took the shape it has today, occupying the majority of College Green and Castle Place (which had been the entrance to the gaol), with a playground quadrangle later formed with the construction of the gymnasium and the Winslow Building, buildings along the Severn Street boundary, and grounds extending towards to the river.

In 1930, Headmaster Cuthbert Creighton bought the remaining plot of land, between School House and the river towpath, and transformed the site into beautiful gardens, dedicated to the memory of his wife Margaret, who had died ten years earlier.

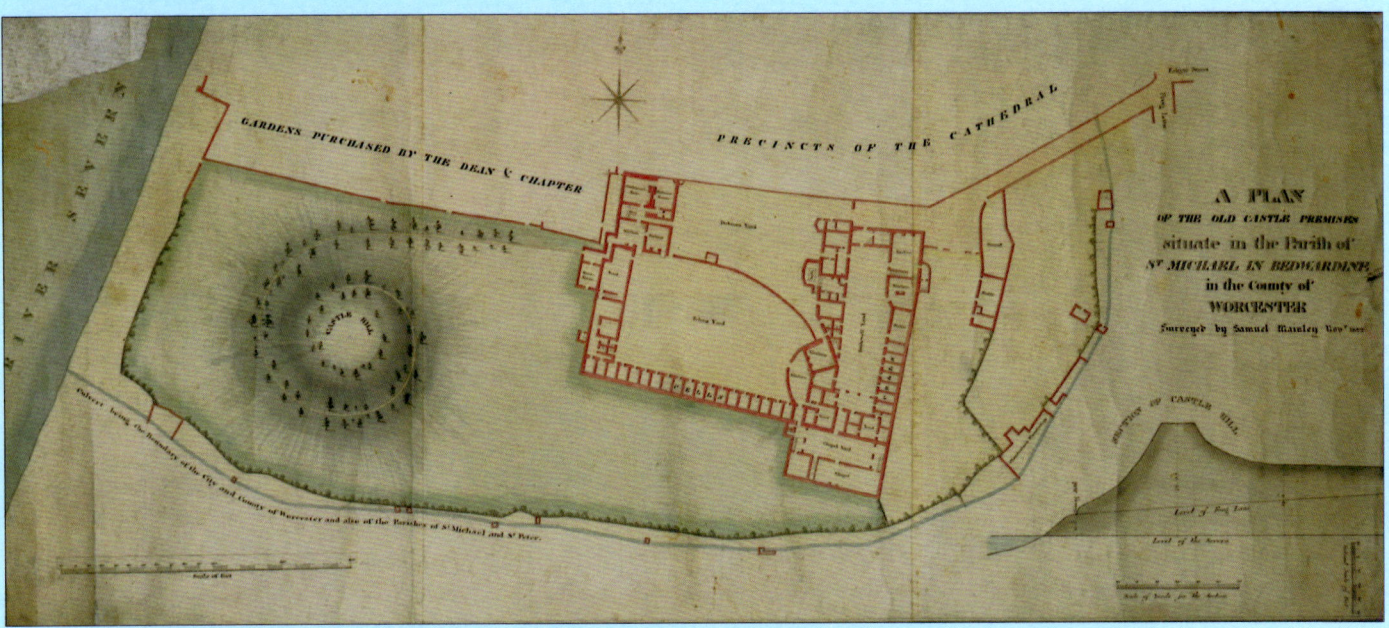

Plan of the site of Worcester Castle and the King's Prison, 1882 - Castle Hill can be seen towards the left of the map

The Creighton Memorial Gardens, opened in July 1931 - this view was virtually unchanged, except for the size of the trees, in 2015

Once completed, Creighton donated the gardens to the school.

Among the interesting features of the gardens are the fountain, above which sits a leaden statue of Sabrina, from a poem by Milton, 'Comus', whose *"moist curls swayed the smooth Severn stream"* and who, taking refuge from her stepmother in the river, became goddess of the River Severn. Leaded dies which surround the fountain bear the signs of the zodiac. The base of the fountain is made from a cider press taken from Creighton's house at Claines. A plaque, near to the fountain, tells the history of the site.

A summer house, or loggia, provided a quiet, shaded place to escape; a plaque bears a Latin inscription, which translates as:

"In 1930, in memory of Margaret Creighton, Cuthbert Creighton had this garden made. May the beauty your eyes behold, reader, recall her, whom beauty delighted."

The summer house fell into disrepair and was demolished; in 1992, the OV Club paid for the summer house to be rebuilt, using the same design as the original.

The south-eastern corner of the gardens is divided by a wall from the rest - this was a private garden, for the Headmaster's use, and easily accessible from the southern end of School House, in which he lived. This was later to become a 'Fourth Form playground' and, after years of being little more than a muddy plot, was given a hard playing surface in 2005, and even a basketball hoop.

An area of grass, nearest to School House, was lost to the increasing demands of car parking in 2003. Other than this, the school gardens, and the view looking back towards the school, changed little between 1931, when the Creighton Memorial Gardens were opened, and 2012. The Michael Baker Boathouse, which flanks the southern side of the gardens, includes a terrace, looking over the lower lawn, and a path through the gardens forms the attractive approach to the main entrance of the Boathouse (see Chapter 9).

Further information about Worcester Castle can be found in Appendix 15: The archaeology of The King's School.

The summer house, rebuilt in the 1990s

*Illustration showing Castle Hill.
The Deanery (No. 10) can be seen to the left of Castle Hill;
the former St Peter's Church emerges behind the hill.*

Aerial photograph, September 2015, showing the Creighton Memorial Gardens connected to the Michael Baker Boathouse

The fountain, centrepiece of the Creighton Memorial Gardens, with its statue of river goddess Sabrina

Vista across the Creighton Memorial Gardens, summer 2015, looking west beyond the River Severn to the Chapter Meadows Playing Fields
Inset: View to the Fourth Form Playground, refurbished in 2005, originally the Headmaster's private garden

L A Wilding- Headmaster 1936-1939

From 166 applicants for the position, Longworth Allen Wilding was appointed Headmaster in 1936, aged 34. Married, and with three young children, Wilding had been an assistant master at St Edward's School, Oxford since 1927. With two degrees from Oxford, experience as an OTC officer, and, with his wife, a good social standing in Oxford, the governors were willing to overlook his lack of boarding house experience.

One of Allen Wilding's first changes had been long overdue. The day boys, who had been treated as a single house, were divided into two houses, to be known as Chappel's House and Creighton's House. The two houses would retain a single housemaster, Frank Thomas, and would still have only one changing room, so the initial benefits were seen in inter-house events, in which each day boy house competed separately from January 1937. Chappel House kept the yellow striped tie, while Creighton House adopted a pink stripe. An immediate effect was to increase the engagement of the day boys, who had often, with good cause, felt on the sidelines of the boarding school.

At his first Speech Day, in July 1937, Wilding urged parents to keep their sons at King's beyond the School Certificate, for at least a year:

"It is at this time that boys pass from the letter to the spirit of learning, and it is at this age that a boy can learn, even by mistakes, to take a position of responsibility and develop powers of leadership and initiative which will make him not only a better wage earner but a better man."

Longworth Allen Wilding

The coronation of King George VI, in the summer of 1937, included a parade of the OTC, involving three cadets from King's, and a Scout Camp at Eastnor Park in which the King's Troop were part of the 10,000-strong Coronation Jamboree, and were met by General Baden-Powell, Chief Scout.

Aerial view from the south-east, 1937. The first of two extensions to the 'Fourth Form' building had been carried out, and the houses in Castle Place (1,2 and 3) had yet to be demolished. Beyond the Cathedral (right of photo) the original College Street and Birdport (later renamed Deansway) could still be seen - most of that area, including Lich Street and the south of High Street, was demolished and redeveloped in the early 1960s.

The strain of taking on the role of housemaster alongside his first headship at a school with an established staff, had started to show in Wilding, who was given a term's sick leave in April 1938. Frank Thomas served as Acting Headmaster, and deputised for Wilding at Speech Day and the OV Dinner.

The Headmaster returned in September 1938, and appeared to be in much better health, cheered by the favourable report which followed the School Inspection in June. However, a far greater and rather more difficult strain was placed on Wilding when, in December 1938, he received a 'Top Secret' notice from H.M. Office of Works. The Government had been making contingency plans, since the Munich Agreement of September 1938, to move Government offices and military installations out of London to the provinces, knowing that Hitler had the capability to strike, even without a formal declaration of war. The buildings of The King's School would be required, in the event of war, for Government purposes, and the school was to be evacuated. Wilding was eventually granted permission to share this information with the Dean, as Chairman of the Governors, and together they appealed against this requisition because of the damage it could do to the school, but this was unsuccessful, due to Government concerns over the 'national interest'. The covert search for a temporary home for the school began, but it quickly became clear that there was no suitable site in Worcestershire. Wilding was familiar with the coast of North Wales, and secured options on two private hotels.

This had come at a significant cost to Wilding, in terms of his reputation and standing with his staff, who increasingly felt that the Headmaster was absent from school rather too often, and that he lacked the necessary qualities to continue as Headmaster. To this end, the assistant masters presented a declaration of no confidence in Wilding to the governors. At this time, most of the governors shared the teachers' opinion, as they were unaware of the secret burden placed on their Headmaster, and, while affronted by the temerity of the staff, they accepted the resignation tendered by Allen Wilding in August 1939, in which he agreed to leave in December.

Events in Europe continued rather rapidly, and the governors accepted the options on the hotels in Criccieth, so Wilding wrote to parents in September 1939, advising them of the relocation of the school and arranged for most of the day boys to attend the Royal Grammar School. The school reduced from 155 to just 95, with most boarders and more than twenty day boys moving with the school. Wilding informed parents of his resignation a few days later.

Allen Wilding travelled to Criccieth with the school, leaving the boys in Creighton's capable hands when he and his family left to return to Oxford at the end of December 1939.

Working as Senior Classics Master at the Dragon School, Oxford, Allen Wilding's most significant achievement was to transform Classics teaching across the country, with his three-part *Latin Course for Schools*, published by Faber and Faber between 1948 and 1952, followed by a fourth book *'Greek for Beginners'*. At least 250,000 copies of his books had been sold within ten years of Wilding's death, in August 1963.

King's Remembered

Basil Eckersley MBE *Castle House 1930-1937*

Basil Eckersley was awarded an MBE in 1946 for service with the Manchester Regiment in Burma. He went on to become a distinguished barrister, with expertise in commercial law and later in maritime arbitration. Basil died in 2004 at the age of 85.

I joined Castle House a little past my eleventh birthday as the youngest member of the school. My elder brother had been a day boy and I remember attending, as a six year old, the Speech Day of 1925 at which Viscount Grey of Fallodon officially opened the Chappel Memorial Reading Room and the new classroom block.

S.D. Strong, who had himself been a Castle House boy and therefore held strong views about its peculiar pre-eminence, succeeded T.E. Rammell as housemaster in 1929. Mr and Mrs Bentley, who took over in 1933, produced a marked improvement in our diet. There were maids in attendance at meal times, our beds were made for us and even our shoes were cleaned. The latter were lined up each evening in the changing room, and woe betide the owner of a pair which had not been removed by breakfast-time. As I recall the punishment for a second offence was usually a beating.

One's primary loyalty was to the House. In Mr and Mrs Bentley, Castle was fortunate. There was more than a touch of the military man in the bearing and, to some extent, in the attitudes of 'Captain Bentley'. He could be severe when occasion required, but he placed trust in his lieutenants and they knew they could look to him for support. However, during my last year as House Captain I always had a lurking suspicion that he found it a subject for mild regret that a house of his should be headed by an individual who had dismally failed to make any sort of a mark with bat or ball or blade, but we got on well enough.

The Lower School was then housed in Edgar Tower which only later became the art preserve of Miss Campbell - who in those days was the only female teacher. If the accommodation was somewhat primitive, it was strategically placed in one not unimportant respect. At the mid-morning break, we were within a stone's throw of the tiny shop in Edgar Street where 'Ma Bishop' administered to the needs of youthful thirst and appetite. The cost of a fresh bread roll, with a bar of whole chocolate inserted in it, was an old penny.

There followed promotion into the Middle School. First into the Lower Fourth, a mixed and disorderly rag bag which proved a permanent strain on the disciplinary powers of Arthur Taylor, a kindly if eccentric soul who owed his nickname of 'Bill Bootlace' to the precarious thread which secured his spectacles to his person. Next the Upper Fourth where the Reverend Whitaker exercised a gentle, but firm influence. Thence into the twilight world of the Remove under R.J. Castley. The home of the Remove was then at the west end of College Hall, with another class usually in session at the further end; 'Bruin' Castley's strong, gruff voice was never in danger of being drowned by whoever happened to be his competitor. Castley's humour was the homely kind which a schoolboy could easily appreciate:

"Please, Sir, my pen has run out."
"Has it? I didn't see it go."

Then it was the Upper Fifth, where Bentley imposed discipline and demanded concentration which allowed no one to forget that there lay ahead a hurdle in the shape of the School Certificate.

Castle House, 1937
Basil Eckersley is seated to the left of Arthur Bentley, Housemaster.

There were many, of course, in those days when the minimum school-leaving age was 14 and where money was tight, who never got beyond the Middle School and who went out into the world without any kind of official qualification.

For me there followed three years in the Modern Sixth. The Classical Sixth, affectionately nursed by A.D. Franklin, monopolised the Sixth Form Room. The Modern Sixth was a loose conglomerate of modern linguists and would-be historians, with the odd scientist somewhere in the wings. What our motley group lacked in cohesion and dignity of surroundings was more than compensated by the good fortune we shared in having as our form master a man of enormous imagination and charm in Alec Macdonald, himself an OV. The breadth of his interests and enthusiasms was of course infectious.

As the crown of England changed hands twice within the space of a year, there came a change in the headmastership of The King's School, with Creighton's retirement in 1936. Rarely can any school have benefited from a headmaster's generosity the like of that to which King's is in Creighton's debt. There are of course tangible memorials in brick and stone, as well as in the garden, which was especially appreciated by the boys who were the first to enjoy it, some of whom had modestly laboured in its transformation from wilderness to a thing of beauty.

Creighton will be best remembered by those who were boys in his time as a vivid personality and as the one man by whom the whole tone of the school was set. The gaunt, striking figure, the quizzical gaze through the pince-nez spectacles, the humour which shone through what on first acquaintance seemed a somewhat formidable demeanour.

The place of Creighton cannot have been an easy one to fill. His successor, L.A. Wilding, was a comparatively young man and this in itself may perhaps have led to a measure of resentment and resistance amongst some of the more senior of his colleagues. I was personally saddened that his headmastership proved to be of brief duration. My own relations with him were always friendly and in my last year, as House Captain and School Monitor, we saw a good deal of one another.

Adapted from an account by Basil Eckersley which was published in *'The King's School, Worcester and a history of its site'*, 1994.

The King's School evacuation of the Second World War

Cyril Havard FRCS (Castle House 1938-41) and Peter Oades (School House 1938-40) recounted the evacuation of the school to Criccieth in 'The King's School, Worcester and a history of its site', 1994; the following account draws largely on their reports.

Growing international tension in the late 1930s had caused the British Government to prepare seriously for the war which was expected imminently. Headmaster Allen Wilding had sought a suitable location to which the school could be evacuated, having been instructed, in secret, by the Government, that HM Office of Works planned to commandeer the school buildings in the event of war. Meanwhile, the O.T.C. prepared the boys, although the cadets may not have fully appreciated the grim intentions behind the 'field days' when the Corps went out into the countryside with old rifles from the Great War, with blank cartridges, to engage in pretend battles.

Wilding sent a letter to all King's parents, dated 7th September 1939:

Dear Sir or Madam,

I much regret to inform you that the government have commandeered the premises of this school. The possibility of this eventuality has been known to the Chairman of the Governors and myself for several months, but we were unable to inform you before for reasons of government secrecy. I am glad to say, however, that we have been able to use this time for securing good accommodation in private hotels in Criccieth in North Wales, in very pleasant surroundings, and what is definitely a 'reception area' which should be very safe.

The Chairman shares my confidence that you will be equally willing to entrust us with your son at Criccieth as here.

Will you kindly let me know - if possible within 48 hours, whether or not we may expect your son at Criccieth on September 21st?

On arriving at Criccieth, School House and Hostel boys should report at the Caerwylan Private Hotel; Castle House boys at the Pines Private Hotel. You may be assured that we will do our utmost to maintain the essentials of school life at Criccieth, and we feel sure that we may count on cooperation of all concerned.

Yours sincerely, L.A. Wilding.

Please reply to me at Worcester. Gas masks must be brought.

The evacuation plan, carefully devised by Wilding, was reported in the Evening News, September 1939

With this communication, the school was informed of the evacuation plans; 89 boys of the 158 were to accompany Wilding to Criccieth. The Headmaster arranged for the others, along with most of the 40 day boys, to be educated at the Worcester Royal Grammar School, thanks to the generosity of Headmaster H.R. Pullinger, who even allowed the King's boys to wear their King's School uniform and cap.

Caerwylan Hotel, Criccieth

O.T.C. Band playing in Criccieth

The strain of managing the evacuation plans, made worse by the requirement to do this in secrecy, had placed a remarkable pressure on Allen Wilding, and he sent a further letter to parents on 12th September:

Dear Sir or Madam,

I am writing with great regret to inform you that circumstances unconnected with the war have led me to resign the headmastership of this school, as from the end of the Christmas term 1939. I am naturally very sorry that this will mean the ending of the happy relations which have existed between us and that I shall not have the pleasure of seeing your son through to the end of his school career. It is however a satisfaction to me to feel that I have been able to settle the school at its new home in Criccieth before I leave.

The governors have accepted the generous offer of the Reverend C. Creighton who preceded me in the headmastership, to return to the school as honorary headmaster for the duration of the war.

Thank you for all your help, which I have so much appreciated.

Yours sincerely, L.A. Wilding.

The Office of Works provided transport to take desks, beds, books, stationery and supplies for the O.T.C. and Scouts to Criccieth, and all was set up ready for the boys to arrive by train on 21st September.

School House, initially under the Wildings, took up residency at the Caerwylan Private Hotel, run by Captain and Mrs Pritchard; boys from The Hostel, with Mrs Pedder (Richard Pedder having been recalled to the Navy) occupied a small house next door, and joined School House for meals in the hotel's dining room. The boarders of Castle House, with Mr and Mrs Bentley, were self-contained within 'The Pines', nearby. Day boys joined one of the boarding houses.

Several of the assistant masters had travelled with the school - Frank Thomas, Sam Strong, Arthur Franklin, Alec Macdonald, B Ward and V Wrigley - finding their own accommodation nearby. H Nicholls was unable to leave Worcester, but his daughter took his place as Secretary for Wilding; similarly, Edgar Day could not leave the Cathedral, and in the absence of a replacement, instrumental music was abandoned. Seargant-Major George Cooper accompanied the O.T.C. and also served as PT instructor.

The boys quickly felt at home in the converted hotels in Criccieth, set in breath-taking scenery. Each pupil had two jars in the dining room, one containing sugar rations, the other butter rations, and the boys certainly felt well fed. The classrooms were in 'The Towers', a disused three-storey hotel later to become an old people's home, located some distance away, beyond a lifeboat station and a milk bar, a popular diversion for the pupils with its penny and ha'penny game machines. The classroom windows had to be painted over within the first few days as local dolphins caused a significant distraction for masters and pupils alike. With the King's boys were a number of German Jews and two Italian refugees; the Italian boys were later taken away because their father had a link to Mussolini's government.

J.G. Greaves, Lord Lieutenant of Caernarvonshire, provided a field for playing rugby; his son-in-law, Colonel G Drage, lent the school the Drill Hall, used by the Local Volunteer Force, as an armoury, indoor training centre and gymnasium. Colonel Drage would attend Speech Day in July 1941, after King's had returned to Worcester.

Allen Wilding left the school at Criccieth at the end of December 1939, to be replaced by Cuthbert Creighton, returning as 'Honorary Headmaster' in January 1940.

Getting around Criccieth, and to local villages for sports and recreation, meant that bicycles were almost essential; the boys made many expeditions into the countryside. On one particular occasion, Peter Oades' OTC contingent went out to celebrate after passing their Certificate A qualification, which would allow them to gain a commission into the armed forces more easily. The boys had gone out during prep time and were concerned to have been spotted by 'Cuth Creighton' driving towards them, but the Headmaster just waved cheerily. The boys also enjoyed their new freedoms to smoke out of the sight of the masters and to *"meet the local female society",* as Peter Oades put it.

English tongues struggled with such names as Caerwylan and Glanwyn, and as one of only two Welsh boys in the school, Cyril Havard had to act as interpreter when bargaining with a local farmer for the use of a field to play rugby. The boys played a particularly memorable match against officers at R.A.F. Penrhos, played not to the roar of a crowd, but to the rumbling of bombers overhead. This was an unusual opportunity for younger pupils to play against grown men, and also the first opportunity to drink beer; B.B. Ward, the sports master, remembered a pressing engagement in Criccieth, leaving the boys to the hospitality of the Officers' Mess - a nervous Squadron Leader bravely ordered fifteen pints. Cricket suffered more than rugby, since the nearest flat surface which could be used as a cricket pitch was on the other side of Porthmadog, almost five miles away. Many boys opted to play golf instead, although the local sheep provided a number of natural hazards.

School House at Criccieth, 1940

The 'phony war', which had made life seem simple to the evacuees, was over by the summer of 1940. Mr Price, owner of the Pines, informed the boys that the Nazis were *"bombing the heart out of Rotterdam"*; the boys watched with horror as Paris appeared at the left hand edge of the war map in the *Daily Telegraph* and slowly, day by day, moving inexorably eastwards.

The O.T.C. band had played the Last Post and Reveille on a balcony of the Memorial Hall in Criccieth on Remembrance Day 1939. Some months later, survivors of Dunkirk started to be brought to Criccieth to recover. The boys were saddened to see men from various regiments, *"without arms or equipment, dispersed to lie, depressed and demoralised, on the grass at the centre of the town. The first sign of returning morale was a sight I shall never forget"* recalled Cyril Havard.

Until the summer, the O.T.C. had enjoyed band practice on the seafront every day, apparently tormenting those living within earshot of the Drill Hall. At this point, however, the O.T.C. took on rather more significance, forming the nucleus of a new L.D.V. (Local Defence Volunteers) branch, later known as the Home Guard. Under the leadership of Captain Sam Strong and Sergeant-Major Cooper, their primary task was to provide night-time defence of Black Rock Halt, located between Criccieth and Porthmadog, due to a fear that there might be a Nazi invasion of the Welsh coast. Members of the Corps were issued with live ammunition for their nightly patrols.

On one occasion, a Blenheim bomber narrowly missed getting back to its base and landed in the sea. The boys were organised into pulling on ropes on the beach to haul the bomber ashore before it could suffer too much damage.

When half term holidays came, the boys were usually given days off to go out on their own expeditions. They would assemble for prayers and a hymn in the morning, and Creighton carefully chose *'Lead kindly light amidst the encircling gloom'* making a joke about the fact that the boys would be wandering off on their own. Worship continued, with the school attending a local church on Sundays, where the only significant change was the much longer sermons to be endured; Reverend T A Cooke encouraged it.

On the last school day in Criccieth, 19th July 1940, Creighton held lists in the Drill Hall and referred to the debt owed by the school to Wilding for his planning *"in circumstances of unparalleled difficulty"*. The Headmaster praised the pupils and staff for the way in which the spirit of the school had survived its exile.

With all of the obvious distractions, it was not uncommon for the boys to have missed achieving sufficient credits in their School Certificate exams to need to resit the following year; the school was able to return to Worcester for the following school year, from September 1940, finding that the school buildings had not been needed after all, as alternative, purpose-built facilities had been constructed elsewhere. The school buildings had not been damaged during this early part of the war (nor would they suffer later), and all the boys who had been evacuated, who numbered around 100 by the summer of 1940, returned home safely. Those who needed to retake their School Certificate were put into a special form, known as the Lower Sixth, taught by 'the Bird', Frank Thomas.

The number of pupils recovered quickly, with 135 boys between the Lower Fourth and the Sixth Form, similar to the number who had been at King's in September 1939, with eight in the Lower Sixth, including both Cyril Havard and Peter Oades.

In a rather poignant ending to his account, Cyril wrote: *"...the rugby XV with whom I played in my last year. I can see all their faces now. A.E. Baldry had left school by then but I remember playing against him in house matches in my first year. He was killed in the RAF. Both Jim Taaffe and 'Granny' Good, the second row against whose backsides I used to push in the days of 3-2-3, were also shot down in the RAF. Peter Hulme, the other wing forward, was killed in northern Germany within weeks of the end of the war while serving in the Worcestershire Regiment. I have lived a life tinged with guilt that they went on to die while I was tucked safely away in Medical School. Sleep well, gentlemen."*

A memorial board was installed in College Hall, designed by Hope Bagenal, which included the name of his own son. Forty-one OVs gained honours and distinctions between 1939 and 1945; there is a total of fifty names on the memorial board.

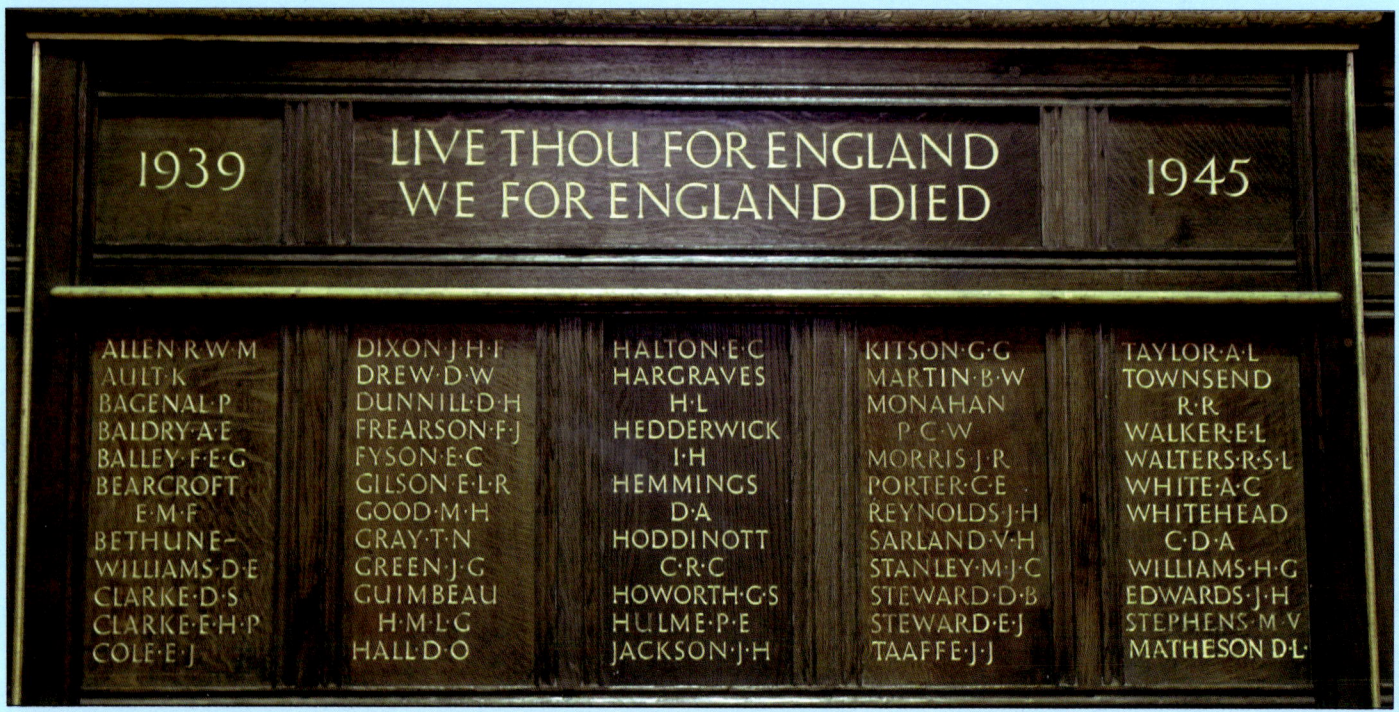

Creighton returns 1940-1942

Reverend Cuthbert Creighton could not have expected in 1936 to return to King's as Headmaster, but he offered his services to the governors generously as Honorary Headmaster, following Allen Wilding's resignation, for as long as the school needed him. His offer was gratefully accepted, and Creighton led the school during its time in Wales from January 1940, bringing the boys home safely to Worcester in July1940, once it was clear that the school buildings would not be needed by the Office of Works.

When school resumed in September, 135 names were on the roll, including thirty day boys returning from RGS and thirty new pupils.

Having returned the school to its home, a number of changes were implemented. To avoid having three Housemasters dealing with ration books, it was decided that all catering would be provided in School House. The day boy houses were reinstituted, with Alec Macdonald in charge of Chappel's and B Ward Housemaster of Creighton's. The Headmaster, living at his home in Claines, was no longer Housemaster of School House; Frank Thomas took over this role.

The school's relationship with the Royal Grammar School had changed, following Henry Pullinger's generosity to the King's School boys during the removal to Criccieth. Little sport could be played due to flooding, but two fives matches between the schools - one at home and one away - ushered in an era of friendly sporting rivalry between the schools, with the first rugby match in 1941 - appropriately, in the new spirit of friendliness, the match ended in a draw.

Further co-operation with RGS took the form of a shared Air Training Corps Squadron from February 1941. The O.T.C. had undergone re-structuring in 1940, with a Senior Training Corps (S.T.C.) operated through universities and a new Junior Training Corp (J.T.C.) at schools. A particular highlight for King's boys at the time was the visit of Fl. Lt. M Boddington (School House 1929-32) who flew his Spitfire to Worcester in July 1941,

The fountain at the centre of the Creighton Memorial Gardens, photographed on a wintry day in 2002

answering questions and performing an aerobatic display over the school.

King's was recovering well from its ordeal by the end of 1941, so much so that Creighton felt able to resign in November, enabling a new Headmaster to be appointed. Due to the ongoing war, the school's 400th anniversary, Sunday 7th December 1941, could not be properly celebrated, but a service in the Cathedral paid tribute to the school, and to Creighton who had served it so well.

Creighton left King's quietly in April 1942, once Ronald Kittermaster took up the position of Headmaster (see Chapter 6). Creighton continued to live at Tutnall until 1944, when he moved to Marlborough, his home until he died in 1963, aged 86.

6: Post-war King's - rebuilding and development

F R Kittermaster - Headmaster 1942-1959

Ronald Kittermaster, with his wife Meriel, moved in to School House in April 1942. When the Summer Term began, King's had a total of 163 boys: 36 in the Lower Fourth, 33 in the Middle Fourth, 31 in the Upper Fourth, 28 in the Lower Fifth, 23 in the Upper Fifth and only 12 in the Sixth Form. The priorities for the new Headmaster were clear: to increase the pupil numbers; sort out the school's finances which had taken a beating during the evacuation to Criccieth; and restore the morale of the eight staff members who had returned to Worcester with Creighton.

Kittermaster's appointment was to follow on from Wilding with Headmasters who did not hold office in the Church of England. Indeed, until 1939, Kittermaster lacked a degree, which he achieved at the age of 40 having studied an external degree course in English with London University, making him only the second Headmaster of King's to have graduated at a university other than Oxford or Cambridge (the other being Stephen Denning who was a graduate of Durham).

The eldest of five brothers, Ronald Kittermaster was born in October 1899 and educated at Rugby School where he excelled in rugby and cricket. A classicist who studied Science and Mathematics in Army Class, Kittermaster passed into the Royal Military Academy, Woolwich from where he was commissioned in November 1918. A distinguished military career took Kittermaster to Ireland and then to India, where he served at the Prince of Wales' Royal Indian Military College, preparing boys for Sandhurst. A transfer back to England led to Kittermaster's appointment by the War Office to The Duke of York's School, Dover as Second Master. A year later, in 1929, Kittermaster accepted the position of Housemaster of Franklin House at Canford School. It was from Canford, following his marriage to Meriel in July 1930 and his graduation from London University, that Ronald Kittermaster was appointed to become the twenty-ninth Headmaster of The King's School, Worcester.

The most immediate task for the new Headmaster was to restore pupil numbers; fortunately, the Summer Term of 1942 saw a surge in applicants, resulting in 59 new boys, easily able to compensate for the 16 leavers, so that the number of pupils on the school roll for September would be 206.

Frank Thomas had been Housemaster of School House, but moved to The Hostel on the arrival of the Kittermaster family, including their five year old daughter. Paul Longland, who now had a son, moved from The Hostel to assist Kittermaster in School House.

A change in cultural outlook

Kittermaster, a keen actor and lover of poetry, was responsible for producing plays at Canford; Meriel was a keen musician. The Kittermasters encouraged Alec MacDonald to stage a production of Shakespeare's *The Tempest*, with female actors provided by the Alice Ottley School, on the Guesten Hall lawn in July, drawing audiences of more than 300 to each of the two performances. Mrs. Kittermaster established a Music Society which met on Sunday evenings to hear recordings of classical music on her gramophone. She was keen to develop music at King's, following a successful School Concert in May, at which

F. Ronald Kittermaster

Edgar Day conducted the School Choir.

Kittermaster's first Speech Day, on Friday 10th July, started with a P.T. Competition, won by Castle House, the prizes for which were presented by A. G. Elliott-Smith, Headmaster of Cheltenham College, whose school had similarly been commandeered by the Ministry of Works and recently allowed to return having shared with Shrewsbury School. Elliott-Smith spoke of his genuine sympathy for the position of The King's School. This was followed by Kittermaster's address to the school and parents in which he asked them, *"to co-operate with the School in encouraging a general cultural background, without which mere examination successes are barren."* Later Headmasters would encourage development of 'well-rounded' individuals; indeed, Kittermaster's sentiment has continued throughout the following seven decades, embellished by the Christian ethos restated by Tim Keyes, resulting in the most recent statement of the school's 'vision' in the mid-2000s: *"To help young people to reach their potential at school in preparation for leading confident, fulfilled and unselfish lives as adults."*

Changes in the wider cultural offering for pupils came quickly, with a Literary Society established by Kittermaster and an Art Circle led by Miss Campbell to complement Meriel Kittermaster's Music Society. A Dancing Club, Play-Reading and Debating Socities all thrived, with day boys joining in alongside boarders.

A joint Sixth Form Club was established between King's, the Alice Ottley School, the Royal Grammar School, the Girls' Grammar School and the College for the Blind, with two pupils from each school forming a committee to organise cultural and social programmes.

Meanwhile, Meriel Kittermaster began to arrange celebrity concerts in College Hall. Arnold Foster conducted the City of Birmingham Symphony Orchestra, featuring Irene Kohler as a solo pianist; there was a concert by folk singer Eve Maxwell Lyte and a seventeenth- and eighteenth-century concert led by Dr Westcott with his harpsichord.

The crowning achievement of this cultural revolution at King's would be the amalgamation of the Choir School with The King's School in June 1944, as detailed in Chapter 7. As well as gaining Choir House and the Choir School's playing field for a nominal rent to the Dean and Chapter, King's would benefit from the additional thirteen boys being taught at the school and the musical prowess which they would add to school life. The three staff of the Choir School (P.F. Davis, Headmaster, having retired) would also transfer to King's. A format for Chorister rehearsals and a schedule for singing at Cathedral services were drawn up within a detailed agreement which ensured consistency in the age of Choristers and standards for entry to The King's School. The Cathedral would benefit from a single, stronger and more financially stable school, and an enlarged Cathedral Choir, comprising ten Choristers and fourteen Probationers.

Expansion beyond the Cathedral precincts

For the first time, in June 1944, The King's School was to be extended beyond its main campus around College Green and the site of the former Worcester Castle. The purchase of Tredennyke House in Barbourne enabled King's to have its own, separate, preparatory school, initially led by Kittermaster's brother David.

Tredennyke House would later be sold, following the purchase of St Alban's House, between Severn Street and Mill Street, in 1951. The pattern for separate preparatory schools had been established, and would make it easier for later Governors to agree to the acquisition of Hawford Lodge in 1996.

A fuller account of Tredennyke House, St Alban's House and Hawford Lodge can be found in Chapter 7.

The end of the Second World War

After six long years, the war in Europe came to an end in May 1945. During this period, forty-one Old Vigornians gained honours and disctinctions for their military service. Fifty former pupils lost their lives fighting for their country, a heavy loss, albeit far fewer than the 82 who died during the Great War; the names of those who died would be commemorated on a board in College Hall, designed by Hope Bagenal and positioned opposite the memorial board for the fallen of the Great War.

Although The King's School had been permitted to return to its home in Worcester in 1940, the Ministry of Works had retained the use of 14 College Green, former home of Canon Wilson (see Chapter 5) adjacent to College Hall. When no longer required for the purposes of war, the house was returned to the Dean and Chapter, who rejected applications for tenancy from others to enable the school to lease the building for an initial period of five years; as Governors, the Chapter was acutely aware of the needs of the school, and of its Headmaster.

Against the background of war, Kittermaster had succeeded in his task of increasing the number of pupils, no mean achievement considering the lack of a school secretary or a bursar to manage the school's properties and finances, and all while serving as Housemaster to the boarders of School House.

Performance of Shakespeare's 'Richard II' in College Hall, 1946

Reorganisation of the school

It was now time to relieve the Headmaster of the significant duty of Housemaster, and he was granted the use of Number 14 as the new Headmaster's residence. The substanital house was too large for the Kittermaster family's needs, and so the upper floor was made available for teaching music.

An apartment was created within the upper floors of the former Headmaster's residence in School House, to accommodate the new Housemaster, Capt. N.C. Bloomfield. A new Masters' Common Room in the bay-fronted room on the upper ground floor (known as 'S4' since the 1990s), and a new office for the secretary and accountant, H.E. Nicholls, in School House allowed more space within the 1899 classroom building at Number 7. Indeed, the former Common Room was to be used as the Headmaster's office, with the remaining rooms now all available for teaching.

The King's School at this time enjoyed the use of College Hall, Edgar Tower, Choir House, The Hostel, Castle House, School House, Numbers 7 and 14 College Green, the 1925 classroom block (extended in 1936) which formed a green quadrangle with the Chappel Memorial Reading Room, a gymnasium and workshop (on the later site of the Wolfson Building) opposite three fives courts, a playground behind School House, and the Creighton Memorial Gardens. There was a preparatory school at Tredennyke House and a boathouse on Hylton Road, in addition to the playing fields on the lower part of the Chapter Meadows, on which Thomas Rammell's cricket pavillion provided changing facilities.

The Direct Grant

Attlee's Labour Government was keen to introduce reforms after sweeping to power in June 1945. Ellen Wilkinson, Minister of Education, sought to have a 'maintained' school in every town: despite the application of the Royal Grammar School, it was The King's School which would continue to receive the Direct Grant. The result of this denial for RGS was transformational - in having to accept 'voluntary aided' status, school terms were lengthened, Saturday lessons abolished and fees were no longer permitted.

King's escaped these changes, although the school would now be required to admit 25% of pupils from primary schools with 'free places' (a significant increase from the 10% required under the previous Board of Education Grant secured by Creighton), with midday meals to be provided for all day boys. This certainly placed a financial strain on the school, although outweighed by the potential loss of the grant, and also created pressure on the dining room of School House which was used for all boarders' meals and had prevously managed to provide lunches for those day boys who needed them. The solution would be to upgrade the kitchen in the basement of School House and to construct a separate Dining Hall for the day boys, for which Kittermaster appealed to the Old Vigornian Club for financial support from the 'Fourth Centenary and War Memorial Fund' established by the Club in 1941. While the work was going on, College Hall was pressed into service as a refectory, in which lunch for 80 day boys was served daily for the first time in centuries, carried across College Green in metal containers by cooks Charlie Passey and Alf Taylor.

Day Boys' Dining Hall, late 1940s
Demolished in the 1970s, its site became an open, grassed area known as the 'Dining Hall Quad'.

The number of maintained schools in England had been reduced from 232 in 1942 to 165 by 1946, with many notable schools, including Warwick School, deciding to become fully independent, fee-paying schools, as they were either unwilling or unable to meet the conditions of the Ministry of Education. Each school would be under the control of an independent governing body, with responsibility for all capital expenditure, and required to submit annual accounts to the Minister. In exchange, a capitation grant was received for each pupil aged eleven to sixteen, with an additional allowance for those in the Sixth Form. Tuition fees for 'free place' day pupils were paid by the Local Education Authority. The school could offer income-dependent financial support towards tuition fees for day pupils, but no financial support was available for boarders.

The additional 'free places' at King's inevitably led to an increase in pupil numbers (by September 1958 there would be 150 free places, rather more than the fifteen offered by Creighton in 1941), which, combined with a doubling of the population of Worcester in the years immediately following the war resulted in a school roll of 611 pupils by the end of Kittermaster's headship.

Teaching accommodation

In July 1949, a School Fete, the first of its kind, was held to raise money for a second extension to Creighton's 1925 classroom building. The building had originally comprised four classrooms, with the addition of an art room and geography classroom in 1936. This new extension, opened in 1950, provided an extra four classrooms, resulting in this building becoming the main classroom building for the school and enabling Number 7 to be used entirely for science teaching. The Sixth Form was now taught in Edgar Tower, with the lower yeargroups taught at St Alban's House.

Beyond the classrooms

Kittermaster's drive to improve the arts at King's resulted in annual dramatic performances, alongside greater interest in poetry and literature, art, pottery, dance and of course, music. The Headmaster himself wrote and produced a number of plays, including a comic opera *The Headmistress* in 1957, in which The King's School of 2007, still a boys' school, was governed by a female Head.

Providing a rounded education also required improvements in sport, achieved through coaching and training, as well as the continuation of inter-House competitions and tournaments against other schools. By 1958, Peter Curle's Hockey XI was able to play an unbeaten season, and the Boat Club raced in eights (following a decision by Kittermaster to move towards larger boats); the Boat Club had performed remarkably at Marlow Regatta during the 1950s, under the guidance of coaches Bob Carlyle and Richard Knight, with King's top of all public schools rowing in IVs. Kittermaster hoped to provide a new boathouse, on the school site, and raised funds, with the support of the Boat Club, at the School Fete in 1958 (an annual tradition since 1956).

Generations of sporting pupils would have rushed down the slope to the Watergate in order to catch the Cathedral Ferry, to avoid the long walk to the Chapter Meadows' playing fields for rugby, football, hockey and cricket. The last 'Betty', as the boat was known (named after Betty Webb, appointed ferryman in 1750 and who held the position for 43 years), crossed the river in June 1958, when the boat was considered to be unsafe and beyond repair.

The last 'Betty' with Cathedral Ferryman Gilbert Morgan, June 1958.

The J.T.C. (Junior Training Corps) and later the C.C.F. (Combined Cadet Corps), as the O.T.C. was known from 1940 and 1948 respectively, became a popular (if not quite mandatory) part of school life, enjoyed by many of the boys in preparation for their National Service on leaving school. Lt. Kittermaster was keen to instill a sense of military discipline in the boys, and was supported in this by a number of servicemen, including Lt.Col. Sheppard who was Commanding Officer from 1946-64. See 'Cadets at King's' (Chapter 5) for further details about the J.T.C. and C.C.F.

Alec Mackie   Choir House 1947-56

School life for me began in September 1947 when, aged 8, I entered Form 1, after three years in the kindergarten at St Mary's Convent. I was joined in Miss A A Campbell's class by two others from St Mary's, John Bayliss and West.

Forms 1,2 and 3 were in what was to become Choir House. Miss Campbell's sister Myfanwy "Miffy" and Miss Forward were the other two form mistresses. The small playground doubled up as a cricket pitch in summer, football in winter and became the venue for the occasional boxing match.

'Woodrow' Wilson was in charge of the junior classes and Wilf Thomas, Bill Bailey, Dan McTurk, 'Jasper' Cash, 'Laddie' Sheppard, Ned Dilks, 'Fritz' Nathan were some of our other teachers here and later in the Lower Fourth.

Discipline, particularly for the day boys, was strictly enforced by the Monitors. They had the power to carry out beatings to punish those who broke the 'rules'. Blotting paper inside your pants helped reduce the sting as you bent over a chair in the Sixth Form Library to receive "six of the best"!

Masters, particularly those who had served in the army during the war, were adept at throwing chalk and the occasional board rubber at boys in the back row who gave the wrong answer or were 'playing up'. Penal drills were awarded for minor misdemeanors which meant after school litter picking and classroom cleaning or supervised 'runs' to the Diglis Wier or Ketch.

When I progressed into the senior school, sport and the CCF were my best 'subjects'. I played hooker in the U15 rugby side. Peter Venables played in the back row and we were coached by Dan McTurk, who had played for London Scottish before the war. In my final term, I was touch judge for the 1st XV.

Cricket was my favorite sport. David Cook was Captain of Cricket when I made my debut for the first XI. We travelled to away matches in Burnham Coaches. Bill Bailey sat in the front and the senior members of the team sat in the back. I remember Vernon Evans offering Mr Bailey a cigarette the moment the coach left the City boundary en route to Shrewsbury School. Bill declined the offer: he was a pipe smoker. Returning from an away match Mr Bailey stopped the coach in Alcester. He told us he was going to the pub for a drink and we could go to "that one down the road but be back in 20 minutes". Henry Shouler led the way! David Westgate was captain in my last year at School and it was a particularly proud moment for me when he awarded me my cricket colours during an assembly in College Hall.

Three generations of Mackies had served in The Worcestershire Regiment and I was naturally proud to wear "The Worcester's" cap badge when I joined the CCF. Parades, inspections and Certificate A and B tests took place every Saturday. Field Days were held each term and the Summer camp was spent at military training areas Castlemartin, near Tenby; Kimnel Park, Rhyl and Catterick

Captain Wilf Thomas, ex Royal Welch Fussiliers, marched my platoon from school to entrain at Shrub Hill station to travel to Rhyl. At the camp each section of eight was allocated a tent and straw filled bedding placed on duck boards. Corporal Peter Meadows was in charge of our tent. On our last night, it poured down and I was awoken by the rain flowing down the hillside beneath the duckboards on which were were sleeping! I will always treasure the memory of the sight and sound of 'Sarge' Barrett shouting "get out of bed and empty your bedding" as the rain poured down at 3.00 am - six hours before we had to de camp and catch the return train to Worcester.

Alec Mackie in CCF uniform on the promenade at Rhyl, 1951.

Our neighbours under canvas at Castlemartin Camp were from the Edinburgh Academy. A piper would march between the tents playing each morning at dawn and each night at 'lights out'. On our last night at camp, the same piper accompanied his friend who stood on a table in the canteen wearing full highland dress and sang a well known Scottish marching song "Four and twenty virgins came down from Inverness".

Bringsty Common near Bromyard became a familiar venue for CCF 'field days'. We were given 'haversack rations'. Corporal Nigel Jones was in charge of my section and he took us to a clearing in the bracken to eat our sandwiches. The clearing was close to the Live and Let Live pub. Too good an opportunity to miss, two of us managed to buy a couple of bottles of scrumpy to take back to the others. The afternoon exercise that day had to be cancelled after the flare fired by 'Sarge' to start the event landed in dry undergrowth and set the bracken alight.

My last day at School before leaving to join the army was to culminate with the Sixth Form Christmas Ball in College Hall. Girls from the Alice Ottley and Girls Grammar School were to be our dance partners. We had three months to learn some basic dance steps so, armed with a wind up gramophone and a Victor Silvester 'teach yourself' dance book, we used the gallery in College Hall as our dance studio on Sunday afternoons taking it in turn to 'dance' as the girl. My partner was Alan Bufton, who had been my opening partner in the 1st XI. Somehow we did manage to learn the waltz and quickstep to dance for real at the Ball, but not with each other!

Happy days and good memories!

Alec Mackie served in The Worcestershire Regiment (1957-60) then became a journalist before working as a media officer for a number of organisations including Hereford and Worcester County Council and Hereford and Worcester Fire Brigade. He retired at the age of 71.

Alec has served the Old Vigornian community as Captain of the OV Cricket Club and Secretary, Chairman and President of the OV Club. He is currently member emeritus of the OV Club Committee. Both of Alec's sons are OVs as are his two granddaughters.

Winslow Building

The Winslow Building, 1958

Alec Macdonald, School Historian, wrote an essay for *The Vigornian* of July 1942, in which he identified an entry for 'Edward Winstow' in Arthur Leach's list of Scholars in the Cathedral Library as 'Edward Winslow', one of the Pilgrim Fathers who set sail for the New World on The Mayflower and among the first New England Governors (see Chapter 2 for further details). It seemed fitting to Kittermaster that a new building at King's should eventually be named in Winslow's honour.

The opportunity for this came late in Kittermaster's headship, when, following criticism in a report by Her Majesty's Inspectors, a need for a new science teaching building was identified in the summer of 1957 as urgent. Kittermaster had planned for a science building, and, to that end, had organised a second School Fete on 9 July 1956 which had raised £6,000. An offer of funding from the Industrial Fund would provide £23,000, some £6,000 short of the projected building cost. A 'Final Urgent Appeal' was issued, raising a further £1,500 and the remainder was borrowed from the school's bank. A steel-framed, glass-clad structure designed by young architect Maurice Jones was built in less than a year, ready for the examinations of July 1958, offering five modern science laboratories (two for Chemistry on the lower floor, two for Physics and one general on the upper floor), two prep rooms and a lecture theatre; the enclosure of the ground floor later created a further two classrooms and the building would be extended in the early 1980s to include three additional laboratories. Physics would occupy the top floor, Chemistry the middle floor, and (by the 1990s) ICT the ground floor; Biology would become the only science to be taught at Number 7 College Green. The laboratories and lecture theatre would undergo significant refurbishment in the 2000s (see Chapter 9); after the original design-life of 40 years had already passed. An occupant for almost all of that period was Keith Bridges (Chemistry 1963-2003) after whom the first refurbished Chemistry laboratory was named.

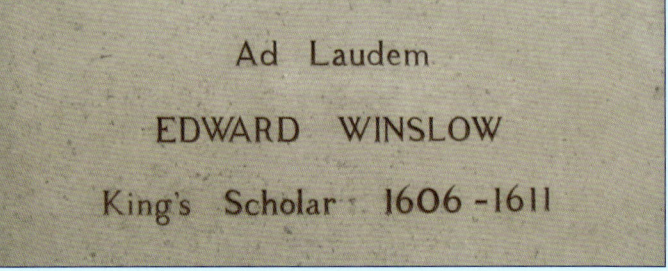

Above: Lessons in the Science Lecture Theatre and a Chemistry laboratory, c.1959

Right: Memorial plaque to Edward Winslow

The Winslow Building was to be the first named after an OV; the next would be the Wolfson Building (1973), and later the Michael Baker Boathouse (2012) - these were named after the respective benefactors.

King's Remembered

David Gillard — Castle House 1947-54

I joined King's in January 1947 as a rather shy, uncertain junior probationer in the Cathedral Choir, from Tredennyke preparatory school which was run by David Kittermaster. Lester Wilson was the kindly, understanding housemaster of Choir House which all junior choir members joined on their arrival at King's (the gym shoe he kept to adminster punishment, 'Happy Harry', was used only in extremis).

Nothing particularly eventful happened to me during my time in Choir, which was a happy house, although I remember that, so soon after the war, the food served to all boarders (in the dining room of School House) seemed to us at the time barely edible. Despite the valiant efforts of Chalie Passey and Alf Taylor, there was, I suspect, little they could do with the ingredients available to them to alter the situation, restricted no doubt by a rather limited budget. As a choir member, you were always late for supper on the weekdays on which Evensong was sung, and so relied on the goodwill of your fellow House members to leave sufficient for a reasonable meal.

Perhaps the first major decision I faced at King's was the choice of boarding house when the time came to enter the senior school. The opinion among my own circle of friends was that School was for the studious, Hostel was populated by a rather feeble group of people, but Castle was for those who aspired to be men, particularly if they had sporting interests (especially rugby, which I liked, and boxing, which I did not!). So Castle it was, under the formidable Housemastership of A.J. Bentley, a somewhat ferocious-looking man whose displeasure at the stupidity of a pupil could be heard over a wide area as he roared: "You poisonous fool, boy!"

Dan McTurk

Bentley was succeeded at Castle House by S.R. Sheppard, who presented a far more human, and perhaps humane, face than his predecessor: certainly his ideas on punishment turned out to be far more lenient. He was quickly named 'check up', as an often used saying of his was, "My word laddie, I'll have to check up on that."

I suppose the 'Mr Chips' of his day - in the sense that he was held in great affection by his pupils - was Dan McTurk, then Housemaster of School House. The essential Englishman in both appearance and manner, he was the only teacher I met who could bring history to life and actually make the lesson enjoyable.

He couldn't abide the use of chewing gum in a lesson he was taking. He would stalk down the room to the offender, waste bin out-thrust, and say: "Put it there chum - you know I won't allow that filthy habit here." On seeing a pupil whose concentration had wandered, he would strike the desk a thunderous blow with the flat of his hand and cry, "Jenkins, don't sit there like a bally drink of water - keep your mind on your work!". I always valued a comment by Mr McTurk on one of my essays that had particularly pleased him. Against a very high mark he had written: "I've waited over a year for this, you blighter - well done indeed!"

First published in 'The King's School, Worcester and a history of its site', 1994.

The Masters, Mistresses and 'Non-teaching' staff

The number of Masters and Mistresses continued to grow during Kittermaster's headship: he inherited eight from Creighton and gained a further three as a result of the amalgamation with the Choir School.

Eleven new Masters were employed during the 1940s: Lester Wilson (1943-63) taught Mathematics and Science; N.E. Dilks (1943-68) History and English; Alex Natan (1944-67) German and Modern History; Stuart Sheppard (1944-68) General Subjects; Harry Ferrar (1946-68) Modern Languages; Dan McTurk (1946-65) English Subjects; Bobbie Cash (1946-73) English and Careers; (L.M.) Bill Bailey (1946-77) Geography; Wilfred Thomas (1947-79) Modern History; Fred Logan (1947-80) Biology; and Richard Knight (1949-78) taught Mathematics.

As described in Chapter 7, Lester Wilson, Bill Bailey and Wilfred Thomas were all involved, along with David Kittermaster, in the eventual establishment of St Alban's as a preparatory school for King's (albeit a journey involving Tredennyke House and the merger with the Choir School and also forming Choir House); Wilfred Thomas became Master of St Alban's in 1955.

Dan McTurk was appointed Housemaster of School House in 1946, replacing Bloomfield after just one year. McTurk was a much-loved teacher of English and history, as described by David Gillard (above). Sheppard succeeded Arthur Bentley as Housemaster of Castle House in 1950. Richard Pedder (Housemaster of The Hostel during the evacuation) served as Housemaster of The Hostel from 1945 until Richard Knight moved from Chappel House in 1958.

During the 1950s, the number of teachers continued to grow, with the employment of several masters who would serve the school for years to come, including historian Peter Curle, who became Second Master in 1978, and whose untimely death just before his retirement in 1986 shocked the school community. Peter Barnett joined the school in 1952, becoming Housemaster of Creighton House in 1958 and then adding Head of Classics to this in 1960, roles in which he continued until 1984.

In 1951, Kittermaster appointed the first full-time Director of Music, Reginald West, former organist at Armagh Cathedral. Following the retirement of Ivor Atkins in 1950, the Chapter had formed a separate house (Number 13) from Number 14 to accommodate his successor; the result was that music practices would no longer be possible in Number 14, and so the house at 7 College Yard was rented for the West family and music was taught there.

H.E. Nicholls continued his work as school secretary until the age of 70, when ill health prompted his resignation. He was replaced in 1958 by Miss Ann Turvey who was appointed School Accountant and Clerk to the Governing Body.

Harry Ferrar, who had replaced Alec Macdonald as Head of Modern Languages in 1946, became Second Master in

Art room and workshop, 1959
On completion of the Wolfson Building in the 1970s, Art and 'C.D.T.' moved into a dedicated home.
This room would be used for careers advice before eventually serving as a library for the Geography Department.

1954, following the retirement of Frank Thomas, remaining Housemaster of Creighton House, but with a generous allowance of seven periods per week to shoulder the new responsibility now delegated to the Second Master of overseeing school business. Macdonald spent two years in Germany, from 1946-48, returning briefly before his death in 1949.

Miss Anne Campbell, who first joined the staff in 1916 (working at the Choir School during its separation from King's), died in service in 1957. Her sister, Myfanwy, who had taught at King's since 1917, retired the same year.

Kittermaster appointed three new rowing men to the staff in 1958: Donald Anderton, Alan Stacey and D.R. Leonard. They continued the good progress made by the KSW Boat Club under Richard Knight, who had taken on responsibility for rowing in 1955 and designed Kittermaster's new boathouse, opened in 1960.

Kittermaster's legacy

The editorial of *The Vigornian* in December 1943 reported: *"In his address in College Hall at the beginning of the term, The Headmaster made us all sit bolt upright in our seats, by telling us that the King's School was going to be the best school in the country. There were many, no doubt, who dismissed this remark as wishful thinking, but we are certain that a large majority regarded his words as an ambitious ideal, for which it was well worthwhile to strive."*

Such was the regard that Kittermaster's pupils had for their Headmaster, it is clear to see why King's became such a popular school for the people of Worcestershire, and how it was that Kittermaster was able to increase the number of pupils to unprecedented levels (by the time of this speech, the number had doubled from 163 to 325; this would almost double again by Kittermaster's retirement sixteen years later).

The desire to offer a broad-based education, not limited to strong academic learning, with an emphasis on the arts and sports, particularly rowing, combined with an ability to inspire confidence in donors to his appeals and an astute grasp of business and finance, enabled The King's School under Kittermaster to flourish. A programme of reordeing of school buildings resulted in the completion of Creighton's 1925 classroom building, a multi-use School House, the use of Number 7 as the 'Biology Block' and the creation of the Winslow Building, has meant that the achievements of Kittermaster would live on for many decades.

In spite of all this, however, the most significant legacy of Kittermaster's headship must surely be the establishment of St Alban's Junior School, later to become King's St Alban's, following the amalgamation of the Cathedral Choir School into The King's School; the abilty for King's to teach younger boys who would in time move into places at the senior school enabled the growth and development of the school during the 1960s and later, securing the school's future.

Craze (1972) reports that *"all who knew Ronald Kittermaster at Worcester bear witness to the tenacity and courage with which he did battle for the School; the virtues of the old games player were very much to the fore. He was also an excellent public speaker and a good occasional preacher. In his talks in College Hall his recurrent theme was the consideration for other people that was the secret of good manners."*

Ronald and Meriel Kittermaster retired to Dorset in 1959, where he died in March 1972, mourned by all who knew him. A new day boy house was named in Kittermaster's honour in 1984.

Old Chapel

The Old Chapel, near Crickhowell in the Black Mountains of Wales, is used as a base for outdoor activities, including an annual camp for pupils in the Lower Remove (Year 9), and for training expeditions for Duke of Edinburgh's Award candidates, and members of the school's Himalayan Club.

The building dates from the late fifteenth or early sixteenth century, and would have served the needs of the hill farmers and shepherds in the upper part of the Grwynefechan valley, with worship following the pattern of the Established Church until around 1700, when the chapel was abandoned. Later, from 1752 until 1775, the chapel was used for regular services by a local Methodist community, after which the chapel was again left empty, often used as a shelter for sheep and cattle. Worship resumed in 1845, this time for Calvinist Methodists. In 1880, the chapel was restored, re-roofed and furnished with pews, by Sir Joseph Bailey (later Lord Glanusk), and the chapel flourished for around 80 years, before depopulation in the area, and improved access to the nearest church, led to the closure of the chapel in 1955.

David Annett wrote about the decision to purchase the 'Old Chapel', and the early use of the Chapel by King's, in a document for the School Archive, in 2002.

In 1963 I had for some time thought that it would be a good thing if the school could acquire a base in remote and unspoilt country in which boys - particularly those from urban and suburban backgrounds - could spend even a short time experiencing the natural world, unadulterated by the material comfort and sophistication which we are apt to describe as civilisation. I enlisted the help of my colleague Dan McTurk, who shared my views, and we embarked on an intermittent and lengthy search for a suitable place. The requirements were that it should be in remote and preferably hilly country, and yet within reasonable driving distance - say 60 miles - from Worcester. This obviously pointed to the Welsh border country, and Dan and I scoured the Marches from Ross to Rhayader without finding anything suitable.

I always spent Saturday mornings in term-time receiving prospective parents and showing them the school. One Saturday my visitors included a doctor from Birmingham with his young family. He happened to mention that they were on their way to spend the week-end at their cottage near Llanbedr in the Black Mountains. I told him of our search, and he said that they would enjoy searching their valley - the Grwyne Fechan - to see if there was anything suitable there, and that they would call in on their way home on Sunday evening to report.

This they did, and their report was that the whole valley had been part of the large Glanusk estate, but that some years ago the Glanusks had sold all the farms and their land to sitting tenants. In the whole valley there was only one unoccupied building, and that was a former chapel, which had not been sold. Without delay I contacted the Glanusk Estate Office and explained what I was looking for. The Agent told me that there was no question of Lady Glanusk selling the chapel and the land surrounding it, for she wanted for sentimental reasons to keep a foot-hold in the valley, but that she might consider a lease, and that meanwhile I was welcome to have a look at the place.

At the earliest opportunity Dan and I collected the key from the Estate Office near Crickhowell, and with considerable excitement went in search of the chapel. All we could see from the lower lane was the ridge of the roof, for the whole intervening ground was overgrown with gigantic bracken about 8 feet high. We forced our way through it, unlocked the door, and an astonishing sight met our eyes. After the last service in the chapel in 1955 the congregation

The 'Old Chapel', with campsite, photographed in 2005

must have walked out leaving everything in its place, and never returned. The furniture was complete, including the harmonium, and even the prayer books on the minister's stall were still there on their red velvet cushions. We felt that we were guilty intruders. (Later we took some of the pews back to the school and put them on the steps of the cricket pavilion). The chapel itself was then a single room with no gallery: at the west end was a small separate room open to the roof and entered from outside. This was where the minister stabled his horse when he rode over from Talgarth or Trefecca to take the service. Surrounding the chapel was a sizeable piece of land bounded by the lane on one side and the river on the other. It was level, and provided more than enough space for the erection of tents and the parking of vehicles. On the slope beyond the river was a young plantation of conifers; these were only a few feet high, and did not cut out the light as they do now. From the moment we saw it Dan and I realised that this was the place we had been looking for, and to our great delight Lady Glanusk agreed to let us have it on a 25-year lease at a modest rent. This was in 1964.

The 'Old Chapel' - with new reed bed in foreground, 2002

Our idea was to keep everything as simple as possible; water was collected from a spring (certified drinkable) on the other side of the lane; light came from Tilley and Hurricane lamps, and heat from oil stoves; cooking was done on Calor gas and an elderly Rayburn discarded by Llangattock Rectory, and the plumbing consisted of a chemical closet in a lean-to shed. The nearest telephone was in the public box on the upper lane. This Spartan regime worked satisfactorily provided that a simple set of rules was strictly observed, and many of the boys found it instructive to learn that water did not always come from turning a tap, or light from touching a switch. In those days we were not subject to the rigid health and safety regulations which operate today, and the school was all-male - though parents and staff wives and families were always welcome, as long as they understood what conditions to expect.

In the early days there was much work to be done, both inside and outside, even to achieve the simple standards at which we aimed. Most of this we did ourselves, with help from the school maintenance staff, and professional help from outside only when absolutely necessary. Anyone who has visited the chapel, especially on a sunny day, will be struck by the beauty of the place, and it does indeed exercise a remarkable spell on many of those who come to know and love it. From the start Trevor and Judy Bailey and their

Camping at the 'Old Chapel' in 1969

Simon Cuthbertson leading a staff team demonstrating a 'team-building' activity to the amusement of pupil campers

family were enthusiastic 'chapel-goers', and poured abundant love and labour into the place. We also had a group of loyal parents who came out frequently to help in many ways. Paul Cattermole, then a House-tutor in St Alban's, was another great supporter, and he went further by organising a group of boys who brought the long-silent bells of Llanbedr church back into ringing condition, and then rang in the New Year on them, to the enormous pleasure of the villagers. He also used to bring a small choir from St Alban's to sing in Llanbedr church, including the wedding service for the squire's daughter.

I cannot remember a single occasion when the villagers of Llanbedr or the farmers in the length of the valley had cause to complain about our presence among them, and some indeed became good friends. Paul Cattermole remembers a visit from the octogenarian Misses Jones from Llangattock, who had been members of the chapel congregation. They were so pleased to see that the chapel was in use by The King's School that they donated £5 to buy a box of tinned food as a reserve in case a party was snowbound there."

The chapel was clearly well-loved, and ideally suited for the school's use. In 1967, the stable was converted into a kitchen and a loft errected above it to provide sleeping quarters for the staff. A telephone broke the total isolation of the site in 1992.

Generations of pupils and staff have enjoyed camping at the 'Old Chapel'. In the 1980s Mike Bentley introduced boys in his Lower Fourth Form to the experience; this developed into the 'Lower Remove Camp' under the leadership of Mike Stevens, which, until 2008, involved a form (of up to 24 boys and girls) camping together. Since 2008, the Lower Remove (Year 9) group within each House, accompanied by the House staff and members of the Upper Sixth, take the two-day camp together. Organised since 2000 by Simon Cuthbertson. Activities include walking through the hills, climbing at a local activity centre, kayaking on the River Wye, swimming in the stream, playing in the woods and camp fires.

The school purchased the chapel and its grounds in 1983, and has since carried out sympathetic improvements to the facilities, including a reed bed, electricity, a new kitchen and running water, pumped into a tank in the loft to supply showers. A rear extension was added with WCs. These 'upgrades' added a basic level of hygiene, safety and comfort to the 'Old Chapel' experience, but, it was widely felt, whilst making it easier for staff to organise camps, it did not take away from either the character and charm of the unique location or the valuable experience, which for so many pupils had been among the highlights of their time at King's. Gone are the days of flushing toilets with buckets of water from the stream and rotas for collection of spring water, but the search for firewood in the forest and the games played in the grounds would remain as popular as ever.

Choir House Camp, summer 2009

The King's School, Worcester   *From 1541 into the 21st Century*

D M Annett - Headmaster 1959-1979

David Maurice Annett was born in Suffolk in 1917, the son of an engineer in the Indian Army. Having won a scholarship to Haileybury College, where he was Head Boy, he progressed to Queens' College, Cambridge with a scholarship in Classics. From Cambridge he was appointed Head of Classics at Oundle School in 1939. During the War, Annett served with the Royal Army Medical Corps and later the Royal Artillery, rising to the rank of Captain after service in India and Burma.

Following demobilisation in January 1946, Annett returned to Oundle, where he gained a reputation as a good teacher who made learning interesting and encouraged pupils to think for themselves. He became a Housemaster in 1948, and married Rosemary, known to all as Romey, in 1953. That year, Romey took up headship of Bredenbury Court, a preparatory school for in Cheltenham, and David was appointed Headmaster of Marling School, Stroud. Their daughter, Rosamund, was born in 1955.

David Annett was appointed to succeed Kittermaster as Headmaster of The King's School, Worcester from September 1959. Kittermaster had worked hard, in often difficult circumstances, to increase the number of pupils and ensure the financial growth necessary to secure the school's future.

In September 1959 there were 627 pupils in the school, an extraordinary achievement under Kittermaster, but the school now needed a significant programme of development and it fell to Annett to tackle this.

The Boathouse

At the start of Annett's headship, the new Boathouse, the vision of Kittermaster designed by Richard Knight, was completed; an opening ceremony took place in May 1960. Two months later, the First VIII won the Junior Eights at Marlow, and rowing at King's went from strength to strength throughout the decade.

David Annett

Rebuilding the House system

By 1959 there were still only two day boy houses: Chappel House, under H.M. Ballance, and Creighton House, under Peter Barnett. The two Houses had a remarkable 157 and 170 pupils respectively, but with merely a changing room/cloak room for each House and two or three small study rooms in the turrets of Edgar Tower for each House to call its own, the accommodation was far below even the fairly basic standard provided for the boarders.

Annett identified the two key issues: a Housemaster cannot hope to provide a good level of pastoral care for so many boys; the accommodation should be of a far higher standard, providing the boys with common areas in which to be together as social groups.

The first issue was dealt with through the separation of the Middle School (the modern Years 7 and 8) from the Houses, and the creation of two new day boy Houses in 1961: Bright House, named after Henry Bright (Master 1589-1627), was created from Chappel House; Wulstan House, named in honour of St Wulstan (Bishop of Worcester 1062-1095) was formed from Creighton House. H. Neill was the first Housemaster of Bright House and Fred Logan Housemaster of Wulstan House. The House colours were to be orange and purple respectively. Each of the four day Houses now had between 50 and 60 boys, all aged between 13 and 18, making it viable for the Housemasters to provide genuine pastoral care for all day boys.

Frank Sutcliffe took over Chappel House from Ballance in 1961; in the same year, Bill Bailey handed over Choir House to Peter Curle. The three older boarding Houses - School House, Castle House and The Hostel - remained under the care of Dan McTurk, Stuart Sheppard and Richard Knight.

The Boathouse, designed by Richard Knight and opened by Mrs W R Scurfield, mother of Hugh Scurfield (Chappel House 1943-54), in 1960

An important appointment

In 1960, Annett recommended to the Governors the appointment of a full-time Bursar, to enable the necessary development of the properties of the school - both in respect of refurbishment of existing buildings and the planning and delivery of new facilities - to be managed. The Governors agreed, and Group Captain T.A.F. Elsdon, O.B.E., D.F.C., recently retired from the Royal Air Force, was duly appointed in June 1960. The management of the school's financial and business affairs was passed from Harry Ferrar to Elsdon, along with his office in 8 College Yard, and the pattern for the relationship between Headmaster and Bursar, which developed further under Elsdon's successors (A.B. Bouldstridge, A. Hickox, D.J. Gilligan and J.G. Bartholomew), was established: the Headmaster was the public face of the school and responsible for its staff and pupils, while the Bursar would take on responsibility for the business, property, legal and financial concerns of the school. As can be seen in Chapter 9, by the turn of the 21st Century, the responsibilities of the two men at the top of the organisation were such that a team of six was needed to form a Senior Management Team, complemented by a Deputy Bursar (Finance), an HR Manager and an Estates Manager, to manage and develop a Foundation of three schools, with a substantial portfolio of properties, nearly 350 staff and almost 1,500 pupils.

Aerial photograph taken in the early 1960s. By 1965 demolition had begun to clear space for City Walls Road, the widening of Sidbury and College Street and a car park off King Street, resulting in the destruction of many fine buildings (and, arguably, some derelict, poor quality housing). The King's School certainly benefitted from the lack of planning control at this time - three of the houses which can be seen in Castle Place were demolished, as were the houses either side of the public house on Severn Street (later the 'Salmon's Leap', which would be demolished in 2009 to make way for The Keyes Building) providing space for the dining hall and modern languages building and, later, the John Moore Theatre. The new Winslow Science Block has pride of place at the centre of the photograph.

The development of the modern King's School

Annett realised that his ambitions for new accommodation would cost a substantial amount of money, and that it would be difficult for him to personally manage the necessary fundraising, even with the support of his new Bursar. A Development Committee of eighteen members, including OVs, a Governor, three senior masters, the Headmaster and Bursar, was set up in the spring of 1961, under the patronage of the Lord Lieutenant of Worcester, the Bishop of Worcester and the Hon. Peter Walker MP. Number 4 Castle Place was rescued from demolition, at a cost of £150, and used as the Campaign Office.

The aim of the Development Campaign was to raise £120,000 in two stages of seven years each. Funds would be raised mainly through the use of seven-year covenants which were acceptable as security by banks and tax-efficient for donors, as well as a series of School Fetes, which had become biennial events from 1956, and the work of a Ladies' Committee of parents, OVs' wives and friends of the school; the Ladies Committee was established by Mrs D. Kinnersley, Secretary of the Campaign from 1962, who had enjoyed earlier success in support of Dean Beck's Cathedral Tower Appeal.

The clearance of dilapidated and derelict housing across the city of Worcester was due to include much of the ancient housing in Severn Street. Keen to seize an opportunity, the school had purchased most the land and properties between the Royal Worcester factory and the river towpath (the cottages at the western end were demolished for the construction of the Boathouse) as well as houses in Castle Place. In one contract seventeen small cottages were purchased by the school for only £2,000. Cassidy, Farrington and Denys, a London firm of architects, was commissioned to devise and submit plans for the development of the new estate.

Projects for stage one would include a new building providing accommodation for the four day boy Houses which would double as eight additional classrooms, a new Music School and an outdoor swimming pool and gymnasium to replace the now decaying wooden gym built in Creighton's time.

Pages from the 1961 Appeal, making the case for a new gymnasium and swimming pool. In the Appeal booklet David Annett described the cramped, insufficient facilities for day boys and proposed a classroom building for Severn Street - a 'New Block' - which was to be realised and would be named the Annett Building in his honour in 2001.

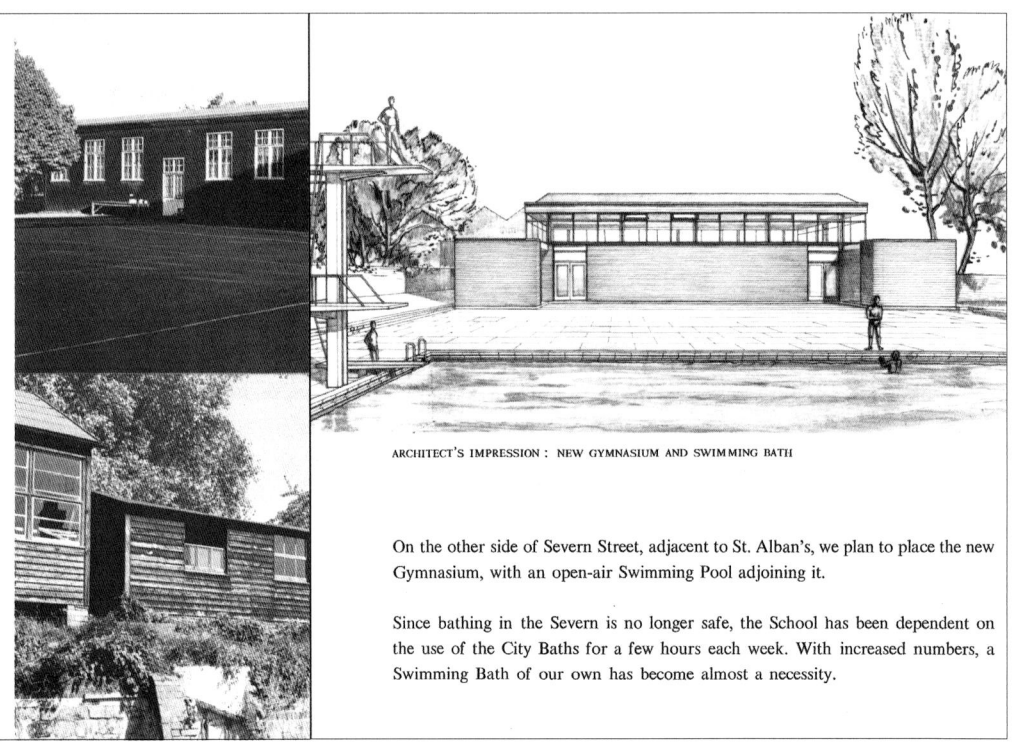

Aerial photograph looking north, taken in 1965 - the Winslow Building completed the quadrangle forming the playground; the plot of land for the planned gymnasium had been cleared ready for use next to the swimming pool - this would replace the old wooden gym to the south of the playground; the New Block (later the Annett Building) stood on the opposite side of Severn Street - to its right would later stand the new dining hall and languages building; at the bottom left of the photo a Victorian terrace of houses had yet to be demolished - the plot would become a playground for St Alban's.

Generous donations and covenants enabled work to begin on these projects almost immediately. The swimming pool would be the first project to be completed on the St Margaret's site; at cost of £18,000 the 84' x 42' pool, with a maximum depth of 9'6", was opened in the summer of 1962. A changing block was included at the site, intended to serve the planned gymnasium, which would sit adjacent to the pool.

Under Kinnersley's leadership, the Campaign had raised more than £57,000 by the end of 1963 from donations, subscriptions and covenants, with an additional £1,000 from the Ladies' Committee and a further £1,300 from the 1962 School Fete. This had enabled work to begin on the 'Day Boy and Classroom Block', known from then (and, in fact, until as recently as 2001 by which time is was far from new and had been superseded by several newer buildings) as the 'New Block', in January 1963. The building was completed quickly at a cost of around £47,000 and occupied immediately, although the official opening was not until 13th June 1964, to form part of the re-styled Speech Day. More on the New Block, later named in honour of David Annett, can be found on the following pages.

The 1964 Fete added a further £1,500 to Campaign funds, which could now be used to finance the development of King's first Music School, in the 'Fishermen's Cottages', the last three remaining dwellings, which would later be connected to the John Moore Theatre. The Music School included a large classroom, a record library, an instrument storeroom and seven small rooms for instrumental tuition and practice. These facilities must have been a wonderful welcome for the new Director of Music, Harry Bramma F.R.C.O., who took over from West in 1964.

By the end of the first stage of the Development Campaign, on 31st December 1967, the total funds raised came to a total of £72,000. More than 60 social functions had been organised, a gymkhana was established at Droitwich which became an annual event from 1964, and a 'Swop Shop' for school uniform was set up, helping parents and raising £425 towards the campaign.

Promoting the 1966 King's School Fete

Annett Building

The largest of the projects identified for David Annett's 1961 Appeal, a 'new block' was proposed to provide four classrooms and day boy accommodation - each of the four day houses (Chappel, Creighton, Kittermaster and Wulstan) would have its own common room, study and House Master's study, along with new cloakrooms, changing rooms and lavatories.

Local builder Spicers Ltd. started construction in January 1963, and completed at a cost of approximately £47,000.

The building, known as the 'New Block', was officially opened by Sir Edward Boyle MP, Minister of State for Education and Science, on 13th June 1964. Sir Edward said much in praise of Direct Grant schools in a speech which was relayed by closed-circuit television to classrooms and College Hall, allowing the whole school to witness the event. A note in the programme described the internal finishes as 'designed to necessitate as little maintenance as possible'.

ARCHITECT'S IMPRESSION : NEW BLOCK SEEN FROM WEST END OF SEVERN STREET

THE PLANS...

We propose to build a new block on the north side of Severn Street backing on to the existing School property. This will contain the new day-boy accommodation, and also four new classrooms. The Upper School day-boys have now been divided into four houses each of about 60 boys ; each house will have its own Common Room, Monitor's Study, and Housemaster's Study. Suitably equipped cloak-rooms, changing-rooms, and lavatories will also be provided for both Upper and Middle Schools.

At a later stage it is the intention to add Music Rooms and Workshops on an adjoining site.

Above: Plans for the New Block in the 1961 Appeal brochure

Right: Shield donated by A Elt (OV) to mark completion of the building

Below: The 'New Block', 1964

The Annett Building, following refurbishment, 2001

During the re-ordering of School House in the 1980s, a new home was found for Wulstan House, and Bright House moved into the basement of the New Block - the house room was used for Classics teaching by Housemaster Bob Stone; the other two houses spread out across the top floor, and the classrooms became the home of the Mathematics Department.

By the late 1990s, the New Block, which seemed dark and outdated, was suffering from structural issues, caused in no small part by the flat roof. The 1998 strategic review of the school (see Chapter 9) considered the possibility of demolishing the building. Fortunately, this proved unnecessary, and a major programme of renovation was undertaken, including the addition of a pitched roof and larger windows.

Re-opened, and renamed in honour of David Annett, in October 2001, the 'Annett Building' provided eight classrooms for Mathematics, as well as a pastoral base for the Fourth Forms, in a bright, modern building. The basement housed a gym and dance studio; in 2014, ahead of the move of these facilities into The Keyes Building, the basement was converted into two further classrooms, which would serve as a home for Choir House, relocated to provide additional space in the Music School.

Left: David Annett at the official opening, 1964

Above: the renaming and re-opening, 2001

Derek Griffiths *Chappel House 1956-67*

I joined King's at St. Alban's Junior School in September 1956, and can't say the three years spent there were enjoyable. I recall in the second year, one boy giggling uncontrollably at a master's joke whose response was to beat him severely. From that day, I kept my head down. On the other hand, we had an undefeated football team for three years and Mr Thomas was a real gentleman and an effective Maths teacher.

Life changed dramatically when I moved to the senior school. My circle of friends widened, the masters treated us with more respect, and attitudes generally were changing; after all it was the early sixties and the whole country was buzzing. The music and fashion scenes were particularly interesting, but caused a major problem involving the school cap. It was a school rule to wear it when outside the school premises and to touch it when you met a master - I never did work out the logic behind this. The cap just did not go with my 'Billy Fury' haircut and was a constant source of punishment for the next three years, until I found a way of balancing it on the back of my head.

The penalty for this offence, and many other minor infringements, was Penal Drill. It could be handed out not only by masters, but also by monitors. You were obliged to stay behind after school for about an hour to do menial tasks, such as cleaning the playground or weeding the school garden, under the supervision of a school monitor. One cold, wet winter evening, we were instructed to remove the moss from between paving stones in the school garden - a very unpleasant task. You can imagine our pleasure when the monitor was severely reprimanded by the school gardener, who had taken a lot of time and trouble to create the effect. On another occasion, we were told to stand still with our arms outstretched - sounds simple enough, but after about ten minutes the pain is excruciating.

'The Mavericks'

Being a local boy, I remained a day boy throughout my time at King's. This gave me a major advantage over boarders who were not allowed out in the evenings until the Upper Sixth. We had a social life outside school - a group would meet on a Saturday night at 'Fletcher's Dance Studio'. Later on, music became an important part of life. Bill Pidgeon, Pete Webster and myself discovered we all possessed guitars and Nick Chance fancied himself as a bit of a drummer. We decided to form a rock group and meet at my home to practice on three cheap Spanish guitars and an upturned waste bin. Our rendition of 'Apache' was incredible. Eventually, these instruments were

Chappel House with Housemaster Frank Sutcliffe, 1966

exchanged for three cheap electric guitars and amplifiers - the drum kit had to wait. We borrowed one for our first live gig in aid of Oxfam, as a group called 'The Mavericks'. We played twenty tunes and we raised a large sum of money for Biafra.

In the Lower Remove, I entered Chappel House under Frank Sutcliffe, who was strict but fair and had a good sense of humour. He was assisted by Rex Hazeldene, Head of P.E. At this time the day-boy houses moved to the New Block and an outdoor pool was built which was freezing cold, especially first thing in the morning. The most popular activity at break-time was cards. We started with bridge and solo, but soon degenerated into three card brag. At Christmas each house held a party which was a fun-packed event and we were even allowed to wear casual clothing. One year Stuart Knee and I decided to write a song for the occasion about several of the masters at King's but it was not altogether polite. Dare we risk it? I chickened out and asked Rex Hazeldene what he thought. "Go for it!" he said, "I'll deal with anyone without a sense of humour".

Another event which began at this time was the 'Beat Meet' - entertainment with a rock band and a trad jazz band and our group played in one or two of them. Girls were invited from the A.O. and The Convent and credibility was lost if you didn't have a partner by the end of the evening.

By now I was having a good time at King's and also surprisingly working reasonably hard. This was not true of everyone. A friend of mine who was academically ahead of me was never really able to fit in. He was reported by a monitor for smoking and was suspended for two weeks. He decided to clean up his act; changed his Chelsea boots for Oxford brogues, had a college-boy haircut and prepared to work. A few weeks later when his housemaster asked him how he tied his tie, he replied, "It's a Windsor knot, sir." "Well, I don't like it - tie your tie in the traditional manner immediately" retorted the master. My friend walked out of the school and moved to the Worcester Technical College.

I remember Nick Taylor (Castle House 1962-67) as a tremendously talented sportsman and Bob Moody (Castle House 1960-65) for his generous sportsmanship. I concentrated on cross-country and athletics and was delighted to be appointed school captain for both. I enjoyed the responsibility and team selection duties, especially if it was raining and Nick was unable to play cricket. I particularly remember when Bob won the senior two-mile cross-country and I won the middle school. He insisted that I have the trophy because my time was faster. I owe Tim Hickson and Rex Hazeldene sincere thanks for extra coaching and encouragement.

The most lasting impression I have of King's is of life-long friendships, Nick Chance and Bill Pidgeon continued to have 'jam sessions', all in B flat because of Nick's change to a saxophone, and I would often meet up with Stuart ('Flea' to his friends) Knee and Chris Blackman. Did I enjoy my time at King's? Well, my son enlisted and I think that says it all.

Derek Griffiths qualified as an accountant, but decided to start his own business and produced cast-iron kitchenware which he sold in his shops in Stourbridge and Birmingham.

Demolition of Numbers 1, 2 and 3 Castle Place in the early 1960s; the school acquired the site with the intention of building there, but the land has never been used for more than parking cars. Number 4 was saved from demolition as it was used as the Campaign Office for the Development Campaign.

David Annett enjoying the fun of the fair at the 1968 School Fete at which a record-breaking £2,465 was raised.

During the first phase of works, the swimming pool, New Block and Music School had been completed, renovation and improvement works had been carried out on the boarding houses, including St Alban's House, the fives courts were repaired, with the addition of a roof and electric lighting, and four tennis courts were added to the playing fields. The school had spent £92,000 on these projects, with a bank loan of £20,000 to cover the shortfall in fundraising.

Stage two of the Development Campaign was launched on 3rd October 1968 with a new committee, including a number of stage one campaign members, to complete the fundraising needed for the second tranche of building projects.

The first priority for the new committee would be to repay the school's £20,000 loan. A Labour Government, hostile to Direct Grant and independent schools, had come to office under Harold Wilson, and it was thought sensible to create an independent trust to manage the school's fundraising and development to protect any funds from the clutches of the government in the event of a nationalisation programme, and so the King's School Development Trust came into being in 1968. Further details about the Development Trust can be found in Chapter 9.

The projects for stage two would be: a new, large School Library, to be created in Edgar Tower; the already-planned gymnasium to be built next to the swimming pool; a new dining hall and kitchens to cater for all pupils in one location and replace the wooden huts; classrooms for teaching modern languages; and a new building to provide a modern workshop and art room.

Two Fetes followed in 1968 and 1970, each setting a new record for profit - in 1970, a total of £2,520 was raised, equivalent to a sum in excess of £37,000 in 2015.

A serious challenge to the Direct Grant faced the school at the hands of the Public Schools Commission and its two Donnison Reports in 1969 and 1970 (more on which can be found later in this chapter); Annett and the Governors issued statements which aimed both to reassure parents of pupils with free places and all those considering donating to the Development Campaign, that the proposed changes, which in effect would have resulted in either conversion to a state-run school or full independence, would take some years to apply in the event they were even accepted. Eventually, after the General Election of 1970, such concerns were allayed by the election of a Conservative Government. Even so, the Trust had raised more than £35,000 by that time, and projects were already under way.

A new School Library was opened in Edgar Tower in 1969, with new shelving, a gallery level, lighting and fitted carpet installed in the two large rooms at the heart of the Tower (a third room, the 'Reference Library' was added later). A selection of the books from the Sixth Form Library (now, of course, 'The Old Library') were brought over and a significant investment in new books was undertaken by Librarian, A.N. Brownridge; the Library had 4,000 books by the end of 1970, with plans to double this number as the level of borrowing increased steadily.

The playing fields had been extended in 1967 with the addition of the 'Fair Field' (between Rammell's Pavilion and Bromwich Road), in exchange for the field at Battenhall which had been the school's as a result of the amalgamation with the Choir School. This upper field was levelled for use as a pitch, with four hard tennis courts constructed; in later years, these courts would double as netball courts and so proved a sound investment by the Trust. In 1968, however, Peter Curle made use of them for winter hockey, as an alternative to rugby.

Sports Hall and Swimming Pool complex, completed in 1971

New School Library in Edgar Tower, 1969

The Winslow Science Block seen across the site of Creighton's gymnasium, demolished to make way for the Wolfson Building, 1972

The much-anticipated gymnasium, or Sports Hall, was completed in 1971. The Sports Hall measured 100' by 54' with a 22' high ceiling. The flooring, a new form of needlefelt, was chosen for durability, and marked out for a variety of sports. An internal balcony which overlooked the swimming pool had been designed to accomodate fencing competitions, although this was never utilised. On King's Day (as Speech Day became known in 1970), 28th May 1971, the £42,000 Sports Hall was opened by Sir Jack Longland (School House 1919-23).

The new Sports Hall rendered Creighton's wooden gymnasium redundant, and it was demolished in 1972 to make way for the next project: a new building to house the Technical Studies (later known as C.D.T. - Craft, Design and Technology) and Art departments which a progressive school now required. Two years earlier, the Wolfson Foundation, established by Lord Wolfson of Marylebone (Creighton House 1942-45), had decided to award a grant of £32,000 to provide a workshop for science and engineering projects with space for an arts centre on the upper level. The delay in construction was due to the process of selecting an architect and then revising plans to incorporate an additional Chemistry laboratory which would be connected to the first floor of the Winslow Building.

Opened in 1972, the Wolfson Building provided modern, spacious facilities for two important subjects as well as the much-needed additional laboratory, and released space in the 1925 classroom building.

Meanwhile, two undercrofts were converted into useful spaces: the undercroft of College Hall was established as a social space for members of the Upper Sixth (the Old Library providing a social space for the Lower Sixth), while the undercroft of the Winslow Building was enclosed to provide two additional classrooms. A Careers Room had also been established, providing advice to pupils considering a range of professions. 5 Edgar Street was acquired in 1974 to house the School Shop and Swop Shop.

This expansion of the school's facilities, including the transformation of boarding houses, day boy accommodation, teaching spaces and purpose-built homes for the arts and sports, had revolutionised the school campus, enabling a level of teaching and pastoral care for a number of pupils which would have been unthinkable in the decades before.

The final project would, perhaps, have an even more important impact on the daily lives of every pupil: a new Dining Hall offering canteen-style lunches and large enough to serve the entire senior school and the middle school in only two sittings. There would be an opportunity to incorporate classrooms on an upper level, as well as a smart meeting room, served by a dumb waiter from the state-of-the-art kitchen below, suitable for conferences and Governors' meetings.

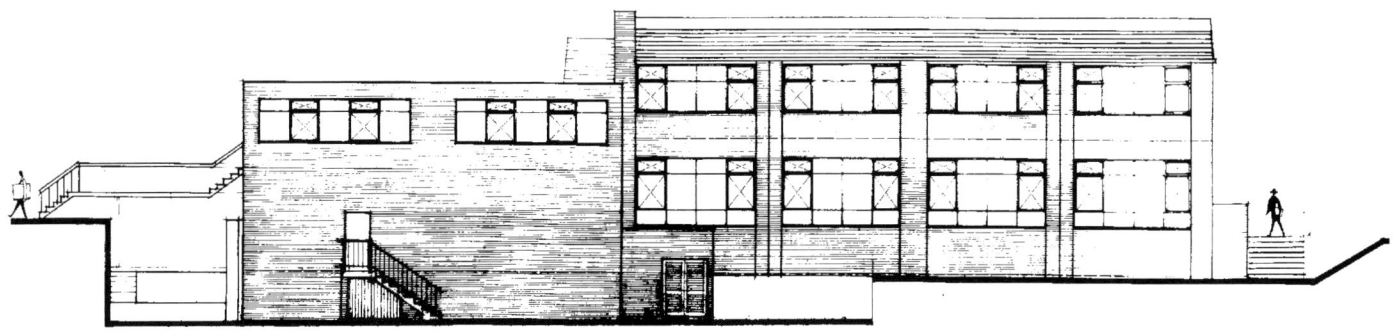

Architect's drawing of the new Dining Hall and Modern Languages building.
The design had to take account of differing ground levels on all sides and the need to retain access to School House and the New Block.

Wolfson Building

The site of Creighton's wooden gymnasium had been identified in the 1960s as the position for a new building to accommodate Craft and Technology (variously described as Woodwork, Technical Studies and C.D.T., but effectively the subject now known as Design and Technology) and Art. Once the Sports Hall was opened in 1971, work could begin on clearing the site and planning the new building.

The Wolfson Foundation agreed a generous grant of £32,000 for the construction of the new facility, which would offer a workshop for engineering and science projects with provision for an arts centre on the upper floor.

The finished building, brought into use in stages during 1973, included a large workshop for wood and metalwork, a materials storeroom and a design room on the ground floor. The first floor offered a large art studio, with a smaller room for textile printing; the Art department was connected into the roof space of Chappel's old gymnasium, providing working space for Sixth Form artists. At the other end of the building, a generously-proportioned new Chemistry laboratory connected via a storeroom into the first floor of the Winslow Building. Much of the equipment and machinery for the workshop was provided by local industrial firms, thanks to the efforts of Mr. S.W.G. Meakin of the C.B.I. The last item to be installed was the computer terminal, which would allow the new subject of Computer Studies to be introduced during the following years.

Peter Baseley (Head of C.D.T.) was quick to exploit the new facilities available, offering a double period of craft teaching to boys in the Middle School, and developed schemes of work for Upper School projects. Andrew Kneen, who had succeeded Tim Vivian as Head of Art in 1972, was provided with a light, airy space for his artists, enabling a high standard (and larger scale) of artwork to be produced.

C.D.T. continued to develop under Peter Baseley throughout the 1980s and 1990s, with computer-aided design increasingly used alongside the teaching of traditional carpentry and metalwork

Art and CDT building
- concept sketch by Philip Bedwin of I.D.C. Ltd., December 1971

skills. After Baseley stepped down as Head of Department, this work was continued by John Whitehouse, who further developed the progressive programme delivered in C.D.T. which had become a strong, popular subject at GCSE and A Level.

In a similar way, on the upper floor, John Exton (Head of Art 1983-94) pushed the standard of artwork ever higher, hosting public exhibitions of increasingly ambitious work. The Art Department expanded beyond the Wolfson Building into the upper floor of the adjacent Royal Worcester Porcelain cafeteria building, to which, under Liz Hand's leadership, the Art Department would eventually move in 2008. For further details about the Art School, see Chapter 9.

By the time of Art's departure from the Wolfson Building, Chris Wilson had taken over as Head of Design and Technology. Computer-aided design was complimented by computer-aided manufacturing techniques, allowing the development of highly complex and impressive projects by pupils at all levels. Wilson's involvement in the expansion of the Design and Technology Department into the upper floor of the Wolfson

Peter Baseley (Head of Technical Studies/C.D.T. 1973-96)
teaching in the workshop, c.1980

John Exton (Head of Art 1983-94) with A Level Art students, c.1990.
This area was in the roof space of the former day boy changing room.

The Wolfson Building, 2015, after refurbishment and the addition of a grand glass porch in 2009

Building helped to drive the contemporary feel to the suite of reconfigured workshop spaces and the new design studios, which, from 2009, were able to accommodate up to four classes in workshop-based activity, with an additonal two rooms for design and other computer-based work. The exterior of the building was also brought up-to-date, with a grand glass porch flooding the modernised lobby with light, and the stylish, new windows offering the same to the workshops and studios. The cost of the project, however, meant that the windows had to be replaced one floor at a time over a two-year period.

A fire escape stairwell was constructed as part of the refurbishment, taking the place of an internal staircase within Chappel's old gymnasium (the main part of which had been used as an additional art room from the late 1990s). This was incorporated into the 'grand piano' shaped Weston Centre, built as part of The Keyes Building, in 2014.

The Wolfson Building was designed to provide state-of-the-art facilities for two subjects which were of growing importance by the 1970s; the redevelopment of the building in the 2000s has provided a modern home for Design and Technology, one of the most popular subjects at GCSE and A Level, driving a surge in the uptake of engineering and design-based degree courses in recent years.

The rise in popularity of Design & Technology led to the reconfiguration of the existing workshop space, as well as the addition of a workshop and classrooms upstairs, offering a bright, spacious working environment.

The Dining Hall and Modern Languages building under construction, 1976. The Day Boys' Dining Hall can be seen in front of the building site. This photograph offers clear views of Numbers 5 and 6 College Green, The Hostel and Castle House; the additions to Castle House are easy to identify from this angle.

In *The Vigornian* of 1977, David Annett described a summer of remarkable changes to the school campus: "...seldom can the school have re-assembled in September to find so many physical changes. Foremost among them is the new Dining Hall. Spacious, light, and remarkably quiet, it provides a striking contrast to the crowded and unsightly 'prefabs' in which we have fed for so long. The new kitchens provide excellent meals with an unprecedented choice of dishes, and upstairs the Modern Language Department, after years of 'making do' in most inadequate accommodation, is now housed in roomy quarters with an impressive array of technological aids.

On the other side of the school we have taken on lease from the Dean and Chapter the beautiful 18th-century house formerly used as the Deanery. This has been renamed College House, and provides on the ground floor Common Rooms for the staff, an office for the Headmaster's Secretary, and an entrance hall which must make a far more pleasant impression on visitors to the school than the brown-tiled passage in the Biology Block. Upstairs are studies for our VI-form girls, and a flat for Mr. and Mrs. Roslington, who are in charge of them. This unexpected addition to our buildings has enabled us to increase the number of girls to 27, of whom six are boarders, and a total of 40 is envisaged.

The old School House Dining Room is now a Lecture Hall seating about 110, with provision for film-projection, thus fulfilling a long-standing need. It has been named Passey Hall in honour of Charlie Passey, who during his 30-odd years as Chef has cooked so many meals for consumption in this room, and who is now enjoying the facilities of the new kitchen.

Much has been achieved, but much still remains to be done. The new quadrangle, freed from the clutter of prefabs, has to be landscaped: the old kitchens have to be converted into Music rooms, and the old Music School into VI Form studies. The Library has long been waiting to take over the third room in the Edgar Tower, which can now be released for this purpose.

Finally, but perhaps most urgently of all, we have to find additional Physics and Chemistry Laboratory space to cope with the unexpected increase in numbers taking these subjects in the VI Form."

Gordon Leah (Head of Languages from 1968), teaching in a Modern Languages 'laboratory', c. 1980

The new, large and airy Dining Hall did indeed mark a significant improvement in catering facilities, as well as enhancing the look of the southern parts of the main campus, as the wooden huts could be removed.

Charlie Passey retired in 1979; the new Caterer would be Nick Witherick, assisted by his wife Heather until their retirement in the early 2000s. Heather Witherick recalled that the Dining Hall would play host to House Suppers, for the day boy Houses as well as boarders and could also be used to stage events. During the late 1970s and into the 1980s, the popularity of the newly-independent school would reach to a large number of overseas students, particularly from Hong Kong and the recently-independent countries of Africa; the arrival of Muslim students posed a challenge for the caterers during Ramadan, when food would not be eaten during daylight hours. Fortunately, the Withericks had a house in Edgar Street, and were able to return to the kitchens, often later than 11.00 pm, to provide meals.

The Dining Hall and Modern Languages building, early 1980s

A special generation of staff

The 1960s saw the engagement of a number of masters whose influence would be felt in later years, including Tim Hickson (Physics 1962-2002, Second Master 1986-2002) and John Turner (Mathematics 1960-1995, Careers Master and later Senior Master). Nick and Heather Witherick were among a large number of new staff to arrive at King's during the 1970s and who would serve the school in many ways during the following decades.

Mentioned by Annett on the previous page are Mr and Mrs Roslington; John Roslington first arrived to teach Physics in 1975, and was joined by Caroline, who would later teach History, and became Housemaster of College House in 1977. John would later establish the Computing / I.C.T. Department, while Caroline would manage the School Archive. They retired in 2009 after a combined total of 65 years' service.

Known to generations of pupils were Peter Baseley (C.D.T. 1973-2003, Head of Departmenr 1973-96) whose passion for woodwork was clear to all his students, and who provided many stage sets in the difficult 'theatre' of College Hall; P.C. Thompson (Classics 1970-2006), remembered affectionately for his insistence on 'finding the verb, boy!' and traditional 'public school' manners; Stewart Davis (Biology 1969-2007), who was Housemaster of Kittermaster House for 18 years from its foundation in 1984 and who commanded the C.C.F. throughout the 1980s and 1990s; Tim Watson (Physics 1969-95) whose energetic coaching inspired many rowers; Peter Diamond (English 1970-92, Head of Department from 1972) who took on the mantle of producing countless school plays; Edward Reeves (Mathematics 1978-2006, Head of Department until 2001) whose passion for Maths inspired many to study Further Mathematics and continue the subject at university; Bob Burkill (Head of Geography 1977-97) who shared his enthusiasm with all; Brian Griffiths (Mathematics 1978-2009) who produced many school musicals and served as Housemaster of Creighton House and later as Head of Careers; Margaret Nott (Biology 1976-2003), whose association with the school began when her husband arrived as Chaplain in 1970, and whose compassion made her an ideal assistant to later Chaplains; and Marc Roberts (Mathematics 1975-2012) who was Housemaster of School House and later Wulstan House for many years, and coached many rugby teams with good humour in his booming Welsh voice.

Many others have come and gone during this time, each making his or her own impression on the school and its pupils, but this generation of teachers, whose dedication and loyalty to The King's School is revealed in their length of service, matched by comparatively few teachers in earlier times, and likely to be matched by few since.

Careers Room in the 1970s

Caterer Nick Witherick serving lunch in the Dining Hall, c. 1980

The first steps towards co-education

As revealed in Annett's 'School Notes' in the 1977 issue of *The Vigornian*, College House had recently opened its doors to welcome Sixth Form girls, both day girls and boarders. College House was indeed the first girls' house, but the first four girls had arrived at King's some six years earlier, in September 1971.

The Vigornian of December 1971 simply had this to say about the enrolment of the first girls: *"We welcomed four girls as recruits to the Science VI in September. Their arrival - which caused less of a stir than was anticipated in some quarters - is not to be taken as the first step towards full co-education: several applications have already been received for next year but at present it is not intended to accept more than a total of about twelve."*

Whether it was intended to be or not, the arrival of Alison Heath, Barbara Cookson, Nicola Bradbear and Catherine Hay marked the start of a regular and growing intake of girls into the Sixth Form. Annett would later describe the decision to admit girls as *"an entirely successful move"*, undertaken to provide education for girls in subjects which *"were not taught or not taught very well"* in girls' schools.

These first girls were based in Number 14, the Headmaster's house, under the care of Romey Annett and, as they were all scientists, the tutelage of Keith Bridges. Initially, a private study - separate from the boys' areas - was provided, but this was abandoned when the girls complained of feeling isolated from their classmates, and the girls were 'assigned' to boys' boarding houses for social activies and after-school study.

The option to lease Number 15 College Green from the Dean and Chapter provided an opportunity to extend the provision of facilities to accommodate the growing number of girls, who, under John and Caroline Roslington's care, flourished as an important part of the school, making their mark quickly. That is not to suggest that there weren't problems integrating girls, even in a small way, into a previously male-only institution, but the girls faced the challenges - boys' behaviour, the attitudes of some (older) masters, the lack of PE and Games options and facilities - coping remarkably well.

The success of the pioneering girls in the 1970s paved the way for full co-education in 1991, although, as detailed in Chapter 8, this was never a foregone conclusion.

King's Remembered

Barbara Cookson — The Hostel 1971-73

Barbara Cookson was one of the first four girls to be admitted to The King's School in the Autumn Term of 1971.

The arrival of girls at King's came as something of a surprise to most of the pupils. I recall telling some friends at the Swan Theatre Youth Group during the summer holidays that I would be going to their school. They didn't believe me.

The first morning I can remember vividly - walking in through the Edgar Tower and kicking the leaves along College Green trying to take as long as possible getting to Number 14 where we had our study. I was still the first of the four to arrive and Mrs. Annett showed me into the study. Later on we filed into the back of College Hall for our first assembly. The hymn was 'Jerusalem'. With all those male voices raised I began to realise I had joined something big!

Quite where we were in the pecking order was a distinct problem. Even the masters did not always know how to behave. I think it was Mr Turner's reaction when I walked into my first class with him that most nearly caused me to flee in panic. We were late (we seemed to spend all our time sprinting up stairs and across College Green and on this occasion probably getting lost as well). When we arrived Mr. Turner and the entire class stood up!

I didn't intend to be a comic turn when I took the part of the Abbess in the 'Comedy of Errors', but the line Shakespeare never wrote for Antipholus on being reunited with his mother - 'Oh Mumsy!' - got a tremendous laugh, but perhaps it was relief that the play was all but over and the audience could get up off the board seats on scaffolding that had been set up in the Sports Hall.

Barbara studied Maths with Theoretical Physics at Cambridge. After university she trained to become a patent agent and later qualified as a property lawyer in London.

Adapted from an article published in *'The King's School, Worcester - and a history of its site'*, 1994.

Gillian Hunt — Castle House 1975-77

I guess having two older brothers who'd been at King's I was better prepared than most of the girls who started in the Sixth Form in 1975. There were only seven of us I think. It is hard to separate the ups from the downs, but there are a number of things which were particularly memorable.

It was such a beautiful environment compared to the 60s' built Girls' Grammar School and, with studies (very cold) at the top of the Headmaster's house, we had complete freedom to wander in and out of school whenever we fancied.

King's was much more competitive academically than I was used to and there were much higher expectations all round. One also had to get the balance right: it was okay to do well, but not okay to appear to work too hard!

The sheer quality of the music was quite daunting, but enjoyable. I have fond memories of rehearsing with the orchestra in College Hall and listening to some superb violin solos from Geoff Webber.

I remember feeling very conspicuous because we had no uniform and we were called by our first names, not by surnames like the boys. I was the only girl in my Physics set and in hindsight I'm very grateful to Mike Croome for being brave enough to sit next to me on day one!

I even remember some of the things teachers said. Mr. Knight, after our first maths lesson, told me and Louise Ward that he didn't expect us to stay in the top set or pass the A Level; we took pleasure in coming first (Louise) and second in the maths exams that year! I can hear Mr. Diamond trying to teach General English to a bunch of us unco-operative scientists, telling me, 'You're not at all like your brother are you?' (Tim had just left to read English at Cambridge).

Gillian [Bryson] Hunt was the first King's girl to be awarded an Open Scholarship to Oxford University. After studying Chemistry for seven years, Gillian moved into IT. She is married to John and has two sons.

The end of the Direct Grant

Harold Wilson's Labour Government (1964-1970) pursued reforms in Britain's education system, seeking to bring maintained and Direct Grant schools under Local Education Authority (LEA) control as comprhensive schools. A review was announced by Anthony Crosland, Education Secretary, in 1965 - the first since the Education Act, 1944. The Public Schools Commission set up two panels: the Newsom Report (1968) considered private boarding schools while the report by Professor David Donnison (1970) dealt with private day schools, Direct Grant and maintained grammar schools.

The Donnison Report recommended that Direct Grant schools, such as The King's School, should be included in the programme for comprehensive education and should no longer charge fees. The Commission had not been in agreement, however, with seven of the nineteen members recommending that a 'full grant' status be awarded to existing Direct Grant schools. In either case, assurance was made that any changes should be phased in so as not to affect the education of pupils already attending Direct Grant schools. This was to be expected, and indeed Annett and Canon Armstrong (interregnum Chairman of Governors between Dean Milburn and Dean Kemp) issued public statements to reassure parents and pupils and to assist the Development Trust in its task of raising funds for stage two of the school's appeal; the Development Trust had been established as an independent organisation in 1968 to protect any funds raised against Government interference.

Fortunately for The King's School, the Conservative Party swept to office in June 1970; Annett wrote of the lifting of *"a great burden of anxiety and uncertainty"* following the appointment of Margaret Thatcher as Minister for Education and Science in Edward Heath's Government in *The Vigornian* of 1970. Thatcher reversed an earlier cut in the capitation allowance, but schools had to reduce their fees to compensate.

This was to be short-lived, however. The return to Government of Harold Wilson in 1974 saw the abolition of Direct Grant Schools. Annett and the Governors had to choose between accepting fully-maintained status (and LEA control) and full independence: in June 1975 it was announced that The King's School would become an Independent School in September 1976, which would, regrettably, be unable to offer free places to academically gifted children from poorer families.

*Above: The Sixth Form girls of 1972-73.
Barbara Cookson stands third from the right
Left: Gillian [Bryson] Hunt, 1977*

Sports, the arts and extra-curricular activities

Amid the seemingly continual changes of Annett's headship, life at King's carried on, and indeed flourished.

A new Head of Physical Education was appointed in 1962, OV Rex Hazeldine, who had been captain of the rugby, hockey and cricket teams while at school, as well as a star athlete. Advances were made in school athletics during the 1960s and rugby was strong, although seldom strong enough to beat the Royal Grammar School.

The OV Club paid £2,500 for an extension to the Rammell pavilion in 1966 at a time when cricket (directed by Henry Searle and then Mike Points) was thriving, with stunning victories against Hereford Cathedral School in 1962 (166 for 4) and RGS in 1964 (bowler N.P. Wilson taking six wickets for eight runs); in the same year, captain C.C. Barlow set a record of 142 not out against King Edward's, Birmingham.

Appreciative of the new Boathouse, Richard Knight's rowing crews enjoyed early success, with the First VIII almost winning the Princess Elizabeth Cup at Henley on the first attempt in 1961. The standard of rowing suffered briefly, however, when a change to the grading of Advanced Level of the General Certificate of Education (the pass grades would now be from A to E - this would continue with A Levels for more than forty years, until an A* grade was added in 2008) resulted in Middle Sixth boys dropping rowing to focus on their examinations in the early 1960s; this led to the Boat Club withdrawing from the Henley Regatta. Richard Gabriel, who had coxed Great Britain in European Championships in 1958, 1959 and 1964, took over rowing at King's in 1967. Within two years, an expanded number of crews were enjoying success at the National Schools Championship at Pangbourne. The new Colts Eight had an almost unbeaten season in 1969.

The new swimming pool, which replaced swimming in the river, provided a great training facility for Paul Cattermole from the 1963 season, with his swimmers setting new records and competing in diving and water polo which were added to Swimming Sports competitions in 1964 and 1966 respectively.

Bell-ringing, 1968, led by Paul Cattermole.
Campanology fell out of favour in the 1980s and 1990s, but a revival in pupil interest was encouraged by Tim Keyes, Headmaster, in the 2000s when a thriving Bell-ringing group was re-established.

The school's musicians were able to enjoy the new Music School from 1965, moving to enlarged premises in the former kitchens in the basement of School House in 1977. The Keys Society, established in 1974, enabled pupils to devise and perform at five concerts each year with minimal guidance from teachers; Keith Bridges took on responsibility for the society in 1976. Concerts and recitals became regular features of the school calendar; a number of recitals by talented school musicians and others had helped to raise funds for a pipe organ, commissioned by Annett, for College Hall. The organ was constructed by Nicholson's and completed in 1969, providing significant benefits to school music, from concerts to assemblies.

The Worcester drama scene had suffered the demolition of the Theatre Royal, Angel Street, and the Public Hall in the Cornmarket in the 1950s; all ten Worcester secondary schools campaigned with the Worcester Society for the Advancement of Music and the Arts (SAMA) for the foundation of a new theatre, led by Sara Knight, wife of Richard Knight. Thirty pupils, three from each of the ten schools, formed the Worcester Schools Theatre Council which met regularly in The Hostel, planning fundraising events to pay for a block of accessible seating for disabled audience members in the planned new theatre. The City Council granted permission and made a plot of land available at The Moors, and building work commenced in 1964: as this was 400 years since the birth of Shakespeare in the Diocese of Worcester, the name 'Swan Theatre' was chosen. The pupil committee developed into the Swan Youth Theatre, which staged a production in the theatre every Easter.

Drama at King's had continued, however, with plays performed in College Hall or the Old Library. A staff production took place every two years. David Annett recalled fondly portraying Eeyore in a production of *Winnie the Pooh* directed by Peter Diamond. Peter Baseley used great skill to create stage sets for these two awkward venues.

The acquisition of the Old Chapel in 1965 provided a base for outdoor activities, with space for fifty boys to camp in the grounds around the chapel. The first pupils to take up this opportunity were the Scouts; Scouting had grown in popularity during the 1950s and 1960s, with two Troops of boarders (one at the senior school, the other at St Alban's) extending to a third Troop for middle school day boys in 1962. Donald Anderton took on the role of Group Scout Master for the King's School Scouts. Five senior Scouts achieved the Queen's Scout Award during the 1960s (the Scout Association's equivalent of the Duke of Edinburgh's Gold Award), the first being P.N. Martin in 1962. The Scouts enjoyed annual visits to Portsmouth and the Norfolk Broads, with camping in Dorset, the Lake District and Snowdonia before the Old Chapel was available, by which time Paul Cattermole worked alongside the Group Scout Master to manage the programme for a significant number of Scouting pupils.

Increasing academic demands on the school timetable led to the senior Scouts becoming Venture Scouts in 1966, restricted to Sixth Formers two years later. In 1969, all Upper Remove boys in the C.C.F. and the Scouts were combined into a C.C.F. Basic Training Year; activities were essentially those undertaken by the Scouts: map-reading, first aid, camping, canoeing, sailing, rifle-shooting and climbing.

The C.C.F. also underwent changes in 1969, with Lt.Col. Bill Bailey and Capt. Wilfred Thomas stepping down. The new Contingent Commander was Arthur Aldridge D.F.C., whose R.A.F. cadets achieved success in examinations and, with Flying Scholarships, a number of cadets gained private pilot licences. Between 1959 and 1970, Tim Vivian commanded a Royal Naval Section, supported by HMS Cambria in Cardiff. There were opportunities for cadets to visit a submarine depot in Glasgow and to sail with the Dartmouth Training Squadron. The Army Section, under Col. S.R. Sheppard, took part in annual camps all around the country, with visits to the British Army of the Rhine in the early 1960s.

A Works Group was established for the boys, which successfully refurbished the western end of College Hall's undercroft as a Sixth Form social club in 1970. During their work two graves were discovered; A.L. Cubberly instructed the boys in careful excavation of a skeleton which, after analysis at Birmingham University, it was revealed was that of a Roman Christian man, aged between 25 and 30, buried between 480 and 700 AD.

Chess had been a pastime for pupils for at least a century, encouraged by all (except for Canon Chappel, who preferred the boys to engage in physical exercise) as a worthwhile, intellectual hobby. Inter-House competitions had been played since 1904; the Senior Chess Team won the Worcestershire Schools League in 1960, which marked the start of a great decade for Chess at King's. In 1967, however, Contract Bridge started to grow in popularity, under the direction of John Turner. The Bridge Club entered the recently-established Daily Mail Schools Bridge Cup Competition, doing well in the first years and achieving second place in 1971.

Choir House study, 1970s

The first school computer terminal was purchased in 1973, housed in the newly completed Wolfson Building. A computer course was offered to Sixth Formers, which developed into a fully-developed Computer Studies course the following year.

The King's School campus as it was at the end of Annett's headship: the New Block (obscured by trees), Sports Hall and Swimming Pool, Wolfson Building and the Dining Hall / MFL building were all developed during Annett's 20 years as Headmaster. His successor, Andrew Milne, would later extend the Winslow Building, add a polythene dome to the pool and take over Number 9 as the Headmaster's residence.

The end of two decades of transformation

During his time at King's, David Annett had hoped to be a liberal force, modernising the school to suit the needs of his pupils in the modern world.

Annett allowed rules to move with the times, following two basic principles: there was no point in having a rule which could not be enforced, and there was no sense in creating rules which would quickly become obsolete. For this reason, he tried to avoid draconian rulings on fashion: hair might be too long one year and then too short the next; trousers might be too wide one year and then too narrow the next - Annett's chosen course was simply to steer pupils away from extremes of fashion. He did fight to keep drug use out of the school during the 'swinging sixties', and also to encourage boys (and girls) to take on leadership roles as monitors and House prefects against a prevailing attitude of freedom and relucatance to boss other people around. Discipline was still severe during the 1960s, but the Headmaster was no longer a man to be feared in the same way as previous Headmasters, thanks in no small part to the welcoming approach of both David and Romey Annett.

The change in the school's culture encouraged many individual successes. Talented musicians, actors and comedians, authors, sports players and captains of industry had flourished at The King's School during the 1960s and 1970s, under the tuition and guidance of Annett and his large cohort of dedicated and enthusiastic teachers, which numbered 51 at the senior school, with a further five at St Alban's, by 1979.

The admission of four girls to the Sixth Form had been a bold move in 1971, which led to increasing numbers and a further change in school culture by 1977, when College House opened to accommodate 27 girls, of whom six were boarders, with plans to increase the total to 40. With the benefit of hindsight, it seems clear that this led to an inevitable move towards making King's fully co-educational, although this was far from certain even ten years later. The courage of the early girls, and the acceptance of the boys to a change in culture, led to a majority of the staff and parents being in favour of steadily increasing the number of girls at King's.

In 1976, King's became an Independent School, receiving no funding from either the Government or the Local Education Authority. This would have resulted in the loss of children from less wealthy families if it had not been for the introduction of the Assisted Places Scheme by Margaret Thatcher's Government in 1981. The state could no longer control school fees, although Annett had imposed only minimal increases during his time.

The changes and improvements to the school campus were hugely significant, allowing an enlarged school (in excess of 770 pupils in 1979) to enjoy a modern education. These changes included new teaching, sports and catering facilities, and improvements to boarding and day Houses. These combined with the restructuring of the Houses to create additional day boy Houses and College House for girls, as well as the separation of the middle school, made the provision of good pastoral care for individuals a reality in a way which could not have been achieved in previous decades. The radical changes to the school's buildings established an enlarged school site, able

David Annett, photographed shortly before his retirement. This portrait hung in the 'Annett Room', a large conference room at the western end of the Dining Hall and Modern Languages building, until the room was redesignated 'The Severn Room', at David Annett's request once the New Block had been named in his honour in 2001.

to cope with growing pupil numbers in the next decade and offering a framework for future developments.

An achievement which cannot be understated is the success of the Development Committee, later the Development Trust, in creating a more cohesive school community of pupils, staff, parents, Old Vigornians and friends of the school, who came together to provide the funding and opportunities for the school to grow and evolve into the modern, progressive school envisaged by David Annett. This school community would continue to grow in importance during the following decades, as evidenced by the support for the SPACE Campaign and the support for pupils and school projects enjoyed by the school in the 21st Century.

David Annett retired in August 1979 to Whitbourne, Herefordshire, where he and Romey were always happy to welcome former pupils and colleagues. David continued to teach occasionally and served as a Governor at Malvern College, as Chairman of the Worcester Civic Society and as Membership and Grants Secretary of the Herefordshire Historic Churches Trust. Romey Annett died in 1996, David in 2004; a memorial service was held in Worcester Cathedral for each of them, with large congregations celebrating the enormous impact they had made on The King's School.

Tim Keyes (Headmaster 1998-2014) addressing pupils, parents, staff, governors and guests at his last King's Day in July 2014.

One of many significant and lasting changes to the school introduced by David Annett was to transform Speech Day into a more public event, centered around a service in the Cathedral. Although the format altered slightly - the ordering of the Headmaster's Report and the Service of Thanksgiving was changed in the early 2000s - King's Day today would be recognisable to those who attended the first King's Day in 1970.

Old Vigornian Club

William Bolland, Headmaster 1879-1896, felt strongly that former King's pupils should meet regularly and form a club.

The first recorded sports fixtures between OVs and the school took place in 1889. An OV XI beat the school team by 9 runs in June, following the defeat of the OV IV by the school crew at the inaugural School Regatta in April.

Bolland galvanised some of those he had taught in College Hall to organise and attend a dinner, which was held in December 1889 at the Bell Hotel, Broad Street. Bolland joined by 18 Old Vigornians, with Rev. James Went (OV 1858-62), Headmaster of Leicester, presiding; other OVs in attendance included Walter Holland, who would later become the first OV Club President (see below), Samuel Southall (OV 1867-72), and Alexander Pearce Higgins (OV 1876-82) who, following a highly distinguished career as a barrister, became a KC in 1919, a Fellow of Trinity College, Cambridge and a member of the Permanent Court of Arbitration at the Hague. The dinner became an annual event, repeated in a similar fashion until 1894, when the dinner, held at the Star Hotel, saw the election of Frank Webb and P.B. Wright as secretaries for the following year's dinner; they were charged with the additional task of forming an OV Club.

A meeting took place on 7th October 1895 in School House, attended by 23 Old Vigornians; a letter had been sent to all former pupils for whom the school had an address. A new 'Old Vigornian's Club' was formed, and a President, Walter Holland (OV 1869-73), elected alongside a Secretary (Frank Webb), Treasurer and a small Committee. The objects of the OV Club were established: to promote the welfare of The King's School, to enable OVs to keep in touch with the school and each other, to maintain an up-to-date register of OVs and their addresses, and organise an Annual Reunion in Worcester. A letter was sent by Frank Webb to all known OVs, giving the names of the officers, a list of the existing 54 members (with an invitation for others to join), and the Rules of the Club. Rule 5 set the annual subscription at 5s, payable in advance and due annually on 7th October.

The first significant task of the Club was to organise the 1895 Reunion Dinner, again held at the Star Hotel, preceded by a General Meeting, attended by 35 OVs, which added five Vice-Presidents and two members to the Committee. William Bolland was invited as guest of honour. The new Headmaster, William Chappel, was invited to the eighth Annual Reunion Dinner the following year. Chappel invited the OV Club to hold their next Reunion Dinner in School House, which duly took place on 13 January 1898. Mrs Chappel received OVs prior to the General Meeting at 6.00 pm, with Dinner at 7.00 pm. This format worked well, and was repeated in 1899.

In 1898, the new Secretary, Anthony Bolland (School House 1852-60) arranged a Dinner in London, held at the Holborn Restaurant, with Walter Holland invited to preside. W.E. Bolland was invited as a guest in 1899 and Chappel the following year. These London Dinners continued while Anthony Bolland lived in London, but lapsed soon afterwards.

112th Annual Reunion Dinner, College Hall, May 2015

There was no Reunion Dinner in Worcester during 1900, mostly owing to the Boer War in South Africa, but the 12th Annual Reunion took place in 1901, returning to the Star Hotel.

Five Oxford OVs wrote in *The Vigornian* of March 1900 of their 'mortification' and 'sense of shame' that the OV Club did not have colours, prevalent in the undergraduate world. In response, the OV Club Committee decided on Club Colours later that year: dark blue and white - the school colours - with chocolate brown. Ties were offered for sale to OVs at a price of 1s 6d, alongside hat ribbons and waist scarves.

Cuthbert Creighton, Headmaster, introduced changes to the OV reunion, first in 1921, when a two-day OV Festival held in June included the unveiling of war memorials and the opening of the Rammell Pavilion; in 1925 a formal 'OV Reunion Weekend' was established, with Speech Day on Friday 10th July followed by sports

*The OV Club flag flying proudly above the Rammell Pavilion, 2011.
Alec Mackie, Member Emeritus of the OV Club Committee, is pictured next to the flagpole.
Inset: Members of the OV Cricket Club, 2011*

fixtures and the OV Dinner on the Saturday and a service in the Cathedral on Sunday.

J Littlebury was elected President ahead of the 1938 OV Dinner, following the death of Colonel Albert Webb; at his request, he was elected for a period of five years - previous Presidents had held the office for life. This arrangement continued until for a number of years, until the term of office was reduced to one year.

The number of members of the OV Club remained small, reflecting pupil numbers at King's: in 1934 there were 551 former pupils and eight Masters who had been made honorary members. The rise in pupil numbers under Ronald Kittermaster's headship (1942-1959) from 352 in 1944 to 611 by 1958 meant that membership of the OV Club, which had moved away from annual subscriptions in favour of life membership, grew to almost 2,000. The subscription remained voluntary and entitled former pupils to receive a number of issues of *The Vigornian* (see Chapter 3) after leaving school.

Administration for the Club had been carried out largely by the school until 1965, when the OVs undertook to do this work themselves, although still with assistance from the Headmaster and the Bursar, and, later, the use of a computer in the Auditor's office. Michael Craze (The Hostel 1919-25) served as Secretary of the OV Club from 1977 to 1995. Craze was succeeded by Michael Page (Creighton House 1960-65), who has continued to serve the OV Club as Hon. Secretary since.

With the advent of co-education from 1971, girls began to join the numbers of the OV Club; wives of OVs were invited to attend the Reunion Dinners from 1972, so that girl OVs would feel more welcome. The first female President was Heather [Windsor] Morgan, elected in 2003, completing the last milestone in the passage of the school to full co-education.

Members of the teaching staff are offered Honorary Membership once they have been at King's for five years. By 2014, more than 225 teachers had been offered, and accepted, this membership of the Club. Honorary Membership was extended to other staff who had given the school exceptional service from 2008; in June 2015 it was agreed that all members of King's Foundation staff (senior school and junior schools, teachers and support staff) would be offered Honorary OV status after five years' service.

The work of the OV Club Committee has been supported by the Foundation Development Office (see Chapter 9) since 2001. The FDO introduced a new database of Old Vigornians, a new magazine, Connect, distributed free of charge to all OVs twice each year, and in 2002 re-introduced the London Reunion Dinner, now an annual event. OV merchandise now includes cuff-links, pashminas, bow-ties, umbrellas, books and prints, and even hand-painted oars.

Larger numbers of pupils, with the senior school having more than 900 pupils from the early 2000s, including many girls, and an increase in staff numbers, have resulted in a much larger OV Club. The Annual Reunion Dinner, held in College Hall since the 1950s, attracted some 200 OVs and guests every year. The Annual Reunion Weekend now includes a lunch, tours of the school, the OV Club AGM, the Reunion Dinner, and a Cathedral service followed by drinks with the Headmaster. Since 2008, Grace has been sung, in Latin, before the Dinner, by an increasing number of former Choristers. The Dinner regularly featured specific year-group reunions, celebrating particular milestones; the first of these was in 2001, when those marking 50 years since leaving King's, returned in large numbers.

Caroline [Horrigan] Krolikowski (College House 1985-87) became the first President to be elected to serve a two-year term in 2008. During her tenure as President, Caroline introduced a revised constitution for the OV Club, increasing the number of committee members and formalising the procedures for elections and other matters.

In 2010, it was agreed to move the Annual Reunion Weekend from the third weekend in September to the May Day bank holiday weekend, switching with the London Dinner, which had taken place in May but would be held in October. This generally resulted in a warmer, lighter evening for the Dinner, and tied in with the May Day Fête, at which the OV Club has a stall.

Sport continued to be of significance to the Club. An annual golf tournament was often held in conjunction with the OV weekend. The OV Cricket Club, which celebrated its 60th anniversary in 2008, continued to play at the main King's sports fields and at King's Hawford. The OV Rugby XV was joined by a Football XI in 2006, which competed in the Worcester League. An OV Netball team enjoyed an annual fixture against the school's senior squad.

In 2013, the OV Club Committee contributed £30,000 to sponsor a large meeting room in The Keyes Building (see Chapter 9). The room, known as 'Vigornian', would be used for club meetings (the first OV Club Committee meeting held here in June 2015), including the AGM. A list of Club Presidents is recorded on a window in 'Vigornian'; this list of Club Presidents can also be found in Appendix 12.

Top: George Clarke (Oswald House 1997-2007) and Sammi Perry (Bright House 2000-07) modelling OV polo shirts and an umbrella for an 'OV Shop' catalogue, 2006

Above: 2003 leavers celebrate a ten year reunion at the Annual Reunion Dinner, 2013

Left: Former Presidents of the OV Club, with current President Rob Richards (Creighton House 1979-84), at the unveiling of the Presidents' Window in The Keyes Building's 'Vigornian' conference room, May 2015

A M Milne - Headmaster 1979-1983

Andrew McNicoll Milne was appointed Headmaster of King's in November 1978, and took up the position after David Annett retired in August 1979. Andrew arrived with his wife, Nicola, and two daughters, then aged 14 and 12.

Born in 1937, Andrew Milne was educated at Salisbury Cathedral School before reading for a degree in Modern History at Worcester College, Oxford. Milne worked his way up the ladder at Oundle School, progressing to Head of History after five years, then serving as a Housemaster before becoming Second Master in 1975.

The 'cool Headmaster'

A keen musician, Milne was a cellist in the National Youth Orchestra and, while at Oxford, was President of the University Music Club, and played with the City of Birmingham Symphony Orchestra. Nicola Milne was also a cellist, and had studied at the Royal College of Music.

It was Milne's love of music, which included playing the trombone, that led to his reputation as a 'cool Headmaster'; while teaching at Oundle School he had set up a semi-professional jazz band. 'The Milne-Macdonald Big Band' performed in the Chapter House in 1980 during the Three Choirs Festival, the first such jazz performance in the festival's history, at a concert which Milne hoped would be the first of many live jazz performances at King's. Indeed, in January 1983, his band performed at King's again, this time to a 500-strong audience in College Hall, where leading jazz trombonist Roy Williams was the headline soloist.

Developing facilities

Milne had inherited from David Annett a school which was still growing, and undertook to improve a number of facilities, including the 'bubble' - a polysphere dome to enclose the swimming pool at a cost of around £13,000, new changing facilities at the playing fields and the extension of the Winslow Building which filled in the ground floor and provided an additional laboratory on each of the first and second floors. Work was also carried out on the boarding houses and Number 9 College Green, which became the Headmaster's House; the purchase of the Old Chapel was completed, and a complex 125 year lease for Number 12 College Green was negotiated, with the Economics department moving in to the upper floor in the spring of 1983. A new classroom block was proposed for the Junior School at St Alban's, but financial constraints prevented this being approved for several years.

Threats to independent education

The improvements to the school's facilities, along with the continuing increase in pupil numbers and a new level of success in public examination results, with new performance records achieved in 1980, 1981 and 1982, continued in the face of much public debate about the future of independent education. In 1981, Margaret Thatcher's Conservative Government introduced an 'Assisted Places Scheme', which largely replaced the Direct Grant system, allowing children from less-affluent families to attend independent schools; initially fifteen Assisted Places were granted at King's, a number which grew steadily during the following decade. The Labour Party, which at that time seemed likely to win the next General Election, opposed independent education, and would certainly have ended the Assisted Places Scheme, but was considering more radical changes to the private schools' sector. Andrew Milne was a staunch defender of

Andrew Milne, the 'cool Headmaster'

independent education, served as secretary of the local branch of the Independent School Action Committee and campaigned throughout 1981 and 1982 in the local media. In December 1982, the county council voted to 'go comprehensive', eliminating 'small g' grammar schools; Milne announced that King's would continue to offer twenty places to the local authority: "The King's School will make every effort to enable academically gifted children from poorer homes throughout the county and indeed beyond, to avail themselves of what the school can offer." Fortunately for independent education, the Conservative Party was returned to power in the 1983 election, and the Assisted Places Scheme was extended and continued until Tony Blair's Labour Government took office in 1997.

'Crime and punishment'

Milne became increasingly concerned about the growing problem of students drinking; ever larger numbers of 15 to 16 years old pupils, not just from King's, but enough to give the Headmaster cause for concern, were being served in local public houses, with publicans claiming they were finding it difficult to assess the ages of their customers. The Headmaster decided to issue those students over the age of eighteen with an ID card - referred to by the boys as a 'pub pass', to enable them to prove their age, in an attempt to stamp out the practice, warning them that "excessive drinking...could ruin their future by affecting examination results."

In a problem which also affected the Headmaster of WRGS, Tom Savage, a number of younger pupils had started to become involved in shoplifting, with some even organising groups to tour local shops. A handful of pupils from both schools were either suspended or expelled.

Milne was keen to use the threat of suspension or expulsion, rather than to rely on corporal punishment - use of the cane was still legal until 1987 (some private schools were allowed to continue with caning until it was completely outlawed in 1999, if they did not receive any form of Government funding - King's accepted pupils under the Assisted Places Scheme, so was legally required to stop using corporal punishment in 1987). Writing in a newspaper article in March 1982, Milne described the value of involving parents as a deterrent and said that he shunned corporal punishment: "What I try and do is find punishments that inconvenience them directly in the context of the crime they committed. They know that if a threat of punishment is made it will be carried out. It is the discipline of personality. It concentrates the mind far more than flogging."

'Conference & Common Room'

Andrew Milne was appointed honorary editor of *Conference*, the magazine distributed to independent schools who were members of the Headmasters' Conference, with a brief to liven up the magazine which had been "getting stuffier and stuffier". He oversaw a change both in title, to *Conference & Common Room*, and in format which aimed to increase the appeal of the magazine to all school staff and to parents and Sixth Formers. Milne's second issue, Summer 1983, featured King's pupils Jo Dow and Alison Nott (later known by the stage name Bella Merlin) in *The Iron and the Oak*, a play written by King's pupil Edward Kemp, who would go on to become Director of RADA in 2008.

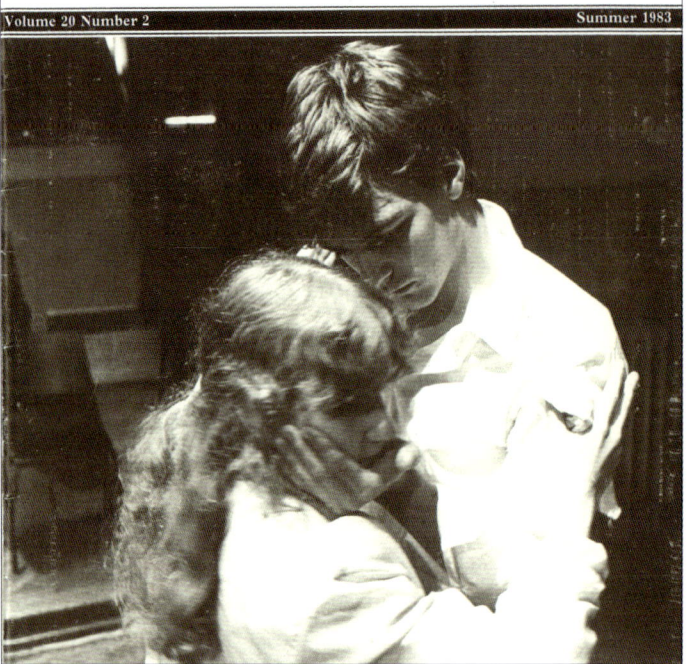

'Conference & Common Room', Summer 1983

Milne's departure

As a Head, Milne was highly regarded by some and unpopular with others – this applied in the common room and with parents; probably because he was a progressive figure compared with his predecessor, and huge changes were taking place in society and in independent schools, many of which were finding it difficult to adjust to these pressures.

It is unfortunate that Milne has been remembered by many for a schoolboy prank. In July 1982, in response to an alleged affair between the Headmaster and the matron who lived at the recently established Sanatorium in College Precincts, some boys painted a trail of red arrows from Number 9 to College Precincts. The matron quickly left King's, taking up a position elsewhere.

The reputation of the school had been damaged by the resulting publicity and Milne had become increasingly unpopular with a faction in the common room. There was also unease on the Governing Body; the Governors had to handle a very difficult situation in a balanced and fair manner. However, in due course Milne realised that he had no option but to resign, which he did in February 1983. Mr and Mrs Milne saw out the academic year with great dignity, leaving King's in July 1983.

Milne subsequently pursued a career in arts administration and was appointed music officer of the Eastern Arts Association in 1984, again rising through the ranks to become director during the restructuring of the national arts organisations in 1992. He travelled to Africa to take up the post of executive director of the Arts Council of Bophuthatswana, where he was said to have been widely respected. On returning to the UK, Milne became Operations Director for the National Lottery at the Arts Council. Survived by his former wife and their two daughters, Andrew Milne died in 1995 at the age of 58.

Andrew and Nicola Milne with Mayor of Worcester, Councillor Albert Wilks, planting the Indian bean tree to the south-east of School House

*Above: Publicity photograph of Andrew Milne, 1979, taken in the school gardens
(the name 'Creighton Memorial Gardens had fallen out of use and would not be re-instated until the 2000s)*

Below: Parents shown around King's in May 1981 - a pupil demonstrates a Van der Graaf generator

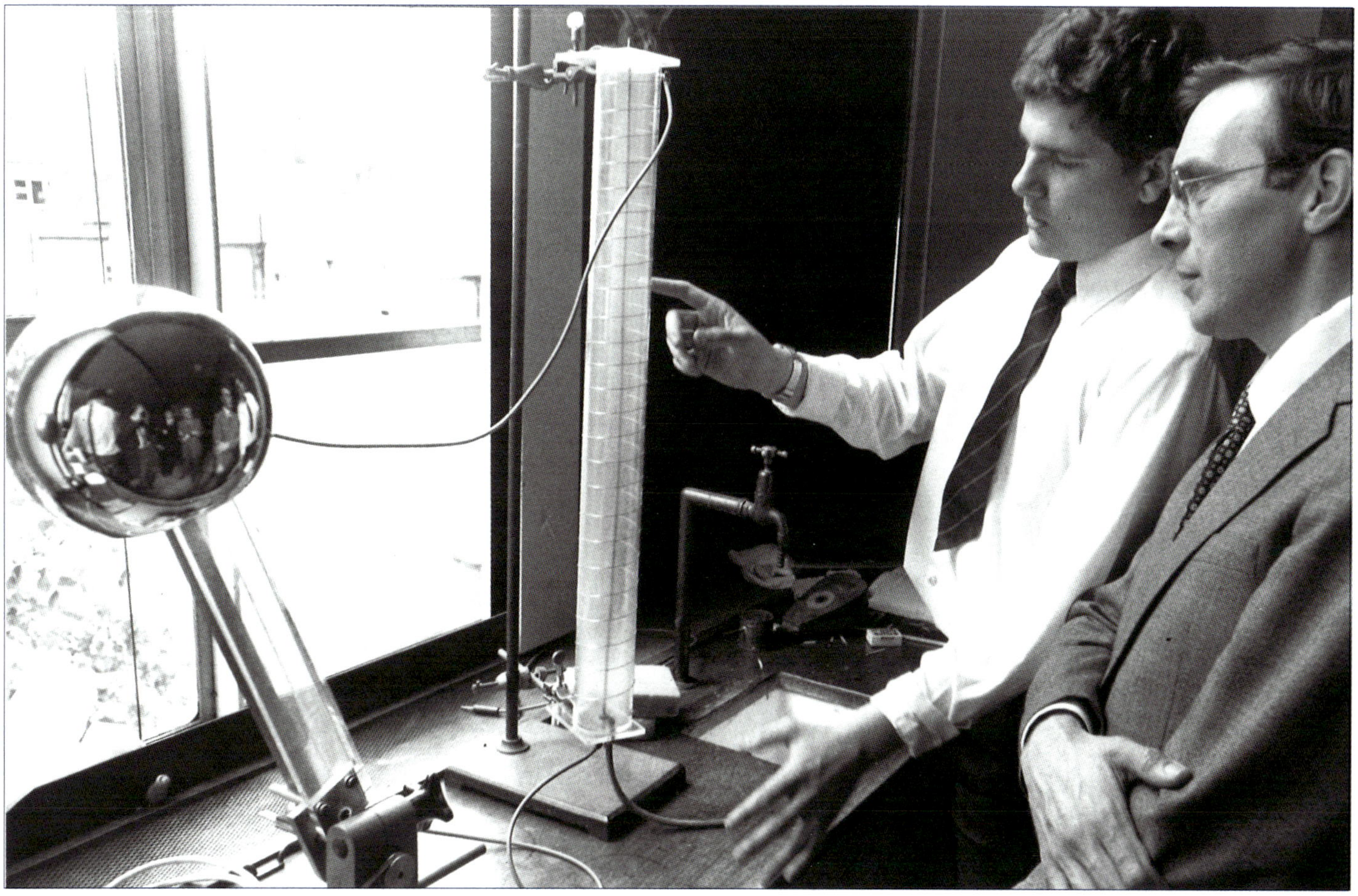

7: Junior Schools

Danny Payne and Galen Bartholomew

The Cathedral Choir School

In establishing the Cathedral Foundation along with his new school in 1541-42, Henry VIII made provision in Statute 25 (see Appendix 1) for ten choristers. These boys were to be educated by a Choristers' Master, appointed by the Dean and Chapter. This then, established the idea of a Cathedral Choir School, quite separate from the King's School, but based in close proximity.

During the 1630s, plans were drafted for a mutually benefical relationship between the 'choristers' and the 'scholars' with proposals, including one endorsed by Dean Potter in 1638, for choristers to be admitted as scholars in return for which the school would provide singers to serve in the Quire on Saturdays and holy days. These proposals were not enacted, but a Chapter Act of 1639 stated that a chorister "may be a King's Scholler".

In an 1818 issue of 'Gentleman's Magazine', an article signed 'MH' described the ten choristers:

"They do not belong as a matter of course to the College School, but by the kindness of the Dean and Chapter they are almost invariably admitted upon the Foundation, and form a part of the forty boys called King's Scholars. In addition to Latin, they are taught writing and arithmetic, but neither the two latter, nor Greek, are required by the statutes... The choristers are instructed in music by the organist."

This arrangement would certainly have been of benefit to the choristers, who would likely have received a superior education from the school than from the organist or choir master of the Cathedral, without placing an additional financial burden on the Cathedral Foundation. In 1835, a Chapter Order insisted that each chorister must be a King's Scholar for the whole time he continued in the choir.

In his 1930s history of The King's School, Macdonald cites an 1854 report "of Commissioners into the State of Cathedral Churches" which refers to a separate choristers' school for sixteen scholars who each received a chorister's salary of £6 19s 2d and free tuition and books. This school for choristers was established in 1852, but discontinued by Maurice Day in 1860. The master of the choristers' school was a lay clerk, paid £30 a year. Macdonald was unable to find evidence of where the choristers were taught.

Certainly by 1882, the strain of having a proportion of The King's School boys being absent through singing duties for large parts of the day, at a time when the school curriculum was becoming more demanding, was such that an entirely separate Choir School was formed. Reverend Herbert Woodward, a Minor Canon and subsequently Precentor, had recommended the idea to the Dean and Chapter, with the support of William Bolland, Head Master of The King's School, and duly established the school from his house in College Yard.

The accommodation was evidently so cramped that Woodward had to share a dormitory with the choristers. A classroom was provided in the Deanery, before the Dean and Chapter agreed to make Number 3 College Green (now known as Choir House) available for the Choir School.

The Dean and Chapter formally became governors of the Choir School, with Woodward as its warden and chaplain. C. B. Shuttleworth was appointed as Master; with his wife

The Choir School in 1911, showing the front and gable additions of 1902 and the Woodward Memorial Extension

he continued to maintain the school for thirty-seven years. Between 1882 and 1909, twenty-two Choir School pupils were awarded King's Scholarships.

Upon the death of Woodward in 1909, a large extension to the school building was undertaken, at a cost of £2,250 raised through donations, as a memorial. This linked Number 3 with the adjacent stable building, which was undergoing conversion work as accommodation for The King's School, in a complementary stonework design by architect Alfred Hill Parker. The extension included a day room and dining room, with a changing room at the rear on the ground floor; a large dormitory, plus a bathroom and laundry were upstairs. A small statue of Woodward stands in a niche on the front elevation of the building.

Following Shuttleworth's retirement, P. F. Davis was appointed Headmaster of the Choir School in 1923. At the suggestion of Cuthbert Creighton (Headmaster of The King's School), Davis began to establish the Choir School as a preparatory school, admitting 'non-choristers' for the first time. Pupil numbers reached fifty. However, by 1942 the Choir School had been losing money for some years, so when Davis reached retirement age, the Dean and Chapter took the difficult decision to transfer the assets, including staff and pupils and the lease for the buildings and a playing field, to the governing body of The King's School, effective 15th August 1943.

Detailed arrangements were thrashed out between December 1942 and June 1944. Arthur Davies, as both Dean and Chairman of Governors of The King's School, had interests on both sides. Ronald Kittermaster, Headmaster, wrote in 1971: *"The drawing up of this agreement gave me a marvellous opportunity of seeing the scrupulous fairness of Arthur Davies at work. He would argue for some time as Dean of the Cathedral and then he would suddenly become Chairman of the King's School Governors and reply to his own arguments."*

The main parts of the agreement were that there should be twenty-four 'singing boys', of whom ten would be Cathedral Choristers and the others Probationers. Those boys older than ten had to achieve the minimum academic standard for admission to The King's School. Whether a boys' voice had broken or not, he would no longer remain in the Cathedral Choir after the age of thirteen, to avoid missing out on his studies. The Choir would rehearse for an hour each day, six days a week, with additional rehearsals for the Three Choirs Festival.

Statue of Precentor H.H. Woodward, Choir House

The Cathedral Choir would sing at Sunday services, with additional evensong services during the week and services on saints' days. In exchange for this, 'Choir House' served as a preparatory school for all King's boys under the age of twelve. Under

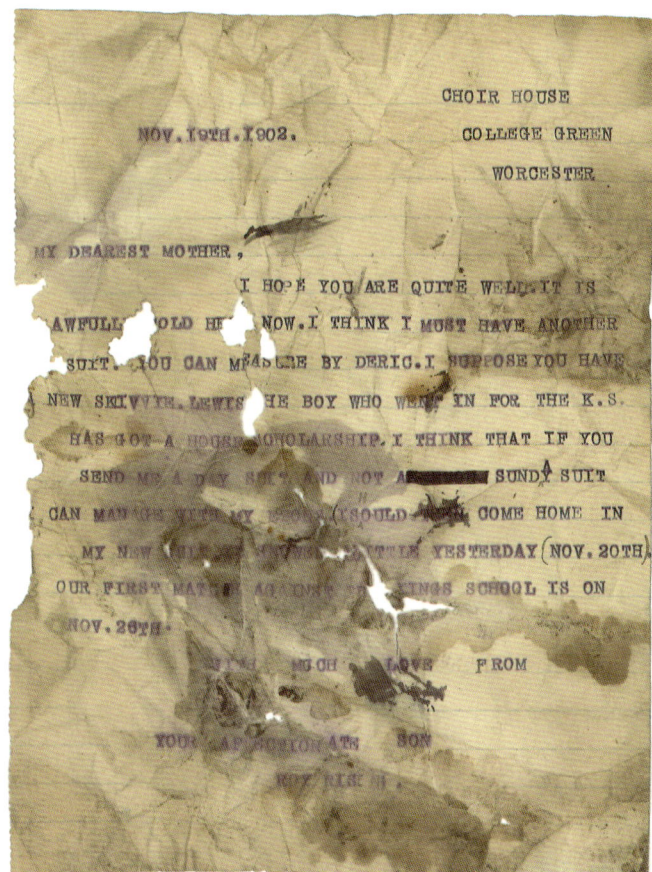

During the extensive reordering works carried out on Choir House during 2000, this letter was found beneath floorboards in the former dormitory. The letter, penned (or rather, typed) by Roy Rising, a pupil of the Choir School, is transcribed below.

NOV.19TH.1902.

CHOIR HOUSE
COLLEGE GREEN
WORCESTER

MY DEAREST MOTHER,

I HOPE YOU ARE QUITE WELL. IT IS AWFULLY COLD HERE. I THINK I MUST HAVE ANOTHER SUIT. YOU CAN MEASURE BY DERIC. I SUPPOSE YOU HAVE A NEW SKIVVIE. LEWIS, THE BOY WHO WENT IN FOR THE K.S. HAS GOT A HOUSE SCHOLARSHIP. I THINK IF YOU SEND ME A DAY SUIT AND NOT A SUNDAY SUIT I CAN MANAGE WITH MY ETONS. (I SHOULD THEN COME HOME IN MY NEW SUIT.) IT SNOWED A LITTLE YESTERDAY (NOV.20TH). OUR FIRST MATCH AGAINST THE KINGS SCHOOL IS ON NOV.26TH.

WITH MUCH LOVE FROM

YOUR AFFECTIONATE SON

ROY RISING.

Housemaster Paul Longland, there were 35 boarders and 40 day boys, including former Choir School boarders. Three staff joined Choir House: Miss Anne Campbell, Miss L Forward and C. M. Thomas; between them they taught two first forms and two second forms.

Kittermaster was pleased with the amalgamation of the Choir School, as reported in *The Vigornian* of July 1944, but that summer saw Longland leave for a position at St. Paul's School.

For further details about Choir House, see Chapter 4.

Tredennyke House, Barbourne Terrace, 2015

Tredennyke House

Coinciding with the departure of Paul Longland, the Tredennyke preparatory school in Barbourne Terrace was considering closing in 1944. Kittermaster persuaded the governors to purchase the school, for which they mortgaged the Tredennyke House building. Tredennyke House was established as an independent junior school for King's, alongside the preparatory school in Choir House, under the headship of his brother, David.

David Kittermaster served as warden of Tredennyke House until 1947, when he was appointed headmaster of Framlingham College's junior school. The Governors considered the best ongoing use for Tredennyke House, and decided upon a gradual change from preparatory school towards additional boarding accommodation, as Choir House had continued under Lester Wilson.

The transition began with the appointment of L. M. (Bill) Bailey (The Hostel 1927-33), with his wife, at Tredennyke. Seven boys were transferred from other houses and were joined by two new boarders. Tredennyke House had a diminishing number of junior boys, with the older boys continuing their allegiances with their former houses by taking part in their teams for school competitions. This continued until September 1948, when the number of boys reached seventeen - enough for Tredennyke House to field its own teams. A house tie of dark blue with "twin light blue and white stripes" had been chosen, as reported in *The Vigornian* of December 1948. By the following year, the transition to senior boarding house was complete, and Tredennyke House now numbered 28 boarders.

The demise of Tredennyke House followed the acquisition of St Alban's House, between Severn Street and Mill Street, which, with the transfer of the preparatory school from Choir House to a new Junior School at St Alban's, left Choir House, on the main school site, vacant and available to house the boarders of Tredennyke, a much less convenient twenty minute walk away through the city to Barbourne.

The building fell into decline after King's sold it in 1951, and for many years was let as a number of bedsits. In the 2000s, however, its fortunes changed as a new owner converted and extended Tredennyke House into luxury apartments.

St Alban's House

St Alban's House, located between the Diglis House Hotel and the Royal Worcester Porcelain factory on Severn Street, had been an orphanage run by the Sisters of Saint Margaret for many decades.

The site had previously been home to the Digley (Diglis) Bowling Green, and was positioned on the opposite side of the ditch (Frog Lane, later Severn Street) to the former Worcester Castle, demolished in 1813 (see Chapter 5). Excavations carried out for the development of the new building at St Alban's in 1990 revealed the site had been a Roman burial ground with the discovery of three human skeletons. The March 1717 *Worcester Post Man* mentioned "...a good convenient House with a Bowling Green and Cherry Orchard..." The house and green were, by 1779, known as the 'Hand and Glove Club', with the house used as lodgings and assembly rooms. The assembly rooms were most likely within the first 'extension' - the wing which runs south to north, connected to the original house by a grand arched doorway.

In 1859, when the 'Diglis Gardens' area was being laid out for development, the house and green was purchased by Cordelia Stillingfleet, who had established a small home and school for oprhaned and destitute girls in nearby Palace Yard, named St Alban's after the parish in which it stood. The orphanage had grown to thirty girls and so the new purchase would allow sufficent space in more suitable surroundings. An 1884 Ordnance Survey map shows the three-storey extension to the main 'St Alban's House', each floor of which consisted of one large room (presumably dormitories), as well as the later, adjoining two-storey wing.

The chapel, separate from the house until a further wing was added in 1908, was built in 1873. A plaque reads: "To the Glory of God and grateful memory of Cordelia Stillingfleet foundress of Saint Alban's Home, 1859".

Following the retirement of Miss Stillingfleet in 1888, nuns from the Sisters of Saint Margaret, based in East Grinstead, Sussex, took over the orphanage, and operated there until 1950. The number of girls had reached fifty, with a small number of boys aged between three and seven years taken in later years. The children were educated at schools around the city, including St Peter's (now a remnant of the Worcester Porcelain factory site off King Street; the adjacent St Peter the Great Church was demolished in 1976). Although an Anglican order, the nuns - and children - made use of a confessional at the east end of the chapel.

The Sisters of Saint Margaret were ready to sell the property in 1951, having closed the orphanage, but would only sell it if a buyer would agree to reatin the consecrated chapel. Royal Worcester Porcelain were unable to make such a committment and, initially, neither was The King's School.

The persuasive arguments of governor Canon Armstrong, a former headmaster, led the governing body to realise that the school's finances were in a better position than for some time and that future development needs of the school might well require some land to be purchased near to the school. St Alban's House, with an adjoining parcel of undeveloped land, known as St Margaret's, was purchased for a 'bargain price' of £22,000 in 1951. The land would later be used for the construction of a swimming pool and, eventually, a sports hall. St Alban's House would become home to the recently established Junior School.

St Alban's Chapel, 1940s

The Junior School at St Alban's

Lester Wilson, with 91 boys, moved from Choir House to the new Junior School at St Alban's House in January 1952. The junior boys were organised into three forms (First, Second and Third Forms). Because of the age range of boys, day boys from 8 to 11 and boarders from 8 to 13, all of the Cathedral Choristers were pupils at the Junior School - the connection with the Worcester Cathedral Choir would remain a key aspect in the life of St Alban's until the present day.

In July 1952, at the first Junior School Speech Day, Headmaster Ronald Kittermaster addressed parents, reassuring them that, although the standard of entry for senior school admittance had risen sharply in recent years, they need not be concerned since the academic standards of pupils at St Alban's were generally higher than those seen in candidates from outside - high praise indeed for the newly-founded Junior School.

Wilfred Thomas was appointed as Master of the Junior School in 1955 and moved into St Alban's House with his wife and young daughter. One pupil's recollections of life at St Alban's during the 1960s can be found on the following pages.

Lessons included Handwriting, Scripture, Mathematics, Latin and French, with soccer played in the winter and cricket in the summer. In the early years, sports were played at a field in Battenhall - a gruelling uphill walk away from school. The boys ate lunch in the senior school dining room in School House. A new playing area to the rear of St Alban's House, known as 'The Wasteland' by the boys, was created by the demolition of a row of houses on Mill Street in the 1970s.

The number of Junior School pupils grew steadily during the 1970s, with two portacabins or 'mobile classrooms' used for many years, one on the 'lower playground' the other next to the chapel. These were finally removed in 1986, with the Third Form pupils taught in the 'fishermen's cottages' on Severn Street (released for use when the music school could move to School House) allowing for class sizes to be reduced to twenty pupils. Entry to St Alban's was still at eight years old; 1990 would see the admission of seven year old boys, with the First Form split into Lower First and Upper First (present-day Years 3 and 4).

The Junior School, following the traditional pattern for public schools, was divided into houses, named after significant figures in the school's history: Canon Armstrong, whose vision had led to the purchase of St Alban's House and whose formidable portrait hangs in the former assembly room; Bill Bailey, who had been housemaster of Tredennyke House; Lester Wilson, first Master of St Alban's; and Wilfred Thomas, Master of St Alban's for twenty years from 1955.

Henry Searle succeeded Thomas in 1975, departing for Rydal School in 1981; Brian Griffiths covered his absence until the arrival of Paul Winter in April 1982.

Although taught at the senior school, 'middle school' boarders (known as the Fourth Forms) slept in dormitories at St Alban's House until 1985, at which time reorganisation following a reduction in boarder numbers saw these boarders move to Castle House; junior boarders remained at St Alban's until 1995.

Michael Abraham took over in 1987 before leaving to establish a junior department at Yarm School in 1990.

St Alban's Junior School, 1957

Mike Fardon

St Alban's 1959-62
The Hostel 1962-68

St Alban's in the early sixties was a predominantly boarding house although part of its population was made up of day boys, commonly known as 'day bugs', who appeared after breakfast and disappeared before tea.

St Alban's was generally known as 'Stale Buns'; if you became a pupil there you would become a 'stale bun' who in that era would look similar to his current counterpart: the short haircut (courtesy Messrs. Skan of Broad Street), short trousers (although baggier), long socks and battered black shoes.

Entry to St Alban's was by examination, a terrifying experience for the candidates, not because of the challenging content of the tests but because of the alien appearance of the invigilating master who wore a black cloak and strutted menacingly around the exam room like a crow. This anxiety was unexpectedly dispelled in one exam when, if memory proves correct, a master caught his gown on the sharp corner of a desk and ripped the fabric, drawing titters from the boys and an embarrassed glare from the master.

An anthropologist would have had a field day at St Alban's. The close-knit community of boys had its own language and customs, no doubt in common with many other similar establishments. On arrival a new boy ('new bug') would be subjected to an initiation ceremony in the dormitory in the form of a cocktail which would have to be manfully swallowed. The recipe of this cocktail remained a closely guarded secret, but it is thought that it contained toothpaste, shampoo, soap and other liquids of unmentionable origin. Other rituals also took place in the dormitory, normally late at night when the teaching staff had taken refuge in bed or at the bar of the Diglis Hotel. These customs included feasting at midnight, drinking bouts (strictly water only), tie flicking and investigating the percussive effects of pillows.

The language used, based on primitive Latin, is also of great interest:

'Quis?'	'Who wants this?'
'Ego'	'I do.'
'Bags I'	'I am claiming that.'
'Veins'	'I don't want that.'
'Cave'	'Look out, you might get a beating, a master is coming!'

As 'beating' has been mentioned, it seems appropriate to add a few words on discipline to complete the picture. Beating boys for even the most minor transgression was commonplace. It took place in a variety of locations including, interestingly, the Chapel vestry. Some masters cheated by putting golf balls in the slipper, but most boys seemed to survive the experience and it was excellent preparation for the Senior School where flogging was very common, not only by the masters but also by the senior boys. But beating was far preferable to writing out 200 times 'I must not stand a glass of water in Jones Minor's bed' – especially if you hadn't.

Daily routine was carried out with military precision. Beds were made in the morning and inspected (hospital corners obligatory). Shoes were cleaned daily and inspected, as also were hands, feet, nails, ears and necks. Shared baths were on the timetable twice a week. Meals were taken in School House and all food was compulsory and had to be eaten, including

The Junior School playground, 1960

the horrendous spam fritters. Some enterprising boys would slip unwanted morsels into blazer pockets (not always their own blazer pockets) for disposal in the School Gardens fountain.

Heating was very basic. In the Great Winter of 1962 the plumbing froze in the dormitories and it became mandatory to keep the plugs permanently in the sinks to prevent them from freezing up. A sound that remains fixed in the mind are the strident tones of the Brummy assistant matron of the time doing her 'dorm' rounds shouting 'ploogs in sinks!'

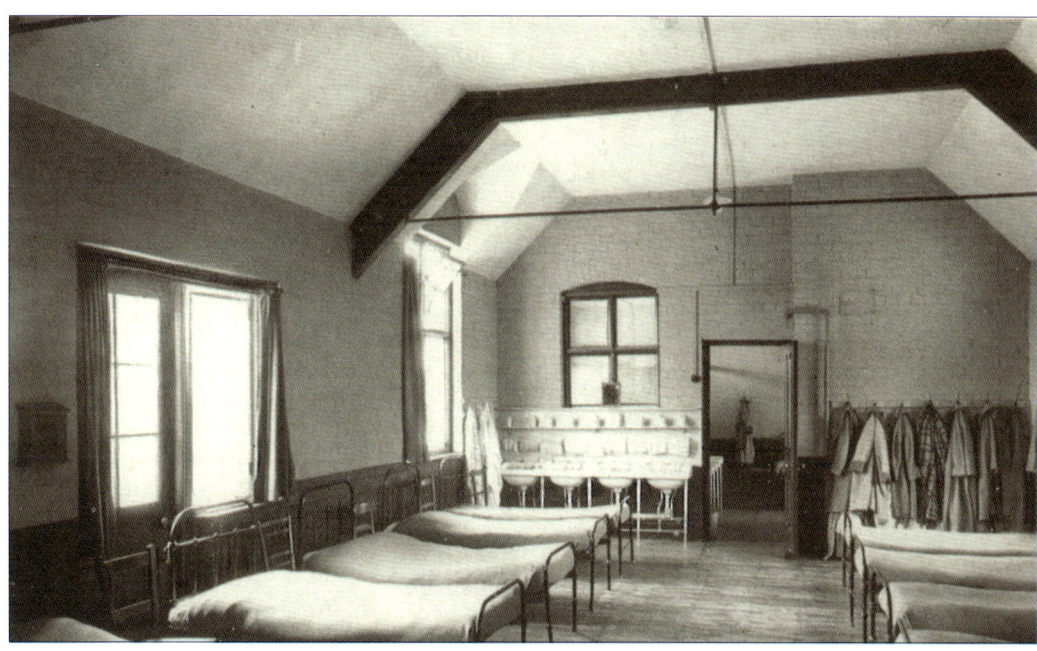

Dormitory at St Alban's

Little did the parents realise it, but the St Alban's boys gained a valuable insight into the feminine psyche. In the first place, there was co-education at St Alban's in the early 1960's. Her name was Caroline Thomas, daughter of Wilf Thomas, the Housemaster, and a very popular girl she proved to be, joining in classes and team games, and wearing the maroon blazer. The other, and possibly deeper insight into feminine psychology, was the 'assistant matron syndrome'. The turnover of assistant matrons at St Alban's was phenomenal; they were young, stunningly beautiful, and the boys would inevitably fall in love with them. When on dormitory duty at night these transitory beauties would float into the Senior 'dorm' and talk about their latest boyfriends - in the most decorous terms of course - while the more 'advanced' boys would offer homely advice.

The education that St Alban's provided was very broad and practical, providing pupils not only with academic knowledge but also giving a grounding in the 'life skills' that are harder to come by in these sedentary days of computer games and social networking. Examples that come to mind include building crystal set radios, assembled from parts supplied by Jack Porter's electrical shop in College Street. These devices involved stringing wire aerials up a tree behind the chapel, and sitting under the tree in the evening listening on headphones to various broadcasts and a great deal of hiss and crackle. Gardening was also popular: not far from the radio station and next to the wall overlooking Severn Street and School House were the boys' garden plots. At the end of every summer term these individual small plots would become the envy of Chelsea as enthusiastic young green-fingered gardeners competed for the annual Garden Cup.

Other activities – 'crazes' as they were called – included marble runs, silkworm culture, pet mice, pet snails, roller skating, racing car tracks and fort construction, to name but a few. Marble runs were particularly inventive. In the third form classroom each pupil had a separate desk with a hole in the top in which to put an inkpot and also a hole in the bottom. This formed the ideal structure for the construction of a 'run' using books, rulers and sound-deadening blotting paper, along which a marble would roll as silently as possible without alerting the teacher. The gentle 'hum and click' of over twenty marble runs operating at the same time is unforgettable.

There were also eccentricities that stay in the memory – the boy who kept his (removed) appendix in a jar in his tuck box for viewing to a select few, the boy who kept a ferret in his tuck box, the boy who made a habit of manually pumping the organ in Chapel and letting the air run out causing it to groan and drop horribly in pitch, the Scouts chaplain who wore shorts in the Chapel services and whose knee caps moved up and down as he read the prayers. This was all part of the St Alban's culture at the time.

What conclusion can be drawn from all this? There is no doubt that life in St Alban's in the early sixties was basic and regimented; but it was also eventful and character building, leaving a legacy of individualism and independence which has greatly benefited its former pupils in later life. Those early years are remembered with affection and also a slight degree of incredulity.

Mike Fardon studied English Literature at London University, and after working for Midland Bank International in London moved back to Worcester where he lectured in Business and Finance. He then went on to establish a publishing company, Osborne Books, based in Worcester. Mike's children, Cathy, Rob, Sarah, Ben and Tom all attended King's during the 1990s and 2000s.

The first girls to join St Alban's, September 1991

St Alban's 'grows up' in the 1990s

The arrival of Neil Gardner as the new Master of the Junior School in September 1990 heralded the start of significant changes at St Alban's - the extension of the school's facilities including the 'new block' and the move to co-education, in parallel with the senior school.

The new block had been long anticipated (Headmaster Andrew Milne had - unsuccessfully - pressed governors to approve it as early as 1981), but was finally constructed during 1990 at a cost of almost £400,000. At the start of construction works, builders discovered three human skeletons, with the site confirmed by archaeologists as the location of a Roman burial ground; one of the skeletons would be displayed at St Alban's until 2012. The new building provided four classrooms, two of which could open into one large room, and a science laboratory. The building was opened on 2nd March 1991 by Peter Walker MP.

During the following summer, and for the next three years, St Alban's House was extended and re-ordered, with a new playground, music and art rooms; former dormitories gave way to upgraded classrooms, staff facilities, changing rooms and a small library. The site was transforming ready for the new challenge facing St Alban's - the arrival of girls in September 1991.

The first thirteen girls joined the Lower First (present-day Year 3) as King's was celebrating its 450th anniversary, at the same time as the first girls joined the Lower Fourth (Year 7) at the senior school. The integration of girls at St Alban's had been well-prepared for and was largely trouble-free. Girls continued to join in the Lower First as the older girls progressed through the yeargroups, so that co-education was fully completed by September 1994.

Boarding ceased at St Alban's in 1995, when junior boarders transferred to Castle House, under the care of Claire Furber.

Opening of the new building, March 1991
l-r: Dr John Moore (Headmaster), Peter Walker MP,
Ray and Joy Turner (Mayor and Mayoress of Worcester),
Neil Gardner (Master of the Junior School)

Above: The new playground and rear extension, completed 1990
Below: St Alban's Junior School, photographed in 1993

U11 Rugby team, 1997-98, photographed with Head of St Alban's, John Allcott

School Chaplain, Reverend Mark Dorsett, leading an assembly in the St Alban's Chapel, 1997

Taking King's St Alban's into the 21st Century

Neil Gardner left St Alban's in 1995 when boarding at the Junior School ceased. He was succeeded as Junior School Head by John Allcott. The school continued to thrive as a happy, successful place, where boys and girls worked together well in a friendly, yet still polite and respectful, manner. The growth in pupil numbers had continued, with more than 180 pupils in 1998.

Changes in the structure of the school following the acquisition of Hawford Lodge Prep School meant that John Allcott relocated to the new school in 1998 as Head of both Junior Schools. It quickly became apparent that this was not a workable scenario, and so Deputy Head Richard Bellfield took over as Head of St Alban's in 1999. Meanwhile, the vacated Master's House had been reassigned as a house for the Bursar, Galen Bartholomew; the only resident member of St Alban's staff would now be Matron, Sylvia Egerton, until her retirement in 2006.

The change in fortune which was evident in the enlargement and expansion of facilities at the senior school at the turn of the century (see Chapter 9) began to make a significant impact on what was, since 1998, King's St Alban's. The most striking change was the construction of a large library, with a new visitors' reception below, opened in 2002 and marking the junior school's half century celebrations. This impressive building, named after Wilfred Thomas, radically altered both the look and feel of the school, providing much-improved access to books and other learning materials, as well as a more modern entrance to King's St Alban's.

As in the senior school, interactive whiteboards were installed in newly-refurbished classrooms; new equipment was provided for science, music, art and DT, and the 'old' computer suite was upgraded at the same time as the junior school was connected to the senior school's IT network.

The Wilfred Thomas Library, built in 2002, provides a striking, modern entrance to the school

Pupils making good use of the Wilfred Thomas Library

Saying Grace before lunch in the Pre-Prep Hall; Year 2 children using an interactive whiteboard; Dance in the Pre-Prep Hall

A decision was taken early on to follow closely the National Curriculum, which meant that children at King's St Alban's were taught broadly the same as children in any other school. The differences at King's St Alban's were the opportunities which could be offered by being part of a much larger organisation - the John Moore Theatre played host to a range of junior school productions; orchestral workshops were shared with the Fourth Forms; outdoor activities and camps were often based at the Old Chapel; access to an indoor swimming pool provided benefits in PE, along with the opportunity to use the senior school's expansive sports facilities. Music, drama and sports staff were shared with the senior school, allowing access to specialist teaching which might not have otherwise been available.

The junior school continued to grow, with three forms of up to 20 pupils in Years 5 and 6 (the standard year group names were adopted in line with King's Hawford). However, the quality of maintained primary schools had improved during the early 2000s, and it was proving less easy to recruit new pupils into Year 3, as the decline in local pre-prep schools (Sunnyside School, opposite Tredennyke House on Barbourne Terrace, closed in 2005) meant that this was no longer, in Worcester at least, a natural age for children to move schools.

Because of this recruitment challenge, action was needed if King's St Alban's was to remain viable in the long term. The brave solution was to invest in an expansion of King's St Alban's by teaching children from Reception (4 years old) to Year 2 (6 years old), which would be established as a 'pre-prep' department and allow children to progress naturally into Year 3.

The Howell Building, Pre-Prep Department at King's St Alban's, 2015, viewed from the Junior School playground

The closure of The Alma public house in Mill Street provided an opportunity for a pre-prep department to be housed within a purpose-designed building, and this was achieved in the Howell Building, named after retiring Chairman of Governors Donald Howell, which opened in 2009. The success of the pre-prep department led to a high demand for places, and so the building was extended, through the purchase of adjoining properties, in 2015, which included the provision of a separate play area for pre-prep children as well as a second classroom for each of the three pre-prep year groups.

Richard Bellfield, with wife Anita, who had been school secretary and later registrar for a number of years, left King's St Alban's in March 2012. Deputy Head Rachel Duke served as Acting Head for a term before a new Head of King's St Alban's, Ian Griffin, was appointed for September 2012.

The opening of The Howell Building, 2009: Richard Bellfield (Head of KSA, 2000-2012), Tim Keyes (Headmaster), Donald Howell (OV and Chairman of Governors 1986-2010), Galen Bartholomew (Bursar) and Alex Roberts (Head of Pre-Prep)

King's St Alban's Junior School, September 2015

Hawford Lodge, 1955-1996

Interviewed in 2010, Douglas Garrad, previous owner of Hawford Lodge, recalled, *"When my wife and I opened Hawford Lodge as a new day preparatory school we didn't really imagine that independent schools would still be in existence 55 years later, but here they still are and here Hawford still is. We knew what we wanted the school to be like – friendly, happy, hardworking, well-mannered and academically successful, a bit of a cliché really. I think we achieved most of this, but how could it continue indefinitely? When King's, under Donald Howell's guidance, took over the school, they took it upon themselves to see that the spirit and the feeling of the place continued in the way we had always wanted it to go. They did a great deal to improve the facilities by building fantastic new classrooms and added splendid modern equipment and facilities. I am not so keen, personally, on the introduction of palm trees to the Worcestershire countryside and on the plethora of signs... but most things I do like very much: the friendliness of the staff, the manners of the children and the general feeling of good nature and success. I am very glad that Hawford is now part of The King's School and so has acquired a history of not 50 years but 500 years. My grateful thanks go to Donald Howell for creating this opportunity for the school my wife and I founded."*

Douglas and Mary Ann Garrad, the school's founders, purchased Hawford Lodge in 1955. Douglas was 29 and Mary Ann 24; they had two boys aged two and three, later joined by two girls who were born in the upstairs rooms of the main house. Douglas had been teaching for four years at Bilton Grange, a prep school near Rugby, and he had been left £6,000 by an uncle which he wanted to spend on a building for a school. There were no regulations at that time – you could just start a school wherever you liked! On a cold day in January 1955 Douglas and Mary Ann looked round Hawford Lodge. It was quite shabby, but they liked the atmosphere and thought it had space and potential, so they bought it. By September 1955 when the school opened, they had signed up 15 pupils.

The Garrads had purchased an interesting property. Hawford Lodge is one of a number of similar Georgian houses in this part of Worcestershire. To its east, on the other side of the road now known as the A449, lies the large and more imposing Hawford House, now converted into flats. The recently re-opened Droitwich Canal is situated on the north side of the property (this was Brindley's second canal opened in 1776).

The residence and estate known as Hawford Lodge was sold at public auction on 23rd January 1843 at the Star and Garter Hotel, Worcester. Copies of the particulars describing the property at that time still exist, along with information about various owners of the property during the late nineteenth and early twentieth centuries. One interesting story relates to a Dutch diamond merchant named Van Moppes, who took the lease on Hawford Lodge for the duration of the Second World War. It is said that Mr Van Moppes kept a large quantity of diamonds hidden in various places at Hawford Lodge and, periodically throughout the war, he visited Hatton Garden to sell these in order to finance the Free Dutch Forces. Despite numerous excavations at Hawford in recent years, diamonds have yet to be found, but there is always hope!

Hawford Lodge School prospectus, 1992
The photograph shows the main house and pupils in their red and grey uniforms.

This then is the background to Douglas and Mary Ann Garrad's venture. They paid £6,500 for Hawford Lodge, £500 more than planned because someone else offered £6,250 after the Garrads had offered £6,000. The Hawford Lodge they purchased had quite a lot in common with the property described in 1843: in 1955 Hawford had electricity only on a 200 volt supply, and water was pumped up from a series of wells and stored in a large reservoir under the courtyard; in dry weather the wells did not replenish sufficiently overnight and water was short. Heating was provided by paraffin heaters, something unimaginable in these days when Health and Safety has to be given so much greater emphasis. As Mary Ann Garrad put it, *"we didn't think about the risks; we were young and excited and felt it was the right time"*. Mains water was not installed until 1963 and central heating for the main building followed in 1966.

It was certainly the right time because the population bulge after the Second World War meant that the new school could grow rapidly and it became highly successful. The school started with one promised child (John Horton aged eight from Crowle), but by the summer of 1955 there were 15 pupils, 46 pupils a year later and, by the summer of 1957 there were 82 pupils. As their first members of staff, the Garrads had appointed John Bartholomew Widdowson and his wife Felicity. John Widdowson, subsequently headmaster of two independent schools in Scotland, was evidently a good first appointment. His post at Hawford was unknown to Galen Bartholomew at the time of his appointment as Bursar in 1996, although John Widdowson was one of his father's first cousins – an extraordinary coincidence which strengthened Galen's resolve to make the merger of Hawford and King's a success.

It was decided to have two forms, 4A and 4B, since this gave scope to add forms above and below. John Widdowson taught mainly Maths and Latin while Douglas Garrad taught most subjects, with Felicity Widdowson teaching Art and Mary Ann Garrad teaching Music as well as preparing school lunches each day. James Herbert wrote recently: *"The most eye-opening things were the teaching styles of Messrs Garrad and Widdowson. We marched round the room conjugating the French verb* j'ai *and were called 'copper bottomed nitwits'!"*

The school day started at 8.50 am and finished at 4.00 pm. However there were clubs most afternoons after school, including a very successful chess club run by Malcolm Darling, who became Second Master after John Widdowson. Most pupils went home on the public bus, which stopped just outside Hawford. On market days (Thursdays) the bus was often full, so the Garrads and Widdowsons occasionally had to ferry pupils home in their cars, and parents were also pressed into service sometimes. In those days there was no restriction on numbers in cars nor any laws relating to seatbelts. The school uniform consisted of a zip-up grey jacket, grey corduroy shorts, a grey shirt, long grey socks, a red tie and a red cap. The emphasis was on a practical and washable uniform, rather than a smart one, but there were also blazers and prefects could wear long grey trousers. Peter Griffiths, one of the 'First Fifteen' founding pupils, recalled: *"In the winter we were allowed to have bonfires in morning break. There were plenty of branches produced from clearing the site and we were allowed a small amount of paraffin carried from the yard storage tank in a saucepan to revive the fire. We then used to stand around it keeping warm."*

Sport and outdoor activities were always important at Hawford. To begin with soccer was played in the Christmas term and rugby in the spring term, but in due course these were swapped. Cricket was the main sport in the summer term and Douglas Garrad and a parent usually drove the cricket XI to matches in two cars. To begin with there were not enough children to form sports teams, but in the first summer term a cricket match was organised, although the opposition didn't turn up so the parents who had come to watch made up a parents' XI. Neil Gaylor, another of the 'First Fifteen' recalls: *"In sport I remember we were beaten so comprehensively in our first rugger matches that our opponents fielded weaker teams the next season and we were greatly encouraged when we began to win!"*

As the school grew, a house system was established, initially with two houses (Greeks and Romans), with two further houses (Medes and Persians) added subsequently. The house system

Hawford Lodge School, 1955: the 'First Fifteen'
Back row: Roger Hirst, Alastair Watson, Richard Denny, Peter Perks, Neil Gaylor, Andrew Jackson, John Wright
Middle row: John de Mierre, Mary Ann Garrad, Douglas Garrad, John Widdowson, Felicity Widdowson, Anthony Williams
Front row: Tim Shaw, Jonathan Goodwin, Peter Griffiths, John Horton, Andrew Beard. (Missing: James Herbert)

King's Remembered

Leanne Sheen *King's Hawford 1993-99*
Wulstan House 1999-2006

My first experience of Hawford Lodge was my scholarship interview. I do not remember it but my mother recounts that I came out of the interview asking why the headmaster (then Tony Race) had laughed. He had asked a simple question: "Leanne, what do you think of team sports?" I answered "I don't know. I don't play team sports. I'm only six."

I did get involved with sport at Hawford, particularly netball (led by Linda Race), as a scar on my knee testifies. It wasn't all about being knocked over though. We always had a lovely tea after each match! I have a special memory of a national netball tournament where we got to stay overnight with hosts. Our cross-country runs on the grounds were also particularly fun, muddy events. On one occasion I was followed by a cow and scrambled to get over the metal gate at the other end of the field. Summer term was all about swimming. I had an ear operation just before starting at Hawford and I was very excited to be finally allowed to learn to swim. I swam my first width in the outdoor pool at Hawford and earned myself a merit in the process!

Until Hawford, my break times at primary school had been spent on a tarmac playground (not playing team sports). One of the unique things about Hawford is its location and setup. Driving up the winding lane felt like entering a different world even though the school was not far from Worcester (or the busy A449). During breaks we played simple outdoor games: conkers, marbles around the roots of the great tree that once stood at the entrance and scrambling under and over the log. We were also allowed into the shrubbery to run around and climb trees. I am sure this must have resulted in a few trips to the kitchen for a plaster. The outdoor nature of the school had its disadvantages though: one day I went home distraught after learning that foxes kill chickens (and why) after our school chickens disappeared overnight.

I do not have much recollection of the academic side of Hawford. However, two things are clear. First, the education at Hawford set me up marvellously for the move to the senior school. The transition was completed with ease. Second, Hawford sparked my love for languages. Prior to languages club at Hawford, which was run by Mrs Roscoe, I had only benefited from a "French for Tots" tape! I followed languages as an academic subject all the way to university but languages have long been an integral part of my daily life, both personal and professional.

A lot of people remember the food from their time at school. Morning break was a rush en masse through the courtyard to the kitchen hatch where we would pick up a glass of milk and our homemade treat for the day such as an iced bun or jam tart. Lunchtimes at Hawford were always very busy with a teacher serving the food at the head of the table and passing it up the table to the pupils. We were fortunate at Hawford to have basic cooking lessons for which we brought in tupperware to take our results home. At the end of one year, our lessons culminated in preparing for a summer picnic and I was tasked with making crisps by hand.

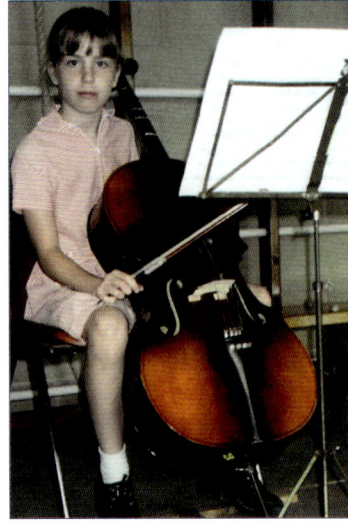

My grandmother drove me to and from Hawford. When I asked her what her memories of that time were, she promptly replied "waiting for you". I was always in some after-school club or other! One year in drama club we performed Mark Billen's 'The Love for Three Oranges'. I think I played Smeraldina as I recall having to hide under a stool for the first part of the play. My grandmother also remembered my cello and specifically it being almost as big as me. I started music lessons at Hawford and enjoyed them immensely (despite having to carry the cello).

I did not carry on drama or music in the senior school to any significant extent. My inner lawyer was already developing and I moved on to activities such as school journalism, debating and helping in the school archives. However, I was always grateful that Hawford had such a vast array of activities as it gave me the opportunity to explore many different interests at an early age.

What did I not miss from Hawford? The red and grey uniform and specifically the thick, red, woolly tights that formed part of our winter uniform. The senior school uniform seemed so much more civilised…

During her time at King's, Leanne was a Queen's Scholar, School Monitor and Editor of 'The King's Herald'. After leaving King's in 2006, Leanne read Modern and Medieval Languages at Cambridge with a year abroad in Paris and Buenos Aires. She is now a lawyer at Allen & Overy in Frankfurt, having completed her legal training in their London and Frankfurt offices.

Cricket match at Hawford Lodge, c.1990

included a very effective prefect system, with a Head Boy and four Heads of Houses, in addition to a housemaster. There was also a star system and boys could be awarded half to two stars, either red for good or blue for bad, in three areas – conduct, industry and manners. The house with the most stars each term won the 'Star Cup'. Manners were hugely important, especially table manners. The dining room was where it is now, but the pupils sat at house tables with a member of staff on each table. Music and Drama were also strengths and verse-speaking competitions were held regularly. These took place in the barn, later known as the theatre, which for many years served as a good school hall and was situated where the Kindergarten is today.

An early project was the swimming pool, built in 1959. Parents were keen on this project but Douglas Garrad felt he could not afford it, at a time when the school was still becoming established. A parent who was a solicitor called a meeting and asked those present to write down on separate pieces of paper how much they were prepared to put towards the swimming pool fund. When these figures were added together, there was more than £1,000 – enough to build the pool. The pool was hand dug by two Irishmen, and it was filled by the fire brigade because the wells could not produce anything like enough water. The Headmaster dived in to inaugurate it and the same pool serves Hawford today. In those days the pool had no filtration system and it was green – as Garrad put it, *"If someone had drowned, you wouldn't have seen a body at the bottom."* It was a different era!

The Cobb was first built as a covered play area, at the suggestion of a teacher named Christopher Cobb, who then tragically died suddenly. Parents again raised the money to build the play area in the mid-sixties and named it in his memory. Later there was further fundraising to turn it into a basic building in the seventies and ultimately into the present-day hall. The classroom block now known as the Garrad Building and used as Science, Language and Art classrooms was originally cattle yards. The walls were not moved but everything else was rebuilt. The acquisition of further farm buildings became the Garrads' present home, known as Lower Hawford. This allowed for further expansion of the school, which had started on the ground floor of the main building, with the Garrad family living on the upper two floors.

Pupil numbers continued to grow in the sixties and seventies to a high point of more than 200. In 1982, Douglas and Mary Ann Garrad retired from the active management of the school and Tony Race took over as Headmaster. Mr Race was already a much-valued and extremely effective teacher and had been a housemaster at Hawford Lodge for some years before taking over as headmaster, a position he held for sixteen years. As the owner, Douglas Garrad maintained control of the business side of Hawford Lodge, and the school retained its special character although, despite the introduction of a lower school, *'Little Hawford'*, and coeducation, there followed a period during which numbers declined steadily and the future as a stand-alone prep school looked uncertain. A number of factors account for this change of fortune, notably the increasing move away from traditional prep schools, with a transfer at age 13, towards junior schools, where the transfer to secondary schools takes place at age 11 in line with the state system. These developments led ultimately to the purchase of Hawford Lodge by The King's School, Worcester in 1996.

Douglas Garrad, with Jim Turner (Head of King's Hawford) and pupils at the turf-cutting ceremony for the Bartholomew Barn, 2015

King's Hawford

How Hawford Lodge became King's Hawford

In 1996 it was relatively rare for a school like King's Worcester to own two junior schools. Yet the purchase of what was then Hawford Lodge, which was agreed late in 1995 and completed in early 1996, was a bold and shrewd move by the King's Governing Body at that time. When King's purchased Hawford Lodge, it was a preparatory school taking pupils up to the age of 13 with 123 pupils and, while it was clear that there was something very special about the Hawford culture, its separate Governing Body realised that a partner was needed to enable much-needed capital investment and to introduce a more modern management approach with a reinvigorated emphasis on academic standards.

The Grammar School, whose junior school was based within their central Worcester site at that time, was in the process of negotiating the purchase of Hawford Lodge with a view to separating its junior school and thus releasing space on its senior school site. Staff at Hawford were concerned, having overheard casual remarks referring to redundancies and potential developments on the Hawford site which they felt to be inappropriate. News of this also concerned the King's Governors because Hawford had for some time been a major supplier of pupils to its senior and junior schools, and relationships between King's and Hawford were close. So it was that the King's Governors entered separate negotiations and, much to the relief of the existing Hawford staff, quickly reached agreement to purchase Hawford Lodge and its site for £540,000 (comprising £425,000 for the site and buildings and a further £115,000 to settle outstanding liabilities).

The long-term potential benefit to King's of having two junior schools feeding 'home grown' pupils into its senior school was obvious; now the challenge was to follow a strategy that ultimately would result in two complementary junior schools with similar standards, both financially successful as separate entities so that neither would deplete the overall resources of the King's Foundation, and seen as equal but alternative routes into the senior school. Hawford would be attractive because of its country setting one mile from the edge of Worcester, while St Alban's would be attractive because it shared the senior

Rear of the main house, 1995

school site with its many facilities, its links to the Cathedral and its proximity to the city centre and the south side of Worcester. The aim was to achieve this while retaining that special Hawford culture often recalled fondly by generations of its old boys, so it was agreed to leave Hawford largely untouched for a couple of years apart from some initial capital investment, in order to see how it fared and to gain a deeper understanding of it. For this period (1996 to 1998), Hawford's Governing Body remained a separate entity, but its composition was changed so that it contained a majority of King's Governors and King's could thus exercise ultimate control. Brian Tait, a long-standing and genial King's Governor and Hawford and King's parent, became the Chairman of the Hawford Lodge Board.

Immediate further necessary expenditure involved repairing the swimming pool, which was empty due to a major leak, some investment in ICT facilities and important structural work to the buildings, notably to the roofs and wiring. The teachers' salaries were being paid at 80% of the public sector rates because that was all that the business could afford, but King's gave an undertaking that this would increase in stages, first to state levels and ultimately to King's levels, but only as the success of Hawford in business terms allowed this. Meanwhile, the King's Governors monitored the financial performance of Hawford separately and authorised all significant capital expenditure. Galen Bartholomew had been appointed Bursar of King's in early 1996 and part of his initial brief was to *"sort out Hawford"*; for those first two years he was the only senior member of staff common to both King's and Hawford, since, with a separate Governing Body, the Head of Hawford did not report to the Headmaster of King's. In September 1996, three weeks after taking up his appointment at King's, Galen Bartholomew was shown round Hawford by Brian Tait; he subsequently remarked that everything he saw there made pound signs flash up in his mind – no surprise since the structural survey had estimated that the cost of urgent repairs alone would amount to £63,000. It was clear that there were many challenges, but the overall aim was to make the necessary changes without losing that Hawford 'spirit' and this always remained uppermost in the minds of decision-makers at The King's School.

Maypole dancing at the May Fete, 2007

King's Hawford within the King's Foundation, since 1996

Following the acquisition by King's of Hawford Lodge, it quickly became clear that there was a need for a structured approach to capital investment at Hawford over many years. This started in 1997 with a major refurbishment of the main roof. The complete rebuilding of what became known as the Garrad Building took place in 1998, followed by annual projects covering the kitchens in 1999 and the changing rooms in 2000. This marked the end of the first phase of capital expenditure covering areas where refurbishment was considered essential.

A significant surge in demand for places at Hawford began and numbers increased during 1997 to about 170. However, these fell back in the next academic year and in summer 1998 there was not a single new pupil registered to start at Hawford the following term. King's had been monitoring developments carefully for two years. The marketplace was clearly communicating a feeling that The King's School should be more proactive in its management approach towards Hawford. The time had come for significant strategic moves to make Hawford Lodge a full part of the King's Foundation and this could not be delayed.

The new strategy now adopted had been drawn up in strict confidence by Galen Bartholomew over the previous few months in consultation with key King's Governors. It was communicated to parents immediately after the end of summer term 1998 by Donald Howell as Chairman of Governors, following approval by the King's Governing Body a week before the end of term. Hawford Lodge would be known by the new name of King's Hawford, with St Alban's being re-named King's St Alban's at the same time. Years 7 and 8 at Hawford were to be phased out, with Hawford becoming a junior school with two forms per year group transferring pupils at 11+, like St Alban's. The separate Hawford governing body was disbanded and the management structure was altered. In future, the new Head of King's Hawford would report to the Headmaster of the senior school for curriculum and administrative matters and to the Bursar on financial, premises and facilities matters; this identical reporting structure for both junior school Heads was subsequently written into the Governors' Scheme of Management and Delegation. The complete refurbishment of what became the Garrad Building, with the prospect of further capital development as the school grew, was also announced, along with a new uniform based on the St Alban's uniform but badged for Hawford. These changes in management responsibility represented an increase in workload for Tim Keyes, who was taking over as Headmaster of the King's Foundation the following term, but he was soon to become a popular and respected figure in all three schools.

The urgent nature of the changes described meant that there was no time to appoint a new Head of King's Hawford, but the solution here, recognised as less than ideal, was to appoint a joint Head of Hawford and St Alban's. John Allcott, who had been appointed Head of St Alban's in 1995, accepted this position and held it for four terms until taking up appointment as Headmaster of Farleigh School. During these four terms, Allcott did much to introduce King's procedures and expectations at Hawford. Bob Middleton took over as Head of King's Hawford in January 2000 and held this position until July 2006, when he moved to become Headmaster of Heathmount School. He oversaw an expansion in pupil numbers at King's Hawford, which was underpinned by a consistent raising of standards. It was his vision that resulted in the completely new and enlarged Kindergarten with its own secure courtyard opposite the Head's house and, by the time he left, Hawford had been part of King's for ten years and its staff were fully assimilated as part of the King's Foundation.

Middleton was succeeded by Jim Turner, who came to King's from Sunderland High School, where he had been Head of the Primary Section for some years. He was also an experienced School Inspector, and quickly identified those areas at Hawford still in need of development. Chief amongst these was the school's academic standards, since King's Hawford's academic performance was still somewhat below that of St Alban's, although the tendency of parents to transfer their children from Hawford to St Alban's at 7+ to give them a better chance of gaining a place at the senior school had stopped some years previously. Happily King's Hawford would become regarded as being equal to St Alban's academically, supported by the annual entrance tests.

Jim Turner, a great enthusiast, championed sport at Hawford, including canoeing on the canal, swimming and camping, as well as the more traditional school sports. He also showed a deep commitment to the arts and made some excellent staff appointments which led to a blossoming of Art, Music and Drama. During his tenure as Head, Hawford was awarded, and has since retained, Artsmark Gold accreditation. Turner worked effectively with the Hawford Parents' Committee, who raised many thousands of pounds for charitable and school projects, the swimming pool enclosure being perhaps the most significant of the latter. Hawford was a national champion in Chess in 2014 and a regional Bridge champion in 2015. The whole school inspection in 2012 showed an outstanding improvement overall and the Early Years inspections have all been rated as 'outstanding'.

The Hawford staff has always devoted much additional time to extra-curricular activities: a hallmark of good independent schools. The dedication of Penny Bradley and Jill Willis to the younger children has been exceptional for many years; generations of children remember them with real affection. An outstanding appointment by Jim Turner was of Dan Peters as Head of Music

Jim Turner with Dan Peters and pupils, King's Hawford Speech Day, 2015

King's Hawford from the air, September 2015, facing south (above) and facing east (below)

Above: The main house, with its modern reception area, stands at the front of the site, with access to the newer buildings beyond. The recently re-opened Droitwich Canal runs to the east of the house (right of photograph).

Below: The scale of recent developments is clear, with a central landscaped area flanked by the playground, Music School and The Cobb. To the south (right of photograph) is the Garrad Building, behind which is the Kindergarten and Head's Cottage. Beyond the gravelled parking area, the Bartholomew Barn is taking shape; the Barn will be surrounded on three sides by the generous school playing fields.

The clock sprire sits proudly atop The Cobb

in 2007 and then Deputy Head in 2011. Peters was to transform Music at Hawford and, over eight years, the peripatetic instrumental take-up increased from under 20% to more than 80%, with consequent high-profile successes at the Worcester Competitive Arts Festival. He also established a highly successful school orchestra and introduced a programme of high-quality performance events, including productions accompanied by a live backing band of children, many of which he wrote and composed himself. His record as Deputy Head and a Maths teacher was equally impressive. Mention should also be made of Rosemary Cook, who was (single-handed) School Secretary to three Heads and who is remembered in the rose garden next to the Music School.

Against this background, the second phase of capital expenditure related to desirable development and expansion of the site, as pupil numbers increased towards the 330 at Hawford in 2015. The following projects were undertaken during the early years of the 21st century on an almost annual basis: the new Kindergarten in the former theatre; a complete overhaul of all the sash windows in the main house; an enlargement of the parking area; a new library; refurbishment of the dining room; a sewage treatment plant; a new music school and classroom block; a new WC block for pupils and visitors; landscaping of the central area; extension and refurbishment of the Head's house; a new administration area and Head's office; refurbishment of The Cobb, which was given a new insulated roof; and a cover and space heaters for the swimming pool so that it could be used throughout the year. Much of the work was carried out by members of the King's maintenance team under the Clerk of Works, Tony Norris, because this was the most cost-effective approach. The determination throughout this programme was to retain the essential character of Hawford. This led to the concept of the Hawford site and its buildings as a mini-village, friendly and unthreatening in scale but allowing young people progressive freedom to move around the site with reduced supervision as they become older.

Some years into his headship, Jim Turner made clear to the Governors that the lack of a multi-purpose hall at Hawford was the only significant deficiency in terms of accommodation which he felt might affect Hawford's future adversely. The Cobb is a very useful space and will continue to be so, particularly for the younger children, but a larger hall for sports, assemblies, drama, music and dance with a sprung floor, changing and kitchen facilities and tiered retractable seating, would be a huge asset to the school. Mindful that building costs were likely to escalate significantly as the economy picked up, the Governing Body commissioned a study and competition: the proposal put forward by Associated Architects won. The site finally chosen from six evaluated was on the upper fields next to the car park. Because of the sensitivity of the site, the design chosen was based on a contemporary architectural version of a traditional barn, which is highly appropriate as the Georgian Listed Hawford Lodge was originally a farmhouse. The Governors authorised expenditure on this project early in 2015, with the hope that it would be completed by the end of 2015, the year in which Hawford celebrated its sixtieth anniversary. The Governors were also delighted to agree to Tim Keyes' suggestion that the new hall should be known as the Bartholomew Barn to commemorate Galen Bartholomew's twenty years of service as Bursar and Clerk to the Governors of King's between 1996 and 2016, and in particular his contribution to King's Hawford.

King's Hawford is a highly valued and successful part of the King's Foundation. Generations of enthusiastic and inspired young people continue to benefit from the school Douglas and Mary Ann Garrad founded in 1955. To paraphrase Douglas Garrad's comments, most of what was intended has been achieved and, crucially, the Hawford spirit has been retained and is very much part of the King's Foundation.

Architect's rendering of the 'Bartholomew Barn', the new multi-purpose hall due for completion in 2015-16 and named in honour of Galen Bartholomew.

8: King's at the end of the second millennium

J M Moore - Headmaster 1983-1998

Following a couple of turbulent years at King's, a steadying influence was needed, and this came in the form of Dr John Michael Moore, who became Headmaster in September 1983.

Born in 1935, Moore was educated at Rugby School and studied at Clare College, Cambridge. His teaching career, as a classicist, saw him progress from Winchester to Radley, where he was Head of Classics and later Director of Sixth Form Studies.

Dr Moore arrived at The King's School with his wife Gill who was involved with European consumer affairs, for which she was awarded an OBE. Moore himself was involved at a senior level of a number of educational groups, including the Headmasters' Conference, for which he chaired the Academic Committee for a number of years, and the Choir Schools Association; he also became a Senior Magistrate for the City of Worcester in 1986.

Big decisions

There would be little opportunity for the school to enjoy sailing through calm waters in the 1980s and 1990s. The return to office of the Conservative Government in the 1983 election ensured that the Assisted Places Scheme would continue, and indeed it was extended during the following ten years, but a significant change in the examinations system would be introduced from 1986.

The General Certificate of Secondary Education (GCSE) was to replace the two-tier qualification system of 'O' Levels and CSEs, as well as the Joint 16-plus examinations. The unified system would offer a single grading system based on that of the 'O' Level grades - A,B and C at 'O' Level would become GCSE grades A, B and C and equivalent to CSE grade 1; D and E grades (for both 'O' Level and GCSE) were equated to CSE grades 2 and 3 respectively and new grades of F and G would be introduced, comparable to CSE grades 4 and 5. The intention was to drive up standards in education, especially in the expanded comprehensive schools' system, with nationally agreed guidelines for courses and examinations - the number of examination boards was reduced from 20 to five. An exacting syllabus would be produced for each course to ensure that teachers and pupils understood the expectations for each grade level, with a focus on practical application of subject knowledge instead of a straightforward test of memory and presentation of information.

This significant overhaul of the education system was just one of many changes introduced by successive education ministers during the following decades, as governments recognised the importance of education both to society and the fast-growing economy, and each sought to mark out improvements and refinements.

Among the next key developments would be the National Curriculum, introduced in 1988, which determined the precise content of each academic subject, and set out schemes for delivery of the content. King's was not required to follow the National Curriculum, either at the senior school or St Alban's, although pressure and expectations from parents would result in the school, with most other independent schools, following the maintained sector in the required curriculum changes.

The school was having to weather these storms of change against a backdrop of troubling finances: boarding schools

Dr John Moore

across England were suffering a decline in popularity during the 1980s, perhaps resulting from parents who grew up in the more liberal 1960s. The number of boarders at King's had fallen significantly, to a level at which School House was, effectively, redundant as a boarding house for boys. However, the number of girls in the Sixth Form, both boarders and day girls based in College House, had incresed significantly by the mid-1980s, requiring a second girls' house. Several staff and governors' meetings had discussed the option of becoming fully co-educational, or at least mixing the day houses for boys and girls, but there was sufficient resistance to delay this level of integration.

Eliot House, established in 1986, was based in Number 12 College Green, with Robert Allum as Housemaster for a large group of day girls; the House took its name from Canon Peter and Lady Alethea Eliot, who had lived at Number 12 from 1965 to 1975.

The question of co-education had been raised, however, and the declining number of boy boarders could not allow the Headmaster to shy away from making two of the most significant decisions in the history of The King's School. Plans would be drawn up during the second half of the decade to shift focus from boarding towards day pupils and to become a fully co-educational school, from the Lower First at St Alban's through to the Upper Sixth.

A number of changes could be made to accommodation at the senior school thanks to the building programme undertaken by David Annett and the acquisition of new buildings by Andrew Milne.

The Chappel Memorial Reading Room (see Chapter 5) was

Aerial photograph of the school, taken in 1985 - the Dining Hall and Wolfson Buildings were established parts of the site; the warehouse on the site of the John Moore Theatre (built 1986) had yet to be demolished [far right of the photo]; the ground floor of the Winslow Building had not yet been filled in and the 'Fishermen's Cottages', home of Oswald House from 1984, did not yet have the obligatory external fire escape; the original summer house was still standing in the gardens [bottom left corner] and the Fives Courts had been enclosed in timber and corrugated sheeting. This photograph was likely to have been taken on a Friday afternoon - C.C.F. cadets can be seen parading on the playground.

redesignated 'New Passey Hall', allowing 'Passey Hall' on the ground floor of School House to be converted into day house accommodation, along with the two dormitory levels above. In 1989, School House began the transition to day boy house, with accommodation on the first (middle) floor of the building. Wulstan House moved in below and Kittermaster above. In turn, this released space in the New Block (later the 'Annett Building', see Chapter 6), allowing better provision for the other day boy houses, Chappel and Creighton. In both School House and the New Block, house rooms could double as classrooms, adding significantly to the teaching space available.

The new Dining Hall was sufficiently large to accommodate serving meals to all pupils, and so the old dining rooms (and kitchens) had been made redundant in 1977. This meant that the lower floor of School House was available for an alternative purpose. The popularity of Music at King's meant that the cramped accommodation in the 'Fishermen's Cottages' on Severn Street, home to Oswald House from 1984, was no longer suitable. A new Music School had been established in the basement of School House in 1977, which expanded into the ground floor in 1988 when the refurbishment of the building was complete. New Passey Hall was used as a large, additional rehearsal space for choirs and orchestras as the number of musical groups increased - a usage that continues in the 'Chappel Memorial Room' (renamed by Tim Hickson by the simple addition of two blue plastic signs in the late 1990s).

The lower level of the Winslow Building was enclosed, and a three-storey extension built, providing additional laboratories. By the late 1980s, one of the ground floor rooms would become a dedicated computer room; the ICT Department would eventually occupy the whole of the ground floor, as well as part of Choir House following conversion of 'the Barn' from study bedrooms in 2000-01.

All of these changes had allowed good use to be made of the school's buildings, with plenty of space for the enlarged Sixth Form, now standing at 240 students. Each of the sciences had dedicated laboratories, Maths, Music, Art, CDT and languages each had its own dedicated facilities. Economics was taught in Number 12 College Green. Geography was beginning to consolidate in the 1925 classroom block - by this stage known as the 'Fourth Form Block'. However, English, Classics, Religious Studies and History were taught in a variety of locations around the school.

The Development Trust identified a number of enhancements which would be desirable to the school's provision in two main

Keith Bridges (Staff 1963-2003) teaching a Chemistry lesson in the Winslow Building - this laboratory would be the first to be refurbished in 2002 and named in Keith's honour at his retirement.

areas - drama and sport. An appeal was launched in 1986, which focussed fundraising on a new theatre, to be built on the site of a warehouse between Wolfson and the Dining Hall/Modern Languages building, and the provision of an all-weather pitch. The campaign was successful, and the spectacular King's Theatre, later named in honour of Dr Moore, which was a rare facility for a school at that time, opened in 1987. The project to construct an all-weather pitch, however, was less successful, as it proved impossible to identify an available, suitable location for which planning permission could be granted.

Sports facilities were otherwise adequate, although by 1991 it had proved necessary to replace the 'bubble' over the swimming pool and make the facility suitable for year-round use by enclosing the pool completely.

Further changes would be needed, however, for the school to become fully co-educational. The decision to implement this historically significant change was taken by governors, after much consultation, in 1989, with an ambitious two-year timetable set for the first girls to arrive in the Lower Fourth and the Lower First at St Alban's.

The 1990s was a remarkable decade for King's - perhaps as significant as the 1880s or even the 1540s! At the start of the decade, King's was, perhaps, a somewhat old-fashioned school, albeit one taking large strides towards a progressive future, with a number of Sixth Form girls but still predominantly a boys school, and with a reasonable proportion of boarders (around 20% of pupils). By the start of the school year in September 1999, King's was fully co-educational and thriving but, importantly, without boarders.

Tim Hickson

*Second Master 1986-2002,
Teacher of Physics 1962-2002, Head of Physics 1971-1986*

Considered a 'legend in his own lifetime', Tim Hickson joined the Physics department in 1962, becoming Head of Department in 1973 and subsequently Second Master until his retirement in 2002.

As a gifted teacher, Tim had been keen to make use of new resources, and pioneered the 'Nuffield Physics' in the 1970s, designed by John Lewis of Malvern College, where he ran teacher training courses in the summer holidays. His association with Lewis also led to his involvement in a 'Science in Society' module for general studies which developed, with other new ideas, into the Diploma of Achievement, taken by King's pupils during the 1980s and 1990s, before the introduction of Key Skills.

In 1997, Tim was awarded the Bragg Medal by the Institute of Physics for 'significant contributions to physics education and to widening participation within it'. The prestige of this accolade could be seen in the programme - other award winners at the ceremony included Tim Berners Lee, creator of the World Wide Web.

As Second Master, Tim was John Moore's right hand man, and he acted as Head to cover Moore in the period immediately following the loss of his wife, Gill, in 1995. Tim would continue to serve Tim Keyes, appointed as the new Headmaster in 1998, supporting his early years in a time of difficult transition for the school, as boarding ended and a new regime of school inspections was due to begin.

Caroline Roslington, History teacher 1977-2009, recalled that it was Tim's involvement in everything at King's,

Tim Hickson was in charge of organising teaching cover - he is holding a 'black spot', the unpopular notice advising a cover lesson put in staff pigeon-holes

where there was nothing to which he would not turn his hand, and *"always with huge charm, energy and enthusiasm, which endeared him to the school as a whole"*.

Generations of pupils would remember straightening their ties and tucking in their shirts as an automatic response to hearing "You, boy!" thundering across the playground; Tim's authority was always balanced with a paternal, supportive nature which never failed to get the best from pupils.

Tim was succeeded as Second Master by Alistair Macnaughton, who recalled being seriously daunted by the shoes he was about to fill when he read the Second Master's job description.

Tim's daughters, Francesca, Katy and Lizzie all went through King's, between the 1980s and early 2000s, and Tim retired in 2002, with his wife, Sheanagh, to their home in Pershore. National Trust property Croome Court gained Tim as a passionate guide, but the draw of King's was still strong, and Tim would regularly return to provide cover and help with exam invigilation during the next ten years.

House Suppers were highlights in the social calendar for the Houses - this was Bright House

Left: P C Thompson's form room (F4) in the 1925 classroom building ('Fourth Form Block'), in which many hundreds of pupils learned Latin, photographed in 1988. Thompson would move into a room in School House in 1992 and insisted on having his 'traditional' furnishings brought into his 'modernised' new surroundings - much to the relief of this room's new encumbent, Eleanor Allen.

Following Thompson's retirement in 2006, his desk and chair were donated to the School Archive.

Right: A more typical 1990s classroom: the dormitory (and original gynasium) at the top of School House, converted into a House Room ('S3') for Kittermaster House in the 1988 and which doubled as Caroline Roslington's History classroom until the 2000s. Wulstan House moved into this room in 2006.

Below: School House centenary plaque which marked the end of the refurbishment of the building and the conversion of School House into accommodation for day boys.

Two aerial photographs taken in 1985.

Above: The photograph shows the four main open areas at the heart of the school site - the 'Dining Hall Quad', Monitors' Lawn, College Green and the Playground - which have given the school its 'campus' feel. The extension to the Winslow Building has been completed [bottom-right], but work has not yet started on the school theatre [bottom-left]. From this perspective it is possible to appreciate the size of Number 12 College Green, which seems so much smaller from the ground. The school site remains dominated, however, by School House - notice the entrance into the ground floor ('Passey Hall') from the Dining Hall quad..

Below: Centred on Edgar Tower, the photograph clearly shows the Chapter House, to the west of the ruined wall which is all that remains of the former Guesten Hall. The connection between College Hall and the other former monastic buildings is evident.

The John Moore Theatre and Drama at King's

Stephan Le Marchand, Teacher of English and Drama from 1983 to the present, recalls the growth of drama at King's, including the development of a dedicated theatre and drama department.

The Old Library was an extremely exciting space in which to stage plays. Performers were so close to the small audience - seventy at a push and a squeeze - that performances were a thrill for everyone. There is no room for dishonesty in actors when the audience can smell the performer. The 1970s and 80s saw memorable productions in that wonderful space of *The Crucible*, *A View From the Bridge*, *Hedda Gabler*, *The Glass Menagerie*, *Black Comedy*, *In Praise of Love*, and *Oh! What a Lovely War*. In the same period there were gripping student-directed stagings of *Waiting For Godot* and *The Birthday Party*. The lighting and sound was controlled from an adjacent room, the English Department bookstore, and the operators had to stand on a stool and look through a window to follow what was happening. The Sports Hall was another venue at this time, Anthony Clemit directing the Lower Remove (Year 9) in *Joseph and the Amazing Technicolor Dreamcoat* there. G&S and other musicals, including *The Boy Friend* and *Guys and Dolls*, were staged in College Hall by Paul Thompson, Peter Diamond (Head of English) and Brian Griffiths; I staged my own adaptation of *The Lion, the Witch and the Wardrobe* for which the Head of Art, John Exton, designed a set. There were productions in the garden of Number 12 of *Animal Farm* and *Mother Courage*, and a special *Romeo and Juliet* in the gardens of College House, with the

The 300-seat auditorium of the John Moore Theatre, 2014

Guesten ruins a magnificent backdrop, one of the windows a spectacular balcony for 'Juliet'. Peter Baseley, Head of CDT, was a tireless and imaginative designer and builder for many of these productions, his set for a modern day *Twelfth Night* located on the Mediterranean coast one of the most memorable. The school was invited to perform on four occasions in Worcester Cathedral: *Mystery and Merriment*, *The Way of the Cross* and *A Winter's Tale* (a musical adaptation of Shakespeare's play by Peter Diamond and Nick Owen, OV), with staff and pupils playing the different generations, were performed in the nave as promenade theatre, and *The Devils* was performed in the Lady Chapel with the passionate support of the Dean at the time, Robert Jeffery.

The special challenges of creating a theatre out of a space intended for something completely different were exciting and inspiring. But the logistical and practical difficulties of working in these spaces meant that there was a real need for a dedicated, purpose built theatre. When the Theatre opened in 1986 a different set of challenges and opportunities presented themselves. With more sophisticated equipment and technology came higher expectations and the opportunity to develop and display other skills and expertise. Chris Charlton, a Sixth Form student, not only understood the lighting system manual but re-wrote it so that mere mortals could follow it. A musical adaptation of Henry Fielding's novel *Joseph Andrews* was a rip-roaring first production, followed soon after by *Cabaret*. Both of these shows made full use of sophisticated lighting and sound systems but had to overcome the problem of the lack of an orchestra pit: there simply wasn't room for one in the design given the limitations of the site. For musical productions, the band has usually been crammed into the space created by retracting a bank of seating on the right hand side

'Tess of the d'Urbervilles', 1998

'Les Misérables School Edition', 2003

of the auditorium. More recent shows have placed the band on a specially erected platform above head height in the wings stage left. Two productions of Les Misérables School Edition, in 2003 and 2012, generated a special excitement not only amongst those involved, but also the whole school and even the wider Worcester community. Other musicals staged in the Theatre since 1988 include *West Side Story* (twice) *Oklahoma!*, *Guys and Dolls* (two senior versions and one junior), *The Boy Friend*, *Anything Goes*, *Me and My Girl* and *Jack The Ripper*, and important members of the production teams of these shows were David Brookshaw (musical director) and Trudie Marskell (choreographer). *For more on Musical Theatre, see Chapter 1.*

For a period in the 1980s and 1990s there was an annual House Drama Festival, in which half of the houses performed student-directed productions in alternate years. The standard varied, but there were spectacular successes: *Twelve Angry Men*, *Forty Years On* and *The House of Bernarda Alba* stand out. Staff pantomimes have happened regularly: *Cinderella* has been a favourite and there have also been a *Jack and the Beanstalk* and a *Little Jack Horner*. We've never got round to doing Russ Mason's favourite, *Aladdin* (or 'Rub it and See'). Staff pantomimes have always sold out: that's what happens when you offer the school community serious drama as opposed to the frivolity of Ibsen or Strindberg.

David Thurlby (Wulstan House 1980-87) was the first Theatre Technician, from 1992, and was responsible for designs, construction, lighting and sound and whatever else was necessary to turn visions into reality. A floating hot-air balloon somehow emerged from stage right in *Orpheus in the Underworld*; daggers on hire from the National Theatre which left a line of blood as you slit someone's throat were used in a memorable production of the 'Scottish Play'; 'Orsino' emerged from the sea to take a (working) shower at the start of *Twelfth Night*; snow fell during a wintry *Much Ado*; neon signs surrounded the Kowalskis' apartment in *A Streetcar Named Desire*, the walls of the apartment suggested by hundreds of bricks borrowed from Underwoods. A full set was hired for *Anything Goes*, only to discover on delivery that we couldn't get it into the theatre: cue the maintenance staff to remove door frames and to use their unique combination of ingenuity and muscle to get things in. They were not quite so successful when they were asked to cut in half a very expensive piece of gauze for the afore-mentioned *Streetcar* only to get the measurements wrong by about 10 feet. Danny Payne, an A level Theatre Studies student at the time, designed and constructed a superb set for a Removes' production of *Tess*, a very powerful adaptation of Hardy's novel: the main concept was to construct furniture and scenery out of blocks of polystyrene sculpted to look like pieces of neolithic stones, the re-configuring of the pieces culminating inevitably in a final tableau of a fully-formed Stonehenge.

During this period, senior productions, House Drama and junior productions fought for slots in the Theatre and there were sometimes as many as nine productions in a year. A change came about when House Drama was discontinued as there was more demand for theatre time as a consequence of the introduction of curricular drama. Initially, Drama was offered as a GCSE subject as an extra to members of the Lower Sixth. This

Cast of staff pantomime 'Cinderella', 2005

produced stagings of *The Real Inspector Hound*, *After Liverpool* and *The Canterbury Tales*. Soon after, Drama became a GCSE option for Years 10 and 11 and Theatre Studies A level was introduced, and a full-time Head of Drama was appointed. In this role, Simon Atkins was responsible for several memorable curricular productions and full school shows, with Fourth Forms, Removes and the senior years.

Soon after Simon's appointment, Chris Crosswell became the new Theatre Manager, and brought his professionalism, expertise and extraordinary stamina and patience to this ever-more-demanding role, helping to raise the standards of school drama by providing designs to inspire inspirational performances. Ingenious and elaborate but always actor-friendly stage sets and lighting designs have shown the students off to the best advantage. 'Rain' fell from above to soak 'Lear' as he raged against the storm; more neon created Times Square in *Guys and Dolls*; magical worlds were created for *A Midsummer Night's Dream* and *The Lion, The Witch and The Wardrobe*.

In 2002-03 the Theatre was refurbished, and named in honour of the recently-retired former Headmaster, John Moore, and a new phase began. King's drama began another new stage of its evolution when the spaces in The Keyes Building became available in 2015. The school will retain the John Moore Theatre whose proscenium arch stage provides the opportunity for spectacle, but will regain in the Wightman Studio in The Keyes Building a space similar to that provided by the Old Library; a space that one hopes will provide again the opportunity for intense and intimate work and more experimental drama.

Below: 'The Lion, the Witch and the Wardrobe', 2007
Inset: 'King Lear', 2005

Above left: Language laboratory, 'French Without Tears', 1986

Above Right: John Roslington and Peter Diamond with The King's Herald *team, who won first prize in the Times-Tandon 'Newsday' competition, 1990. John Roslington continued to enter teams of students throughout the 1990s and 2000s, with* The King's Herald *achieving distinction level in the 'Newsday' competition in most years.*

450th anniversary celebrations

The seven new schools established by King Henry VIII in 1541 shared a year of celebrations to mark their 450th anniversary in 1991.

John Exton, Head of Art, designed a special badge to mark the anniversary, which was used on the cover of the 1991 issue of *The Vigornian*. The insignia is reproduced below. The Development Committee organised a special anniversary May Day Fête; a commemorative issue of *The King's Herald* was produced on the day. A series of watercolours by local artist David Birtwhistle was commissioned, with prints and greetings cards sold in their hundreds. The anniversary prompted an interest in the school's history among pupils, a group of whom would work with Caroline Roslington to produce *The King's School, Worcester - and a history of its site*, the first edition of which was published in 1994.

The culmination of the celebrations was a concert at the Royal Albert Hall with the choirs from all seven 'King's Schools' founded or re-founded by Henry VIII. After the concert, the Headmaster had the opportunity to meet Her Majesty Queen Elizabeth II with a number of King's pupils.

The King's School, Worcester would have cause to recall its 450th anniversary year for another significant reason - the first girls were admitted to the Lower Fourth in September 1991, as the school moved towards full co-education.

Right: Special badge designed by John Exton

Far right: Programme for the commemorative concert held at the Royal Albert Hall

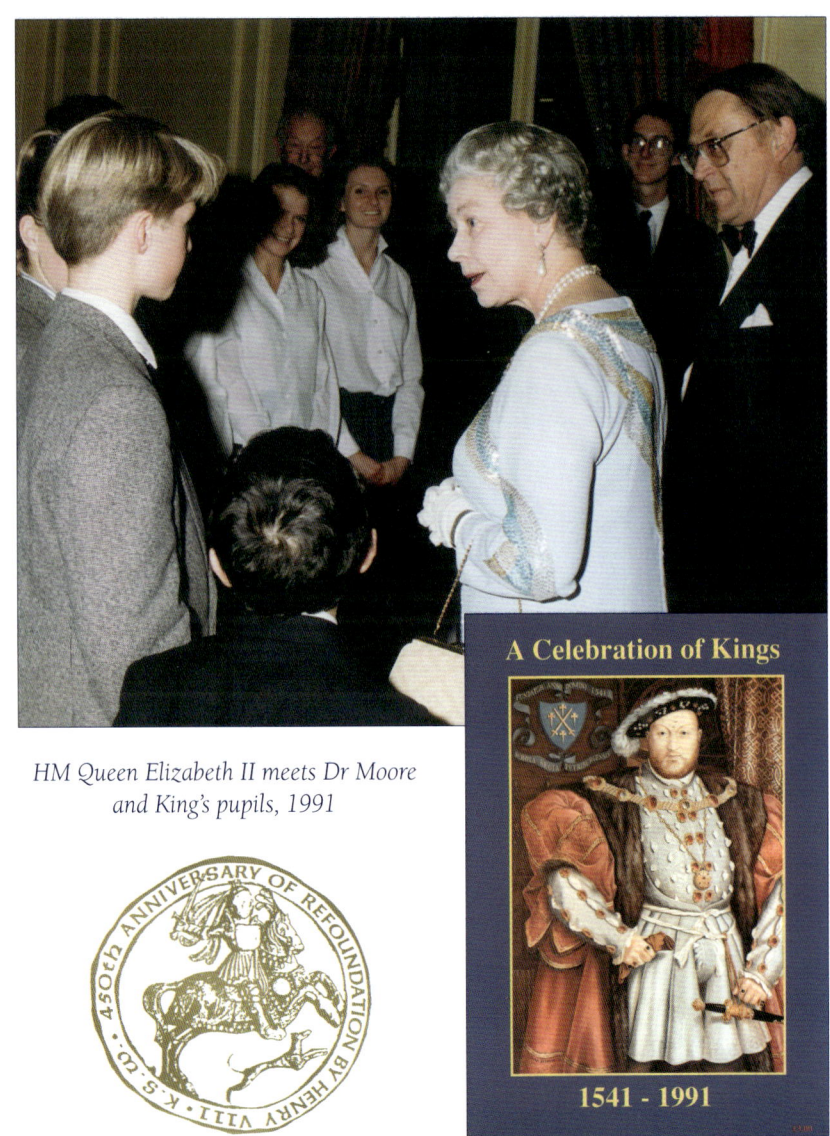

HM Queen Elizabeth II meets Dr Moore and King's pupils, 1991

'Girl Power' in the 1990s!

Following the success of integrating girls into the Sixth Form, the Governors and Headmaster decided to convert King's into a fully co-educational school in 1989 and set an ambitious timetable for the school to be ready to welcome girls into the Lower Fourth (and the Lower First at St Alban's Junior School) by September 1991. New changing and toilet facilities would be needed as female pupils would no longer be 'contained' within College House and Eliot House; indeed, Eliot House would no longer be required, as girls would be integrated into the other houses. College House would remain for girl boarders from the Lower Remove up to the Sixth Form under the care of Sarah Le Marchand (supported by husband Stephan), while younger girls could board alongside the boys in Castle House.

To oversee the task of preparing the school for co-education, a new post of Senior Mistress was created to which Patricia Sanger (later Patricia Stevens) was appointed in September 1990. No small part of her role was to win the support of those staff and parents who were unhappy at the decision, and this was achieved in good humour; Patricia paved the way for an apparently painless transition.

The first cohort of 11+ girls duly arrived in September 1991 and quickly integrated into the life of the school. The relatively small number grew year by year throughout the 1990s, with further girls joining at 13+ from 1993, until the proportions of girls and boys in each year group were roughly similar.

The Games department had been divided into Boys' Games and Girls' Games in 1984 with Nicky Anstey appointed to champion girls' sport at King's. Girls' sports - netball, hockey, tennis and rounders - thrived, with particular success in girls rowing crews.

The final symbol of the fully co-educational school was the appointment of the first female Head of School, Jennifer Pearce, in 1998.

Above: The first girls to join the Lower Fourth, September 1991
Below: The same cohort leaving the Upper Sixth, 1998

Patricia Stevens

Senior Mistress 1990-2004

Patricia Sanger arrived at King's in September 1990 to take up the new position of Senior Mistress, with the special responsibility to oversee the move to co-education. It's difficult to imagine exactly how much work must have gone into making this transition happen so seamlessly. Her guiding principle was simply that girls and boys are different but equal. Even so, the move to co-education was not easy, not least because there was some opposition to the idea amongst members of staff. The opponents were successfully converted, one so successfully that Patricia married him. Sadly, Mike Stevens became ill, and in 2004 Patricia retired to care for Mike full time.

In the Senior Management Team, Patricia played a crucial part, working closely with Tim Hickson and Alistair Macnaughton. Her readiness to listen and her wise counsel made her an excellent staff mentor. She chaired and sat on many committees and steering groups. She was Lead Inspector for criminal records; Child Protection Officer; she was in charge of staffing. She was responsible for setting up little girls' boarding. She was given a number of poisoned chalices including Review and Development and Inset; indeed Inset didn't exist here at King's until Patricia took it on. The Staff Handbook she produced was a tome of impeccable thoroughness.

Patricia was also a passionate and much-loved member of the English Department, inspiring a generation of students and offering wisdom, good humour and warm companionship to her colleagues.

King's Remembered

Lauren Pruden-Lawson   *Chappel House 1991-1998*

I had always wanted to go to King's. I was lucky enough to experience places like the Old Chapel from the age of 4 or 5 years. I just loved it and knew King's was the place for me: there was just one problem; they didn't take girls! However, by the time I got to 11, they had realised that girls were the way forward!

I was in L4D and am still in touch with the friends I met on day one. As there were only a few girls, we had to be resilient, confident and outgoing. We forged strong relationships that will last a lifetime.

I loved everything about King's. The sport, the teachers and the stunning Cathedral (although I only started to appreciate that when I was a little older).

We girls settled in quickly and over the years, we made our mark.! Many teachers had huge influences on me; Brian and Sheena Griffiths got me through huge amounts - relaxed conversations on long walks in Wales and more intense discussions in the Maths classroom. Stephan Le Marchand was the reason I went to Oxford University; without his constant support and encouragement I would never have applied. Andy Guest showed me how to push myself on the river and in the gym as I followed his tough training regime. Being president of OUWBC [Oxford University Women's Boat Club] was one of the best experiences of my life.

Building dens with Miss Jaques [later, Fiona Short] during the Lower Remove Activity Week, team building activities on the Upper Fourth Activity Week, winning a medal at National Rowing Championships in Scotland, falling in the river! and opening my A level results with Stephan Le Marchand will be memories I will treasure for the rest of my life. King's is an amazing school - so much so I went on to teach there for four years [Biology, 2007-2011].

The school is about so much more than exam results. It is about making sure you are ready for 'life'; building friendship, skills and confidence.

Lauren is pictured, centre, in the photographs on page 167.

Jessica Page   *Chappel House 1994-1999*

I came to King's from the Alice Ottley in 1994 - the thought of going to school with 'boys' was a novelty! We were only the second year of girls to go all the way through the school but you wouldn't have thought it. We had equal numbers of girls and boys in our houses and classes and we were rarely treated differently (except for Mr Thompson calling me 'Miss Page' rather than 'Page'). I had many highs as well as lows at King's: unfortunately, due to the school still being integrated, there was an element of bullying which many pupils didn't feel they could raise with certain teachers, because of the slightly archaic attitude that still existed at the time.

We were encouraged in sport and PE lessons. I was lucky enough to represent the school in a range of sports throughout my time: athletics, at which I was chosen to represent Worcester county; rounders; tennis; and especially netball (which I still play to this day) in which we enjoyed success at both district and county levels.

Playing the role of 'Nancy' in the 1996 school production of Oliver! was a wonderful experience - using the school's incredible theatre, having singing lessons, the amazing costumes and performing on stage for nearly a week! Following that experience I was involved in every school and house production until I left!

As far as academia went, I knew the path I wanted to take: the arts side - English, drama, classical civilisation, etc. My house master Mr LeMarchand was an incredible inspiration. My GCSE maths teacher Mr Bentley, although eccentric, got me through my coursework and exams meaning that I could go on to study the subjects I wanted. My biology teacher Miss Featherstone helped me out with her patience, extra tuition and guidance (even if she was the only teacher to give me a detention!)

In my sixth form years, I was lucky enough to go on a classical civilisation trip to Greece which still sticks in my mind as one of

Jessica as 'Nancy' in Oliver!, 1996

the most informative, fun and relaxed school trips. Bob Stone regaling us with stories in Ancient Greek, the slightly ropey hotels, the amazing historical sites, including where the first Olympic Games were held, the Temple of Dionysus and all the museums. Being 17, I really didn't appreciate it as much as I should have done, so I went back in 2007!

My time at King's was not all perfect, but it got me into my first choice university and I now work in the field in which I chose to study. I am still close friends with many Old Vigornians, from a number of graduating classes, as King's forged great friendships and camaraderie.

Jessica studied Film, Television and Radio at University of Wales, Aberyswyth before embarking on a career in television planning with MTV, BBC, NBC Universal and CNBC Europe in London. She returned to Worcestershire in 2015, with fiancé Darren, to pursue TV and film production work with Capture Production Studios, based in the USA.

The end of Saturday morning school

The decline in boarding at other schools, along with decreasing numbers of boarders at King's, led to a decision - hugely popular with pupils, as King's was by then the only school teaching on Saturdays in Worcester - to end Saturday morning lessons, from September 1993.

Rather than abandon school on Saturdays altogether, and to allow the boarders to use the time constructively, participation in activities on Saturdays became compulsory. A range of activities and clubs, from CDT to astronomy, sprang up or made use of the extra time available on Saturday mornings, while sports fixtures continued to be played on Saturday afternoons. Mandatory attendance ceased from 1999, but many activities continued to operate at weekends, including the Duke of Edinburgh's Award, drama rehearsals and sports training.

John Turner, Senior Master with John Moore at the presentation of cheques worth £6,000 to charities from the proceeds of the 1995 Charity Walk. A sponsored walk, organised by Brian Griffiths and John Wheeler, took place in years between School Fetes. The May Fete enjoyed something of a heyday during the 1980s and 1990s, when huge crowds flocked to what was one of Worcester's major events.

Early days of the Information Age

John Roslington, Physics master since 1975, had a keen interest in computing, and introduced microcomputers to a mostly reluctant group of Sixth Formers in the early 1980s, in lunchtime and after school sessions. Early pioneers included Dylan Smith (The Hostel 1980-90) who built an e-mail system and an adventure game and went on to work for IBM in the USA.

The Apple Macintosh made computing more accessible for students, and provided a mouse which made desktop publishing possible. A team of students produced the first issue of *The King's Herald* in 1988, an entry in the *Times International Newsday Competition*, which required the team to produce a

David Willmer teaching an IT lesson in 'the Mac Room', 1995

newspaper in a day; the school enjoyed much success with *The King's Herald* in the 1990s, winning awards for each entry.

Younger pupils were taught to use word-processing software and their Maths teachers encouraged use of spreadsheets and programming tools in the new computer rooms on the ground floor of the Winslow Building. Elsewhere, BBC Micros provided software for science and geographical experiments.

In September 1997, Roslington introduced A Level Information Technology to the curriculum, leaving Physics to become Head of IT, and opening a third computer room to accommodate classes for what would quickly become a popular subject. The appointment of Jean Vivian as ICT Co-ordinator in 1998 encouraged the use of new technology and resources in other departments; she was also responsible for training all teaching staff in the basic use of computers, the Internet and office applications. After Roslington's retirement in 2009, the A Level course ceased and Vivian would take over the ICT Department, introducing new activities including coding and animation.

By the late 1990s a network of around 50 computers had grown up in the Winslow Building, with a large colour laser printer and projectors in the IT rooms, computers in Chemistry and Physics laboratories, and spurs to further clusters of computers in the Wolfson Building, for CDT, and the Geography department, managed by Nick Dart, IT Technician and later Network Manager. Some of the older BBC computers were still in use in Biology, and a computer was available in the Common Room, as well as for the Headmaster and secretaries.

David Willmer created a database on his Archimedes computer to help produce the school timetable - in time, this developed into 'ReportWriter' used by all staff for writing end of term reports. A new school database, 'Asyst' was introduced by Julian Thould, administered by Willmer, which, in part, led to the gradual move towards Windows PCs.

Reverend Mark Dorsett leading a house assembly in the Quire, 1997. Houses would take turns to have a Friday morning assembly in the Cathedral, in addition to College Hall assemblies every Monday and Thursday.

All change for the new millennium

Dr Moore, a well-respected Headmaster for almost three generations of pupils, retired in August 1998. In the years since, John Moore came to be regarded as having been 'a safe pair of hands', although the significance of the changes which the Headmaster had overseen, working alongside a governing body led since 1986 by Donald Howell (see Chapter 9), cannot be overstated. The King's School of 1983 was hybrid boys' boarding and day school and a relatively small number of girls in the Sixth Form; sport, particularly rugby and cricket, often dominated school life, although music and drama were starting to flourish. The school's finances were less than secure, with the Assisted Places scheme in its infancy; the O Level was the qualification achieved by most students, before moving on to A Levels.

Moore's successor Tim Keyes (see Chapter 9) inherited a large, fully co-educational school, with a small number of remaining boarders, but with plans in place for an imminent end to boarding, and development of the disused boarding houses envisioned. The school was thriving in the arts and sports, and academic standards were increasing, even taking account of the new, and frequently changing, GCSE courses and the new modular A Level courses being introduced for new subjects such as IT and Business Studies. Many school buildings had been refurbished, with the significant addition of the Theatre and the enclosure of the swimming pool. Finance remained a difficult subject for the school, with the Assisted Places phased out from 1997, so a new development campaign would surely be needed to renovate and extend the school's campus. The Junior School - that is, King's St Alban's - had become co-educational and been expanded, and joined by Hawford Lodge, now 'King's Hawford'.

Tim Keyes, assisted by Bursar Galen Bartholomew, who had been appointed in 1996, thus serving two years with Moore, would have a range of substantial issues to address, and quickly, but the foundations of the changes that would be brought in by his successor during the years that followed, had been laid

Dr John Moore, J.P. in College Hall, 1998

during the 1980s and 1990s by John Moore.

Moore retired to his home in Ombersley, from where he continued to serve as a Justice of the Peace. Returning to King's infrequently after his retirement, as is the usual practice, John Moore did return, along with David Annett, for a celebration to mark the end of boarding in July 1999 and again in January 2001 for the re-opening of Choir House (see Chapter 4). The John Moore Theatre was named in his honour following refurbishment in 2003, at a ceremony attended by the former Headmaster, whose health was deteriorating. John Moore died in 2005; a memorial service was held in the Cathedral, attended by many of his colleagues and former pupils.

The last boarders at King's, 1999

'Bye Bye, Boarders'

The end of boarding at The King's School was among the most important decisions the governing body could have made. During the 1980s and 1990s, the number of pupils boarding at King's, and at many other schools around the country, declined. School House had already been converted into a day boy house, with the building made available for other teaching and pastoral accommodation, including a new Music department, in 1989. In 1995, Choir House would complete its conversion into a day house, taking in pupils from other the day houses which had grown in size significantly since the transition to co-education.

Peter Iddon with The Hostel, 1992-93

In 1997, the recently-appointed Bursar, Galen Bartholomew, presented to the Governors the business case for ending boarding, a still contentious issue with a number of important opponents, not least the Headmaster. The Governors decided to support the arguments for the future benefits to the school rather than clinging to a tradition which would surely have died out eventually anyway. An announcement was made that new boarders would not be admitted from 1997, clearing the way for a gradual end to boarding. Castle House closed in 1997, ending junior boarding.

In September 1998, the last boarders from The Hostel moved into the vacant accommodation on the upper floors of Choir House, under the care of Peter Iddon, the last Housemaster of The Hostel, with the pupils of Marie Arthurs' Choir House below. This allowed for the reordering work needed to convert The Hostel into the school's new administrative centre, Hostel House, ahead of the summer 1999 deadline to return College House to the Cathedral. The final girl boarders left College House in July 1999 along with the last boys from The Hostel, and their building was duly returned to the Dean and Chapter when the Headmaster, secretaries and staff Common Room moved into Hostel House in September.

It was to be the end of an era for life around College Green and for some, including John Moore who remained sceptical, the school would seem the poorer for it. However, as can be seen in Chapter 9, this proved a remarkable opportunity for the school to grow in numbers and to improve its accommodation significantly in the years that followed.

End of boarding party, 1999

The King's School, Worcester   *From 1541 into the 21st Century*

A century of sport at King's

Sport at King's in the 21st century has come a long way since its beginnings in the Victorian era. From low-level recreational games through a regime of physical training to a range of elite competitive sports and a philosophy of encouraging participation by all in individual and team sports.

Rowing is known to have been a recreational activity for boys at King's as early as the 1850s, when records show that the school owned a 'four-oar boat'. William Helm, Headmaster 1856-1860, died at the age of 24 after a vigorous session of rowing on the river. An incident involving the near drowning of two boys when their boat was swamped by the wash of a steam tug boat; the boys, who couldn't swim, were rescued by one of the rowers, Tom Baxter, son of the Second Master, who was awarded a Bronze Medal by the British Humane Society.

The Boat Club was established in 1877 (see Chapter 3), primarily to promote the use of the river for leisure and recreation. The first School Regatta, in April 1889, was opened by a race between an Old Vigornians' IV and the school IV, with the school IV beating the OVs' IV by two lengths. An annual race against Hereford Cathedral School, on the Severn, started in May 1891 from the Dog and Duck Ferry to the Grandstand (about half a mile) - King's won by almost a length in 2'42. Other than this sort of informal event, the Boat Club didn't actively train rowers for racing until after the First World War.

The Vigornian of 1879 records a suggestion by a tennis enthusiast to gain permission from the Chapter to use College Green as a lawn tennis court. The editor's sharp reply retorts that "We fancy that the writer's enthusiasm has carried him away and led him to forget what the College Green is...".

The trend for competitive sport in schools hadn't gathered momentum until the early Victorian reforms of Dr Arnold, of Rugby School, who advocated a model of moulding 'character' and turning the English schoolboy into a Christian gentleman. Organised games were central to the new model for public schools, such as those founded at Malvern, Cheltenham and Marlborough. At King's, boys had played 'mob football' in the Cathedral cloisters, and rough games fives and hockey in the

Boys waiting to start the Ketch Run, 1910

Cathedral Gardens. Three of the modern Headmasters of King's, Bolland, Chappel and Creighton, had been educated at Marlborough, and brought the philosophy of sport, as a remedy for laziness, with them to Worcester.

Bolland was particularly fond of cricket, and, often to the despair of the oarsmen, favoured the development of cricket. The sport, in an early form, had been played occasionally at the school since the 1860s, using the public gardens of the Arboretum, and sometimes even the Pitchcroft racecourse, as a makeshift cricket pitch, before a rented pitch was acquired on the eastern bank of the river near to Diglis Lock. This field was liable to flooding, uneven and with no decent access, so in the 1880s, Bolland decided to lease the south-west corner of the Chapter Meadows from the Cathedral, which would, during the next few years be shared with Worcestershire County Cricket Club which moved to the site in 1891 from Boughton Park. While still liable to flooding, and somewhat unlevel, the access from New Road was significantly improved, and the first pavilion was built here in 1889, built from the same subscription funds which paid for the building of the two fives courts on the newly-defined playground (see Chapter 4), formed on the site of the Worcester Prison when development began for School House (see Chapter 5 and Appendix 15).

The top floor of School House included the school's first gymnasium from 1889, but an increase in the number of boarders led to its conversion into a dormitory in 1897. This was replaced by a wooden gym on the southern side of the playground in 1901, paid for by subscriptions and partly in memory of those who had fought and died in the Boer War in South Africa, 1899-1901.

The first recorded cricket match between the School XI and the Old Vigornians' XI took place in June 1889, the OVs winning by 9 runs. Two years later the 1st XI, which included all three of Bolland's sons, beat the OVs twice in the season. The fixture list was small, with occasional matches against Bromsgrove and Cheltenham, and memorable matches in the grounds of Spetchley House against a team of soldiers from Norton Barracks, which the school side usually lost. Chappel was also a keen cricketer, and encouraged the boys by arranging for them to be coached by the County wicket-keeper, after the County side took up residence at New Road.

King's boys had played both Association football and rugby football, on a similarly informal basis in the 1850s and 1860s,

1st XI Football Team, 1902

The Rammell Pavilion, opened in 1921

using the Diglis Lock field; in the 1870s, rugby football was adopted as the main winter sport, and was played at the Chapter Meadows pitch during the 1880s. Rugby, or indeed any sport, was not compulsory for day boys, most of whom abstained, so what games could be played would often feature teams of just eight or nine-a-side, far short of the required fifteen for a proper match.

Athletics and fives were more popular sports than rugby football, because they were individual events and so more easy to organise in a small school where filling places for a team sport was often difficult. In 1894, a Cycle Club was introduced as part of the Athletics programme by Richard Beach-Hicks; the highlight of season was a 10 mile cycle race.

Thomas Rammell arrived at King's in September 1891, and was disappointed to see the poor state of rugby, at that point hampered by a water-logged pitch which had recently flooded. He considered alternative solutions, including using the playground for practice; however, the hard surface was not suitable for this purpose, although would be ideal for Association football, which had the additional benefit of only needing eleven players to form a full team. Rammell proposed moving from rugby football to association football, with practice and games on the playground when the pitch was unavailable. Head of School, H.M. Conacher, who supported Rammell's arguments, discussed the matter with a representative of each form, and gained approval for the change. 'Football' was adopted as the main winter sport from 1892 until 1921, when the school was large enough to support teams for rugby.

By the turn of the century, sport and physical education was still very much 'in development', with many reports in *The Vigornian* of lack of interest among the boys, particularly the younger ones; much skiving and slacking; and the rivalry between rowers and cricketers. Following Chappel's arrival, a Games Committee was formed in 1897, charged with the task of organising sport throughout the school.

Athletic Sports were the basis of inter-house competitions, with the first shield awarded to the winning house, School House, for the 1904 Sports. Later, in 1905, a 3.5 mile cross-country race was added, the 'Ketch Run', which was an annual event until 1928. A Gymnastics Cup was introduced in 1905, offered by the OV Club, also won by School House.

It was in the 1920s that King's started to play rugby matches against Bromsgrove School and King Edward's School Birmingham, annual fixtures which have continued ever since. An annual 'derby' against local rival WRGS (later, RGS Worcester) was initiated in the 1940s, but didn't attain the status given to it in recent years until the 1960s.

Hockey and tennis were also played by the boys, but as less important sports, much less was recorded about them until more recent decades.

Rammell, who, as well as rugby, was also in charge of cricket, designed and paid for a new pavilion, opened in 1921, dedicated to those who "learnt to play the game for their school, played it also for their country during the years 1914-1918. *Haec olim meminisse juvabit* ['These things one day it will be a pleasure to remember' from Vergil's *Aeneid*]." A third fives court was added to the existing pair of courts on the playground when they were refurbished in the early 1920s, and the building was also dedicated as a memorial to the fallen OVs of the Great War.

The gym was replaced by a larger facility paid for by Creighton in 1929, and designed to embrace the physical education ideas of the time with little apparatus and plenty of floor space; Creighton's gym was refurbished in 1947, and following the latest theories about physical training, was fitted out with beams, ropes, wall-bars and other equipment.

Over time, the Chapter, as Governors of the school, had agreed to fund the levelling of a larger area of the playing fields, extending up towards Bromwich Road with more usable ground, with additions made particularly during the headship of David Annett, including a hard surface for four tennis courts.

The Boat Club moved from its boathouse on Hylton Road to a new building, designed by Second Master and keen oarsman,

Creighton's gymnasium, built in 1929 and refurbished in 1947. The gymnasium was demolished in 1972 to make way for a day boy changing room and the Wolfson Building.

1st VIII crew launch a boat at the opening of the boathouse, 1960

1971 by Sir Jack Longland (School House 1919-23), whose career in education, broadcasting and mountaineering earned him a knighthood in 1971.

The arrival of the first four girls to the Sixth Form in 1971 would usher in an era of change for sport at King's. Two of the girls joined the boys for hockey and all four girls formed their own rowing Girls' IV. As more girls joined the school during the 1970s and 1980s, hockey was established as a separate girls' sport (boys' hockey stopped shortly after the re-introduction of football in 1994), and netball was introduced, with rounders in the summer. Other sports, including rowing, tennis, basketball, fencing and athletics, were open to both girls and boys. The hard surface at the playing fields, used for tennis, now doubled as netball courts.

Richard Knight. Occupying the south-west corner of the school campus, on the site of a terrace of dilapidated cottages, the boathouse had to make best use of a site "of no known geometric shape". The new boathouse was opened in 1960 by Mrs W Scurfield, mother of rower Hugh Scurfield (Chappel House 1943-54) who would later become Chairman of the Development Trust and instrumental in raising support for the later Michael Baker Boathouse. Rowing was going through a period of rapid development, competing in regattas at Marlow and Henley, and, thanks to the new facility, able to race with VIIIs as well as IVs. The success of rowing continued through the following decades, with a 1990s girls VIII achieving no fewer than 25 regatta wins at junior and senior level, including the National Championships of 1996, 1998 and 1999.

By the 1960s it was clear that the provision of facilities for sport was still inadequate, and the 1961 appeal (see Chapter 6) included a new swimming pool and a sports hall to replace the gym, which was approaching the end of its useful life, as well as new changing facilities. The swimming pool opened in 1962, with the sports hall completed later and opened in

Andrew Milne arranged for a new block of changing rooms to be built at the playing fields in 1981, which was extended to provide decent changing facilities for girls (who had to use the Rammell Pavilion in the 1980s and 1990s) in the mid-1990s; it was also during Milne's headship that the first of two polysphere 'bubble's was installed to enclose the swimming pool, allowing it to be used year round. Due to subsidence issues to the pool side of the sports hall, remedial work was carried out in 1990, and the opportunity to fully enclose the swimming pool was taken, as well as adding new changing rooms for the girls. The 'new' indoor pool was opened by Peter Luff MP in 1991.

Sailing had featured among the early activities of the Boat Club, but a separate Sailing Club was established in the 1970s by keen sailor John Roslington, who built up a small fleet of dinghies and took crews sailing at the Severn Sailing Club, near Bredon.

Paul Witherick (Chappel House 1974-84) recalled that *Boggy's* (Marc Roberts') regime of training for his 1st XV rugby team was harsh, involving after-school practices on Monday, Tuesday and Thursday evenings, as well as during Games on Wednesday, with a match after school on Saturday afternoons. He was glad to be part of the rugby team but sometimes envied the boys playing hockey who seemed to have a much easier time.

The 1986 School Appeal included a desire to create an all-weather pitch at the playing fields, to get around the problem of often water-logged pitches, which, with a larger school, was becoming more problematic than ever. The enormous cost of constructing such a facility above the flood-line ensured that this would be unlikely to proceed. Eventually, in 2007, as part of the school's partnership with Bishop Perowne College, a site for the all-weather pitch at Merrimans Hill was agreed, and construction could finally begin. The pitch opened in 2010, dedicated to the memory of Peter Curle, Second Master 1978-86, whose vision this project had been.

A multi-gym, with weight training equipment, was first set up in 1982, in a garage which stood next to the front porch of School House; this was demolished during the 2001 remodelling of the New Block (see Chapter 6) which, as the Annett Building included a new weights room and

Cricket 1st XI, 1955

Sports Day, 1961

Rugby - undated, but possibly 1950s

Gareth Edwards CBE (Welsh RFU player, declared the 'Greatest Player of All Time' by 'Rugby World' in 2003) opened the new pavilion in 1983, pictured with 1st XV Captain, Stuart Preston (School House 1977-83) and Headmaster Andrew Milne

Mixed Hockey, 1983

Basketball on the playground in the 1970s in front of the fives courts which had been enclosed in the 1960s

U13 Netball Team, 1993

a fitness centre which replaced the room of cardiovascular training equipment in the Porcelain Works building, set up in the 1990s.

By popular demand, football was reintroduced as the spring term sport in 1994, quickly replacing boys hockey. An annual fixture against WRGS was established, played at Worcester City FC's St George's Lane ground, and the sport flourished under the leadership of Chris Haywood.

Andy Guest, Head of PE from 1988-2002, introduced A Level PE to the school curriculum which incorporated study of physiology and anatomy with sporting theory and practice. This became a popular subject option, taught in the Fishermen's Cottages (former home of Oswald House), and heralded a new serious approach to sport and physical education at King's.

Rugby had particularly suffered in the 1990s as a result of co-education, which reduced the pool of available players and diverted some of the focus the sport had received, along with the re-introduction of football which made rugby sevens unviable for a number of years, particularly when King's faced boys' schools, including RGS Worcester, Solihull and Warwick School. Nicky Wilson had established a Girls' Games Department in 1991, offering hockey, netball, tennis and rounders, but the feeling that girls sport was a 'special interest' and not worthy of proper resources persisted for some time.

King's resisted the recent trend of offering sports scholarships, where élite athletes are encouraged to join a school, often at Sixth Form level, to bolster teams. One reason for this was to avoid pupils who had played in 'A' teams throughout their school careers being pushed out in the Sixth Form by 'bought in' players, an admirable aim, favouring 'home grown' players, although King's teams often found themselves facing challenging sides with many élite players.

These negative influences did not, however, cause long-term problems for sport at King's. The introduction of pre-season training in the late 1990s, first for rugby in Scotland and Ireland and later for hockey and netball, saw a renewed drive to improve the performance of school sports teams. Dedicated heads of sports were appointed, under the oversight of Andy Guest and then Jonny Mason, Director of Sport, appointed in September 2002.

Increasingly ambitious sports tours allowed senior rugby teams to play in South Africa, the USA and Canada; cricketers travelled to Jersey each year and often as far as Sri Lanka or Barbados; netball and hockey tours often visited Australia, at the instigation of Ollivia Beveridge, Head of Netball from 2007, who hailed from Tasmania.

An unprecedented period of high achievement in sport started early in the new millennium and was still continuing by 2015. An invigorated 1st XV rugby squad was captained by Harry Nuttall in 2011-12, and enjoyed a terrific season, winning 21 of their 25 matches and reaching the semi-final of the prestigious Daily Mail Cup; the following year's 1st XV, captained by George Jeavons-Fellows, achieved similar success, winning 14 of their 16 games and reaching the last sixteen in the Daily Mail Cup competition. In the same year, the rugby sevens team won 37 of their 39 games, winning all five of the tournaments entered and getting through to the quarter finals of the national competition, played at Rosslyn Park.

The highlight of the rugby season, however, remained the fixture against RGS Worcester, played at the Worcester Warriors ground, Sixways, since 1999 when Dan Cullen (Chappel House 1992-99) led King's to a 15-10 victory, and always drawing a large crowd of supporters for both teams. King's managed to hold its own in this match, known since 2008 as the 'Modus Cup', with frequent victories.

Not to be outdone by the boys, the senior netball team reached the national schools finals in 2012, 2013 and 2014, and younger teams enjoyed a great run of success at district, county and West Midlands levels. Similarly, a series of good wins in hockey at all age groups

The swimming pool was covered by a polythene 'bubble' until construction of a permanent roof, enclosing the pool, in 1992. Photographed in 1990.

1995-1999 Girls IV which represented England in 1998 and 1999; the crew were National Champions in 1996, 1998 and 1999 and enjoyed 25 regatta wins at junior and senior levels

and levels left that sport primed for future success. A 'Super Netball' fixture, between King's and RGS Worcester, played at the University Arena, University of Worcester, was introduced in 2015.

Team victories were just part of the story of post-millennial sport at King's, however; for a school which does not focus primarily on sport, a surprising number of individual sportsmen and women enjoyed success at national and international level.

Zac Purchase (Oswald House 1997-2004) competed at international rowing events, becoming world lightweight single sculling champion in 2006, ahead of selection as a member of Team GB for the 2008 Olympic Games in Beijing, where he won a gold medal with partner Mark Hunter in the Mens Double Scull event; at the London 2012 Olympic Games he followed this success with a silver medal in the same event at Eton Dorney. Zac was awarded an MBE in 2009.

Rower Zac Purchase (Oswald House 1997-2004), Olympic gold medallist at the ceremony to name a boat in his honour, 2008

Sophie Le Marchand (Chappel House 1996-2007) had the distinction of being the first girl to play in the 1st XI cricket team, which she did for three years, and was selected for the England U21 and England Academy teams, playing in the European Championships and against South Africa, Pakistan and New Zealand, as well as for the MCC against India. Sophie later captained the women's cricket team at Oxford University and went on to play cricket for Somerset and Bath, alongside playing football for Kikk United FC.

Luke Narraway (Oswald House 1997-2002) became the first full King's rugby international since the 1980s when he was selected to play for England against Wales in the Six Nations competition at Twickenham in 2008, having played professionally for Gloucester RFC since leaving King's.

Ross Laidlaw (Oswald House 1998-2002), 1st XV Captain of Luke's team, held the points record of 240 for a King's season, and went on to play professionally for Bristol, London Irish and Plymouth.

Sammi Perry (Bright House 2000-07) represented England in the U17 and U21 sides, competing in the World Youth Netball Championships. From 2005 to 2009, Sammi played for the University of Bath's Superleague Netball team.

Andrew Boyce (School House 2011-13) played rugby for Worcester Warriors while still at school as a member of the club's Elite Player Development Squad, and was selected to represent England in the U18 team during the 2012 season.

As well as team sports, athletics developed as a serious sport, with athletes competing successfully at district, county and regional levels. The traditional sports days gave way to a series of sports afternoons, one for each of the Fourth Forms, Removes and Seniors (Fifth and Sixth Form); due to the scale of the events with such a relatively large school and the level of ability of many of the competitors, the events are no longer held at the playing fields but instead at Nunnery Wood Sports Centre.

A new boathouse, funded by a hugely generous gift from a former King's rower Michael Baker (Choir House 1948-55), opened in 2012, providing a stunning new home for the KSW Boat Club, with additional gym training facilities alongside enhanced boat storage and function spaces.

Sports facilities were further expanded in 2015, with the opening of The Keyes Building (see Chapter 9). In response to the serious overloading of the sports hall, which had been used in a carousel of facilities for PE since the 1990s when the timetable reached full capacity, and high demand for fitness training facilities, the new Sports and Performing Arts Centre had at its heart a four-court multi-purpose sports hall, with a new cardiovascular training suite and weights room, with new changing facilities attached. A new indoor climbing wall with a gallery would allow abseiling, and the grand entrance steps leading up to the playground (styled as 'Castle Court' in 2003) from Severn Street, recorded the achievements of many King's sporting teams through the decades.

Other sports developed and grew in popularity, as the Sixth Form were allowed a greater choice of recreational sports in the 2000s; fencing, badminton, basketball, canoeing, water polo, golf, equestrianism, volleyball, swimming, fitness training and cross-country were among the sports available by 2014. Emphasis on participation in exercise and physical activity became more important, alongside the higher level of competitive sport enjoyed by more élite athletes, recalling the intentions of Bolland, Chappel and Creighton in following the model school ideals of the 1850s.

See also: 'KSW Boat Club', Chapter 3
'Michael Baker Boathouse' and 'The Keyes Building- sports and performing arts centre', Chapter 9
Appendix 11: Sports Captains

Swimming Pool, 2015

Girls and female staff taking part in a 'Race for Life' in aid of cancer charities, 2015. They stand on the steps of the pavillion next to the athletics track, rebuilt in 2010 following a fire.

Sports Hall in The Keyes Building, 2015

2011-12 1st XV rugby and 1st VII netball squads, who achieved national recognition, photographed in the Creighton Memorial Gardens with the 'prow' of the Michael Baker Boathouse, which juts out over the towpath, in the background.

Rowers training in the Michael Baker Boathouse, 2012

CV training and weights suite in The Keyes Building, 2015

9: Taking King's into the 21st century

T H Keyes - Headmaster 1998-2014

Timothy Harold Keyes, M.A., arrived as Headmaster of King's at the age of 43, from the Royal Grammar School, Guildford, where he was Deputy Head and taught Classics. Tim brought with him his wife, Mary Anne, who would teach Maths and Science at King's St Alban's, and their two sons, Sam and Bill. Tim's niece, Philippa, joined them at Number 9 College Green for eighteen months, giving the Headmaster an insight into teenage girls to which his previous experience in boys' schools, and with sons, had not exposed him before. Tim and Mary Anne sent their elder son, Sam, to RGS Worcester, until the Sixth Form at which point he attended King's, and their second son, Bill, was a pupil first at King's St Alban's and then at King's.

Like his predecessor, John Moore, Tim Keyes had a particular interest in higher education and the HMC (Headmasters' and Headmistresses' Conference), serving on the Board of UCAS as a representative of the independent schools' sector and on the Universities' Subcommittee of the HMC. He also shared a common interest in European affairs, and was keen to involve the school in the EU's 'Comenius Project', developing a relationship with Dom Gymnasium in Magdeburg, Germany, where he spent much of his sabbatical in the summer of 2009.

Tim and Mary Anne are devout Christians; Mary Anne became a Reader in the Church of England and both were actively involved in parish life at the Church of St Philip and St James, Hallow, where Tim was an enthusiastic bell-ringer - a hobby he developed into a popular activity at King's. Mary Anne led a revived Christian Union, with Chaplain Mark Dorsett, often hosting meetings at Number 9 and leading 'away weekends' at the Gaines Centre, near Broadwas. The school's relationship with Worcester Cathedral became, perhaps, stronger than ever, with a School Eucharist held in the Crypt every Wednesday before school, alongside regular services for the whole school at the start and end of each term and to mark significant religious festivals. A firm relationship flourished between King's and fellow C of E Foundation School, Bishop Perowne Church of England College, on Merriman's Hill, Worcester, independent of the later requirements of the Charities Commission that private schools should share facilities and expertise with state schools. The two schools shared a common strength in the performing arts and, since 2010, an All-Weather Pitch, built in the grounds of Bishop Perowne College but funded by King's; a number of shared activities also developed, including debating, Maths and Latin.

A school on the edge of change

By the time of John Moore's retirement in July 1998, the first group of girls to join King's in the Lower Fourth (Year 7) had just left the Upper Sixth, and girls made up 47% of the total number of pupils. The decision to end boarding had resulted in the remaining boy boarders living in Choir House, which was entirely a day house by that time, in the care of Peter Iddon, and the last girl boarders living with Sarah Le Marchand in College House. College House, which had been the 'front door' to King's since the 1970s, was about to be handed back to the Dean and Chapter, and work was under way to convert The Hostel and the Old Library into the school's new administrative centre. Boarding had been scheduled to end in July 1999 when

Timothy Harold Keyes, with wife Mary Anne and sons Sam and Bill, shortly after arriving at King's in 1998

its closure had been announced at the end of 1997, and the last 11 boarders duly departed at the end of Keyes' first year as Headmaster.

Among Tim Keyes's first impressions of King's was that *"the school premises felt a little tired, particularly School House, with so many walls and stairs, and there was no clear school entrance - Castle Place felt like a tradesmen's entrance"*. The recently appointed Bursar, Galen Bartholomew, had similar impressions of *"derelict Fives courts, antiquated boarding facilities and aged minibuses"*.

The decision by the new Labour Government in 1997 to end the Assisted Places Scheme, which had enabled so many pupils from less privileged backgrounds to benefit from a King's education, had made a serious impact on pupil numbers, with only 72 pupils joining the Lower Fourth in September 1998, compared to previous incoming groups of at around 100. This, along with the great reduction in the number of boarders, and the poor state of many buildings, in particular those which had been boarding accommodation, gave a distinct feeling of austerity, and even the prospect of staff redundancies.

This should not suggest that Keyes saw the school as being in a state of decline; there was much to feel positive about. The first girl Head of School, Jenny [Pearce] Easterbrook, led his first group of monitors, which also included the talented Allan Clayton, later to become a famous name in the world of opera. Relations between staff and pupils were strong, with older members of staff setting the tone of behaviour and breadth of commitment. The school's pastoral system, campus, ancient buildings and traditions were positive assets and the school was highly-regarded.

Building on the school's strengths would require a significant shift in a number of areas, and the looming inspection, the first to be undertaken by the Independent Schools Inspectorate, due in 1999, certainly added to the sense of urgency.

The process of change

King's had been led by a Headmaster and Second Master (Usher) since the school was founded in 1541. This resulted in a highly autocratic style of leadership which was ill-suited for a modern school; King's was already a large organisation, with three schools in its Foundation; the senior school had 79 teachers and 825 pupils. An important structural change had been implemented the year before Keyes arrived with the establishment of a formal 'Senior Management Team', comprising the Headmaster, Second Master (Tim Hickson), Bursar (Galen Bartholomew), Senior Mistress (Patricia Stevens) and Director of Studies (Julian Thould); this group would share the management of the school, working in a 'cabinet-style' with frequent meetings to consider carefully all aspects of school life.

An early task was to prepare for the school's first Inspection, undertaken by Julian Thould and Patricia Stevens. There had not been any regular monitoring of the school and there was no 'handbook', few committees or regular meetings. Julian and Patricia worked hard to implement these, as necessary aspects of the inspection process.

The staff were *"on the mature side"*, with only two teachers in their twenties and only three Heads of Department appointed within the previous few years - Mark Dorsett (Religious Studies and Chaplain), Richard Geary (Chemistry) and Andrew Longley (Geography). The staff was very experienced but somewhat averse to change, which required careful handling. A system of continuing professional development (CPD), which included in-service training (INSET) and a process of review and development for staff, first for teachers and later including support staff, was required, and responsibility for this fell to Patricia Stevens, whose role in overseeing the integration of girls was now complete and became primarily one of caring for the welfare of staff and of pupils, in respect of 'child protection'.

Sarah Le Marchand was given the new role of 'Head of Sixth Form' from September 1999, with the dual aims of promoting the Sixth Form at King's, and increasing the number of candidates for 16+ entry to the school, and supporting students through the UCAS service for university applications, which had become a significant and onerous responsibility for House Tutors. A second new post, that of 'Head of Fourth Forms' (Years 7 and 8) was created in 2000 and filled by new member of staff Jackie Golightly, the purpose of which was to oversee the Fourth Form Masters and Mistresses (Fourth Form Tutors from 2006) and assist them in providing a distinct and supportive experience for those in the 'middle school', between joining King's at 11+ from one of the Junior Schools or from outside and moving up to the Houses in the Lower Remove (Year 9); the role was taken over by Andrew Longley in September 2001.

Meanwhile, the move to Hostel House was completed, offering staff significant new facilities and with more office space to allow room for the new administration which would be needed. Much of the rest of the buildings were decorated, as a 'quick fix' to improve the appearance of the school while plans were considered for full refurbishments.

Tim Keyes's feelings of *"elation and relief"* when, in November 1999, the Inspection Report stated that King's was a good school, were followed by embarrassment that he should ever have doubted it. The pointed remark from the Lead Inspector that *"I've never been in a place where there was so much paint drying"* was an accurate reflection of how much had needed to be done in such a short time. This was followed by the cheering recruitment figures for the following September, showing that the incoming Lower Fourth would again number around 100 pupils.

The school curriculum

A number of new A Level courses had been introduced during the last years of John Moore's headship: Business Studies (alongside Economics, by Russ Mason) and Information Technology (by John Roslington) in September 1996, with Theatre Studies (by Rosemary Diamond and Stephan Le Marchand) and Physical Education (by Andy Guest) added in September 1997. English Language was later introduced to complement English Literature. Social Biology was dropped from the curriculum in 1999 to allow a greater focus on Biology. Religious Studies was removed as a compulsory GCSE and later transformed by Mark Dorsett into 'Religion and Philosophy', which boosted the number of students opting for the subject.

The new A Levels set the school in good stead for the Government's 'Curriculum 2000' initiative, which saw the end of traditional, linear A Level courses, with examinations at the end of the second year, and the introduction of 'modular' courses, with more frequent examinations and teacher-assessed coursework. It would quickly become the established practice for the majority of students to select four subjects to study for one year (AS Level) and then continue with three of these subjects for the second year (A2 Level). Whilst allowing students a chance to study a fourth subject, this did result in the loss of some 'extras' which had been offered to our Sixth Form, including GCSE Drama and additional languages, Italian and Russian. The modular courses enabled students to 're-sit' exams several times if necessary, with the aim of improving grades; the unfortunate effect of this was that, for some, the 're-sit' would draw focus away from the exams for their current modules, so the results could suffer. The scheme also introduced examinations very early on during the A Level course, sometimes seen as detrimental to both teaching and learning. It was decided in 2012 that January module examinations would no longer be taken at King's, to alleviate this pressure; the Department for Education decided that the 'new' exam system, both for A Level and GCSE courses, would be replaced by a return to the 'old' system from 2015. A proposed International Baccalaureate system was not implemented by the DfE, although much talked about in the early 2010s; an 'EBacc', not offered by King's, encouraged Sixth Form students to study a range of subjects, including English, Maths, a science and a language.

Further changes would affect the Sixth Form curriculum at King's, with the addition of 'Government and Politics', offered as an A Level course in 2009 by Peter Gwilliam, Head of History; English Language replaced the two previous A Levels offered; Information Technology, seen as an outdated subject, was dropped in 2010. Students in the Sixth Form were able to study for a GCSE in Philosophy from 2013 and could choose to take an AS Level in Critical Thinking, a new subject which focuses on analytical skills, much sought after by universities. 'Key Skills' replaced the 'Diploma of Achievement' which had aimed to broaden students' horizons, in a similar (though probably better) way to 'General Studies'.

Changes were also made to the range of GCSE courses at King's. GCSE Drama, which had been an 'extra' for the Sixth Form before the advent of A Level Theatre Studies, was introduced as a GCSE option for the Upper Remove (Year 10) from 1999. Religious Studies, which had been taken in the Upper Remove, a year earlier than most examinations, became optional and was moved to the Fifth Form (Year 11), along with Additional Maths GCSE.

The GCSE system came under fire in the media during the 2000s, with exams believed to have become easier, and coursework considered to be too simple. This led to the adoption of the IGCSE (International GCSE) standard by many schools across many subjects. At King's, IGCSE courses had replaced GCSE courses in Maths, English, French, German, Spanish, Biology, Chemistry and Physics, by 2014, with other subjects expected to follow suit during the following few years.

The changes in the exam systems, at both levels, have had an impact on the school's fortunes in the School League Tables, published annually by national newspapers to compare exam results. When first introduced in the 1990s, King's didn't generally perform well against other schools, and John Moore made it a policy to ignore League Table positions, as they did not reflect the level of achievement for individuals or the overall quality of education offered by the school. However, the League Tables persisted and parental awareness of the relative positions of King's and its local competitors meant that King's would have to take them seriously. The quality of teaching and learning at the core of the King's education meant that over a few years, King's quickly outperformed its local rivals, and, from the early 2000s was the highest-placed at GCSE in the city and at A Level in the county for a number of years, despite changes in the exams and the introduction of the (more difficult) IGCSE courses.

Developing the campus for the future

During 1997, the Bursar had commissioned a full survey of the school site. Amongst other things, the report showed that boarding was taking up 11 % of the total floorspace to accommodate a forecast 11 boarders in the academic year 1998-99. The end of boarding would provide an unprecedented opportunity for the school to consider the use of its buildings, and to provide new facilities to accommodate its future growth.

A strategic review of the senior school site was then commissioned by the Governors, and this was carried out by Richard Slawson and John Christophers of Associated Architects, a Birmingham-based architectural firm introduced to King's by Galen Bartholomew, the Bursar who had been appointed in 1996. A report, which formed the basis for a ten-year plan, was produced in the summer of 1998, addressing the immediate concerns of the Governors, the Bursar and the newly-appointed Headmaster.

The key issues to be addressed involved the loss of Number 15 College Green, which was to be replaced as the school's administrative centre by Number 5, and the report included proposals for the reordering of The Hostel, to be vacated that summer, and the Old Library (see Chapter 4); the anticipated demolition of the 'New Block' which had passed the end of its design life (see Chapter 6); the relocation of Oswald House and Bright House along with providing new accommodation for English and Classics (this would be found in Choir House, Chapter 4); provision of a new library, a Sixth Form Centre, additional sports facilities and the need for better changing areas and a replacement for the Tuck Shop, on the corner of Edgar Street and Severn Street. The increasing pressure on car parking spaces, with the demand for greater energy efficiency

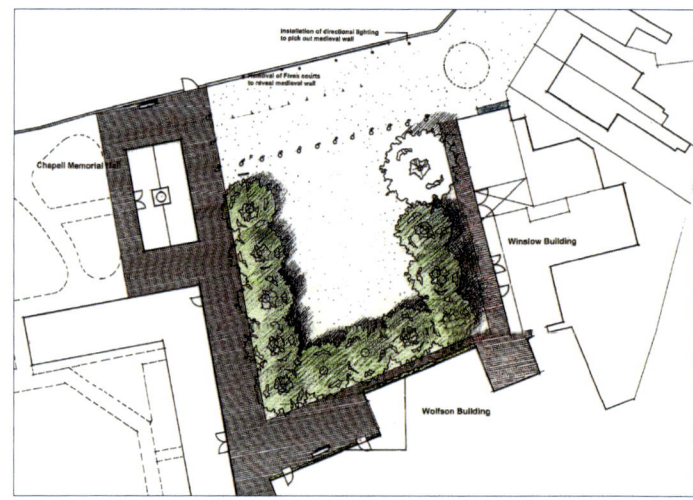

Above: Concept drawing for the new 'Castle Court'
Below: Workmen laying the new yellow stone surface, August 2003

and concern for the historic nature of the school's environs were also considered.

The development of the school site was overseen by the Bursar, Galen Bartholomew, whose background in industry and construction and sense of history provided great support to Donald Howell, Chairman of Governors from 1993-2009, who, with Tim Keyes, was enthusiastic about the opportunities for expansion and renovation. The largest building project during John Moore's time as Headmaster had been the construction of the School Theatre (see Chapter 8), and the projects already envisaged for the start of the new decade would amount to far more than this; careful management would be needed in this, both logistically in terms of access to buildings and facilities during works, and financially, to ensure that the development would be affordable. Key relationships developed, between the school (Bartholomew, Keyes and Howell) and the architects, particularly John Christophers, John Jones (Quantity Surveyor), Chris Guy (Cathedral Archaeologist), Archaeologist Mike Napthan (whose reports on the findings of archaeological work at the School House and Severn Street sites can be found in Appendix 15), and the Dean and Chapter, whose co-operation was invaluable.

After the re-ordering of Hostel House, the next building to be developed was Choir House, which would house the English and Classics departments in spacious new accommodation, along with a new Health Centre, replacing the Sanatorium in Castle House, and space for Bright House (in the eaves of the building) and Chappel House on the ground floor. A new ICT suite, named after Enigma code-breaker Alan Turing, provided a much-needed facility for access to computers and the new online learning tools available.

A further ICT suite, equipped with specialist software and equipment for teaching modern languages, was created from two classrooms in the languages building. This provided a huge enhancement to the teaching facilities of the MFL department.

Although numbers 1, 2 and 3 were demolished decades before, planning restrictions meant that the dilapidated house at 4 Castle Place had to be retained and restored. The house was refaced in sandstone and refurbished as a home for a resident caretaker, Fred McFee, who joined the school in 1998.

After surveying the 'New Block', it was determined that structural repairs could be carried out and a positive prognosis for the building was given. In 2001, a complete transformation of the building was undertaken, including replacement of the old-fashioned windows and the addition of a striking pitched roof, to create the Annett Building (see Chapter 6), which provided a base for Fourth Form pupils, a gym and dance studio for the PE department and eight large classrooms, an office, storeroom and departmental library for Mathematics.

4, 5 and 6 Castle Place following restoration of number 4, photographed in 2015

Funding for the adaptations needed for full co-education had come mostly from the sale of buildings which would no longer be required - the former Sanatorium at 7 College Precincts, the Uniform Shop at 11 Edgar Street, moved to the back of the former Porcelain Works building on Severn Street, and the Tuck Shop, whose functions were incorporated into the Dining Hall. However, funding for projects during Keyes' tenure as Headmaster would come from a combination of strong cash flow, arising from an increase in pupil numbers, along with some limited and prudent borrowing.

The disused and unloved Fives Courts were demolished in 2003, opening up the playground, which would be redesigned as 'Castle Court' and would become a pleasant, open space, free of cars and surrounded by trees and benches - a much more welcoming approach to the school. The potential damage caused to the castle wall by the Fives courts meant that the rear wall was rendered, which also protected the roof windows of the Reprographics department, located behind the wall. New school gates would be added around the campus later, with a sliding gate across Castle Place and modern gates to replace the former School House gates from College Green; these would add significantly to the security of the school site out of hours.

The Theatre, which by 2001 was already 25 years old, underwent a refurbishment, including repainting of the auditorium to a more suitable dark blue, and updating of the lobby area and green room. The Theatre was named in honour of John Moore, whose foresight had provided King's with such a significant and, at the time, unusual, facility, and re-opened in 2003. An air-circulation system was installed in 2008, funded by the King's School Parents' Committee.

A new Library had been planned for some time, and School House was identified as the most suitable location, with the large rooms available and its position at the heart of the school campus. This would be a very large project, in size, complexity and cost; a fundraising campaign was undertaken by the Foundation Development Office to help meet the cost, projected to be more than £1,600,000; the campaign raised £190,000, including a generous grant from the Wolfson Foundation. Before building could start, however, the Music department needed to be relocated from the lower floor of School House; Castle House was transformed into a new Music School which was opened in July 2003 by Stephen Cleobury.

Once the Library had moved out, Edgar Tower provided space for A Level artists, while work on the new Art School was carried out. The former Porcelain Works canteen on Severn Street, purchased in 1991 for a mere £99,000, had been used by the Art department for some years, as Sixth Form studio space and a gallery, the department having long-since outgrown its home in the first floor of the Wolfson Building. The Uniform Shop, at the back of the building, was closed, with the business transferred to 'Schooltogs' in New Street. The poor quality rear extension to the Edwardian building was removed, to be replaced by an impressive glass and brick structure, linked in to the original building, in which the timber roof beams were exposed. The resulting Art School is a light and airy space, with a double height gallery, large studios, and individual spaces for A Level artists.

During this time, a complete refurbishment of each of the school's thirteen science laboratories, in the Winslow Building and Biology Block, was also carried out, employing a specialist design and installation company. The technicians' prep rooms in Chemistry and Physics were also refurbished. Once the laboratories were finished in 2006, the Science Lecture Theatre, on the first floor of Winslow, was upgraded, with modern, more comfortable seating and enhanced ICT and presentation facilities.

The Wolfson Building was refurbished next, providing additional space for Design and Technology, which after the departure of the Art department in 2007, now occupied both floors. A grand, double-height, glass and steel entrance porch was installed at the east end of the building, and a fire escape staircase added to the west end, which was designed to be joined into the, already

School Archive

An informal School Archive was established by Peter Gwilliam and Caroline Roslington in 1993, with a handful of boxes in an upper room in Edgar Tower. A Sixth Form Archives Club, comprising Alex Nicol, Paul Overton, James Roslington, Essi Sadeghi-Dehkurdi and Julian Wood, carried out research into the history of the school and its site, resulting in the publication of *'The King's School, Worcester - and a history of its site'*, edited by Caroline Roslington, in 1994.

An official School Archive began in 1997, housed in rooms at the top of School House, and managed by Caroline Roslington. During the following years the collection of artefacts and records grew, and the School Archive developed into a wonderful resource for the school.

A new home for the School Archive was found in 2007; the western side of Edgar Tower, formerly part of the School Library, comprises a permanent exhibition space, with an adjacent store room and work space for the Archivist and pupil members of the archive clubs.

The work of the School Archive expanded during Caroline's tenure as Archivist, especially after her retirement from the History Department in 2009. Researchers and archivists from other organisations, including the Commonwealth War Graves Commission, and local historians developed relationships with what quickly became established as a nationally important archive. Requests for information from OVs and their families were handled regularly, and many OVs have returned to King's to view the collections and share their memories of the school.

An Oral Archive was started to capture these memories for posterity, along with talks by Barnabas Group speakers, and addresses in College Hall and the Cathedral; by 2015, the Oral Archive included contributions from more than 20 OVs, with recollections of King's going back as far as 1946.

A regular feature of the Annual OV Reunion Dinner has become a display from the School Archive of the history of the school, alongside photographs and Vigornian extracts for year groups marking particular milestones at the Dinner. Displays and materials provided for other events, including lunches, reunions and building openings, always prove popular.

The role of School Archivist was taken over by Pauline Baum in 2011, when she moved from the School Library. Since that time, and with the assistance of Pauline Wright (Hon OV), the work of the School Archive has continued to grow and flourish.

Thousands of items have been catalogued, ranging from school registers and prospectuses to gas masks, caps and canes. The *Vigornian* magazine has been converted into a digital, searchable format, which is in itself a valuable resource for many, including the Foundation Development Office, which works closely with the School Archive.

Two very popular clubs continue to allow pupils to come face-to-face with the history of King's, a Sixth Form Archives Club and 'Raiders of the Lost Archive' for younger pupils. The young archivists help to catalogue new items, many of which are donated by the OV community, prepare displays and respond to requests for information.

A major project, *'King's in 100 Objects'* was started in 2012, with pupils, staff and OVs invited to suggest objects (or places, pieces of text or photographs) that would sum up the school for them.

To mark the centenary of the First World War, the School Archive embarked on a number of projects, including posting extracts from the diaries of OVs involved in the war on Twitter, alongside more traditional exhibitions and talks.

Pauline Baum retired in February 2015, passing on the stewardship of the School Archive to Harriet Fisher.

Caroline Roslington pictured with members of the Sixth Form Archives Club, 2008

Above: Sixth Form archivists at work, 2015
Below: School Archive exhibition room, Edgar Tower, 2013

Pauline Baum with the 'Raiders of the Lost Archive', 2014

Castle Court, 2015

anticipated, Keyes Building, which would include a new prep room for the technician.

Classrooms were redecorated in other buildings, including the 'Fourth Form Block' (1925 classrooms, with later extensions), home to Geography and Religious Studies, where a new Geography Library included much-improved ICT resources, and also Number 12 College Green, the base for History, Politics, Economics, Business Studies and the Chaplaincy. The Dining Hall was refurbished in 2002, offering a wider choice of school lunches, and the Chappel Memorial Room's cupola was painted gold when that building was refurbished in 2002.

As the end of the first ten-year 'master plan' for the school campus approached, it was clear that, whilst so much had already been achieved, there was still more to do; the number of pupils had continued to increase and, by 2007, stood at 928, and the number of staff had grown to 157, including 63 support staff. This put tremendous pressure on certain facilities, including the Sports Hall, gym, dance studio, changing areas, Sixth Form study spaces, meeting rooms, used for conferences and assessments as well as meetings, the Dining Hall and the John Moore Theatre, as well as car parking. Growth in the number of pupils studying languages at GCSE and A Level meant that many of the languages teachers were unable to teach in the MFL building.

'The Salmon's Leap' public house, located on Severn Street, between the Art School and John Moore Theatre, and behind the Wolfson Building, unexpectedly came up for sale in 2006. With permission granted to purchase the adjacent car park, used for the Theatre, which had been leased for many years, the Governors gave consent for the school to purchase the building, with its extensive garden, as well as the car park, and a large plot of land was now available for the school to build on.

In a plan reminiscent of the 1880s designs for School House (see Chapter 4), Associated Architects devised a scheme to include accommodation for as many of the school's outstanding needs as possible. The ambitious design for a 'Sports and Performing Arts Centre' would incorporate a large, multi-purpose sports hall, a new gym, dance and drama studios, an underground car park, a new entrance foyer for the John Moore Theatre, complete with new green room, additional changing facilities, additional classrooms, a Sixth Form Centre, meeting rooms and an indoor climbing wall. A courtyard to the rear of the Wolfson Building would open access to Wolfson and the Art School, and the new building would link with the John Moore Theatre. A striking bronze frontage, to reflect the supposed Bronze Age settlement under the site, would follow the curved boundary of the plot, with a roof-line echoing the former Royal Worcester Porcelain factory buildings opposite. A grand set of steps would lead from Severn Street to Castle Court, and provide the long-desired 'front door' for the campus, missing since the late 1990s. A major fundraising campaign, the largest undertaken by the school, was launched, with a target of £1,000,000, the remainder of the funding to come from borrowing, planned to be repaid within five years due to historically low interest rates, and retained surpluses, the result of careful financial management during the previous few years.

Following extensive design and budget meetings, over nearly seven years, which, despite some compromises, enabled virtually all the previously identified needs to be met, the contract was signed early in 2013. This happened to coincide with the lowest point in the building industry's slump, following the 2007 recession, allowing the final cost of the project to come in at £9.5 million -some £4 million cheaper than a 2010 estimate of £13.5 million. The SPACE, as the building was known during its development, would include a large conference room (named 'The Vigornian Room' in recognition of a substantial contribution made towards the project by the OV Club) which would, in time, replace the Severn Room, allowing for the expansion of the MFL Department. Additional classroom space would also be available in the lower level of the Annett Building, where the gym and dance studio would no longer be required.

Improvements to the Winslow Building included a modern science lecture theatre and refurbished laboratories

Thanks in no small part to the Foundation Development Office's 'SPACE Campaign', the funds were successfully raised and a ground-breaking ceremony took place in May 2013. Just twelve months later a topping out ceremony marked the completion of the building works in May 2014, with fitting-out completed ready for the building to be named The Keyes Building after the Headmaster whose vision helped to form The King's School of the 21st century, and opened on 20th June 2015.

The other two items included in the second ten-year plan were both sports facilities - an all-weather sports pitch and a new boathouse, and both were completed before construction of the 'SPACE' got under way. The first of these was enabled by the partnership between King's and Bishop Perowne College, built at Merrimans Hill, on land provided by Worcestershire County Council and funded by The King's School. This fulfilled a long-term ambition to provide a year-round surface for sports, and the All-Weather Pitch, dedicated to the memory of Peter Curle, opened in 2010.

A generous donation from Old Vigornian Michael Baker of more than £2,500,000 enabled the school to plan and build a new boathouse. The stunning Michael Baker Boathouse transformed the south-western corner of the school campus,

All-Weather Pitch at Bishop Perowne Church of England College, Merriman's Hill, opened in 2010

Foundation Development Office

Among the key priorities given to Tim Keyes on his appointment as Headmaster was to focus on fundraising, both to build bursary funds following the end of the Assisted Places scheme, and to generate finance for much-needed capital projects at King's.

To this end, the Foundation Development Office was established in 2001, with Carol Bawden at the helm from 2004. Carol had strong connections with the school, having been a sister of King's pupils in the 1960s and a King's parent in the 1980s. Carol described the role of the Foundation Development Office:

'Rather than the accustomed 'smash and grab raid', a one-off appeal within a designated time frame, we were looking to emulate the American model of 'development' as an important element of the school's strategy. The fundamental difference was the concept that long-term successful fundraising only happened when time, energy and effort was given to understanding who the people are in our community and gaining their trust and respect. 'Friendraising' needed to precede 'fundraising'.'

The FDO would work closely alongside the Development Trust and OV Club. There are a number of facets to the work of the office, but two key objectives: to build and strengthen relationships within the King's community, and to seek philanthropic support from all areas of that community for means-tested bursaries and contributions towards capital projects.

Achieving the first of these two objectives involved communicating with Old Vigornians and former parents and encouraging them to reconnect with their alma mater. The 'Connect' magazine was introduced in January 2001 and is sent free of charge to all OVs, Hon OVs and former parents. It aimed to inform readers of important school events and news, reunion events, the work of the School Archive and news from OVs. Working closely with the OV Club, the FDO assisted in the organisation of the Annual Reunion Weekend and promoted school events which were of interest to the community. A second annual reunion, a dinner in London, was re-established in 2001; the FDO also organised a programme of regular events around the country and overseas. These included two highly successful events in the USA, hosted by Michael Pimley (The Hostel 1961-71) in 2008 and 2012, reunions in Hong Kong and Malaysia in 2009, and in Paris and Sydney in 2011.

The Barnabas Group was founded by the Headmaster in 2008 to build on the legacy of St Barnabas, a Christian missionary and "the son of encouragement" (Acts of the Apostles 4:36). Distinguished OVs, who have excelled in their chosen professions, were invited by the Headmaster to join this group and to speak to the school in College Hall of their experiences (see Appendix 10). OVs and parents were also involved extensively with careers, work experience and young enterprise and encouraged to return to share their knowledge and expertise with current pupils.

The second objective is further divided into two large tasks: raising long-term bursary support and financing capital building projects. King's had a proud tradition of providing opportunities for academically gifted and talented children to receive a high quality education regardless of their families' ability to pay; the Direct Grant and Assisted Places schemes helped to facilitate this, but since this type of support had been withdrawn by successive governments the school needed to provide its own funding.

The school had no endowment funds and one of the challenges was to create a capital resource which could be invested in a flexible manner and from which bursaries could be funded. The Enduring Bursary Fund was established in 2011 thanks to the gift of £1,000,000 to the school from Michael Baker (Choir House

Guests at the 2012 USA Reunion, hosted by Michael Pimley at his home in Princeton, New Jersey

Sophie Whitworth and Carol Bawden, photographed at a 2008 event to mark Henry VIII's 500th birthday, and celebrate King's Scholars

The Weston Centre, a Sixth Form social space within The Keyes Building, opened in 2015

1948-55). The fund continued to grow and support a substantial number of bursaries each year.

The Fellowship Bursary Scheme was set up in 2006 by Andrew Underwood (School House 1977-87) to encourage OVs and friends of King's to join together to share the cost of supporting a bursary. These funds were spent as they were received and a number of well-established groups were able to fund bursaries.

The first major capital campaign for the FDO ran from 2004-05 to support the development of a new Library in School House; the 'School House Fund for Academic Excellence' saw an appeal to OVs from School House; the FDO also conducted a telephone campaign in 2005 using pupils and parents to call members of the community. This, along with a generous grant from the Wolfson Foundation, achieved the campaign objective of raising £190,000 towards the £1.6 million cost of the project.

Shortly after completion of this appeal, Carol Bawden stepped down as Foundation Development Director. She continued in a consultative role, and, through her close work with the Baker family, she was able to realise their dream of funding a new boathouse for King's for which they donated a further £2.5 million.

Sophie Whitworth, an experienced marketing manager, took over the school's development strategy. In addition to building on Carol's work with OVs and increasing bursary support, one of Sophie's priorities was to mastermind an appeal to raise £1,000,000 towards the cost of the planned 'Sports and Performing Arts Centre', and so 'The SPACE Campaign' was born. Following a variety of initiatives, The SPACE Campaign was highly successful and, with almost theatrical timing, achieved the £1,000,000 target at the 'Fireworks Finale' event in August 2013.

The FDO, assisted by Alice Brunt since 2012, continued to work closely with the community reuniting friends, bringing OVs back to King's, promoting the school's aims and ensuring that a King's education would be available to many gifted children, regardless of their families' finances, for generations to come.

The 1541 Society was founded in 2003 to bring together all those who had supported the school in a major way whether through donations or by making a legacy pledge to the school, or who had given of their time and expertise to campaigns and projects. The first society meeting took place in Edgar Tower in 2007 and since then it gathered on an annual basis to meet with the Headmaster and be updated on the progress of the school and the plans for the future.

The SPACE Campaign's 'Fireworks Finale' ended with an auction, hosted by Will Kerton (Oswald House 1982-92), at which the £1,000,000 target was reached

opening onto the Creighton Memorial Gardens and providing breath-taking views up and down the River Severn. The Boathouse opened in April 2012. Michael Baker gave a further £1,000,000 to establish a bursary fund; his family's extraordinary generosity transformed the school and the lives of many of its pupils.

Landscaping work around the campus improved the outdoor spaces, with seating and trees in a new 'Library Square' to the west of the Monitors' Lawn, new courtyards behind the houses on College Green and in front of the Annett Building, and a new surface and facilities for the Fourth Form Playground. New paving and planting alongside the Long Gallery of School House improved that area, as did a canopy to shelter the daily queue outside the Dining Hall, funded by the KSPC. New lighting accompanied new CCTV cameras around the campus, with the low level lighting in both Castle Court and the Creighton Memorial Gardens being particularly atmospheric. A system of 'heads-up' mapping, in the form of monolithic signs around the site, was designed to guide parents and visitors to key school locations.

The Fourth Form Playground, refurbished in 2005

'Library Square' at the western end of the Monitors' Lawn, 2015.
Creighton's quadrangle between the Chappel Memorial Reading Room, the 1925 classrooms and the rear of The Hostel and Castle House had been brought up to date.
The double-height glazed entrance leads to the Long Gallery, from which the Library is accessed over a glass bridge.

Aerial photographs of the senior school campus, September 2015.

These images show the extent of development in Severn Street, from the Art School to the Michael Baker Boathouse, undertaken between 1962 and 2015. The scale of The Keyes Building, which links Severn Street with Castle Court can be fully appreciated from above.

Edgar Tower is shrouded in scaffolding for the restoration work which had recently begun.

School House - a new Library for King's

The much-loved library in Edgar Tower (see Chapter 2) had been confirmed by two school inspections to be too small and inaccessible for what, by the early twenty-first century was a large school over a large campus, of which Edgar Tower was on the periphery.

Plans were set in motion under the librarianship of Alison Scaiff, and developed further by Pauline Baum, with the full support of the management team and Governors, to relocate the library to a more central position, and it was decided that the lower floors of School House, which would be vacated by the Music department once it moved into Castle House in 2003, would offer both sufficient space and the central location required. Associated Architects devised a scheme which would see the northern entrance of School House transformed into a grand lobby for a new 'Long Gallery' which would be built along the eastern side of the ground floor. Full-height glass doors would lead to a glass bridge and into the main area of the Library, through enlarged bays, previously ground floor windows; a staircase would lead down to a double-height space for reading and periodicals, a large computer suite and teaching room for Sixth Form use, office and workspace for the librarians

Entrance to the Library from the Long Gallery over the glass bridge

and Head of Sixth Form, and accommodation for the Careers department on the lower level.

Once the plans were approved, two major projects needed to be completed: an archaeological survey of the site, which was completed by Mike Napthan (see Appendix 15), and a fund-raising campaign, the first capital campaign to be undertaken by the Foundation Development Office, under Carol Bawden's leadership. The campaign included parent-to-parent phone calls, an appeal to Old Vigornians, particularly those from School House, and a bid for funding from the Wolfson Foundation, which would provide a significant contribution to the cost of installing the 'technology' into the building. The names of many of the donors are etched into the window at the southern entrance to the Long Gallery.

Construction was under way by 2005, and due to the central position of the building, and the need to continue to use the upper floors and southern end of School House, caused significant disruption. There can be little doubt, however, that the project was enormously beneficial for the school and its pupils, and a great success.

The stunning architecture of the Library, with the glass bridge, cantilevered shelving and extensive use of wood, achieved four architectural prizes, including a coveted Royal Institute of British Architects Award in 2006.

In August 2006 came the move from Edgar Tower. A commercial removal team was employed - they had just moved the Ashmolean Library's books, which was a sound precedent. In a smooth operation, the contents of the Library, including more

The main floor of the Library, with doors to the McTurk Room

The school motto, from Sophocles, in the Long Gallery of School House
"I learn what may be taught, I seek what may be sought, my other wants I dare to ask from Heaven in prayer."

Southern aspect of the Long Gallery. The Indian Bean tree, planted by Headmaster Andrew Milne, is in the foreground.

than 15,000 books, were slid down the stairs of Edgar Tower in less than two days on wooden planks; the spiral staircase became a helter-skelter for boxes of books, packed in sequence from the shelves.

Following a remarkable amount of work, the Library opened on the first day of the autumn term, 2006, complete with books, DVDs, periodicals and more than 30 computers.

Notable school figures are celebrated in the Library: the lower floor computer suite is named the 'Bolland Room', after William Bolland (Head Master 1868-79), whose grandson David Bolland (School House 1932-37) was able to visit the Library before his death in 2013; a large quiet study room on the ground floor is known as the 'McTurk Room', after Dan McTurk, Housemaster of School House, 1946-62; a bronze bust of Henry VIII (see cover photo) was sculpted by Martin Lorenz (School House 1945-50) and presides over the periodicals area. A stained glass panel in the Long Gallery, 'The Tree of Knowledge' was created by Anthony Bolland (School House 1952-60), great-grandson of William Bolland, and features ancient and contemporary forms of writing floating across a tree of knowledge, with a ladder representing a child's journey into knowledge, pictured right.

The Library was opened by poet Roger McGough in October 2006, and under the stewardship of Pauline Baum, assisted by Pauline Wright, developed quickly into a well-used, popular and peaceful space, at the very heart of the school.

Pauline moved to the School Archive (and so, back to Edgar Tower) in 2011, and was succeeded as Librarian by Annabel Jeffery. Pupils could enjoy access to a range of resources, with more than 200 books borrowed each day, a quiet working space, and a number of activities including a book club with more than 40 members.

'The Tree of Knowledge' stained glass panel, created by Anthony Bolland (School House 1952-60) which was installed in the Long Gallery of School House in 2009

Teaching and learning

Developing the school campus undoubtedly provided a more attractive environment, but the key focus was to provide the highest possible standards of teaching and learning producing pupils who "felt comfortable in their own skin", to use Tim Keyes' expression, and who could naturally develop into high academic achievers. Many departments, including English, Mathematics, Geography, Religious Studies (later renamed 'Religion and Philosophy') and the sciences, had modern, refurbished classrooms within single buildings, centred around departmental libraries and studies.

Additional space for teaching in the new buildings helped to change the way in which many subjects were taught. The Art School provided small, individual studios for A Level artists, alongside larger studio spaces and exhibition space; provision of computers in the Art School allowed teaching of digital image manipulation. Design and Technology gained computers for CAD (computer-aided design) software and space for new equipment, including a laser-cutter and milling machine, enabling ever-more complex and intricate projects to be produced. The new Music School included a large cluster of keyboards connected to computers with recording and notation software, radically enhancing the teaching of musical composition techniques. Of course, teaching of PE benefited from the many new facilities, most centred around The Keyes Building from 2015.

Placing the Library at the heart of the school campus was perhaps the most significant of these changes, as it enabled wider use of the resources, both by pupils for recreational reading and private study, and during taught lessons - ample space for computer terminals with access to online resources was provided alongside a collection of more than 10,000 books, periodicals and multimedia resources.

Perhaps even more so than the Library, the use of technology within the classroom has transformed teaching across the school. In the 1980s, some teachers made use of overhead projectors and slide projectors, but, even by the late 1990s, there were very few computers in classrooms, other than those in the IT department, whose use was largely restricted to those studying IT or, because of their location in the Winslow Building, Chemistry and Physics. The introduction of interactive whiteboards - the first was piloted in the lecture theatre by Russ Baum in 2002 - revolutionised the classroom environment; to run an interactive whiteboard required a computer and a projector, and these quickly spread around the school, so that, by 2014, almost every classroom had this equipment installed, and the remaining rooms had projectors or digital displays.

The new technology offered teachers alternatives to 'chalk and talk' - the traditional writing on the board, working through text books and dictation of notes - with a wealth of subject and topic-specific resources available, including presentations, video clips, notes and digital experiments. New teachers had often learned to make use of the content-rich resources while training, and the younger staff quickly embraced the new technology, leading many of the 'more established' teachers with them. In later years, the use of portable 'tablet' devices introduced yet more interactivity into the classroom environment. The computer network infrastructure was expanded significantly, with fibre optic cables laid under the playground and from building to building, connecting the computers, which by 2014 numbered

Ethan Sugden (Creighton House 2004-11) was among the first to receive the 'King's Certificate' from Professor David Green, Vice-Chancellor of the University of Worcester, 2010

more than 700, with central network servers, holding terrabytes (TB) of data, sharing printers and providing Internet access; much of the network resources were accessible for pupils and staff from home, via an electronic 'gateway', from 2012.

Access to such tools in the classroom, and with virtually all the pupils having computers and Internet access at home, altered the function of the ICT department; a teacher was less likely to take a class to an ICT room to look at online resources or type essays, so these facilities were more often used for coursework and using interactive software. With ICT embedded across the curriculum, ICT lessons could be devoted to specialist skills such as video animation and programming, rather than use of word processing, presentation and spreadsheet software.

New technology had a significant impact on the teaching of languages; a 'Multi-Media Centre' was created in the MFL building in 2002, offering a network of computers interconnected and attached to a teacher's console, allowing individual, paired and group conversational skills to be developed, alongside the use of interactive, dedicated software.

Of course, technological advancements were not the only developments in the school curriculum. Coursework, also called 'controlled assessment', was introduced or extended for all GCSE subjects and many A Level courses, altering the flow of work and the balance of the examinations during the courses. There were also changes in the subjects on offer. Syllabus changes, along with differing requirements of exam boards, led to many departments opting to follow IGCSE courses, which were seen as more rigorous than the GCSE courses they replaced.

In the Fourth Forms, Years 7 and 8, all pupils would take English, Maths, ICT, Biology, Chemistry, Physics, Art, Design and Technology, Drama, Geography, History, Religion and Philosophy, Music, Latin, Languages (German, Spanish and French on a carousel, with pupils choosing two from Year 8), PSHE (delivered by Form Tutors), PE and Games.

In the Lower Remove, Year 9, Classical Civilisation could be taken as an alternative to Latin, and Dance was introduced. PSHE Days, of which there were three in each year, were introduced as an alternative to teaching this in individual classes.

For the Upper Remove and Fifth Form, Years 10 and 11, compulsory subjects were English (both Language and Literature), Maths, the sciences (Biology, Chemistry and Physics, taught as separate subjects but with the option of taking a 'dual award' examination) and one modern language, all of which were studied to GCSE/IGCSE level. Optional subjects included Geography, History, Religious Studies, Classical Civilisation, Latin, additional languages, Art, Design and Technology, Drama and Music. All pupils continued to have weekly PE and Games, and participated in the PSHE Days.

In the Sixth Form, each student would study four subjects in the first year, with most 'dropping' a subject after AS Level at the end of the Lower Sixth. The subject options, in 2014, were English Literature, Mathematics, Further Mathematics, Biology, Chemistry, Salters Chemistry, Physics, Physical Education, Religion and Philosophy, Classical Civilisation, Latin, History, Government and Politics, Economics, Business Studies, Geography, Art, Design and Technology, Drama and Theatre Studies, Music, Spanish, French and German. Critical Thinking, a new subject aimed at training students to develop analytical skills, was offered as an AS Level. All students would also take part in PE and Games lessons, and take the Key Skills course, which replaced the 'Diploma of Achievement' as a general studies-style course, broadening students' knowledge and experiences, including time for careers guidance and university applications.

The Careers department, headed by Brian Griffiths and later by Stephan Le Marchand, offered information to pupils from Year 9 to the Sixth Form on careers as well as university and vocational courses. A Business Conference involved all members of the Lower Sixth and was followed by a week of work experience. In the Upper Sixth, the focus here, as in houses and Key Skills, was on university applications - Sarah Le Marchand, Head of Sixth Form, co-ordinated UCAS applications and the processing of examination results, personal statements and academic references for more than 140 students each year.

Learning Skills, a new department, introduced by Joanna Lucas in 2010, focused on developing 'study' skills and provided additional support for many pupils, particularly, though not exclusively, for those with special educational needs - dyslexia, discalculia and others - throughout the school.

Universities had reported an increasing difficulty in differentiation between strong A Level students; King's had long sought to develop 'rounded' individuals, and, to help students demonstrate this to universities, Richard Chapman, Senior Deputy Head, introduced a new 'King's Certificate for Skills and All-round Achievement' scheme in 2010. In partnership with the University of Worcester and the Hereford and Worcester Chamber of Commerce, the King's Certificate encouraged each member of the Lower Sixth to set a number of targets - academic performance, development of an extra-curricular skill, service to the wider community, presentation skills and meeting a new challenge - with opportunities during the year to review and reflect on progress; successful candidates would receive their certificates at a ceremony in College Hall. The Extended Project Qualification (EPQ) also offered students an opportunity to demonstrate advanced research skills and academic prowess, requiring members of the Upper Sixth to produce a 5,000 word dissertation on a subject of their choosing.

Below: Members of the 2010 Comenius Project group outside the European Parliament, Strasbourg

The Art School

The Art department at King's had a proud reputation for excellence from the 1980s onwards, having moved into the comparatively spacious Wolfson Building in 1973, under the guidance of John Exton, Head of Art from 1983.

Liz Hand, who joined King's as an Art teacher in 1991, became Head of Art in 1993 and oversaw an explosion of arts activity during her 21year tenure as Head of Art and later also Creative and Performing Arts Co-ordinator.

One increasing focus had been encouraging pupils to exhibit work, and exhibitions were mounted regularly in Worcester Cathedral, the Malvern Theatres and a new gallery created in the John Moore Theatre; work was also displayed in the Dining Hall. Highlights were the A Level and GCSE Exhibitions each year, showcasing the very high standard of work.

John's annual GCSE trip to Cornwall continued, and Liz also offered art tours which included such destinations as Amsterdam, New York and China.

Liz had been keen to make art as inclusive as possible, and King's entered the national annual 'Big Draw' competition from 2006 - pupils, staff and families took part every year, and the school's first entry won an award presented by illustrator Quentin Blake at a ceremony at the British Museum. Specialist workshops encouraged pupils, with their families, to explore textiles, jewellery and sculpture. Life drawing classes, for A Level students, developed drawing and observational skills. Clubs for younger pupils allowed expression and nurtured creative flair. Artists-in-residence worked with pupils of all ages to develop particular skills.

An *Arts Alive! Festival* took place in 2002, opening up the creative and performing arts to pupils and staff across the school in a full week of workshops, performance and exhibitions; the festival was so popular it was scheduled to be repeated in a three year cycle, along with similar *Words Alive!* and *Science Alive!* festivals.

Above: A Level Art Studios
Below: Official opening of the Art School by artist Derek Nice

The massive expansion of art made it clear that a larger home would be required, and plans were drawn up to convert the former Royal Worcester Porcelain Works canteen, which had been bought in the early 1990s, and used by A Level artists. Work commenced in 2007, with A Level students moving to the recently-vacated Edgar Tower and younger pupils having classes in a portacabin. The short period of disruption was certainly worthwhile, as the resulting Art School provided a stunning gallery space, named after artist Sir Terry Frost, large studios for Fourth Form, Lower Remove and GCSE classes, including a large textiles area, and individual studio workshop spaces for A Level artists. A departmental library with computers for digital art further enhanced the facilities. The building was opened by Cornish artist Derek Nice, a former artist-in-residence, in February 2008.

The new Art School provided further opportunities for exhibitions, and Liz invited a large number of professional artists to mount exhibitions, including Mark Spray, Carole Waller, Ione Parkin and Phil Whiting, many of whom also ran workshops and lectures for pupils. Student exhibitions could also be mounted in the Art School, both in the Sir Terry Frost Gallery and the large studio spaces.

The performance of King's artists at both GCSE and A Level continued to be remarkable, with an unbroken 100% pass rate for many years, with most students achieving A* and A grades.

The reputation of the arts at King's, and Art in particular, had become widely recognised, and Liz handed a thriving, successful Art School on to her successor, Georgina Terry, when she retired in 2014.

The Art School, opened in February 2008

King's and Queen's Scholars, 2005

Student involvement

The role of School Monitors was developed, with training weekends for new Monitors devised by Richard Chapman, from 2008. Monitors were appointed, usually an equal balance of boys and girls, as well as a Head of School and one or two Deputy Heads of School. A list of Heads of School can be found in Appendix 10. Monitors continued to process into assemblies in College Hall, sitting on the stage to either side of the Headmaster and Deputy Heads, with each giving an address to the school at an assembly during the autumn and spring terms.

The system of House Prefects and Heads of House which existed in the 1980s and 1990s, where a Head of House would organise activities and even take Roll Call, was reformed, with each house appointing two Heads of House, a boy and a girl, who supported the work of the House Tutor in leading the house at events and developing a strong community.

King's and Queen's Scholars remained an important part of the school, leading Cathedral services and setting an example to pupils.

A School Council was established with representatives of all years meeting with senior staff each term to discuss important issues.

Rewards and sanctions

Among the first changes introduced by Tim Keyes was a system of 'merits', announced to pupils at one of his first College Hall assemblies. Merits ('blue papers') were awarded to pupils for good work, positive behaviour or particular, small achievements. Initially the scheme was applied across the whole school, to the amusement of many in the Sixth Form, and the concern of some staff; later, merits were awarded only up to the Fifth Form, but were always most successfully received in the Fourth Forms, where Andrew Longley presented certificates to those achieving 10, 20, 30, 40 or even, rarely, 50 merits within each year. By 2013, the blue paper had been largely phased out, as merits were awarded electronically, using the SIMS database.

Headmaster's Commendations were introduced later to recognise exemplary work and higher level achievements and improvements; pupils would meet the Headmaster in his office, and their achievements were recorded in a book kept there.

Conversely, a new system of reporting bad behaviour and poor school work was needed. Red papers were issued and passed to House and Form Tutors when a teacher felt it necessary. This, with an 'On Report' book issued when a significant number of red papers had been received, replaced the previous 'Satisfecit' cards, to monitor pupils' progress towards satisfactory behaviour.

Detentions were used as a means of dealing quickly with specific issues; most offences would lead to an after-school detention on Wednesday evenings, while more serious offenders would be required to attend a Saturday morning detention.

Suspension and expulsion remained the ultimate sanctions, used less frequently by Tim Keyes than by his predecessors; Tim admitted that his most difficult moments included the four occasions when he had no option but to ask a parent to remove a child from King's on disciplinary grounds.

Structure of the school

The senior school continued to be formed of seven year groups, which divide broadly into three - the Fourth Forms, the Removes and Fifth Form, and the Sixth Form; pupils in the Removes and Fifth Form and students in the Sixth Form are all members of one of the eight houses, while the Fourth Forms are smaller groups, of around 22 in six forms in each of the two years.

By 2014, King's had still yet to formally adopt the 'National Curriculum' year group names, so the following names were in use:

King's name	N.C. year	Pupil age
Lower Fourth	Year 7	11-12
Upper Fourth	Year 8	12-13
Lower Remove	Year 9	13-14
Upper Remove	Year 10	14-15
Fifth Form	Year 11	15-16
Lower Sixth	Year 12	16-17
Upper Sixth	Year 13	17-18

In the Fourth Forms, pupils would study all subjects, taught mostly in form groups, with the same model continued into the Lower Remove, although some subjects would be dropped at this stage and the pupils would have chosen which main language to take to GCSE level. During the Lower Remove year, pupils would select GCSE options and proceed to study these subjects, along with PE and Games, during the Upper Remove and Fifth Form, when the GCSE exams would be taken. During the Fifth Form, A Level subjects would be chosen, intially four subjects for the Lower Sixth, with most students dropping one of these four for the Upper Sixth year; Sixth Form students would also study Key Skills and take part in PE and Games.

The school day was made up of eight periods, each lasting 35 - 40 minutes, and, although the timings of the school day varied during the past few years, in 2014 the pattern of the day was as follows.

8.30 am	Registration in forms and houses
8.40 am	Assembly, Cathedral Service or Form/House time
9.05 am	Period 1
9.45 am	Period 2
10.20 am	Morning break
10.40 am	Period 3
11.20 am	Period 4
11.55 am	Lunch for Fourth Forms (until 12.25 pm)
12.05 pm	Period 5 for Lower Remove - Upper Sixth

Sue Hincks

Senior Deputy Head 2007-11, Second Deputy Head 2004-07, Acting Head 2009

Sue Hincks arrived at King's in 2004 as Second Deputy Head, taking over much of the work of the Senior Mistress, Patricia Stevens. With a first class degree in Modern Languages and Modern History, Sue's first teaching post was at The King's School, Peterborough, where she was involved in the 450th anniversary celebrations shared by all of the King's Schools (see Chapter 8). Sue moved to Marlborough College where she was Head of French and Head of Junior Scholars, and then to Gresham's School, Holt where she was Head of Languages for seven years.

Sue quickly established herself as a knowledgeable, reliable and resourceful member of the Senior Management Team, with a passion for organisation and eagerness to ensure that school policies and procedures were kept up-to-date in readiness for the 2005 Inspection.

Tim Keyes recalled: "Sue joined the senior team in 2004 and then in due course, when Alistair Macnaughton moved on to be Head of King's Gloucester, became the first woman to hold the role of what used to be called (but for obvious reasons could no longer be) Second Master, and is now called Senior Deputy. She left in the year in which King's celebrated 40 years of girls in the Sixth Form at King's and twenty years of full coeducation. She was herself instrumental in ensuring that the school is a balanced coeducational establishment.

She was acting head for a term in 2009 when I was on sabbatical. I know that my colleagues look back on Sue's term in charge as dynamic and refreshing and will have seen it at the time as evidence that she was more than ready to run her own school.

Sue will be remembered by her colleagues for her intelligence, meticulous organisation, extraordinary capacity for hard work, generosity with her time and patience in assisting with a whole range of personal and professional concerns, not to mention her readiness to sing, dance or take part in a staff panto. She is remembered by those whom she taught as a dynamic, unconventional and caring teacher and by the school as a whole as someone who could express her displeasure in no uncertain terms from the stage in College Hall at one moment and at another spend hours trying to find the best way round a pastoral difficulty. She was clear in her expectations to staff and pupils alike – you knew where you stood with Miss Hincks, and that was reassuring.

She was a superb administrator and improved many systems and policies in the school. That eye for, and interest in detail is rare in someone who is also so adept at seeing the bigger picture. Sue is also a very creative thinker and brought in many good new initiatives, not least as the Chairman of the staff Strategy Group.

Those to whom she taught French and German, or who were in her highly successful Quiz teams, knew well her sense of fun and determination to make time spent at school as positive as possible. When a trip, home or abroad or a language exchange was short of a member of staff, she would frequently and without fuss offer to fill the gap. She also led trips of her own, including one to our partner school in Magdeburg.

She richly deserved her promotion to be Head of the Girls' Division of Bolton School."

12.45 pm	Period 6 for Lower Remove - Upper Sixth
1.05 pm	Period 6 for Fourth Forms (until 1.45 pm, then break)
1.20 pm	Lunch for Lower Remove - Upper Sixth
2.15 pm	Registration in forms and houses
2.25 pm	Period 7
3.05 pm	Period 8
3.40 pm	End of school

With eight periods in each day, the school week had 40 lessons in total, although many of these would be used as 'double lessons', running for 75 minutes, particularly for the sciences and Games, and more often for the Sixth Form. Members of the Sixth Form would receive eight taught periods per subject, as well as two double sessions of Key Skills, a double Games lesson and two periods of PE; the rest of the time would be used as study periods with students encouraged to use the School Library and departmental libraries for their own work. For a pupil in the Fourth Forms, each day's timetable would usually include English and Maths and one of French, Spanish or German, probably with a double science lesson - Biology, Chemistry or Physics, and possibly either PE - which might be swimming, gymnastics, indoor ball games or fitness training - or Games, which could include rugby, football or cricket for boys, netball, hockey or tennis and rounders for girls; rowing was an option from the Lower Remove upwards, with many other sports for Sixth Formers.

School lunch changed significantly in the early 2000s. While pupils were still permitted to take two items, the choice of meals grew tremendously, with the introduction of a pasta bar, salad bar, jacket potatoes, selection of sandwiches and wraps and fresh soup to complement the main courses, and with a selection of fruit and yoghurts providing a healthier alternative to the traditional puddings, although, of course, the hot crumbles, pies and cakes always remained popular.

From the start of the Lower Fourth, pupils were encouraged to take part in clubs and activities, some of which, like the choirs and orchestras, would meet at lunchtimes, necessitating an 'early lunch card'; some would run at weekends, particularly sporting activities and those like Model UN which had conferences at various host schools and the Duke of Edinburgh's Award with regular training expeditions; the majority took place after school - the regular Friday afternoon C.C.F. Parade continued, alongside sports practices and fixtures and D&T and Art clubs. It would be unusual for a willing student not to find an evening event to attend or take part in each week, with a staggering number of concerts, theatre productions, lectures, parents' evenings (attended by pupils in older year groups from 2012), sports fixtures and other events for particular activities and groups.

Successive Governments proposed changes to the format of the school year, which, with a long summer holiday - at King's still seven weeks by 2014 - was proving difficult for many parents and put increasing pressure on students sitting ever more public exams in a narrow time period. These changes have yet to be introduced formally, and certainly not at King's, so the school year continued to start in the first week of September, with a ten-day break starting in late October, and the Christmas holiday running from mid-December to early January. With a week for half term in February and late May, and three weeks for Easter, the year ends with King's Day in early July.

The pastoral system
The Houses

Following the end of boarding, College House, Castle House and The Hostel were no more, leaving eight day houses - Bright, Chappel, Choir, Creighton, Kittermaster, Oswald, School and Wulstan.

In 1999, each house was led by a House Tutor, supported by two Assistant Tutors. Between them, the staff were responsible for the 70 or so pupils in the House, ranging from Lower Remove (Year 9) to the Upper Sixth; the House Tutor would generally take responsibility for UCAS applications, and the three tutors would each take charge of the pastoral care of a third of the pupils in each year group. With the increasing number of pupils in the houses, and the increasing number of teachers able to shoulder pastoral responsibility, the team of tutors for each house was enlarged, with one Assistant Tutor allocated to each of the five year groups, allowing a horizontal as well as vertical system for monitoring pastoral and academic progress, releasing the House Tutor to focus on UCAS applications, assisted by the Head of Sixth Form, and on organising house events. In 2011, the role of Assistant Tutor was re-designated as Year Group Tutor, to define the role more clearly. Practice varied between houses, but in many cases, the 'YGT' would stay with the same group of pupils as they progressed through the house; others developed specialisms, taking care of a specific year group.

In a change to the previous practice of Prefects appointed by the House Master or Mistress, each House Tutor would now appoint two Heads of House, a boy and girl, who would lead the house in activities, and assist the house staff in maintaining standards of behaviour within the house. The duties would vary between houses, but could no longer include tasks such as taking roll call, now 'registration', as this was legally the responsibility of a teacher. Indeed, the system of registration also changed, with the traditional paper registers replaced by an electronic system in 2010.

The houses continued to take part in a number of inter-house competitions, the House Music Competition being easily the most popular and most hotly-contested. The House Drama Festival was dropped in 1999, due to the strain on the Theatre, which now accommodated more curriculum drama; several other events quickly filled the gap, including a quiz, debating and basketball competitions. The houses also adopted charities, organising events throughout the year to raise funds.

Twice-weekly assemblies in College Hall saw the whole of the upper part of the senior school together; the assembly would often include an address by a monitor, or visiting speaker - during Alistair Macnaughton's time

Rev. Dr. Mark Dorsett, Chaplain, King's Day 2014

School Photograph, 2014, which included more than 940 pupils

as Senior Deputy Head, an interview with a distinguished visitor became a regular feature of assembly, a tradition continued subsequently. Assembly would also include notices and announcements of achievements by the Headmaster, as well as occasional singing practice when the hymns were sounding less in tune than they should! Four of the houses attended a short service in the quire of the cathedral each week, led by the Chaplain. Pupils were invited to attend a weekly School Eucharist, in the Crypt.

The Fourth Forms

The Fourth Forms, Years 7 and 8, had long been treated as a largely separate part of the senior school, almost a 'middle school', although this term had fallen out of use at King's during the 1980s. This separation became more defined when the role of 'Head of Fourth Forms' was established in 2000, with the purpose of assisting with recruitment at 11+ and introducing the pupils to the senior school, preparing them for life in the house system. Jackie Golightly was the first to hold the position, before Andrew Longley took over in September 2001. Each form was the responsibility of a Form Master or Form Mistress (called Form Tutors from 2006) and comprised between 19 and 24 pupils. Keyes had inherited four forms in each of the Lower Fourth and Upper Fourth year groups; this increased to five forms in 1999, which grew to six forms by 2003; in 2009, a particularly large year group, the Lower Fourth was expanded to seven forms, though this only lasted for one year. This was a remarkable achievement, particularly considering that this took place at a time during which the Assisted Places Scheme was phased out.

The form would be taught most subjects together, moving around the school between classrooms, with the exception of Maths and English, which were split in ability groups, and MFL, where pupils took part in a carousel of languages before selecting a language to follow. PSHE was delivered by Form Tutors.

The form met in its form room each morning and afternoon for registration, and twice each week would attend an assembly in the John Moore Theatre, usually led by the Head of Fourth Forms. Additional short services would also take place regularly in the cathedral. During 'Form Time', members of the Upper Sixth would sometimes join a form as mentors, to help address any concerns faced by younger pupils. From 2002, each Lower Fourth form went on an activity day, early in the school year, often at Top Barn Activity Centre, near Hallow, which helped to create bonds between members of the form, and develop the relationship with the Form Tutor.

When the Annett Building was re-opened in 2001, the classrooms became home to the Lower Fourth forms, with a Fourth Form Office staffed by a dedicated secretary; a Deputy Head of Fourth Forms was introduced to support the Form Tutors and the Head of Fourth Forms, as the demands of pastoral care steadily increased. The Upper Fourth's form rooms remained in the 'Fourth Form Block', as it was known, although more recently referred to generally as the 'Geography Block'.

The Lower Remove

The Lower Remove, Year 9, had become a significant transitional year, as pupils left the familiarity and close-knit community of the Fourth Forms to be placed into one of the houses. To make this transition easier for the pupils, the houses undertook 'bonding activities', taking their lead from the Fourth Forms, with many going to the Old Chapel. A new position of Lower Remove Co-ordinator, held by Tom Sharp, ensured consistency of pupil experience, as well as co-ordinating house allocations, with the Head of Fourth Forms, and organising internal school exams.

The traditional 'Lower Remove Camp' to the Old Chapel changed in format in the early 2000s, with the Heads of House joining

Fourth Form lunch in the dining hall, 2007

the Lower Remove pupils and the House Tutor and Year Group Tutor, helping to integrate the younger pupils into the house.

The Lower Remove pupils, as in the Fourth Forms, continued to be taught in form groups; in the Upper Remove they would be studying their GCSE subjects so would be taught in sets.

In 2014, a proposal for separating Year 9 from the house system was considered. The role of the Lower Remove Co-ordinator would be extended so as to be similar to that of Head of Fourth Forms, with the pupils being registered in forms as well as being taught in forms. The advantages of this would be to ease the transition from one pastoral structure into the other and to reduce the overall size of the houses, which by now approached 90 pupils each, putting pressure on the house accommodation, as well as other important facilities including College Hall, where the Houses all met twice each week for assemblies. Earmarked as a decision for the new Headmaster, it seemed likely that this proposal could be implemented by 2016 or, as an alternative, the number of Houses could be increased from eight to ten.

Physical and spritual well-being

In addition to the pastoral support available to pupils through the Form Tutors and house staff, the Chaplain, Mark Dorsett, continued to offer spiritual support and guidance to pupils. A Chaplaincy Centre was set up in Number 12 in 2006, providing a base for the Chaplain and a quiet space for individual reflection.

This service was complemented by the appointment of a school Counsellor, who attended King's for a few hours each week to see individual pupils, by appointment.

The Health Centre, located in Choir House from 2000, provided health advice for pupils as well as first aid and medical treatment.

Beyond the classroom

During Tim Keyes' time as Headmaster, a large variety of extra-curricular activities developed, alongside a growth in sports and the arts.

The Combined Cadet Force (CCF) continued to hold weekly parades each Friday, and, under the leadership of Nicole [Featherstone] Essenhigh (College House 1986-88), attracted more cadets than it had since it was a compulsory part of school life. Cadets could choose to join the Army or RAF Sections, and would have opportunities to take part in a number of camps and competitions; orienteering competitions became a particular strength, with several successful teams over a few years. For more on 'Cadets at King's' see Chapter 5. SSI Dave Grinnell assisted in the operational running of the CCF, and also supported other activities, including the Duke of Edinburgh's Award Scheme and kayaking (see below).

Another major activity which enjoyed increasing popularity was the Duke of Edinburgh's Award Scheme, offered at Bronze, Silver and Gold levels, for pupils ranging from Lower Remove to Upper Sixth. By 2012, guided by Simon Cuthbertson and a large cohort of staff, around 150 participants were working to reach their next levels. The range of activities involved covered volunteering, skills and physical challenge sections of the award, requiring regular commitment over several months. Training for

Helen Jones (Kittermaster House 1999-2006) on the climbing wall, 2003

expeditions often took place at the Old Chapel, but also went as far afield as Snowdonia and the Lakes and the Peak District. Around 15-20 students each year completed their Gold Award, which they received at St James' Palace from Prince Philip himself.

The Old Chapel (see Chapter 6) continued to serve as a base for Lower Remove Camps, which included walking, climbing and kayaking among the activities offered.

King's relationship with New College Worcester (for visually impared students) developed from providing scribes for examinations to joint ventures, including an expedition to Iceland.

The Himalayan Club, which celebrated its 20th anniversary in 2013, was established by John Walton and taken on by Josh Hand (Chappel House 1991-2001) from 2013. The club encouraged dozens of pupils, parents and staff to trek through amazing terrain, including expeditions to Turkey and Tanzania as well as India and Nepal; in the process, more than £250,000 was raised for the King's Himalayan Trust.

Climbing continued to be a popular physical challenge at King's, with the climbing wall on the western end of the Fourth Form Block so heavily utilised that a new, state-of-the-art indoor climbing wall, with abseiling gallery, was included in the Keyes Building.

Other outdoor activities included kayaking, fencing and an Equestrian Team, which competed successfully at a number of show-jumping events. The Sub Aqua Club, established by Frank Loveder (Head of Chemistry 1987-97) and taken on by parent John Kingsley, trained for diving expeditions which took members as far away as the Red Sea; King's St Alban's teacher Jonathan Bailey later took on organising the club.

Skiing trips continued to take large numbers of pupils to the French and Swiss Alps each year. Closer to home, Basketball enjoyed something of a renaissance with junior and senior teams, and Judo classes ran every Saturday morning in the sports hall.

Under the oversight of Director of Sport, Jonny Mason, appointed in 2002, sports at King's enjoyed a period of growth and successes at all levels. Rowing particularly grew in stature, with an increase in the number of pupils participating; the KSW Boat Club took part in an increased number of regattas, including their own King's Regatta. The Michael Baker Boathouse provided a superb base for rowing, and for the large number of charitable activities undertaken by the KSWBC, many of which supported

Himalayan Club Expedition to India, 2011

C.C.F. cadets celebrating a range of competition successes, 2007

'Cardiac Risk in the Young' after the tragic early death of rower and previous Head of School Scott Rennie (Bright House 1993-2002) in 2009.

Senior rugby teams competed in several tournaments each year, and, in 2011-12, reached the semi-final of the prestigious Daily Mail Cup. The annual derby against RGS Worcester was played at Sixways, home of the Worcester Warriors, from 1999. Rugby Sevens was introduced and achieved early success. Football had been re-introduced in 1994 and quickly replaced boys' hockey; under Chris Haywood's leadership, it became more popular and enjoyed an annual fixture against RGS Worcester, played at St George's Lane until 2013, when Worcester City FC's ground was demolished.

The appointment of Ollivia Beveridge as Head of Netball in 2007 saw the continuation of the success of girls' sport established by Nicky (Anstey) Wilson; netball teams at all levels competed successfully in local championships, and the senior team reached the national schools' finals in 2012, 2013 and 2014. A renewed focus on Hockey, under the stewardship of Sarah Parkinson-Mills, Head of Girls' Games from 2012, saw early progress in local competitions, with the girls benefiting from the All-Weather Pitch at Bishop Perowne College.

Athletic sports became an ever larger affair, with sports days taking place at Nunnery Wood Sports Centre, and separate events for Fourth Forms, Removes and Seniors (Fifth and Sixth Forms).

Above: Young Enterprise company 'Swish', 2008
Left: Jean Vivian receiving the school's award as the first Young Enterprise Centre of Excellence, 2012

King's participated in the European Union's 'Comenius Project', with pupils encouraged to work on projects with others from schools across the EU. Particularly close links developed with Dom Gymnasium in Magdeburg, Germany. Participants undertook activities as varied as an election campaign on educational systems to devising a new sport, 'Comball', and enjoyed several visits and conferences, also building language skills.

The programme of MFL exchanges continued, with annual visits to Le Vesinet and Lille in France, Memingham and Berlin in Germany, and Zaragoza in Spain, involving hundreds of pupils, mainly from the Removes and Lower Sixth. A student-led MFL Society re-formed, offering events from cheese and wine evenings to summer parties with boules. 'Recreational' language learning opportunities included the chance to learn Japanese (led by pupil John Richardson, Wulstan House 2001-07) and Mandarin taught by Irene Bartholomew.

One of the largest success stories among the activities offered at King's was the Young Enterprise programme. The scheme became so popular for the Lower Sixth that students had to apply to join from 2008, forming one of five companies (six from 2014). Under Jean Vivian's enthusiastic guidance, King's companies competed in regional contests, with many getting through to West Midlands finals, and one company, *Just Desserts*, making the national final in 2002. A new scheme, 'Mini Enterprise' was launched in 2010, encouraging fifty members of the Upper Fourth (Year 8) to start small ventures, before King's joined the 'Young Enterprise Tenner Campaign' which started in 2013. Sir Geoffery Mulcahy (Chappel House 1952-60), Chief Executive of Young Enterprise, presided at a ceremony in 2012 at which King's was named as the UK's first 'Young Enterprise Centre of Excellence' and Jean Vivian was awarded the Young Enterprise Gold Award for services to Young Enterprise.

Student journalism continued to flourish, with John Roslington's *The King's Herald* reaching Distinction level each year until the competition ended in 2007; *Term Time* magazine was introduced as a replacement, offering a team Sixth Formers the challenge of producing a magazine in a day. *Stepping Fourth* was launched in 2001 giving a journalistic platform to keen Fourth Form reporters and editors.

A Debating Society was joined by a Model United Nations group, which attended conferences to represent the views of other nations in debates and committees. An Amnesty International group supported victims of regimes around the world. Philosophy Club encouraged pupils to consider arguments and 'Questions' offered a contemporary approach to religious matters, complementing the work of the Christian Union.

The 2006 The King's Herald team with Leane Sheen (Wulstan House 1999-2006) as Editor

Michael Baker Boathouse

The Michael Baker Boathouse was to be the fourth boathouse used by the KSW Boat Club, replacing Richard Knight's boathouse, at the south-west corner of the school site, which opened in 1960. Galen Bartholomew, Bursar, recalled: *"The boathouse had served the school well, but the Boat Club had outgrown the accommodation, so many boats had to be stored outside. In addition, the old boathouse had suffered structural problems that had resulted in the south wall shifting on its damp course."* Clearly, the building would need to be replaced at some stage, but a remarkable offer of a gift from Michael Baker (Choir House 1948-55), a keen rower while at King's, allowed the school, and its architect, John Christophers of Associated Architects, to start to plan for an iconic new home for the Boat Club. As Christophers said at the time, *"A unique site demands a unique building. Although it might have been 'safe' in this special and sensitive place to design something that appeared vaguely Victorian, the new boathouse needed to do something more than that."*

Andrew, Nicky and Pam Baker at the opening, 2012

Working closely with the Baker family, Carol Bawden, Director of Development, whose brother Iain Furniss (Castle House 1958-61) had rowed in the first King's VIII to go to Henley in 1961, encouraged Michael, with wife Pam and children Nicky and Andrew, to be involved in the design; they were keen to embrace the architect's vision of a building in the shape of a boat, making the best use of the available site, built with strong environmental credentials.

Archaeological work was carried out in 2010, under the watchful eye of Mike Napthan, and revealed a number of Corinthian capitals, leading to the discovery that the site, which had been derelict fishermen's cottages when acquired by the school in the 1950s, had once been a stonemason's yard; it was understood that this stonemason had been responsible for the spire of St Andrew's Church, known as the 'Glover's Needle'. The stonework was incorporated into the entrance lobby.

At the suggestion of Galen Bartholomew, it was agreed that it would be desirable to have access to the boathouse from the school campus, and a connection was made between the upper level of the Michael Baker Boathouse and the Creighton Memorial Gardens, aligning the entrance with the pergola in the gardens and the view across to the 'Glover's Needle'.

The building was to be composed of three parts: the lower level serving as space to store and work on boats, constructed from robust English-bond brickwork, appearing to grow out of the embankment; the upper level with changing facilities and a large area which could be used as a training suite or for functions, capitalising on the stunning views up and down the river, opening on to a timber balcony which joined the new boathouse to the gardens. The upper level, in contrast to the boat storage area below, appeared to float, with a prow cantilevered above the towpath; the 'boat' was clad in sweet chestnut timber laths, which quickly weathered to a silver-grey colour, set at a shallow angle to emphasise the dynamic shape of the building.

Sustainability had been central to the design, which used Passivhaus principles, solar panels, triple glazing and a wood pellet boiler. The building achieved EPC A rating, virtually carbon-neutral.

Boat storage in the lower level, 2012

The 'prow' of the Michael Baker Boathouse jutting out over the towpath towards the River Severn.

The initial donation from the Baker family was £2 million for the boathouse, with a further £1 million donated for bursary funds; when the projected cost of the building rose to £2.5 million, the family had little hesitation in meeting this extra cost.

The stunning Michael Baker Boathouse was opened in April 2012, with a ceremony which included the naming of a boat. Unfortunately, Michael Baker was too ill by the time the building was finished to attend the ceremony, but his family acted on his behalf.

The Michael Baker Boathouse won a prestigious RIBA West Midlands Award in 2013, but more importantly, quickly fulfilled both of its two main functions - providing a modern, large home for the KSW Boat Club and a space in which school functions could be held, making the most of the building's position, with views across the gardens towards the Cathedral and, beyond, the Glover's Needle. The Boat Club had a proper home, with training taking place most days and a number of charity events held there, including 24-hour Ergo Challenges, many in support of C.R.Y., the KSWBC's chosen charity. Between 2012 and 2014 many important school functions had already been held in the magnificent upper floor and terrace, including the Fireworks Finale of The SPACE Campaign and OV Reunion events.

For more on the KSW Boat Club, see Chapter 3.

In 2012, Carol Bawden produced a book The King's School Worcester Boat Club - Anecdotes and Memoirs 1877-2012 *to celebrate the opening of the Michael Baker Boathouse, which provides a fuller record of the development of the building.*

King's started to become established as a centre for chess, while a bell-ringing group took advantage of the opportunity offered by Worcester Cathedral to develop an interesting hobby.

The School Library started a pupil book club, 'WRAITH', while the Literary Society organised occasional play readings and theatre visits, growing out of the 'Library Evenings' of the 1980s and 90s. The School Archive offered pupil historians and curators the chance to explore the school's history; the Battlefields trip to Belgium and northern France continued to take pupils to the sites of trenches, graveyards and memorials to those lost in the Great War.

An increased focus on charity work, raising funds and awareness for important causes, was supported by the Sixth Form Charity Committee - Pink Day, Green Day and a range of other activities, from cake sales to concerts were organised by the students, with two key highlights each year being a senior citizens' Christmas party and a summer party for children from a local special school. The Sponsored Walk and May Day Fête continued in alternate years, raising a great deal of money for charities, and, in the case of the Fête, organised by the KSPC, for school projects. A total of more than £20,000 was raised for good causes each year between 1999 and 2015.

The creative and performing arts, led by Liz Hand as Arts Co-ordinator, introduced 'Arts Alive!' and 'Words Alive!' festivals, celebrating the arts with pupils from all year groups, usually during a full week of activities. Many pupils took individual LAMDA Speech and Drama lessons, in addition to the drama clubs which led to three school productions, for different age groups, each year. Chris Crosswell, Theatre Manager, introduced a Technical Theatre Club, and the biennial Dance Showcase continued with Dance Clubs at all levels. A new DADA (Dance and Dramatic Arts) Society was formed. Art Clubs included life drawing classes, open studios and an Animé Club, complemented by the Digital Media offered by the ICT department. The Art School entered the national 'Big Draw' competition each year, awarded first place on two occasions, and offered regular workshops to pupils and their families. The student-led 'Keys Society' organised and performed in high-quality concerts each half term, adding to the programme of musical performance which included termly School Concerts and regular Young Performers' Concerts.

Several of the academic departments introduced new activities, with clubs for ICT, History, Classics and Maths; the Maths department also set up a regular series of Maths Team

Mandarin Club, taught by Irene Bartholomew

Religion and Philosophy tour of the Holy Land, 2013

Challenges, in some years competing against other schools, and a 'Countdown' competition. Pupils enjoyed success for several consecutive years in the national Maths Challenge competition.

Science Club engaged pupils with topics in Biology and Chemistry, while Physics enthusiasts could take part in electronics and robotics clubs. A series of lectures at Birmingham University was available to A Level scientists. The Engineering in Education Scheme (EES) enabled a group of Sixth Form students to design a solution to a real-world engineering problem, as part of a national competition. In a similar way, the 4x4 in Schools Challenge involved a team of pupils designing and building a 1:10 scale 4x4 vehicle - the King's team won the national competition in 2013 and were crowned world champions in 2015.

Geography fieldwork included regular visits to study the geomorphological features of the Gower peninsula and urban development in Birmingham, as well as a popular trip to Cadbury World for the Lower Remove (Year 9), to learn about globalisation. Politics students enjoyed an inaugural visit to Washington D.C. in 2013, although the Drama exchange programme to Notre Dame Academy in Worcester, Massachusetts ended in 2004. Religion and Philosophy students could join a trip to The Netherlands, which included cleaning war graves with pupils from around Europe, and a large group travelled to the Holy Land in 2013.

Community Service, which encouraged pupils to take an active role in helping others, grew in popularity. A mentoring scheme was introduced for Sixth Formers to work with new pupils in the Lower Fourth (Year 7), and a number of students offered assistance at King's St Alban's and King's Hawford, as well as other local primary schools.

The competitive scene in Worcester

In 2004 a King's Governor received an unexpected approach from the then Chairman of The Alice Ottley School (AO) and three other senior Governors, proposing a merger of the two schools. A meeting with four senior King's Governors was arranged and, while it was clear that the AO Governors were absolutely serious, King's Governors were concerned to note that no other AO Governors were aware of the proposal, nor were the AO Headmistress or Bursar!

Like many other girls' schools, the AO was experiencing significant difficulties, which for the AO had intensified once the Grammar School had followed King's and become fully co-educational. When asked why the AO Governors were not approaching the Grammar School next door, the reply was that the AO was felt to be far closer to King's in terms of culture. The AO exam results, which a mere 10 years previously had been the best of the three schools, had declined sharply and this in turn had led to poor recruitment, which was resulting in increasing financial pressures.

The King's Governors held an Extraordinary meeting – the first since the purchase of Hawford Lodge – and agreed in principle to a merger in which the King's Governing Body would become responsible for running both schools, with Springfield remaining co-educational, with a separate division based in Britannia House for girls only aged between 11 and 16 (Years 7 to 11), and with a joint co-educational sixth form based on the King's site. An element of single sex education would thus have been retained under this proposal and the intention was also to retain the name and goodwill associated with the Alice Ottley.

Unfortunately the then Chairman of the AO had seriously misjudged the situation and his fellow Governors did not support him. The AO Governors elected a new Chairman, a very distinguished international businessman, and the reformed board decided to soldier on independently, with a view to marketing the school more effectively as a girls only institution and thereby increasing pupil numbers. However this did not work out either and three years later the AO merged with the Grammar School becoming RGSAO initially, although the AO was dropped soon afterwards with the merged school being known simply as RGS Worcester.

Mergers are often difficult and it can take many years to meld the cultures of two different organisations together. A merger between King's and the AO would inevitably have led to a reduction in our combined exam results (as happened to the Grammar School after its merger with the AO) at the very time that the King's results were forging ahead. It would also have placed huge extra pressures on Tim Keyes and Galen Bartholomew at a time when changes were being made successfully at King's in so many areas. In a number of respects, therefore, King's perhaps had a lucky escape: its Governors and management team were left to focus their efforts on driving up academic and pastoral standards on the King's site without any dilution of management energy.

In 1998, King's had four forms of entry at 11 plus, while the Grammar School had five forms of entry, the Alice Ottley had three forms of entry and St Mary's Convent had two forms of entry. In 2007, at the time of their merger, the Grammar School commented that it was now the largest independent school in Worcester. Since that time numbers at King's have increased modestly, but currently RGS Worcester is substantially smaller than King's. Following the closure of St Mary's Convent in 2014, one can judge the overall decrease in the number of independent school places in Worcester since 1998: from 14 forms to 10 forms of entry at 11 plus over a period of 16 years. In the years ahead it seems clear that prospective parents will look for schools offering excellent academic standards combined with high quality pastoral and extra-curricular provision; in short good quality and value, but not necessarily the cheapest product, although the cost of providing independent education is likely to become an increasingly significant issue.

Parents' Committee

Galen Bartholomew

Over the past fifty years, the Development Committee, the Development Trust and the Parents' Committee have all contributed to raising money for the school's development. The remarkable expansion of the school and its facilities over this period has been in no small part due the fundraising efforts of staff, parents, friends and pupils, including the crucial contribution from the various appeals that have been run by the school.

The Parents' Committee has also served an important social function through its fundraising activities. The annual Christmas Ball, invariably oversubscribed, is a great opportunity for parents to enjoy each other's company, with a few members of staff in attendance as well, particularly those with children in the school. The biennial School Fete is another occasion when the school comes together and welcomes the local community to join in the festivities. In the other year, the School Walk raises funds for local charities, supported by the Parents' Committee, who provide refreshments. Other events organised by the Parents' Committee include regular quizzes in the Dining Hall with fish and chip suppers.

Initially the School Fete was purely for fundraising, notably for the much-needed facilities identified by David Annett soon after his appointment as Headmaster. More recently, part of the profits have gone towards substantial donations to local charities, with the remainder being spent on a large number of projects to benefit the school. The largest of these was more than £70,000 towards the Old Chapel's extension. Other major donations include two each of £30,000 for greatly improved ventilation in the John Moore Theatre and towards the SPACE Campaign for The Keyes Building. Smaller donations over the years have benefited the school community in many different ways.

A crucial part of the whole process has been the fun and camaraderie which comes from helping the Parents' Committee, along with a lot of hard work! Over the years parents have been generous with their time supporting a variety of projects. A succession of officers, particularly the Chairs, have worked tirelessly to meld the committee into a happy and effective group and the school is very much in their debt.

The Common Room

During the past twenty years, the profile of the teaching staff changed significantly. Gone were the days of teachers who stayed at one school for most of their careers with the retirements of long-serving staff members, including Tim Hickson (Physics and Second Master 1962-2002), Keith Bridges (Chemistry and The Hostel 1963-2003), Paul Thompson (Classics and Fourth Form Master 1970-2006), Bob Stone (Classics and Bright House 1984-2009), John Roslington (Physics and College House 1975-2009) and Caroline Roslington (History 1977-2009), leaving Peter Iddon (English and The Hostel from 1980), Stephen Le Marchand (English, Drama, Careers and Chappel House from 1983) and Russell Mason (Economics, Business Studies and Marketing Director from 1984) as the longest-serving staff.

King's appointed a range of new teachers to replace the retiring staff, and this included a large proportion of newly (or recently) qualified teachers, whose enthusiasm and familiarity with modern techniques and new technology energised many of the 'older' staff, and brought down the average age of the teaching staff considerably. Many of these new teachers were women, altering the gender balance of the Common Room - in 2013, 49 of the 98 teachers were female, an exact 50:50 split. However, full 'equality' was still some way off, with only seven of the 26 Heads of Departments being women by 2014.

Perhaps the department most affected by this change was Classics - for many years the preserve of *'grumpy old men'* (Bob Stone's words) - which by 2012 was taught by a *'quartet of friendly and approachable younger women'.*

The Masters' Common Room had been established as a members' club when staff numbers grew significantly in the 1930s and 40s but lacked a formal constitution until after the departure of Andrew Milne as Headmaster in 1983. A new constitution was devised and accepted for the Common Room Club in the early 2000s, with support staff admitted as associate members, with optional full membership on payment of a monthly levy. Kate Appleby served as Common Room President from 2004 until 2007, when John Wheeler took on the role. Russ Mason was elected to the post, which is responsible for organising social events and taking Common Room issues to senior management, in 2013.

Social events for members of the Common Room included Christmas parties from 2001, held at school and at local hotels; skittles evenings and theatre outings. Staff pantomimes had been organised occasionally since the 1970s; Danny Payne revived the idea in 2004, producing *'Cinderella'* with Lorraine Guy in the title role, and, after a suitable interval, *'Jack and the Beanstalk'* in 2013, with principals including Catherine Cantin, Alice Briggs and Mary Anne Keyes and Andrew Maund as 'Dame Gaga', with a supporting cast of more than twenty from King's and King's St Alban's, raising £3,000 for The SPACE Campaign.

Below: the Teaching Staff, photographed in July 2014, which numbered almost 100 teachers - a list of roles can be found in Appendix 14.

Front row: Richard Geary, Mark Dorsett, Mark Poole, Sarah Le Marchand, Steven Bain, Stephan Marchand, Peter Iddon, Duncan King, Tim Keyes, Jon Ricketts, Russ Baum, Russell Mason, John Wheeler, Richard Davis, Chris Gallantree-Smith, Tom Sharp, Vanessa Gunter, Trudie Marskell

Second row: Matthew Parkin, Richard James, Chris Atkinson, Alison Hines, Chris Wilson, Christine Battrum, Jean Vivian, Jo Clark, Andrew Longley, Anthony Gillgrass, Simon Cuthbertson, Chris Haywood, Simon Atkins, Monica Longley, Ian Robinson, David Haddock, Andrew Maund, Richard Ball

Third row: Rosie Shearburn, Alan Deichen, Elaine Friend, Sarah Bradley, Joanna Lucas, Anne Sansome, Lois Haddock, Anne-Marie Simpson, Rachael Worth, Jonny Mason, Lorraine Guy, Eric Lummas, Rachael Rutter, Graham Gunter, Donna Salkeld, Mike Newby

Fourth row: Gemma Holden, Alice Briggs, Emma Watts, Ronan Head, Jules Price-Hutchinson, Claire Horacek, Josh Hand, Katie Beever, Andrew Kerley, Adrian Ford, Jim Chalmers, Claire Neville, Gwyn Williams, Helen Holden, Jo Wootton, Josh Gardiner, Jenny Hewitt

Back row: Nick Rosewell, Sarah Stuart, Will Joyce, Oliver Heydon, Nicola Sears, Sarah Parkinson-Mills, Beth Darby, Olivia Rothbury, Rhiannon Lewis, Neela Brennan, Jon Sarriegui

Missing from photograph: Peter Gwilliam, Jerry Owen, Fiona Short, Nicole Essenhigh, Sue Stone, Lin Brighton, Lucy Walmsley, Jill Knipe, Catherine Cantin, Rachel Stanley, Richard Mardo, Claire Brown, Rachael Graff, Tom Jeavons, Simon Taranczuk

Administration of the school

Governors

King's had been well-served by its governing body in the years since Bolland's 'New Scheme' of 1884 (see Chapter 4), with governors from a range of backgrounds, bringing a variety of skills and areas of expertise, who have been dedicated to the school and its future success, often serving for many years. Among those who gave significant service during Keyes' headship are Lady Morrison, David Barlow, David Finch, David Mills, Brian Tait and David Wright, a number of whom are former parents or Old Vigornians or both. None of these, however, could have given more than Donald Howell, OV, appointed as a governor on his thirtieth birthday in 1973, who led the governors as Chairman for 24 years from 1986 (see panel, below). Donald handed over the reins to Hugh Carslake, a former King's parent, in 2010, who would lead a governing body comprising almost half women and with the Dean, The Very Reverend Peter Atkinson, as Vice Chairman.

The King's School adopted new Articles of Association in 2003, incorporating the school as both a private limited company and a charity; the name of the school was legally established as 'The King's School, Worcester' and rules relating to the school's governance were formalised. There would be a maximum of seventeen governors, including the Dean of Worcester as an ex-officio member; the Bishop of Worcester nominates a member of the Church of England and the Chapter may nominate a further six, though there is no requirement for these to be from the Church. Oxford University Council also nominates a governor, with the remaining eight members co-opted.

Since its establishment in 1972, a number of governors served on a 'Finance and General Purposes Committee', with senior members of school staff; the primary focus of this body has been the financial control of the school's budget, including the setting of fees, salaries and levels of capital expenditure, but the committee also considers the long-term objectives of the school and matters relating to buildings and property. Since Donald Howell's retirement in 2010 a separate Chairman has led the F&GP committee. Following a recommendation in an independent review of the governing body, a separate Education Committee was formed in 2008, with the task of overseeing the school's academic policy, referring to the Director of Studies and Academic Deputy Head, as well as those staff responsible for curriculum areas. Individual governors were often given specific areas of focus: for example, Lady Morrison was given special responsibility for the Junior Schools.

Donald Howell

Chairman of Governors 1986-2010, Governor 1973-2010
St Alban's 1953-55, School House 1955-61,
Head of School 1960-61

The retirement of Donald Howell as Chairman of Governors at King's in 2010 was marked by a reception at King's St Alban's, where Donald's relationship lasting almost 60 years had first begun. Tim Keyes addressed the gathering, outlining his gratitude for Donald's dedication and years of service to the school; the following is an excerpt.

"No one can rival Donald for the combination of length of close association with the school, commitment to it and time given on its behalf.

He was part of an extraordinary generation of pupils at King's who went on to become leaders in their chosen fields. For Donald, it was firstly Engineering at Imperial College London which led, in due course, picking up accountancy on the way, for which the school will always be grateful, to working as a Managing Director as part of GEC under Arnold Weinstock.

Donald has played a central role in helping the school to develop the site, always having the knack of seeing when the time was right for a particular development. He was at King's as a pupil when the Winslow Building was erected 52 years ago with a shelf-life of 40!

Given that the school had such inadequate accommodation in so many areas when Donald was a pupil here, it is very much to his credit that he has never taken the line that the sort of projects that we have undertaken in recent years are an extravagance. His earlier experiences here, however, have given him a very clear 'no gold taps' philosophy which has served us very well indeed at times when architects may occasionally have been in danger of using us to indulge their flights of fancy.

One of his many gifts is an eye for detail and another is his consultative, but decisive leadership. It was Donald's quick-thinking and strong lead that led to the purchase of King's Hawford. It was his determination to make us focus on our needs clearly, and then taking the right opportunity, that led to the purchase of 'The Alma' pub which, in September 2009, became the Pre-Prep for King's St Alban's which has been named, in Donald's honour, 'The Howell Building'.

Having led us with equal conviction to buy 'The Salmon's Leap', he has made us think very carefully about our plans for the new Sports and Performing Arts Centre and it is partly because he has tested our rationale for this combination of facilities at various points along the way that we are so confident that it is the right time for this project."

Galen Bartholomew, Bursar since 1996, recalled his great appreciation for Donald's significant contribution to King's, writing in 2010: *"Though Donald's professionalism has been exemplary, working for him has been great fun. As Chairman, Donald, while being very supportive, has kept his distance, recognising that there should be a gap between the top person and those who work for him. Governors meetings have been good-natured and inclusive... The Governors take a strategic and largely non-executive role, except when what Donald calls 'a touch of the tiller' is required. It is inconceivable that the name of Donald Howell will ever become separated from the history of The King's School, Worcester."*

The King's School Worcester Development Trust

Sophie Whitworth

In 1968, the Development Committee, which had been responsible for running a series of fundraising initiatives on behalf of the school throughout the 1960s (see Chapter 6), set up an independent trust to administer the proceeds from appeals and to lend the money to the school free of interest to be spent as circumstances required. J B Cavenagh was elected as the first Chairman and the original trustees were O R Craze, W G Cullis, C W Holder, T T Howell, J P Pimley and P C Underwood. The first project to be financed through the Development Trust was the new library in Edgar Tower in 1969 which was followed by the provision of a 'hard surface' including four tennis courts.

O R Craze took over as chairman from 1970-74 and, in 1972, the objectives of the Trust were outlined to the community at a party in College Hall, with the stated priorities being: a new dining hall; a properly equipped suite of teaching rooms for modern languages; and a new music school. Funds were raised for the Trust through a Covenant appeal, through the efforts of the Development Committee and a range of fundraising events including the School Fête. T T Howell took over as Chairman in 1974 and led the Trust through a period of great activity in the building work at the school. He was particularly active in seeking covenant revenues alongside the usual fundraising activities. He also understood the importance for the Trust to build up an 'endowment' for the school. In 1975, he outlined the need for a separate fund to enable the school to award 'assisted places' each year to replace the Direct Grant scheme which was to be abolished.

In 1986, T T Howell resigned as Chairman of the Development Trust when his son Donald (School House 1955-61) was appointed as Chairman of the Governors, as he felt that the legal independence of the Trust from the school might be compromised. He was succeeded by Peter Underwood just as the school embarked on a major new campaign *'Building for an even better education'*. A full time campaign director, former member of staff Ian Brown, was employed and ran a campaign which raised more than £400,000, providing the school with a state-of-the-art theatre.

The need for a bursary fund had been somewhat alleviated by the introduction of the Assisted Places Scheme in the 1980s in place of the Direct Grant. When the scheme was abolished by the Labour Government in 1997, it was clear that the establishment of some sort of endowment for bursaries was imperative if King's was to continue its long history of providing opportunities for pupils from all sorts of backgrounds, regardless of their means.

In 1999, the new Headmaster, Tim Keyes, outlined his development objectives: a bursary fund, new libraries at each of the three schools, a new kindergarten at King's Hawford, a new music school, a formal entrance to the school, and a new indoor sporting arena.

The way was led by Michael Pimley (The Hostel 1961-71) who, in celebration of his father's association with King's, established the *John Pimley Bursary Fund* in 1999 which provided personal support for three Sixth Form bursaries.

One of the first initiatives for the Headmaster was the establishment of a Development Office and the renewal of the Development Trust to meet the new objectives.

In 2003, Peter Underwood, who had overseen the trust for 17 years, died and former Second Master Tim Hickson took over as Chairman briefly, to be followed by David Mills (The Hostel 1944-53) who joined the Trust following the departure of Barbara Curle (Hon OV) and W G Cullis, who had served as a Trustee for 36 years. The Trust was enlarged to include representatives from all areas of the school including the Common Room, the Governing Body, parents and Old Vigornians. It included family members from three of the original trustees : Donald Howell, Andrew Underwood (School House 1977-87) and Michael Pimley. In 2005, Hugh Scurfield (Chappel House 1943-54) was appointed as Chairman.

The School House Library Campaign became the first priority for the FDO and Trustees but in 2005 the Trust received a large bequest from Basil Eckersley (Castle House 1930-37) which enabled them to offer funding for several full fee bursaries. Alongside this, the *Fellowship Bursary Scheme* was introduced to encourage groups of OVs to join together and through regular donations to support pupils.

By 2009, the KSW Development Trust was already providing funding for eight full fee bursaries when it was notified of an extraordinary donation from the Michael Baker (Choir House 1948-55) and his family of £3.5 million - £2.5 million to finance development of a new boathouse and £1 million to establish a bursary fund.

Hugh Scurfield, with guidance from the Investment Committee, led by Fanos Hira (Oswald House 1980-87) and Penny Hope, Deputy Bursar, was determined that the fund should be invested to provide the maximum amount of bursary support and so the *Enduring Bursary Fund* was born, the objective being to preserve the value of the capital but avoid the restrictions of an endowment and thereby allow much greater flexibility for investment. This vision proved critical in the years that followed; whilst interest rates remained at a record low, the fund thrived and from an initial capital value which would support 120 full fee places if fully expended, it would now be able to support substantially more. In 2012, Hugh Scurfield completed seven years as Chairman. He had guided the Trust through a time in which it had become an increasingly important part of the King's Foundation, having provided a major contribution to the new library, established the Enduring Bursary Fund, financed the Michael Baker Boathouse, and provided regular bursary funding through individual contributions from the community.

Andrew Reekes (Choir House 1964-69) took over the chairmanship, also becoming a Governor in 2015, with a remit to guide the Trust and Foundation Development Office through The SPACE Campaign. With the opening of The Keyes Building in 2015, the Trust could focus on providing funding for means-tested bursaries.

Between 2001 and 2014, the number of bursaries the school was able to fund increased three-fold. This was an important contribution but still far below the levels of support provided through the Direct Grant and Assisted Places schemes. In his final term as Headmaster, Tim Keyes asked that anyone wishing to mark his departure should do so by contribution to a bursary; two new 'Keyes Bursaries' were awarded in 2014.

The School Governors and Senior Management Team, July 2014

Front row (seated):
Tim Keyes - Headmaster; Hugh Carslake - Chairman of Governors; Dean Peter Atkinson - Vice-Chairman;
Galen Bartholomew - Bursar and Clerk to the Governors.

Second row:
Ian Griffin - Head of King's St Alban's (standing); Russ Baum - Director of Studies; Jane Jarvis and the Hon. Lady Morrison - Governors;
Duncan King - Acadmic Deputy Head; Carolyn Mellor - Second Deputy Head; Jim Turner - Head of King's Hawford (standing).

Third row:
Jon Ricketts - Senior Deputy Head; Keith Harmer, Mark Atkins, Rob McClatchey, Michael Clarke, John Vickerman, Helen Swift,
Paul Walker, Jeremy Goulding, Laurence Green - Governors.

(Absent from photograph: Douglas Dale, Patricia Preston and Canon Alvyn Pettersen - Governors)

King's Support Staff, photographed in May 2014

Fifty-five members of staff, with jobs ranging from catering to maintenance, admissions to healthcare, ICT Support and Librarians to groundskeepers and C.C.F, bursarial and secretarial staff to the School Archive and Foundation Development Office.

The nature of the different roles, and varying working patterns of the support staff meant that only around half of the total could be present - absent from the photograph were the cleaning staff, many of the catering team and several others, including secretaries and bursary staff; if all had been present, more than 100 people would have appeared in this photograph. A list of names and roles can be found in Appendix 14.

The King's School, Worcester *From 1541 into the 21st Century*

Galen Bartholomew

Bursar and Clerk to the Governors 1996-2016

Appointed in 1996 with an extensive remit to transform the fortunes of The King's School, Galen Bartholomew had a greater impact on the following twenty years of life at the school than many would have expected of a Bursar. Galen held a keen interest in the development of the three schools' facilities, working closely with surveyors, planners and architects, as well as managing the increasing number of support staff, being responsible for the Foundation's finances and serving as Clerk to the Governors.

Donald Howell, Chairman of Governors 1986-2010, recalled working with him:

"It would be difficult to overstate the importance of Galen's contribution to the success of the King's Foundation over the period 1996 to 2016. I shall always be grateful for his advice, support and loyalty to me while I was chairman during the first fourteen of those years. His tenure has been characterised by modesty, professionalism, very hard work and meticulous attention to detail. He has throughout this time displayed a warm, caring interest in the King's community and those closely associated with it. Together with his Chartered Accountant Deputy, Penny Hope, he has prudently stewarded the school's finances and led its non-academic departments for which he has recruited excellent supporting staff. Since the ending of boarding in 1999 freed up more than 10% of the school's floor space, he has project-managed the ensuing huge programme of reordering, refurbishing and extending the school's accommodation and facilities. In doing this so expertly, and tackling many problems so successfully, he has drawn on his previous experience of working in an international contracting company and on his own practical knowledge of building, having at one time constructed his own house out of a dilapidated stable block in Great Missenden! He has had the knack of recruiting external professional advisers who have given first-class service to the school, perhaps most notably Associated Architects and John Christophers of that firm who has had such an outstanding influence on our buildings. Governors have also benefited from Galen's interest and expertise in strategic planning – particularly his ability to analyse the activities of competing local schools and to forecast their likely future moves. My wife and I have greatly appreciated the continuing warm friendship and hospitality given to us over the years by Galen, his most supportive wife Irene, and their son James."

The full governing body would meet once each term, with additional meetings of the 'F&GP' and Education Committees each term. In his capacity as Clerk to the Governors, the Bursar, Galen Bartholomew, was responsible to the Chairman for organising meetings, preparing papers and ensuring communication between governors; the Headmaster, Bursar, Deputy Bursar and Senior Deputy Head along with the Heads of King's St Alban's and King's Hawford, attend meetings, reporting on their areas of responsibility.

Senior Management Team

Since its establishment in 1997, the Senior Management Team underwent a number of personnel changes, mostly the result of retirements and progression to other schools. Julian Thould moved on from Director of Studies at King's to become Headmaster of King Edward VI School in Southampton in 2001. Russ Baum joined the school from Wisbech Grammar School to replace him. Tim Hickson (see Chapter 8) retired as Second Master in 2002, succeeded by Alistair Macnaughton who served as the first 'Senior Deputy Head' until 2007, when he left to take up the headship of King's Gloucester. Patricia Stevens (see Chapter 8) retired in 2004, and her position of Senior Mistress was replaced by 'Second Deputy Head', a role taken by Sue Hincks. Sue progressed to the position of Senior Deputy Head in 2007 and, after covering the Headmaster's absence during his sabbatical in 2009, left to become Head of the Girls' Division of Bolton School. A similar path was followed by Richard Chapman, who joined King's from Warwick School as Second Deputy Head in 2007 and took over from Sue Hincks as Senior Deputy Head in 2011. Carolyn Mellor was appointed as Second Deputy in 2011, alongside Jon Ricketts, appointed to the role of Academic Deputy Head, following an evolution of the role of Director of Studies. When Jon succeeded Richard Chapman as Senior Deputy Head, the vacant position of Academic Deputy was filled by Duncan King, who joined King's in 2014.

The Senior Management Team, or 'SMT', met for a total of around four hours each week, and discussed all areas of school business, including academic matters, staff issues, recruitment, budgets and site development.

To assist in forming long-term plans, an annual 'strategy day' allowed members of the SMT to have a full day of discussion, away from the school, to which various senior members of staff were invited to discuss key issues. Alongside this, each Head of

Senior Management Team of 2002-2007:
J G Bartholomew (Bursar), S E Hincks (Second Deputy Head),
T H Keyes (Headmaster), A K J Macnaughton (Senior Deputy Head)
and R C Baum (Director of Studies)

Department produced an annual development plan, recording progress and identifying areas for improvement during the following school year.

A number of committees were established, each to focus on a specific area of school life, chaired by a senior member of staff. In 2014, the committees covered areas as diverse as Marketing, Health and Safety, Library, Uniform, Higher Education and ICT, with a large of number of staff, both teachers and support staff, involved in the decision-making process.

Support staff

One of the more significant changes in the daily life of the school has been the growing role played by the support staff. The 1984 issue of *The Vigornian* recorded the names of five 'non-teachers': Bursar, Sister, Caterer, Headmaster's Secretary and Accountant, although there were certainly more than just these individuals, below the names of the 55 teachers. A similar list in the 2014 issue included 96 members of support staff alongside the 98 teachers.

The Headmaster's Secretary, Christina Swainston since 1999, was joined by two School Secretaries, a Receptionist and an SMT Secretary, with additional secretarial staff for the Fourth Forms, Music Department and Marketing. The Bursar appointed a Deputy Bursar, Penny Hope, in 1997, to whom day-to-day responsibility for financial matters was delegated; Penny was assisted by a team of five staff in the Bursary, where the HR Manager is also based. The role of School Registrar became a full-time position in 2008, and Vickie Peckston oversaw an overhaul of the recruitment system, working closely with colleagues in Marketing.

The introduction of the SIMS school database in 2004 required a specialist database manager; the growth of this system into other areas included the administration of public examinations, so on the retirement of Marc Roberts in 2009, who had been examinations officer for some years, it was decided that this role should be given to a specialist member of the support staff.

The Foundation Development Office had comprised at least two, though often three, full-time members of staff, while another new department, 'Design, Media and Reprographics', successfully established by Sarah Marshall in 2000 and developed by Danny Payne (School House 1992-99) from 2008 to 2014, employed a full-time assistant to provide a document production service, and self-service copying facility for staff, alongside the Head of DMR who produced school publications, designed various marketing materials and managed the senior school website.

Prior to moving to DMR, Payne had established an IT Support Team, to service the spreading and evolving network of computer equipment. Pete Hodson took over as IT Systems Manager in 2008, overseeing the Network Analyst and two full-time IT Technicians. By 2014, IT Support was responsible for maintaining a network of more than 760 computers (almost entirely Windows-based PCs) including central servers, as well as printers, data projectors (one in almost every classroom), interactive whiteboards and tablet computers, across the three schools in the Foundation.

A team of two or three Librarians managed the School Library, assisting and encouraging pupils with a large body of books, media and online resources, while a Careers Librarian supports the work of the Head of Careers, providing access to a range of careers and university guides and organising the annual Lower Sixth work experience week and a programme of careers lectures and workshops. In the School Archive work was divided between cataloguing artefacts and data and locating resources for events, and meeting OVs and encouraging pupils to explore the history of their school.

The catering operation had grown enormously by the end of Nick and Heather Witherick's tenure in the kitchens, and an upgrade to the Dining Hall facilities, and the variety of meals offered, resulted in a doubling of the number of school lunches being served each day. The Dining Hall took the place of the Tuck Shop in terms of providing break time drinks and snacks

Design, Media and Reprographics, 2012.

The department sits between the rear of Hostel House and the medieval castle wall, which was left exposed during contruction in 1999.

for pupils, and opened daily from 8.00 am for breakfast until 5.00 pm for pupils to wait after school. In 2014, a team of eighteen staff supported Iain Cunningham-Martin, the Catering Manager.

Tony Norris was appointed Clerk of Works in 1996, having worked as an electrician on a number of projects at King's, including wiring the Theatre, over the previous 18 years, and managed the maintenance team, often numbering six or seven men plus Caretaker Fred McFee and one or two gardeners, overseeing the work of many contractors operating on site, from window cleaners to electricians and plumbers to network cable installers, across the three schools. Tony retired in 2013, succeeded by Jim Hawkins, in the new position of Estates Manager; he in turn was succeeded by Adam Winter (Chappel House 1989-94). A team of two or three ground staff, led by Phil Tyrell from 1981, maintained the playing fields, ensuring the pitches are in the best possible condition, despite the increasingly regular floods. Nicky McNamee managed a cleaning staff of more than 20. A Health and Safety Adviser, working one day per week, reported issues of concern and provided training for staff.

Tony Norris, Clerk of Works 1996-2013, celebrating his retirement with Galen Bartholomew, Bursar

The Health Centre in the rear courtyard of Choir House, 2015

The Cleaning Staff, May 2014
A list of names and roles can be found in Appendix 14.

Two school nurses, including Claire Furber who first joined the Sanatorium sisters in 1989, operated the Health Centre, providing first aid and urgent medical care for pupils at school, as well as healthcare advice and organising inoculation programmes. The well-being of pupils, alongside the work of the Chaplaincy, was supported by a professional counsellor, who meets pupils for private appointments.

Specialist science technicians worked in each of the three science departments, preparing experiments, maintaining supplies and looking after the laboratories. Technicians assisted in the running of the Art and Design & Technology departments, including mounting regular exhibitions. Languages assistants supported pupils with individual and small group tuition, as well as supervising the MFL multi-media centre.

A cover supervisor provided additional cover for staff absences from 2005; a supervisor looked after Sixth Form students in the library's Bolland Room and in the Dining Hall.

When David Thurlby left King's in 2001, Chris Crosswell, a professional stage designer, was appointed to manage the John Moore Theatre. His work in building impressive sets and designing sound and lighting schemes added enormously to the already high standard of King's theatre productions.

In 2009, SSI David Grinnell also became *de facto* Transport Manager, overseeing the maintenance of the fleet of six minibuses, arbitrating over double-bookings and ensuring that servicing and minibus driving tests are carried out. By the time the Michael Baker Boathouse was opened, the role of 'boat man' had evolved into a full-time Boathouse Manager, to maintain the large fleet of boats and other equipment and facilities, as well as training crews, alongside other dedicated coaches.

The Keyes Building - sports and performing arts centre

The Keyes Building, viewed from Severn Street, 2015, rubbing shoulders with the Art School

The development of the greatly anticipated Keyes Building, a project matched only in terms of ambition by the construction of School House 120 years earlier, was finally completed in the spring of 2015. The Keyes Building was opened by Tim Keyes, after whom it is named, on 20th June 2015.

King's had long hoped for an opportunity to build a second sports hall and a drama studio to complement the existing facilities. Such an opportunity arose when 'The Salmon's Leap' public house in Severn Street, between the Art School and John Moore Theatre, was put up for sale in 2006. The site was purchased, providing King's with a large plot of land for development.

Original concept image for 'The SPACE', 2009
The glass atrium linking the new building with the John Moore Theatre and the MFL department were lost when the development was scaled back. The 'Norman' colours for the large glass bays were changed in the 2012 redesign, after Neolithic and Iron Age discoveries during archaeological work.

The scheme devised by Associated Architects would incorporate the new sports hall, along with gym space, separate dance and drama studios, changing facilities, a new lobby and green room for a re-ordered John Moore Theatre, a link to MFL with additional teaching rooms, a Sixth Form Centre, meeting and conference spaces, offices and storage, an indoor climbing wall and an underground car park, as well as providing an impressive new entrance to the school by way of a grand staircase leading from Severn Street up to Castle Court. In this way, the building would provide solutions for many of the issues identified in a second 'ten year plan' for the senior school campus in 2008, alleviating a number of key pressure points in the school's accommodation and facilities.

The Sports and Performing Arts Centre would be the largest building project ever undertaken by the school, and would cost almost as much as the previous ten years' of development and refurbishment projects combined, with a projected budget of £13.5 million. The 'SPACE', as it quickly became known, was to have a curved frontage of stained glass panels, coloured to reflect the Norman heritage of the Severn Street site, and the intention was to have two phases of construction, allowing immediate use of the major facilities, with the Sixth Form Centre, some of the classrooms and the links with the John Moore Theatre and MFL department to be completed up to five years later, allowing time for fundraising.

A major fundraising appeal, 'The SPACE Campaign' was launched in 2011, with a target of £1,000,000. The Foundation Development Office ran many initiatives, ranging from a Silent Auction and black-tie dinners to a glass panel sponsorship campaign and a staff draw. The whole school community became involved, with a staff pantomime, dance showcase and

Demolition of 'The Salmon's Leap' and the Nissen huts, April 2009. The cleared site was used as a staff car park, and a temporary boat yard during construction of the Michael Baker Boathouse, until the end of 'The SPACE Campaign', when construction could begin.

*Construction of The Keyes Building, 2013
This photograph is a 'still' taken from a live webcam which allowed the school community to see building progress.*

*John Weston, Chairman of the SPACE Leadership Group, 'breaks ground' with Tim Keyes at the SPACE site, May 2013.
The fomer day boy changing room can be seen before its demolition.*

a gala performance of *'Les Miserables School Edition'* making contributions, fundraising carried out by the King's School Parents' Committee and the Old Vigornian Club, and donations from current and past parents, individual OVs and sports teams, staff of the three schools and Governors. The names of donors are included around the building, with many etched into panels on the Severn Street frontage, and some of the larger donations recognised in the names given to specific facilities. With perfect timing, The SPACE Campaign reached its target on the day of its 'Fireworks Finale' event in August 2013, which included a live auction in the Michael Baker Boathouse.

During the archaeological work, overseen by Mike Napthan (see Appendix 15), it became clear that the development site was significantly older than had been thought previously. In fact, evidence of a large Bronze Age settlement was discovered, one of the most significant such sites in Europe. This, along with a concern about the need to gain use of the facilities as quickly as possible, and the desire to reduce the total cost of the project, led to a reworking of the plans in the summer of 2012.

The frontage of the redesigned building would now respond to the much older history of the site, and would no longer have the wall of stained glass panels; the new entrance lobby and green room for the John Moore Theatre were lost, although a linking corridor would still allow access between the theatre and the studios; the link with MFL was lost, but additional space was made for classrooms within the new building, and the new conference space would allow the existing 'Severn Room' in the MFL building to be converted into teaching space. Crucially, however, the project would be constructed in a single phase and would be delivered within a revised budget of £10 million.

A ground-breaking ceremony took place as part of the OV Reunion Weekend in May 2013; exactly a year later, OVs and other guests were invited to attend a 'topping out' ceremony, at which the building received its new name.

In the time between, the concrete slab, on which the building sits, was poured, the steel frame erected, using an enormous crane which dominated the skyline for most of 2013 and 2014, the timber sections completed, walls built, the roof put on and windows installed.

During the summer and autumn, The Keyes Building was fitted out. Specialist contractors installed the three-storey climbing wall, the sprung floor of the dance studio and the state-of-the-art equipment for the drama studio. ICT equipment, including digital signage, was installed throughout the building. Delays to the final completion meant that the building was not handed over until Easter 2015, several months later than planned, but all who attended the opening on 20th June 2015, and the staff and pupils who began to use the new facilities, could see that it had been well worth the wait.

The Keyes Building provided much needed additional facilities for sports and the performing arts, extra teaching space for MFL, a superb indoor climbing and abseiling facility, a courtyard garden connected to the Art School for displaying students' sculptures, a reception area with a link to the John Moore Theatre, parking for 36 cars and secure cycle parking and, not least, an impressive new entrance to the school campus. The 'Weston Centre', named in honour of John Weston who was a major contributor in terms of both time and money to The SPACE Campaign, connected to The Keyes Building and comprising the 'Castle Court' section of the development, includes a Sixth Form study and social space and improved meeting, conference and seminar rooms as well as a prep room for Design and Technology. Not only have the new facilities provided more space, but additional space was created around the campus: the new sports hall is also to be used for examinations, allowing greater use of College Hall throughout the year; the gym and dance studio released space from the Annett Building, providing additional classrooms for Maths and accommodation for Choir House, which moved from Castle House providing more rehearsal space in the Music School; office space was freed in 5 and 6 Castle Place; and the Severn Room could be converted into teaching space. The maintenance staff moved into the 'Fishermen's Cottages' on Severn Street.

The school's perimeter along Severn Street was completed and an unloved area of the site transformed into a striking building with facilities which will serve the school well for many years to come.

Above: The Crow Dance Studio and the Wightman Drama Studio with gallery and large control room

Below: The Vigornian meeting room and the Weston Centre

The birch-clad exterior of the Weston Centre, with brightly-coloured ventilation panels, forming a sweeping curve to draw visitors into The Keyes Building. The glass-roofed atrium shelters the entrance; below it, steps lead down to Severn Street.

Images of the sports facilities can be found on pages 178 and 179; a photograph of the official opening can be found on page 225.

Rory Johnson — Bright House 2003-09

I think that the time I spent at King's could be described as a time of change and modernisation, although that had already begun before I arrived. By then, it was pretty much equal numbers of boys and girls. Links with the past still remained: I remember Mr Thompson still smoked his pipe and devoted entire Latin lessons to discussing the royal family. Various other long standing and charismatic teachers gradually left, including Mrs Appleby, Mr Stone, Mr Griffifths, Mr Davis and Mr Roberts. They all had quirky little things that made them stand out; few teachers that I was taught by in my last year had been at King's long enough to have developed this mysterious 'legend' status.

The physical appearance of the school changed in many ways, with a brand new library, improved DT facilities, a new art building and boathouse. The rusty old sheds behind the DT block had been demolished to make way for a smart new sports building. I remember when I began having science classes in old, wooden-furnished laboratories that are now all fitted out with gleaming metal and plastic.

Thankfully, some traditions stayed very strong. The association with the Cathedral and the role of the King's and Queen's Scholars, the Himalayan Club, sports tours, excellent plays and concerts, the CCF and many other aspects of school life have remained the same over the decades.

The friendly house atmosphere, with its healthy rivalries and allegiances and the development of teacher-pupil relations as pupils move up through the school, and the respect among pupils of different ages, that is helped by having roles such as monitors, heads of house and school, has remained at King's when at many other schools this has been lost.

I remember playing rugby on waterlogged pitches, in the snow, in the pitch black - a seemingly mandatory requirement of the schoolboy game that hasn't changed. Some traditions such as the RGS Match remained, but have been updated from a few huddling around a wet, dimly-lit training pitch to thousands of spectators watching a massively publicised game in a brand new premiership stadium. Rowing especially, but all sport, seems to have become almost scientific in its preparation with diet, nutrition supplements and highly intensive training routines playing a key role, even down to schoolboy level, a development which I'm not sure I totally support.

Some good new traditions have taken hold, particularly the work of the recently created Sixth Form Charity Committee that managed to incorporate various events into the school calendar, including Pink Day, the Fort Royal garden party and the Christmas party for the old folks.

Rory Johnson exercising the 'traditional' right of the Head of School to graze sheep on College Green (thought to have been invented by Tim Hickson in the 1980s!), Leavers' Day 2009

'Pink Day' became an annual event in the mid-2000s - organised by the Sixth Form Charity Committee, members of the Sixth Form raised funds for breast cancer charities, with events ranging from pink cake sales to a 1st VII Netball v 1st VII Rugby netball match. The 'pink ribbon' photograph was a firm tradition, this one taken in 2012.

A guiding vision

Of increasing importance to public organisations in the last decade has been a 'mission statement', setting out the aims of the organisation and providing a framework and context for strategy planning. King's adopted a formal mission statement.

"Our aims and aspirations in more detail are that:
- *Every pupil fulfils his or her academic potential.*
- *Teachers and pupils pursue excellence in teaching and learning.*
- *Our pupils develop a love of learning, both individually and with others, and acquire a wide range of learning skills.*
- *We create an environment in which pupils are confident in their ability and increasingly ready to take responsibility for their own learning.*
- *Every pupil receives excellent pastoral care within an ethos of tolerance and mutual respect rooted in Christian values.*
- *Pupils develop relationships with peers and adults in a way that prepares them for life beyond school.*
- *Pupils acquire a sense of responsibility and self-discipline.*
- *Pupils benefit from a wide range of opportunities for leadership and the management of others.*
- *We work closely with parents so that they are well informed about the progress of their children and we can work together as effectively as possible in the best interests of the pupils.*
- *We ensure good continuity of care between the Junior and Senior Schools.*
- *Our pupils participate in a variety of physical activities and experience a sense of well-being and self-confidence that arises from good health and fitness.*
- *Our pupils benefit from a comprehensive personal and social education that helps them to lead happy and fulfilling lives.*
- *Our pupils are well prepared for Higher Education and subsequent employment as a result of the teaching opportunities, advice and support that they receive at this school.*
- *Our pupils learn the value of teamwork and the importance of mutual support within and across year groups.*

Upper Sixth mentors working with Fourth Form pupils

- *We provide a varied range of activities beyond the curriculum.*
- *Pupils discover and develop their own skills and interests at school in preparation for adult life.*
- *All pupils be adventurous and participate in a range of activities, appreciating the rewards of teamwork.*
- *All be given the opportunity for personal achievement and fulfilment in a way befitting their own aspirations.*
- *Our pupils develop a moral, spiritual and aesthetic awareness that makes them receptive to the world around them, bringing with it a sense of wonder and openness to the most important ideas in our own and other cultures.*
- *Through bursary support, these opportunities are made increasingly available to children from families who could not otherwise afford to send them here.*
- *Our pupils have regular opportunities to hear / meet and learn from representatives of key institutions in the local community, and further afield, and learn how they themselves can increasingly, as they grow older, be contributors to this community through giving of their time, skills and commitment.*
- *The school recognises the crucial importance of its staff in pursuing the aims above and, as a good employer, undertakes to relieve them wherever possible of duties which could be done by non-teaching staff, as well as provide them with induction, support and training, appropriate to their career stage, and ongoing review and development, thereby enhancing their career progression.*
- *We encourage in all members of our community a degree of spiritual literacy that will enable them to articulate their own values and beliefs, whilst having an informed understanding of, and respect for, those of others. Whilst we respect the right of each individual to form their own religious identity, that occurs here within a community rooted in an inclusive Church of England environment and in the context of regular acts of communal worship. We seek to offer a vision of Christian prayer, scholarship and service rooted in our belief, derived from the principles of the Benedictine monastery that was once on this site, in the importance of the community for the flourishing of each individual."*

Kayaking - one of the activities enjoyed by pupils at the Lower Remove Camps

The school's vision was more simply summarised as:

"To help young people to reach their potential at school in preparation for leading confident, fulfilled and unselfish lives as adults."

Getting the word out

Communication, both within the school community and promoting the school to the outside world, has changed significantly in the 21st century, alongside the technology which made it possible.

E-mail

While the pioneering use of e-mail might date back to the 1950s, by the late 1990s King's had a handful of e-mail addresses, used only by senior staff and ICT 'enthusiasts'. E-mail accounts became more widely used during the following decade, but not all King's staff used the service until it became 'compulsory' in 2010; e-mail then became established quickly as the primary means of communication between staff, even replacing most of the 'notes in pigeon-holes', and then with parents - concerned parents were suddenly given the means to contact tutors and teachers at all hours, which led to much concern for the staff; guidance on the use of e-mail quickly followed.

A new system, known as 'SchoolComms' was introduced in 2010, allowing the school office to send virtual letters home to parents without the need to print and distribute hundreds of copies. Alongside this an eNewsletter was developed which kept parents, and potential parents who could subscribe to the service, informed about school news and events, sent electronically each week.

Publications

The *Bulletin*, introduced by Patricia Stevens in the 1990s, was replaced partly by the weekly *eNewsletter*, but also by a 'glossy' magazine named *K*, sent out twice each year to parents from 2011. The FDO had produced a newsletter for OVs called *Connect* since 2001, and this received a makeover at the same time, following the style of 'K'. Both of these magazines were produced by Design, Media and Reprographics, which also took over publication of *'Vigornian'* in 2011 (see Chapter 3). An *Arts Programme* was published three times each year, distributed to parents and through arts and tourism venues around the county, promoting the creative and performing arts at King's.

Above: The annual Primary Schools' Quiz, 2009, won by Nunnery Wood Primary School

Below: King's banners appeared at arts and sports locations around Worcestershire - this one was at the David Lloyd gym, 2014

Website and social media

Promotion of the school, which traditionally relied on newspaper advertisements and word of mouth, also benefited from new technology. The school website, initially developed by John Roslington in the late 1990s, was identified as a key tool for marketing the school and underwent several 'upgrades' and redesigns by specialist companies. By 2012, when the latest website was unveiled, a complex 'content management system' supported a system built around the idea of sharing news and events - a steady flow of news stories was produced and published online, included in the *eNewsletter* and shared on *Facebook* and *Twitter*, the most widely-used social media platforms. An increased emphasis was placed on *Twitter* particularly in 2013, resulting in many individual accounts operated by staff from all areas of the Foundation, each promoting items of interest to different audiences - pupils, parents, OVs, prospective parents and even other schools.

Marketing

Under the direction of Russ Mason, in the role of Marketing Director, a highly-focussed marketing operation developed, transforming the ways in which the school promoted itself to prospective parents. Specialist design agencies created branding schemes for the school, which were rolled out across newspaper adverts, hoarding banners and the new, stylish

College Hall set up for an Open Morning, 2010

A selection of school publications and prospectuses

prospectuses for the schools. Working with Design, Media and Reprographics, this branding was pushed out across all areas of communication, from minibus livery to headed paper, from the website to business cards and from magazines to name badges. The school insignia was first registered as a trademark in 2003. The new prospectuses were joined by DVD prospectuses at various levels, and these, with other video clips, would often be shared online.

The school began to sponsor other organisations and events, as part of a programme of 'soft' marketing; *'Sport on Monday'* in the *Worcester News* saw pages of King's banners appear in the newspaper each week, and the school entered partnerships with theatres and sports teams, promoting the name of the school and the website - the centre of the marketing strategy. King's also hosted a number of events each year for local primary schools, including a quiz, netball tournament and Maths Olympiad.

It had long been realised that the best way to market the school to new pupils was to invite families to visit the school, so all of the marketing tools available pointed to the website, which in turn encouraged visitors to attend an open event. The most important events for recruitment were the three Open Mornings held each year, one of which was specifically targeted at 16+ recruitment into the Sixth Form. The operation was 'beefed up', with additional resources put into new display equipment, a keynote address by the Headmaster and a full tour of the school campus - even during the difficult economic climate following 2008, a typical Open Morning would attract upwards of 120 families to King's. A series of 'Taster Mornings', first introduced in the early 2000s, aimed to cement the attraction to King's by inviting potential pupils to return for a morning of activities.

Local rivals

For centuries King's enjoyed a rivalry with the Royal Grammar School, now RGS Worcester, on the rugby and cricket pitches, in disputes over scholarships and names, over recruitment and, more recently in School League Tables. In 2014 this rivalry continued, with annual sports fixtures, now across a range of both girls and boys sports, and sometimes fierce marketing targeted at potential parents of the schools, who had competed ever harder during a time of economic recession since 2008. The difficult merger of RGS Worcester with the Alice Ottley School left King's able to draw 'clear blue water' between itself and its traditional competitor, but the old rival remains a serious competitor and, like King's, had a new Headmaster from September 2014.

King's had often 'punched above its weight', and as a co-educational day school in a relatively small city it continued to do so, performing well academically and with key strengths in recent years in rowing, netball and rugby sevens, with teams which have often reached national championships.

In 2013, The King's School, Worcester was placed 35th nationally, in a league table of independent day schools, by *The Sunday Times* - a remarkable achievement for a school which has undergone a transformation from the small, boys boarding school of 70 years earlier, and testament to the success of the changes introduced under the headships of David Annett, Andrew Milne, John Moore and Tim Keyes.

Enduring relationships

It always seemed to be important that King's should be recognised as a significant partner to other institutions in the city. Being situated in the heart of Worcester it was very much to the advantage of King's pupils that the school should be involved in Worcester life. The school's relationship with sporting clubs (notably the professional Rugby, Cricket and Basketball clubs - Worcester Warriors, Worcestershire County Cricket Club and Worcester Wolves, respectively) had been based on the passionate support of so many King's pupils for these teams and on the regular assistance given by the clubs to the school.

The dramatic new approach to the school, through The Keyes Building, with a view to Worcester Cathedral, 2015

The same could be said of local cultural institutions including *Worcester Live* (with whom the school worked on many drama projects) and Malvern Theatres.

King's raised large amounts of money over time for local charities. This had been a two-way benefit since it was central to the school's purpose to encourage its pupils to be unselfish in their outlook. *St Richard's Hospice*, *Acorns Hospice* and *Sight Concern* had been regular local partners in this respect, alongside the campaign to establish a Worcester Breast Unit. Representatives of these and other charities were regular speakers at College Hall assemblies.

Educational partnerships had been a very fruitful area at the start of the 21st century. The growth of the University of Worcester in size, confidence and range of courses in recent times was a matter of great pride for the city. The school worked closely with a number of its departments and looked to a future of further initiatives of this sort. Tim Keyes was awarded a Fellowship of the University of Worcester in 2012. The close connection between King's and Bishop Perowne Church of England College began almost by accident when King's was looking for a site on which to build an all-weather pitch. A lengthy negotiation with the County Council over the lease of land at the school was well worth the resulting facility, but just as valuable was the steady development of shared activity with staff and pupils at Bishop Perowne in a range of subjects and activities. Regular adventurous trips, taking in destinations including Morocco and Iceland, in which King's students accompanied visually impaired students from New College Worcester were transforming experiences for all involved. King's also worked very closely with a number of local primary schools. One sent pupils to King's each week to work with Sixth Form artists. Two others welcomed groups of King's pupils weekly at lunchtime to read or work with their children. The annual Primary School Quiz and Maths Challenge competitions were just two examples of a much wider set of activities that brought primary school pupils to King's, allowing them to work with or be coached by King's staff and students.

Among the school's international partners, as well as those schools with whom King's operated language exchanges, the schools involved in the EU-funded *Comenius Scheme* became regular and welcome visitors to Worcester over a period of more than ten years, and King's pupils enjoyed reciprocal visits to work on common projects to Germany, France, Holland, Spain, Poland and the Czech Republic. Visits to the European Parliament and meeting with MEPs in both Brussels and Strasbourg were particular highlights. The partnership between King's and the German school in this project, the Domgymnasium in Magdeburg, was particularly fruitful and led to biennial joint trips to a small village in Holland in which there is a joint Dutch and German centre for reconciliation based in a youth centre next to a large German war cemetery – an unlikely destination for a school trip but one which proved a most fulfilling experience for all who took part and was a rare example of a trip with students from a school in another country to neutral territory.

A legacy for the future

Tim Keyes announced his decision to retire in May 2013, allowing time for the governors to appoint his successor and a smooth transition for the school.

After sixteen years as Headmaster, The King's School which Tim Keyes handed over to Matthew Armstrong was a significantly different school to the one he had taken over in 1998, having undergone a long period of significant change and development.

The school had become a fully co-educational day school, with an excellent record of academic success, splendid facilities and positive relationships both internally and with the wider community, and formed part of a Foundation with two junior schools, providing education for children from the age of two to eighteen.

In September 2014, the number of pupils at the senior school exceeded 950 for the first time, almost 300 of whom were in the Sixth Form and 125 had joined King's at Year 7; across the school, the boy : girl ratio was now 55 : 45. An additional 210 pupils, aged from four to eleven, attended King's St Alban's, with King's Hawford having 330 pupils aged between two and eleven.

The school's teaching staff was younger, enthusiastic and dedicated, assisted by a team of almost 100 members of support staff, running school facilities and providing services including catering, ICT support and transport. The school curriculum was expanded to allow greater choice and specialisation for pupils, with twenty A Level subjects and more flexibility in languages and sports. A wide range of extra-curricular activities continued to flourish while academic performance was stronger than ever before.

The senior school campus had been transformed in a way that previous Headmasters could barely have imagined: the old boarding houses made way for new classrooms, administration space and a Music School; School House provided a home for a Library at the heart of the school; a new Art School allowed for expansion of Design and Technology, and refurbished science laboratories and the lecture theatre added to the renaissance of the site. The Michael Baker Boathouse and The Keyes Building completed the new facilities, providing much needed space to accommodate the larger school, which could now better meet the needs of all its pupils.

Supported by the Foundation Development Office, relationships with OVs were strengthened; the Development Trust achieved new levels of support through campaigns for capital projects and bursaries; the KSPC raised the profile of the school as well as much-needed funds for smaller projects. External relationships were also nurtured: the partnership with Bishop Perowne CofE College resulted in shared activities and the all-weather pitch; the Comenius Project led to a close relationship with Dom Gymnasium, Magdeburg; the new University of Worcester became a key partner in Sixth Form projects.

The Christian ethos of the school had been brought to the fore once again, with closer links to the Cathedral, a broadened Chaplaincy and a focus on charitable support.

There could be little doubt that The King's School of 2014 was a thriving, well-managed school, fit for the future, and the role of Tim Keyes, who retired with Mary Anne to Ledbury in August 2014, in delivering this transformation cannot be understated.

Tim Keyes holding the 2014 school photograph

Aerial photographs taken in September 2015.

Above: The King's School, Worcester, viewed from the west - a vista which shows the green, leafy nature of the campus. Unfortunately, the size of many of the trees obscures a number of school buildings in this photograph.

Below: The expanse of Playing Fields across the Chapter Meadows, showing three pavilions and numerous pitches for rugby, football and hockey, the hard-surface for netball courts and rowing on the River Severn.

M G Armstrong - Headmaster from 2014

Matthew Gavin Armstrong joined King's from Charterhouse, where he had served at different times as Assistant Headmaster (Academic) and Assistant Headmaster (External Relations). He studied at New College, Oxford, where he gained a degree in Medieval and Modern Languages and his PGCE. He started his career at Lancing College, where he taught French and German and also studied for an M.A. in Renaissance Studies at Birkbeck College, London. After a spell in the city working as a Business Analyst for McKinsey & Co. he returned to teach at Winchester; while there he also gained a B.A. in English Literature, again from Birkbeck. He is married to Kate, and lists skiing and mountaineering among his interests.

Commenting on his appointment in 2013, Matthew Armstrong said *"The warmth of the school, its close connection with Worcester Cathedral, its academic distinction and its focus on all-round education combine to make it a very special place. I am fortunate to be taking over from Tim Keyes, who has led King's with such distinction, and I look forward to building on his good work."*

The major programme of building development came to an end for the foreseeable future with the completion of the Keyes Building on Severn Street and the Bartholomew Barn at King's Hawford. The former had been designed to address all the major deficiencies of the senior school site, such as the lack of a Sixth Form centre, and will also offer extra opportunities for pupils at King's St Alban's. Nevertheless, nothing stands still: future developments will require changes and continuing investment in facilities, quite apart from the need to maintain the school to an excellent standard.

The work of the Foundation Development Office has assumed increasing importance. The greatest challenge it faces is to continue to raise funds for bursaries so that pupils whose parents are unable to afford the fees are still able to benefit from a King's education. Keeping in touch with Old Vigornians and welcoming them back to King's is all part of this process.

The school maintains the view that young people thrive on academic success and a rounded academic education is at the core of what King's aims to offer its pupils. The wide range of performing arts, sports and other extra-curricular activities,

Matthew Armstrong meeting members of the Lower Sixth in the Creighton Memorial Gardens, March 2014

underpinned by excellent standards of pastoral care, aim to produce rounded young people who will go into the world aware of what they can offer rather than what they can take from life.

Armstrong's first year witnessed a smooth handover, thanks in part to the strong support from the Governing Body and senior staff. During his first year, the decision was taken to add an extra house in September 2015 taking the number of houses to nine.

In this globalised age, the school continues to foster friendships around the world, with pupils continuing to broaden their horizons on extra-curricular tours and on language exchange programmes in France, Germany and Spain. Notre Dame Academy in Worcester, Massachusetts, with which King's has maintained an exchange since 1998, returned in 2015 to give a concert in College Hall.

Change presents opportunities, and new leadership can bring a fresh perspective and positive, creative ideas to an institution. Matthew Armstrong has demonstrated that he understands the culture of King's and what makes it special and inclusive: with this appreciation of the things which make the school so very special, The King's School, Worcester appears to be in good hands as it enters the next chapter in its history.

Opening of The Keyes Building, 20th June 2015
Cutting the ribbon, from left to right: Carl Nichols, Chairman of the King's School Parents' Committee;
Professor David Green, Vice-Chancellor, University of Worcester; Toby Thomas, Head of School; Hugh Carslake, Chairman of Governors;
Roy Padden, Chairman, Old Vigornian Club; Julia Seymour, owner, Diglis House Hotel; Jonny Mason, Director of Sport;
James Launder, Year 6 pupil at King's Hawford; Tim Keyes, Headmaster 1998-2014; Madeleine Hales, Year 6 pupil at King's St Alban's;
Donald Howell, Chairman of Governors 1986-2010; John Christophers, Associated Architects; Jules Price-Hutchinson, Head of Drama;
Professor Michael Clarke, a Deputy Lieutenant for Worcestershire; Galen Bartholomew, Bursar; and Robin Walker MP.

Appendix 1: King Henry VIII's 1541-42 Statutes founding The King's School

As described in Chapter 1, a number of Statutes were signed by King Henry VIII (thought to have been written by Archbishop Cranmer), which re-founded the Cathedral Church of Worcester from the dissolved St Mary's Priory and established a 'Cathedral Grammar School' within the new Cathedral Foundation, in 1541-42. Of these, and other Letters Patent establishing the foundation and school, several had particular bearing on the operation of the new school, and these are set out below.
The text has been taken from 'Documents Illustrating Early Education in Worcester 685 to 1700' by A.F. Leach.

25 The Choristers and their Master

We decree and ordain that in our church aforesaid there shall be at the election or nomination of the Dean, or in his absence the Subdean, and Chapter, 10 choristers, boys of tender age with clear voices and fit to sing, to serve the choir, minister and sing.

For their instruction and education as well in modesty of behaviour as in skill in singing, we will that besides the 8 clerks before-named, one shall be elected by the Dean [etc.] and Chapter, of good character, upright life and skilled in singing and playing the organ, to diligently employ himself in teaching the boys in playing the organ at the proper time and singing divine service. And if he shall be found negligent or idle in teaching he shall after three warnings be deposed from office. And he shall be bound by oath faithfully to discharge his office.

26 Of the Grammar Boys and their Teachers

That piety and good letters may in our church aforesaid for ever blossom, grow, flower and in their time bear fruit for the glory of God and the advantage and adornment of the commonwealth, we decree and ordain that there shall always be in our church of Worcester, elected and nominated by the Dean, or in his absence the Sub-dean and Chapter, to be maintained out of the possessions of the church, 40 boys, poor and destitute of the help of their friends, of native genius as far as may be and apt to learn. We do not wish however that they shall be admitted as poor boys of our church before they have learnt to read and write and are moderately learned in the rudiments of grammar, in the opinion of the Dean, or in his absence the Sub-dean, and the Head Master;

And we will that these boys shall be maintained at the expense of our church until they have obtained a moderate knowledge of Latin and have learnt to speak and to write Latin. The period of four years shall be given to this, or if it shall so seem good to the Dean or in his absence the Sub- dean, and the Headmaster, at most five years and not more.

We will further, that none shall be elected a poor scholar of our church who has not completed his ninth year or has passed the fifteenth year of his age, unless he has been a chorister of our church of Worcester.

But if any of the boys is found to be of remarkable slowness and stupidity or of a character to which learning is abhorrent, we will that after a long probation he shall be expelled by the Dean, or in his absence the Sub-dean, and another substituted, lest like a drone he should devour the bees' honey. And here we charge the consciences of the masters that they shall bestow the utmost possible labour and pains in making all the boys progress and become proficient in learning; and that they allow no boy who is remarkable for the slowness of his intellect to remain uselessly too long among the rest, but shall report his name at once to the Dean, or in his absence the Sub-dean, so that he may be removed and another more fit be elected in his place by the Dean, or in his absence the Sub-dean, and Chapter.

We decree also that the Dean, or in his absence the Sub-dean, and Chapter shall elect one learned in Latin and Greek, of good character and pious life, endowed with the faculty of teaching, to instruct in piety and adorn with good learning those 40 boys of our church and all others whatsoever who come to our school to learn. He shall hold the primacy in our school and be called the Head Master or Chief Teacher.

In the second place we will that the Dean [etc. as above] shall choose another of good character and pious life, learned in Latin and endowed with the faculty of teaching, to teach the boys under the Head Master the first rudiments of grammar, and therefore to be called the Lower Master or Second Teacher.

These two teachers of the boys we will shall diligently and faithfully follow the rules and order of teaching which the Dean and Chapter shall think fit to prescribe. But if they are idle or negligent or found unfit to teach they shall after three warnings by the Dean and Chapter be removed and deposed from office. And they shall promise on oath that they will faithfully perform all things belonging to their function.

32 Of the celebration of Divine Service

That Prayers and petitions may continually be done in our church decently and in order, and that every day the praise of God may be celebrated with singing and thanksgiving, We decree and ordain that the minor canons and clerks, with the deacon and subdeacon and the master of the choristers, shall perform the divine offices in the choir of our temple, after the fashion and rites of other cathedral churches; except that we do not wish them to be bound to sing offices in the night.

We order also that every day, as well fast days as others, mass of the Holy Ghost shall be celebrated in the temple early in the morning at 6 o'clock, in a place to be assigned for that purpose by the Dean. Moreover we will that on all principal feasts, the Dean, and on the greater doubles the Vice Dean, and on other double feasts the rest of the canons, each in his rank, shall perform the divine offices. We decree also that none of the canons or others ministering in the choir shall enter the choir during the divine offices without a habit proper for the choir.

We decree further that both teachers of grammar shall be present in choir on feast days clothed in garments befitting the choir; one of them having the seat next in choir above the minor canons, and the other next below the minor canons.

Moreover we will that the grammar boys who are maintained at the expense of the church shall be present in choir on feast days, and diligently do whatever duty is imposed on them by the Precentor; unless they have been otherwise directed by the Head Master. And these boys too we will shall on every day in the year when the sacred mysteries are performed at High Mass be present at the elevation of the body of the Lord, and stay there till the singing of the Agnus Dei is done; and meanwhile, two and two, meditate and say the Psalms "Have mercy upon me, O God," and "God be merciful unto us," and the Lord's Prayer and "Out of the deep have I called," with the prayer "Absolve, we beseech thee."

We will also and decree that as soon as we pass from this light, a funeral service for our soul shall immediately be done in our church of Worcester, all the canons and other ministers of our church, the scholars and poor men being summoned to it, and the day of our death shall be written in the Statute books, so that on the anniversary of that day obsequies and masses shall for all time to come be celebrated for us.

39 Prayers to be said in school in the morning

At 6 o'clock in the morning the usher shall go into school, and with all the scholars of the school in turns say the Psalm (xxi.) The King shall rejoice in thy strength, O Lord. Lord have mercy upon us, Christ have mercy upon us, the Lord's Prayer, and lead us not into temptation, etc. O Lord, shew thy mercy upon us, etc. O Lord save the King, etc. Be a strong tower, O Lord, etc. Let the enemy have no advantage, etc. Lord hear our prayer, etc.

Prayers to be said in school in the evening

At 5 o'clock, when about to leave school, they shall say in turns the Psalm (cxxxiv.) Behold, now praise the Lord, etc. Lord have mercy upon us, Christ [etc.]. Our Father, etc. Rise Lord and help us, etc. Lord of all power and might, etc. [Collect for 7th Sunday after Trinity] with the prayer, Lighten our darkness, we beseech thee, O Lord, etc.

40 Of the School and Classes, and the order to be observed in it

The usual qualities which are found in an architect and other overseers of works in pressing on their work, namely, industry and diligence, ought also to be found in pedagogues and teachers of the tender youth, that they may as it were enter into a friendly conspiracy and contention between themselves and imbue thoroughly the scholars committed to their trust with piety and good letters; and not to study their own advantage or indulge their own love of ease so much as to look on their proficiency and the public benefit, so that they may be seen to do their duty fairly in everything. And this they will be able to do much more successfully if they endeavour sedulously to follow the order we have prescribed.

The whole number of the scholars shall be divided into five or six ranks or classes. The Under Master shall teach the three lower, and the Head Master the three upper classes.

No one shall be admitted into the school who cannot read readily, or does not know by heart in the vernacular the Lord's Prayer, the Angelic Salutation, the Apostles' Creed and the Ten Commandments. Those who are wholly ignorant of grammar shall learn the accidence of nouns and verbs, as it were out of class. When they have learnt these they shall be taken into the First Class.

In the First Class they shall learn thoroughly by heart the rudiments in English; they shall learn to put together the parts of speech; and to turn a short phrase of English into Latin; and gradually to approach other easy constructions.

In the Second Class they shall learn a little higher; they shall know the genders of nouns and the inflections of verbs written in Latin; they shall run through Cato's verses, Aesop's Fables, and some Familiar Colloquies.

In the Third Class they shall endeavour to make correct varyings on the nouns and anomalous verbs, so that no noun or verb can be found anywhere which they do not know how to inflect in every detail. In this form too they shall make Terence's Comedies, Mantuanus' Eclogues, and other things of that sort thoroughly familiar to them.

These classes the Under Master shall have the care of, gradually instilling and inculcating the lesser rudiments into his pupils so as to make them fit and prepared to receive higher instruction.

The usher shall come into school at 6 a.m. and immediately after saying his prayers to God which we have prescribed, shall make his scholars say by heart daily one of the eight parts of speech until they are ready in each. Nor shall he omit on any other day to dictate to his pupils an English sentence, and that a short one, which he shall teach them to turn exactly into Latin, and to write it carefully in their parchment note-books.

In anything to be done in the school the Under Master shall be subject to and shall obey the Head Master;

and shall consult him on the method and plan of teaching; so that they may both agree in their zeal for the profit of the scholars. Both too shall endeavour to teach their pupils to speak openly, finely and distinctly, keeping due decorum both with their body and their mouth.

In the Fourth Form the boys shall be taught to know the Latin syntax readily; and shall be practised in the stories of poets, and familiar letters of learned men and the like.

In the Fifth Form they shall commit to memory the Figures of Latin Oratory and the rules for making verses; and at the same time shall be practised in making verses and polishing themes; then they shall be versed in translating the chastest Poets and the best Historians.

Lastly, in the Sixth Form they shall be instructed in the formulas of the Copiousness of Words and Things written by Erasmus; and to learn to master varyings of speech in every mood, so that they may acquire the faculty of speaking Latin, as far as is possible for boys. Meanwhile they shall taste Horace, Cicero and other authors of that class. Meanwhile they shall compete with one another in declamations so that they may leave well learned in the school of argument.

These classes principally the Head Master shall try to polish in Latin.

He shall come into school by 7 o'clock to perform his duty of teaching thoroughly. He shall too every other day make some English sentence into Latin and teach the flock committed to him to change it into many forms.

Moreover let him understand that he has charge of the whole school. So every week he ought to visit the whole flock, once, twice or three times, and diligently test the abilities of the scholars and ascertain their progress in learning. If he shall prove any of them after testing them in every way to be slow and wholly strangers to the Muses, he shall warn their friends not to let them, being wholly unfit for letters, waste their time in vain and fill the places of others. But those he shall find to be fit and industrious he shall, at least three times a year, call up to the higher forms, namely from the first to the second, from the second to the third, and so on as each shall be thought fit. This shall be done in the presence of and after consultation with the Under Master in the case of those who are entrusted to his care.

Moreover at 6 p.m. the scholars shall return to school and until 7 p.m. shall do their repetition and render to their fellow pupils who have become ripe in learning, several masters also being present, whatever they have learnt through the day.

When leave to play is given they shall play and sport together, not wandering about here and there, lest they incur loss of character, and their minds become set upon other things, and estranged from learning. And they shall not practise any games which are not of a gentlemanly appearance and free of all lowness.

Lastly, whatever they are doing in earnest or in play they shall never use any language but Latin and Greek.

Appendix 2: Chronology of King's School events

1541	Foundation of Cathedral Grammar School (The King's School) by King Henry VIII
	Appointment of John Pether as first Schoolmaster
1542	Opening of the Cathedral Grammar School
	Walter Graver/Graner appointed as first Usher
1547	School marked the death of Henry VIII
1555	Appointment of Roger Colbourne as Master
c. 1555	Destruction of 'The Majestas', College Hall
1557	Appointment of Thomas Bradshaw as Master
c. 1560	School moved to College Hall
1575	State Visit by Queen Elizabeth I
1585	Appointment of Henry Maye as Master
1589	Appointment of Henry Bright as Master
1627	Death of Henry Bright
	Appointment of Henry Moule as Master
1637	Removal of the school to the Charnel Chapel
1642	Re-instatement of the school in College Hall following petition to Parliament
1644	Appointment of John Toy as Master
1646	Replacement of John Toy by Commonwealth Goverment with John Hardinge
	Schoolmaster's House (near 7 College Green) established
1650	The King's School dissolved
1653	Appointment of Thomas Barfoote as Master
	Re-opening of The King's School
1660	Re-instatement of John Toy as Master by Restoration Government of King Charles II
1664	Appointment of Thomas Stephens as Master
1665	Bequest by John Meeke (OV) to establish Meeke Scholarships to the University of Oxford
1666	New Statutes introduced by Dean and Chapter
1667	Appointment of John Wright as Master
1673	First 'inspection' of school undertaken by Dean and Chapter
1687	Geography added to school curriculum
1695	Death of John Wright
	Appointment of Benjamin Slater as Master
1700	Death of Benjamin Slater
	Appointment of John Medens as Master
1707	Renovation of Schoolmaster's House
	Appointment of William Betterley as Master
	Chapter Order prohibits playing football on College Green
1733	Death of William Betterley
	Appointment of Thomas Miles as Head Master
1755	First use of College Hall as a venue for the Three Choirs Festival
1767	Lowest recorded number of pupils (20)
1768	Death of Thomas Miles
	Appointment of Thomas Goodinge as Head Master
1770	Chapter Order provides for shorter school days
	Chapter Order prohibits playing in cloisters
1776	Resignation of Thomas Goodinge
	Appointment of John Bennett as Head Master
1777	Resignation of John Bennett
	Appointment of John Griffin as Head Master
1778	Stable loft (No. 4) leased as Scholars' dormitory
1788	Visit by King George III to College Hall for Three Choirs Festival concert
1813	Death of John Griffin
	Appointment of William Porter as Headmaster
1820	Appointment of Allen Wheeler as Headmaster
1832	First awards of School Prizes
1837	Appointment of Octavius Fox as Headmaster
	Establishment of separate School for Choristers
1838	Appointment of first Second Master (replacing the position of Usher)
	Modernisation of school hours, to between 9.00 am and 4.30 pm
	Formal establishment of School Prizes
1852	Appointment of Stephen Denning as Headmaster
1856	First appointment of a Third Master
	Appointment of William Helm as Headmaster
1860	Appointment of Maurice Day as Headmaster
	Closure of Cathedral's School for Choristers
1865	Cadet Corps established in conjunction with RGS
1866	Bryce report for Endowed Schools Commissioners suggests amalgamation with RGS
1867	Town council meeting to discuss the Cathedral School's finances; petition to Parliament on behalf of Worcester Cathedral School
1868	Cadet Corps disbanded
1872	Appeal to Dean and Chapter to provide additional accommodation for school, resulting in removal of orchestra staging and discovery of 'The Majestas' in College Hall
1874	Re-opening of Worcester Cathedral after restoration works
1877	Foundation of KSW Boat Club
1878	First edition of *The Vigornian* published
	Construction of a fives court on playground (western end of Cathedral)
1879	William Bolland appointed as Headmaster
	Gas lighting installed in College Hall
	First School Concert
1880	Reduction in number of Scholars from 40 to 20
	Schoolmaster's House evacuated due to diphtheria
	Lease acquired for Cripplegate House, St John's, as temporary accommodation for Headmaster and boarders

1881	First draft of 'New Scheme' by Charity Commission
	Choristers transferred to Choir School
1882	First cricket match played at New Road playing field
	Schoolmaster's House at Number 7 condemned
	Sixth Formers first entered for 'Higher Certificate'
1883	Revised 'New Scheme' proposed
1884	'New Scheme' legally separated the school from Worcester Cathedral, providing buildings and land for development and increased endowments
	'Worcester Cathedral Grammar School' formally adopted as name of the school
	School song 'Floreat Schola Vigorniensis' introduced for Speech Day
1885	Start of restoration work in College Hall
	'Castle Gardens' site given to school under New Scheme, creating playground and space for School House
	Fifth Formers first entered for 'Lower Certificate'
1886	Construction of School House started
	First school excursion to London
1887	Completion of restoration work in College Hall
	Composition of new school song *God bless our College School* to mark re-opening of College Hall
1888	Opening of School House
1889	Public debate on amalgamation with RGS
	First school regatta for KSW Boat Club
	First Old Vigorian Dinner
	Inaugural OV v King's cricket match
	Fives Courts built on playground
1890	Announcement in Parliament that amalgamation with RGS would not go ahead
1891	Association Football adopted as main winter sport
1892	Building at Number 7 destroyed by fire
1894	Cycling Club introduced
	School able to use laboratory at Victoria Institute
1895	Establishment of Old Vigornians Club
1896	Appointment of William Chappel as Headmaster
	First selection of School Monitors by Headmaster
1897	Games Committee established to organise sport
1898	First OV London Dinner held
1899	New classrooms built at 7 College Green, including laboratory, Headmaster's office and Masters' Common Room
	School gates built on driveway to School House
1900	First (unofficial) use of name 'Worcester Cathedral King's School'
	Number 5 College Green rented as a hostel for unmarried Masters
	OV Club colours established
1901	Transfer of ownership of College Hall back to Dean and Chapter
	New 'Castle House' leased from Dean and Chapter
	First gymnasium built on playground
1903	Opening of Number 5 College Green as 'The Hostel'
1904	First inter-house competitions held (Athletics, Chess and Gymnastics)
	House colours adopted
1906	Extension of Castle House
1908	Stables at Number 4 College Green acquired for use as Sixth Form Library
	Canon Wilson appointed as acting-Headmaster
	Scout Troop formed
1909	Officer Training Corps (OTC) established at King's with Armoury at Number 4, incorporating Scout Troop and Shooting Club
	'Sixth Form Room and Reference Library' opened
	The Hostel and Castle House first compete separately, with individual house colours
1910	School inspection by the Board of Education
1913	Revisions made to 'New Scheme'
1914	Purchase of 'Noah's Ark' boathouse
1919	Cuthbert Creighton appointed as Headmaster
	Direct Grant awarded by the Board of Education
	Natland opened as a boarding house
1920	First telephone installed
	Advanced Classics course officially recognised
1921	Old Vigornian Festival held
	Unveiling of memorials to OVs lost in the Great War
	Opening of Rammell Pavilion
	Rugby adopted as main winter sport
	Destruction of 'Noah's Ark' boathouse
	Lease acquired for Edgar Tower
1922	Electric lighting installed in school buildings
	Third fives court added as Great War memorial
1923	Opening of boathouse on Hylton Road
1925	Opening of Chappel Memorial Reading Room and new classrooms
	First OV Reunion Weekend
	Speech Day moved from October to June
	Repositioning of school sundial from College Green to Monitors' Lawn
1926	Advanced Modern Subjects course recognised
1927	Choir School enlarged into full preparatory school with younger pupils transferred from The King's School
1929	Gymnasium built on school playground
1930	Purchase of land from Dean and Chapter, by Cuthbert Creighton, to form school gardens dedicated to his late wife
	Number 9 College Green leased from Cathedral

	New Scout Troop formed
1931	Opening of Creighton Memorial Gardens
	Reduction in Direct Grant due to Great Depression
1932	Natland closed
1935	Extension of 1925 classrooms to add art room and geography classroom
	First school play produced in College Hall
1936	Appointment of Longworth Wilding as Headmaster
	Separation of Day Boys into two houses: Chappel House and Creighton House established
	Publication of *A History of The King's School Worcester* by Alec Macdonald
1938	Headmaster informed of Government plans to take control of school buildings
	Frank Thomas de facto Acting Head during Wilding's absence
1939	Evacuation of school to Criccieth
	Thirty day boys taught at RGS
	Resignation of Longworth Wilding
1940	Cuthbert Creighton returned as Honorary Headmaster
	King's School returned to Worcester
	Frank Thomas appointed as first 'House Master' for School House
	First sports fixture (fives) played against RGS
1941	Celebration of the 400th anniversary of the founding of The King's School Worcester
	First rugby match between King's and RGS
1942	Ronald Kittermaster appointed as Headmaster
1943	Incorporation of Choir School into The King's School
1944	Tredennyke House acquired as Junior School
1945	Number 14 College Green used as Headmaster's house
1947	Refurbishment of gymnasium
1948	OV Cricket Club established
1952	Acquisition of St Alban's House and transfer of younger pupils to form a new Junior School
	Tredennyke House sold
1958	Completion of the Winslow Building, including Chemistry and Physics laboratories and a science lecture theatre
1959	Appointment of David Annett as Headmaster
1960	Opening of boathouse
	Purchase of land on Severn Street for swimming pool, gymnasium and New Block
	Appointment of first full-time Bursar, T Elsdon
1961	School appeal launched
	Bright House and Wulstan House established
	Formation of Middle School as distinct 'Fourth Form' pastoral system
1962	Swimming pool completed
	Demolition of houses in Castle Place
1963	Southern end of ground floor of Winslow Block enclosed
1964	Opening of 'New Block'
	Twenty-five year lease for the Old Chapel acquired
	First four tennis courts established at playing fields
1965	Extension to Rammell Pavilion
	Extension to Castle House
1966	Refurbishment of St Alban's House
	Refurbishment of fives courts
1967	Additional land acquired for playing fields
	First Careers room established
1968	Conversion of Edgar Tower rooms to form classrooms and a new library
	King's School Development Trust established
	Climbing wall added to Fourth Form block
	McTurk Memorial Reading Room established in School House
1969	New library opened in Edgar Tower
	Organ acquired for College Hall
	Four hard surface tennis courts constructed
1970	First King's Day celebrated
	Discovery of graves in undercroft of College Hall
1971	First four girls admitted to the Sixth Form, based in Number 14
	Opening of gymnasium on Severn Street
1972	Opening of Wolfson Building for Craft, Design and Technology
	Appointment of A.B. Bouldstridge as Bursar
	Publication of *The King's School Worcester 1541-1971* by Michael Craze
1973	Art Department relocated to Wolfson Building
	First computer course offered to Sixth Formers
1975	Amplification system installed in College Hall
1976	The King's School Worcester elected to remain independent following the announced abolition of the Direct Grant system
	Completion of Dining Hall and Languages building
	Conversion of former dining room in School House as 'Passey Hall' lecture room
	Establishment of 'Economies Committee'
1977	Establishment of College House, based in Number 15, for Sixth Form girls
	Withdrawal of Direct Grant
1978	Refurbishment of School House, including move of Music Department to the basement level
	Rifle range built behind Dining Hall
	Centenary issue of *'The Vigornian'*
1979	Appointment of Andrew Milne as Headmaster
	Number 9 College Green used as Headmaster's house, Number 14 returned to Dean and Chapter
	Refurbishment of Choir House
1980	Appointment of A. Hickcox as Bursar
1981	Acquisition of Number 12 College Green
	Introduction of Assisted Places Scheme

	'Pub Pass' introduced for students aged over 18
1982	Appointment of Derek Gilligan as Bursar
	Multi-gym set up in garage of School House
1983	Completion of changing rooms at playing fields
	Appointment of John Moore as Headmaster
	Economics Department established in Number 12
1984	Kittermaster House and Oswald House established
1985	Castle House closed as a senior boarding house and opened as a Fourth Form boarding house
1986	Donald Howell appointed as Chairman of Governors
	Opening of Eliot House for Sixth Form girls, based in Number 12
	Launch of appeal for school theatre
	Introduction of GCSEs to replace 'O' Levels
1987	Completion of school theatre
1988	First edition of *The King's Herald* newspaper
1989	Decision by Governors to move to full co-education in 1991
	Purchase of the Old Chapel
1990	Appointment of Patricia Sanger as Senior Mistress
	First national award for *The King's Herald*
	Appointment of Neil Gardner as Master of the Junior School
	Archaeological work at St Alban's uncovers Roman human remains
1991	First girls admitted to Lower Fourth (Year 7) and Lower First at St Alban's (Year 3)
	Girls' Games Department established
	Eliot House closed
	Work to enclose swimming pool completed
	New classroom block opened at St Alban's
	National celebration of 450th Anniversary of the seven King's Schools
1993	The King's School Himalayan Club founded
	End of Saturday morning school
1994	Publication of *The King's School, Worcester - and a history of its site*, edited by Caroline Roslington
	Football re-introduced as spring term boys' sport
1995	Junior boarders transferred to Castle House
	Appointment of John Allcott as Head of the Junior School
1996	Acquisition of Hawford Lodge Prep School and establishment of new Governing Body
	Appointment of Galen Bartholomew as Bursar
	Business Studies and Information Technology A Levels introduced
1997	Decision by Governors to end boarding in 1999
	Closure of Castle House as a boarding house
	Establishment of School Archive
	Theatre Studies and PE A Levels introduced
	Inaugural Drama Exchange with Notre Dame Academy (Worcester, Massachusetts)
	Decision to end Assisted Places Scheme announced
	First school website launched: www.ksw.org.uk
1998	Appointment of Tim Keyes as Headmaster
	Full merger of Hawford Lodge with King's
	Establishment of King's Foundation, comprising The King's School, King's St Alban's and King's Hawford
	Appointment of John Allcott as 'Head of Junior Schools'
	First female Head of School, Jennifer Pearce
	Strategic Review of school campus undertaken
	Closure of 'The Hostel' and re-ordering work undertaken on Numbers 4 and 5 College Green to form Hostel House
	Appointment of Simon Atkins as first Head of Drama
1999	First school inspection by Independent Schools' Inspectorate
	Closure of College House and Choir House as boarding houses - end of boarding at King's
	Sale of properties in Edgar Street (Uniform Shop and Tuck Shop) and College Precincts (Sanatorium)
	Relocation of School Office, Headmaster, Bursary and Common Room to Hostel House
	Number 15 College Green returned to Cathedral
	Sarah Le Marchand appointed as first Head of Sixth Form
	GCSE Drama introduced
2000	Appointment of Richard Bellfield as Head of King's St Alban's
	Appointment of Bob Middleton as first Head of King's Hawford
	Opening of Garrad Building at King's Hawford
	'Curriculum 2000' introduced modular A Levels
2001	Establishment of Foundation Development Office
	Appointment of Carol Bawden as FDO Director
	Re-establishment of Development Trust with Hugh Scurfield as Chairman
	Re-opening of Choir House after re-ordering work
	Bright House and Chappel House moved into Choir House building
	Creighton House relocated to Castle House
	Oswald House relocated to School House
	Opening of Annett Building, formerly the New Block, after reconstruction and refurbishment
	Re-establishment of annual OV London Dinner
2002	Refurbishment of theatre and opening as 'John Moore Theatre'
	Installation of new College Hall heating system
	Refurbishment of Dining Hall
	Construction of Wilf Thomas Library at King's St Alban's
	Opening of Kindergarten at King's Hawford
	Opening of Multimedia Centre for MFL

	Appointment of Jonny Mason as first Director of Sport
	First interactive whiteboard piloted
	100th Annual Old Vigornian Club Dinner celebrated in College Hall
2003	Incorporation of The King's School, Worcester
	First female President of the OV Club elected
	Demolition of fives courts to create Castle Court
	Opening of Music School in Castle House
	Beginning of partnership with Magdeburg Cathedral School, Dom Gymnasium, Germany
2005	Archaeological work at School House reveals a number of Roman artefacts
2006	New Library opened in School House, including reinstatement of the McTurk Room as a library and study space
	Purchase of Salmon's Leap public house, Severn Street
	Kittermaster House relocated to Choir House
2007	First female Senior Deputy Head, Sue Hincks
	Refurbishment of Wolfson Building
	Learning Skills Department established
	Appointment of Jim Turner as Head of King's Hawford
2008	Opening of Art School
	Appointment of Sophie Whitworth as Foundation Development Director
	Establishment of School Archive in Edgar Tower
	Celebration of Henry VIII's 500th birthday
	Purchase and demolition of The Alma public house, Mill Street
2009	Opening of all-weather pitch at Bishop Perowne Church of England College
	Expansion of King's St Alban's with opening of Howell Building as Pre-Prep department
	Appointment of Hugh Carslake as Chairman of Governors
	CCF celebration of 100 years of cadets at King's
	Launch of The SPACE Campaign
	Chappel House relocated to School House, Creighton House relocated to Choir House
	Sue Hincks appointed as first female Acting Head during Keyes' sabbatical
	A Level Government and Politics introduced
	Opening of Music School at King's Hawford
	Demolition of former Salmon's Leap public house for groundworks and excavation at the SPACE site
2010	Archaeological work undertaken at the SPACE site reveals an Iron Age rampart and various late-Neolothic and Bronze Age artefacts
2011	'Young Enterprise Centre of Excellence' awarded
	Andrew Reekes appointed as Chairman of The King's School Worcester Development Trust
	OV Annual Reunion Weekend moved to May
	Appointment of Jonathan Ricketts as first Academic Deputy Head
2012	Opening of Michael Baker Boathouse
	Fifth roof installed on College Hall
	'King's in 100 Objects' project launched by School Archive
	Appointment of Ian Griffin as Head of King's St Alban's
	King's St Alban's celebrates 60th Anniversary
	Social media presence formally established via Twitter and Facebook
	Publication of *Vigornian* moved to July
	Appointment of first Estates Manager
	Appointment of first HR Manager
2013	Ground-breaking on Severn Street for 'SPACE'
	First eNewsletter published
2014	Appointment of Mathew Armstrong as Headmaster
	Public grant awarded to Dean and Chapter for repairs to Edgar Tower; launch of 'Make Your Mark' campaign
	OV Club plaque installed at St George's Church (Ypres, Belgium) as memorial to mark centenary of the Great War
	Refurbishment of Number 9 College Green
	Relocation of Choir House to Annett Building
	Establishment of 'School Improvement Advisory Committee'
2015	Opening of The Keyes Building, sports and performing arts centre
	Opening of Weston Centre
	Development of the Bartholomew Barn undertaken at King's Hawford
	King's Hawford celebrates 60th Anniversary
	Re-establishment of Castle House
	Launch of rebranded school website
	Launch of major bursary appeal to fund 'forty scholars' by the time of the school's 500th Anniversary
	Preparations for the celebration of the 475th Anniversary of the foundation of The King's School, Worcester
	Publication of 'The King's School, Worcester - From 1541 into the 21st Century'

Appendix 3: Names and badges - the identity of the school

*The official insignia of The King's School, Worcester in use since the late 1990s.
The stylised text form was created by marketing designer Paul Kilvington, to which the shield was later added to form the full 'logo'.
The colours, typefaces and shield design evolved through a number of revisions into its present form. The joining of the ligature of the 'g' and the apostrophe has been controversial since its inception in the mid-2000s.*

Names given to The King's School, Worcester

THE GRAMMAR SCHOOL
Used in the statutes which founded the school in 1541 and through much of the 16th century, but fell out of use due to confusion with the Royal Grammar School (now RGS Worcester).

WORCESTER CATHEDRAL GRAMMAR SCHOOL
This name appeared in the New Scheme of 1884 and was the school's official name until 2003.

KING'S GRAMMAR SCHOOL
This name first appeared in 1558, in a charter granting lands to what we would call the Royal Grammar School, where the 'King's Grammar School' is mentioned.

QUEEN'S GRAMMAR SCHOOL
Used during the reign of Queen Elizabeth I.

FREE SCHOOL
Common name for the school during the 16th and 17th centuries.

THE COLLEGE SCHOOL
In use between the 17th and 19th centuries, though this title first appeared in the 16th century.

FREE GRAMMAR SCHOOL
The name used for the school by Parliamentarians during the Civil War and Republican era.

CATHEDRAL SCHOOL
Used mostly in the 18th century.

ROYAL GRAMMAR SCHOOL
This title is used in a 1781 letter of recommendation for John Harwood for the role of Usher from Worcester College, Oxford; the school now known as the Royal Grammar School did not receive that name until granted a Royal Charter by Queen Victoria.

WORCESTER CATHEDRAL KING'S SCHOOL
The title of the school adopted by William Chappel (Headmaster) at the start of the twentieth century. Although 'The King's School' was in common use throughout most of the century, the change in name was never legally made, so this title was unofficially the name of the school until 2003.

THE KING'S SCHOOL
Common use during 20th century. School is referred to as 'one of the King's Schools', when listed with King's Canterbury, etc.

KING'S, KING'S WORCESTER and KSW
Shortened forms of the school's unofficial name.

THE KING'S SCHOOL, WORCESTER
Following incorporation as a limited company in 2003, the name of the school was legally changed - this is the current official name of the school, although often used (incorrectly) without the comma.

REGIA SCHOLA VIGORNIENSIS
The traditional Latin name for the school. Whilst unlikely to be heard used nowadays, the name appears in this form around the shield device, and it is from this name that Old Vigornians get their title.

Insignia and badges

The school's coat of arms is derived from those of Worcester Cathedral - the Cathedral Church of Christ and the Blessed Virgin Mary. In turn these derive from those of Bishop Godfrey Giffard (1268-1302). The Cathedral's arms are 'argent, torteaux 4 3 2 1, on a canton azure the Virgin with Child'.

The 'torteaux' (dots) represent the ten parish churches which comprised the City of Worcester at the time of re-foundation if the Cathedral Church by King Henry VIII:

- St Michael, a 'peculiar' of the Dean and Chapter serving College Precincts and the Old Palace, located within the Cathedral cemetry (close to the present-day war memorial) and the parish church through which the Cathedral Foundation maintained a link with city parishioners; demolished in 1843 - the replacement on College Street was demolished in 1965;
- St Peter, in St Peter's Street, off King Street, until demolition in 1976;
- St Alban, Deansway, which has been 'Maggs Day Centre' since 1984;
- St Helen, at the south end of High Street, is now under the jurisdiction of All Saints Church;
- St Martin, The Cornmarket, known as 'Old St Martin's' since the opening of a new church on London Road in 1911;
- St Swithun, The Shambles, retained its Tudor tower but was otherwise rebuilt in the 1730s. The church was adopted by the Churches Conservation Trust in 1977;
- St Andrew, Deansway, partially demolished to create a garden of remembrance in the 1940s, is known locally as 'the Glover's Needle' in reference to the city's former leather and glove-making industries;
- All Saints, a thriving, evangelical church at the junction of Deansway, Broad Street and Bridge Street;
- St Nicholas, The Cross, was de-consecrated in 1989 and has been a popular bar since the mid-1990s;
- St Clement, which relocated to western bank of River Severn in 1822.

Traditionally, the canton would have obscured the upper-left torteau.

Early forms of the school's shield, which displayed either nine or ten torteaux, used a variety of layouts within differently shaped shields; a number of examples are shown below.

The use of 'King's Worcester' in a stylised text arrangement, set alongside a lozenge-style variation of the shield, to form the school's official insignia, has been used in its current, official version since 2008. Variations are used for the junior schools, where 'Hawford' and 'St Alban's' replace the word 'Worcester'; the main version is used for the school, the foundation and the Development Trust.

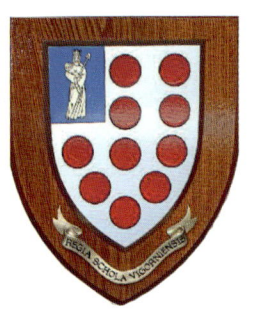

A range of styles for school shields used during the past fifty years. The number of torteaux has varied between nine and ten; the figure of the Virgin Mary has usually depicted her with a halo, although this has sometimes been replaced by a crown.

The current school insignia (right) and 'official' variations (below).

The 'official' colours used for the school are navy blue (Pantone® 281C) and red (Pantone® 485C); the typefaces used for the insignia are a specially-modified variation of 'ITC Berkeley Oldstyle' (King's) and 'Myriad Pro' (Worcester), used as the two typefaces for many school publications, including this book.

Appendix 4: Headmasters and their deputies

Masters and Headmasters

Year	Name
1541	John Pether, M.A.
c. 1553	Roger Colbourne, M.A.
1557	Thomas Bradshaw, M.A.
1585	Henry Maye, M.A.
1589	Henry Bright, M.A.
1627	Henry Moule, B.A.
1644	John Toy, M.A.
1646	John Hardinge, D.D.
1653	Thomas Barfoote, M.A.
1660	John Toy, M.A.
1664	Thomas Stephens, M.A.
1667	John Wright, M.A.
1695	Benjamin Slater, M.A.
1700	John Medens, M.A.
1707	William Betterley, M.A.
1733	Thomas Miles, M.A.
1768	Thomas Goodinge, D.C.L.
1777	John Bennett, B.A.
1777	John Griffin, M.A.
1814	William Porter, M.A.
1820	Allen Wheeler, B.D.
1838	Octavius Fox, M.A.
1852	Stephen Denning, M.A.
1856	William Helm, B.A.
1860	Maurice Day, M.A.
1879	William Bolland, M.A.
1896	William Chappel, M.A.
1919	Cuthbert Creighton, M.A.
1936	Longworth Wilding, M.A.
1940	Cuthbert Creighton, M.A.
1942	Ronald Kittermaster, B.A.
1959	David Annett, M.A.
1979	Andrew Milne, M.A.
1983	John Moore, M.A, Ph.D., J.P.
1998	Timothy Keyes, M.A.
2014	Matthew Armstrong, M.A.

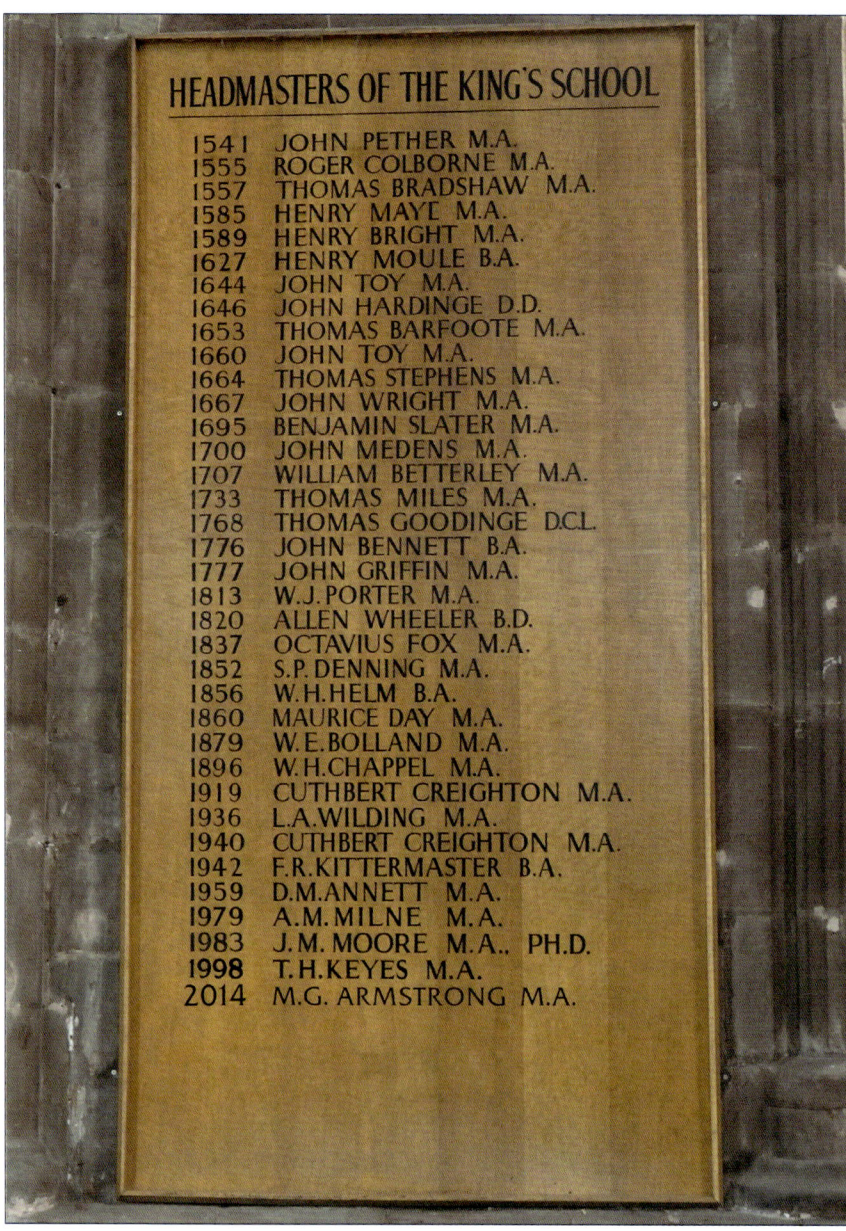

The longest-serving Headmasters were Henry Bright (1589-1627) and John Griffin (1777-1813), serving a remarkable 38 and 37 years respectively. During the past century, the longest-serving Headmaster was David Annett (1959-1979) for a comparatively short tenure of 20 years.

Two men have held the position of Headmaster twice: John Toy (1644-1646 and 1660-1664) and Cuthbert Creighton (1919-1936 and 1940-1942). John Toy fled Cromwell's government at the end of the English Civil War and was re-instated as Headmaster at the time of the Restoration of the monarchy. Cuthbert Creighton retired in 1936 but agreed to return as Honorary Headmaster following the resignation of his successor, Longworth Wilding, during the time of the school's evacuation to Criccieth; he stood down after the school had returned to normalcy and a new Headmaster, Ronald Kittermaster (1942-1959), was appointed.

Longworth Wilding was the first Headmaster not to be ordained, although this requirement had been dropped under the New Scheme of 1884.

A number of Headmasters have made significant impressions on the school, with many of their achievements in guiding the school recorded in this book. Among the most 'important' in the history of the school are: John Pether (1541-1555), the first Headmaster; Henry Bright, a renowned scholar, under whose headship the school grew in both national reputation and size - there were approximately 150 pupils by the time of his death; William Bolland (1879-1896), whose 'New Scheme' effectively refounded a poor school into the present, thriving institution, and whose vision saw the construction of School House; William Chappel (1919-1936) and Cuthbert Creighton, whose building programmes saw a level of expansion which would have been previously unthinkable; David Annett, who undertook a massive programme of development, opted for independent status at the end of the Direct Grant scheme and introduced the first girls into the Sixth Form; John Moore (1983-1998), who oversaw the move to full co-education, the end of boarding and the end of Saturday morning school; and Tim Keyes (1998-2014), during whose leadership a significant development of the school campus allowed for an increase in pupil numbers and a revival in the fortunes and prestige of the school.

Ushers

The Usher was appointed to work alongside the Master, as one of the two teachers provided in the Letters Patent, in which The King's School was set up with the Dean and Chapter. The appointment of the Usher was made by the Dean and Chapter, until the New Scheme of 1884. All were clergymen and many went on to take up a parish after leaving King's. Three Ushers, Henry Maye, Henry Moule and John Wright, went on to become Headmasters of The King's School.

Year	Name
1542	Walter Graner (Graver), B.A.
1545	Richard Allen
c. 1550	Humphrey Harwood (Horwood)
1559	John Cox (Cockis), B.A.
1561	Humphrey Harwood (Horwood)
1575	Henry Maye, M.A.
1580	Lawrence Alcock, B.A.
1582	Hugh Butcher, M.A.
1584	Thomas Inglethorpe, M.A.
1589	Henry Moule, B.A.
1627	Thomas Taylor, M.A.
1644	Thomas Hunt, B.A.
1653	Richard Hoare
1660	Thomas Hunt, B.A.
1661	Stephen Richardson, M.A.
1662	John Wright, M.A
1664	Thomas Greaves
1667	John Baker, M.A.
1670	Joseph Walker, M.A.
1674	Samuel Davies, M.A.
1677	Thomas Roberts, M.A.
1686	William Cox, M.A.
1696	Robert Jones, M.A.
1704	William Fellows, B.A.
1707	Thomas Smith
1719	Thomas Miles, M.A.
1730	John Hughes
1731	Samuel Pritchard, M.A.
1738	Thomas Whitefoot, B.A.
1745	Thomas Pixall, M.A.
1768	-
1771	William Wormington, B.A.
1784	John Harwood, M.A.
1796	Thomas Shirley, B.A.
1803	William Stafford, M.A.
1809	Richard George
1813	Cornelius Copner (Sr)
c. 1816	Cornelius Copner (Jr)
1821	Robert Saunders, B.A.

The appointment of Thomas Baxter, in 1838, was to the position of 'Second Master', rendering the title 'Usher' obsolete. Henry Moule, who served for 38 years under Henry Bright, holds the record for the longest service of any Usher, Second Master or Deputy Head.

Second Masters

Year	Name	Year	Name
1838	Thomas Baxter	1874	Harman Ogle, M.A.
1872	Alfred Beaven, M.A.	1876	Desmond Sampson, M.A.

Under the New Scheme of 1884 the position of Second Master was abolished. An honorary status of Second Master was awarded to Henry Clarke in recognition of length of service. From Clarke's death in 1900 until the appointment of Harry Ferrar in 1954, the position was held by the longest-serving member of the teaching staff.

Year	Name	Year	Name
1883	Henry Clarke, M.A.	1954	Harry Ferrar, M.A.
1900	Thomas Rammell, M.A.	1968	Richard Knight, M.A.
1929	Reginald Castley, M.A.	1978	Peter Curle, M.A.
1934	Richard Whitaker, M.A.	1986	Tim Hickson, B.A., F.Inst.P.
1935	Frank Thomas, M.A.	2002	Alistair Macnaughton, M.A.

Senior Deputy Heads

The position of Second Master was replaced with that of Senior Deputy Head, following the appointment of Sue Hincks, in 2007.

Year	Name	Year	Name
2007	Sue Hincks, M.A.	2014	Jonathan Ricketts, B.Sc.
2011	Richard Chapman, B.Sc.		

In 1990, Patricia Sanger (later Patricia Stevens) was appointed as Senior Mistress, with the specific brief to oversee the integration of girls with the move to co-education. She worked alongside John Turner who, as Senior Master, had responsibility for academic matters. In 1997, the academic importance of the role of Senior Master was recognised in a new form as Director of Studies. Following Patricia Stevens' retirement in 2004, the position of Senior Mistress (still responsible for girls' issues but with a wider role in personnel issues for staff) was renamed to Second Deputy Head. This move cleared the way for the position of Second Master to be updated as Senior Deputy Head in 2007. In 2011, the role of Director of Studies was split, with a new Academic Deputy Head appointed to support the academic departments.

Senior Mistress

Year	Name
1990	Patricia Stevens, M.A.

Senior Master

Year	Name
1988	John Turner, M.A.

Directors of Studies

Year	Name
1997	Julian Thould, M.A.
2001	Russell Baum, M.A.

Second Deputy Heads

Year	Name
2004	Sue Hincks, M.A.
2007	Richard Chapman, B.Sc.
2011	Carolyn Mellor, B.A.

Academic Deputy Heads

Year	Name
2011	Jonathan Ricketts, B.Sc.
2014	Duncan King, B.Sc.

Simplified management structure for The King's School

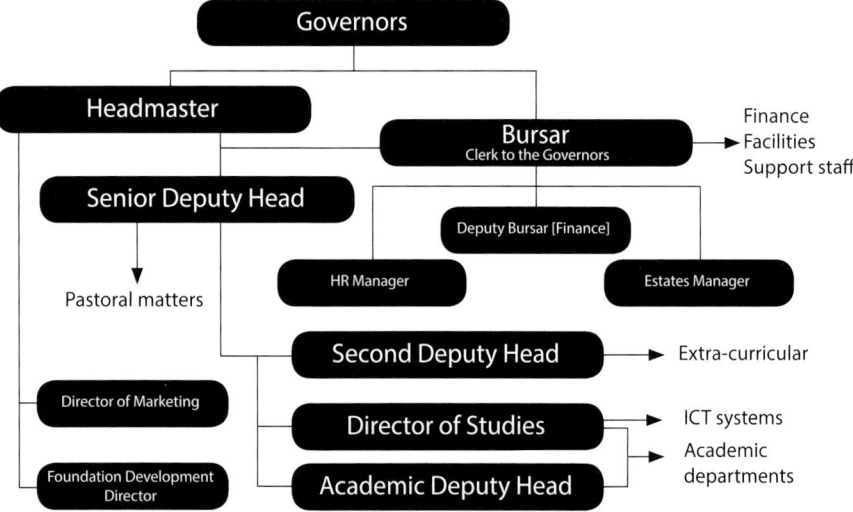

Appendix 5: The Houses at King's

School House

Formed: 1888
Eponym: School House building
Location: School House
Type: Boarding (boys) 1888-1989
    Day boys/boarders 1989-91
    Day pupils (mixed) since 1991
Tie: Navy with sky blue stripe

Housemasters / House Tutors:

1888	William Bolland
1896	William Chappel
1919	Cuthbert Creighton
1936	Longworth Wilding
1940	Frank Thomas
1942	Ronald Kittermaster
1945	N G Bloomfield
1947	Dan McTurk
1962	Alan Stacey
1980	Marc Roberts
1989	Steve Bain

Castle House

Formed: 1902
Closed: 1997
Reopened: 2015
Eponym: Castle House building
Location: Castle House 1902-97
    The Keyes Building since 2015
Type: Boarding (boys) 1902-85
    Fourth Forms (mixed) 1985-97
        and Juniors (mixed) 1995-97
    Day pupils (mixed) since 2015
Tie: Navy with red stripe

Housemasters / House Tutors:

1902	Thomas Rammell
1929	Sam Strong
1933	Arthur Bentley
1950	Stuart Sheppard
1965	Michael Points
1980	Robert Allum
1985	Robert Fleming
1995-97	Claire Furber
2015	Monica Longley

The Hostel (Hostel House)

Formed: 1903
Closed: 1999
Eponym: The Masters' hostel
Location: The Hostel 1903-98
    Choir House 1998-99
Type: Boarding (boys)
Tie: Navy with green stripe

Housemasters:

1903	Reginald Castley
1934	Arthur Franklin
1935	J H L Burnett
1938	Richard Pedder
1940	Paul Longland
1942	Frank Thomas
1945	Richard Pedder
1958	Richard Knight
1973	Keith Bridges
1990	Peter Iddon

Day Boys

1904	Richard Beach-Hicks
1921-36	Frank Thomas

Natland

Formed: 1919
Closed: 1932
Location: 49 Battenhall Road
Type: Boarding (boys)
Housemaster:

1919	Robert Whitaker

Chappel House

Formed: 1936
Eponym: William Chappel, Headmaster
Location: Edgar Tower 1936-61
    New Block (Annett) 1961-2001
    Choir House 2001-09
    School House since 2009
Type: Day boys 1936-91
    Day pupils (mixed) since 1991
Tie: Navy with yellow stripe

Housemasters / House Tutors:

1936	Frank Thomas
1939	[Suspended during evacuation]
1940	Alec Macdonald
1944	N E Dilks
1951	Richard Knight
1958	Howard Ballance
1961	Frank Sutcliffe
1969	John Turner
1988	Stephan Le Marchand
2009	Susan Stone
2013	Josh Hand

Creighton House

Formed: 1936
Eponym: Cuthbert Creighton, Headmaster
Location: Number 9 1936-61
    New Block/Annett 1961-2001
    Castle House 2001-03
    School House 2003-09
    Choir House since 2009
Type: Day boys 1936-91
    Day pupils (mixed) since 1991
Tie: Navy with pink stripe

Housemasters / House Tutors:

1936	Frank Thomas
1939	[Suspended during evacuation]
1940	B Ward
1945	Stuart Sheppard
1950	Jasper (Bobbie) Cash
1951	Harry Ferrar
1958	Peter Barnett
1984	Brian Griffiths
1996	Kate Appleby
2009	Lorraine Guy

Choir School / St Alban's House

Formed: 1943
Closed: 1995
Eponym: Cathedral Choir / St Alban's House
Location: Choir House 1943-51
    St Alban's House 1951-95
Type: Boarding (boys)
Tie: Red with white stripe

Housemasters:

1943	Paul Longland
1944	Lester Wilson

From 1952, the Housemaster of St Alban's House was also de facto Master-in-Charge of the Junior School.

1955	Wilfred Thomas
1975	Henry Searle
1982	Brian Griffiths
1982	Paul Winter
1987	Michael Abraham

In 1990, Neil Gardener was appointed as Head of the Junior School. Details of subsequent Heads of St Alban's and King's St Alban's can be found in Appendix 6.

Tredennyke / Choir House

Formed: 1944
Eponym: Tredennyke House / Choir House buildings
Location: Tredennyke House 1944-52
Choir House 1952-2003,
Castle House 2003-14
Annett Building since 2014
Type: Boarding (boys) 1944-75
Day boys/boarders 1975-95
Day pupils (mixed) since 1995
Tie: Tredennyke House -
Light blue with white stripe
Choir House -
Navy blue with double white stripes

Housemasters / House Tutors:

1944	David Kittermaster
1948	Bill Bailey
1961	Peter Curle
1978	Ian Brown
1988	Russell Mason
1993	Jonathan Martin
1998	Marie Arthur (day pupils)
1998-99	Peter Iddon (boarders)
2003	Monica Longley
2015	Richard Chapman

Bright House

Formed: 1961
Eponym: Henry Bright, Headmaster
Location: New Block (Annett) 1961-2001
Choir House since 2001
Type: Day boys 1961-91
Day pupils (mixed) since 1991
Tie: Navy with orange stripe

Housemasters / House Tutors:

1961	Hugh Neill
1964	Donald Anderton
1988	Bob Stone
2003	Mark Poole
2012	Chris Haywood

Wulstan House

Formed: 1961
Eponym: St Wulstan
Location: New Block (Annett) 1961-89
School House since 1989
Type: Day boys 1961-91
Day pupils (mixed) since 1991
Tie: Navy with purple stripe

Housemasters / House Tutors:

1961	Fred Logan
1980	Tim Watson
1989	Marc Roberts
2002	John Wheeler
2014	Adrian Ford

College House

Formed: 1977
Closed: 1999
Eponym: College of Canons, Choristers and Scholars
Location: College House (The Guesten)
Type: Sixth Form girls (day/boarders) 1977-92
Boarders (girls, Lower Remove - Upper Sixth 1992-99

Housemasters / House Mistresses:

1977	John Roslington and Caroline Roslington
1992	Sarah Le Marchand

Kittermaster House

Formed: 1984
Eponym: Ronald Kittermaster, Headmaster
Location: New Block (Annett) 1984-89
School House 1989-2006
Choir House since 2006
Type: Day boys 1984-91
Day pupils (mixed) since 1991
Tie: Navy with sky blue and yellow stripes

Housemasters / House Tutors:

1984	Stewart Davies
2002	Richard Davis

Oswald House

Formed: 1984
Eponym: St Oswald
Location: Fishermen's Cottages 1984- 2000
School House since 2000
Type: Day boys 1984-91
Day pupils (mixed) since 1991
Tie: Navy with red and white stripes

Housemasters / House Tutors:

1984	Mike Stevens
1999	Lynda Ghaye
2009	Christine Battrum

Eliot House

Formed: 1986
Closed: 1992
Eponym: Canon Eliot
Location: Number 12 College Green
Type: Sixth Form day girls

Housemaster:

1986	Robert Allum

Appendix 6: Junior School Heads

Tredennyke House

1944 David Kittermaster
1948 Bill Bailey

Choir School

1943 Paul Longland
1944 Lester Wilson

St Alban's

1952 Lester Wilson
1955 Wilfred Thomas
1975 Henry Searle
1982 Brian Griffiths
1982 Paul Winter
1987 Michael Abraham
1990 Neil Gardener
1995 John Allcott

King's St Alban's

1999 Richard Bellfield
2012 Ian Griffin

Hawford Lodge

1955 Douglas Garrad
1986 Tony Race

King's Hawford

1999 John Allcott
2000 Bob Middleton
2006 Jim Turner

Appendix 7: School Motto

τὰ μὲν διδακτὰ μανθάνω,
τὰ δ'εὑρετὰ ζητῶ,
τὰ δ'εὐκτὰ παρὰ θεῶν ᾐτησάμην.

The motto was suggested to the school by Dr Henry Philpott, The Right Reverend the Bishop of Worcester, who addressed the audience at the re-opening of College Hall following restoration in 1887. Philpott was speaking about the importance of Greek to a boy's education and his surprise that King Henry VIII had not included any instruction for the teaching of Greek in the school's founding Statutes. He offered the following words, his personal mantra based on the words of Sophocles: *"There are three sources of knowledge for all of us - one is to learn what can be taught us by other people, the other is to search for what we can find out by our own exertions, and the third is to pray for what can only come from Heaven, and can only be given by God."* He then offered the Greek text (reproduced above), with this translation:

"I learn what can be taught me by other persons. I search after what can be, found out by my own exertions. The wisdom that cometh from Heaven I pray for continually."

The first official use of the school motto is in *The Vigornian* of November 1887 (pictured in Chapter 3) where it appears, with a typing error, below the name of the magazine. The motto appeared in most subsequent issues of *The Vigornian*, as recently as 2010.

The motto is inscribed on the Headmaster's desk in College Hall, donated by Sir Ernest Bird, and in the Long Gallery of the Library in School House, where it is accompanied by an updated translation, as printed on the first page of this book.

Appendix 8: School Songs

'Floreat Schola Vigorniensis'

The School Song, written by Rev. W E Bolland for Speech Day in 1884, marking the reformation of Worcester Cathedral Grammar School under his 'New Scheme'. The song was set to music by Precentor Vine Hall, Warden of the Choir School and Bolland's Master of Music.

Vine Hall's musical setting was lost and the School Song fell out of use. To mark the retirement of David Brookshaw, Director of Music 1989-2013, a new arrangement was composed by Peter Shepherd (Bright House 2006-13) and performed by a choir of senior musicians and Old Vigornians at the 110th Annual Reunion Dinner in College Hall. The musical setting is reproduced here.

Floreat Schola Vigorniensis,
Floreat sanctae ecclesiae ministra;
Floreat Schola Vigorniensis.
Semper fideli subolem datura,
Tutamen urbi veniens in aevum,
Floreat Schola Vigorniensis.

These Latin lyrics can be translated into English as:

May Worcester School flourish,
May the handmaid of the holy church flourish;
May Worcester School flourish.
A future giver of young to the ever faithful city
And of safe defence for time to come,
May Worcester School flourish.

Floreat Schola Vigorniensis

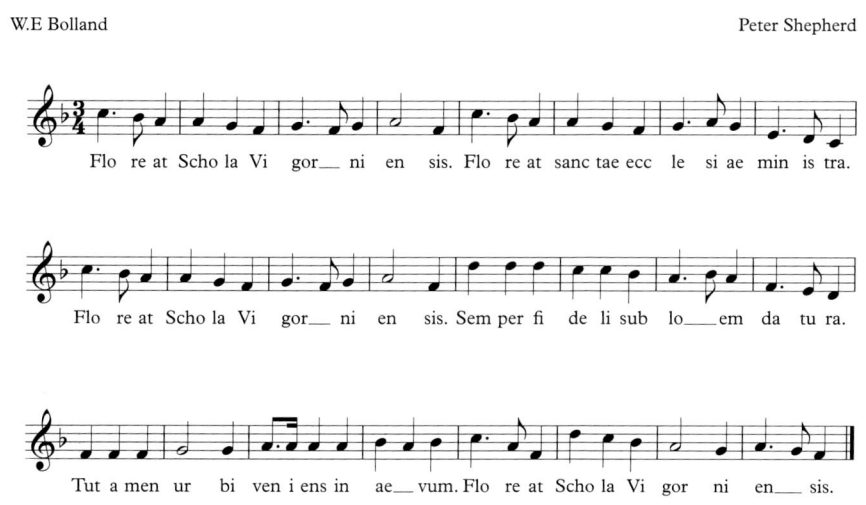

Score for Peter Shepherd's setting of Floreat Schola Vigorniensis
(provided by Simon Taranczuk)

'God bless our College School'

The 're-opening' of Worcester Cathedral Grammar School, following the restoration of College Hall, in 1887 was a grand occasion for which Rev. W E Bolland commissioned a second song. After Earl Beauchamp declared College Hall re-opened, the school's 'Singing Class' performed the song, written by Rev. Isaac Gregory Smith of Great Malvern and set to music by OV A.J. Caldicott.

Where Severn winds its stately course
Beside the spreading meads,
Where Wulstan's minster tall and grey
Nor flood nor tempest heeds,
Where stands the Faithful City, far
Renowned in days gone by;
God bless the old Cathedral School!
With heart and voice we cry
God bless our College School!

In days long past the brothers here
Were pacing two and two,
Adown the cloisters in their cowls
And robes of sable hue.
The past, receding, fades and dies;
But Hope's undying light
Discloses still through breaking clouds
The triumph of the right.
God bless our College School!

Shine on, fair star! we need thy ray,
Here, here, it must begin,
The lifelong warfare to be waged
With misery and sin.
'Tis old, and yet for ever new,
The teaching of the past,
That only they who strive shall wear
The victor's wreath at last.
God bless our College School!

Appendix 9: School Prizes

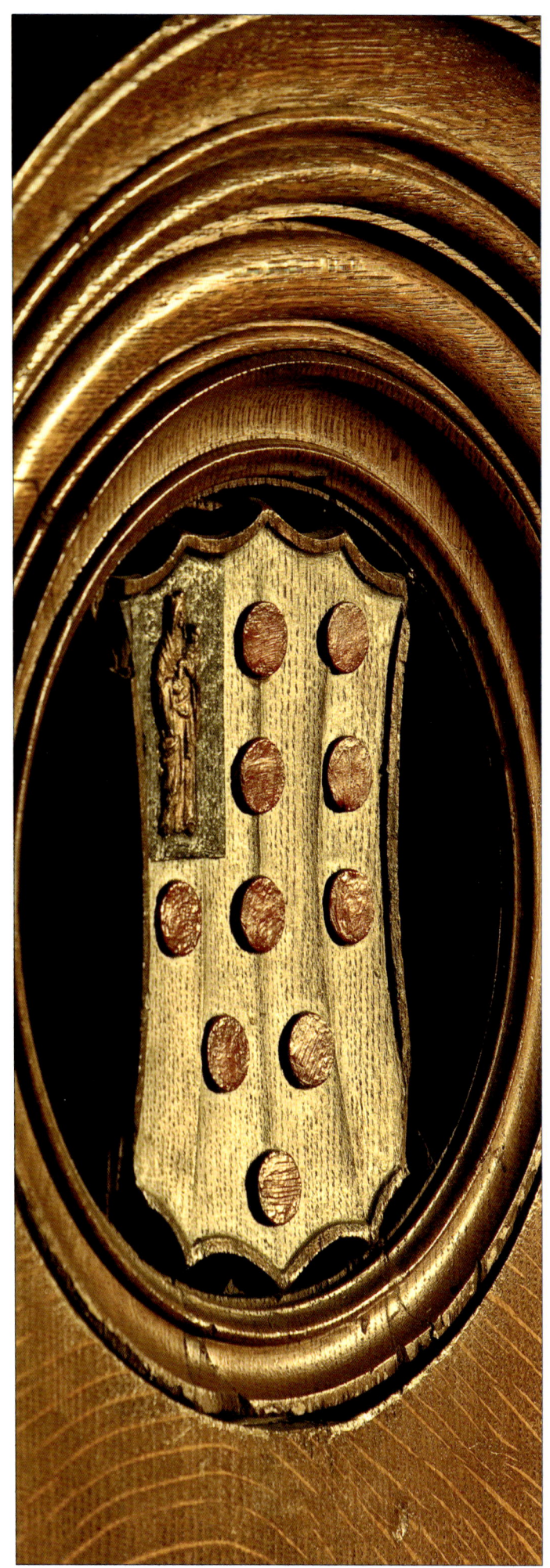

Since the mid-2000s, School Prizes have been awarded to members of the Upper Sixth in the Cathedral on King's Day in recognition of achievements in academic, sporting and extra-curricular aspects of school life.

The first School Prizes were awarded in 1832, formalised under Octavius Fox (Head Master 1838-52) by a Chapter Act of 1832, when a total of £5 was awarded by the Dean and Chapter for distribution as book prizes "amongst the most deserving boys".

For the past few decades, and under the adminstration of the Director of Studies since 1997, the prizes have taken the form of book tokens, purchased by the school. A number of prizes are named in honour of specific individuals.

On King's Day 2015, the following School Prizes were awarded:

Religion and Philosophy
English
Poetry: The Diamond Prize
Geography
History: The Henry Wood Prize
Politics: The Ashley Shameli Prize
Classics: The Maurice Day Prize
Latin
French
German
Spanish
Economics: The Rabjohns Prize
Business Studies
Music
Extra-Curricular Music
Drama
Extra-Curricular Drama: The Cobb Prize
Mathematics
Further Mathematics: The Reeves Prize
Physics
Biology: The Cavenagh Prize
Chemistry
Art
Design and Technology
Physical Education

An award is made to the Senior Scholar, with awards from the Old Vigornian Club for service to the school. Sports prizes are also awarded, including the *Matthew Surman Cup* for rugby, named in memory of a Wulstan House pupil, who died in 1996.

The Diamond Prize (Poetry) is given in honour of Peter Diamond, Head of English 1972-92; *The [Mrs.] Henry Wood Prize* (History) is named for the author of *'The Channings'* (see Chapter 3); *The Maurice Day Prize* (Classics) is named after the school's Headmaster 1860-79; *The Reeves Prize* (Further Mathematics) is named after Edward Reeves, Head of Mathematics 1978-2001. Other prizes are sponsored; the origins of the names of others are no longer clear - *The Cobb Prize* (Extra-Curricular Drama) is named in memory of Christopher Cobb, a master from Hawford Lodge (see Chapter 7).

Awards are made at the Final Assembly in College Hall each year for each academic subject studied by each year group; a prize for Critical Thinking is made to a member of the Lower Sixth.

Appendix 10: Heads of School

Records exist for the role of 'Head Boy', and later 'Head of School', from 1932 although, unfortunately, there are gaps in the records. The name of each Head Boy or Head of School is listed below, with the school year and the name of his or her House. Jenny Pearce was the first female Head of School, 1998-99.

1931-32	Philip Shrimpton	Castle House
1932-33		
1933-34		
1935-36		
1936-37	David Bolland	School House
1939-40	Denis Bendall	Castle House
1940-41		
1941-42		
1942-43		
1943-44		
1944-45		
1945-46	Lloyd Rankin	Castle House
1946-47	Richard Brown	Castle House
1947-48	Andrew Hambling	School House
1948-49	Barrie Smith	Castle House
1949-50	Martin Davies	School House
1949-50	John Brushfield	School House
1950-51	Graham Jackson	School House
1951-52		
1952-53		
1953-54	Michael Senter	Creighton House
1953-54	David Cook	Creighton House
1954-55	Mr Ive	School House
1955-56	Roger Thorn	Creighton House
1956-57		
1957-58	Nick Cotton	School House
1957-58	Cleo Reynaud	School House
1958-59	John Reddick	Choir House
1959-60	Christopher Eames	The Hostel
1960-61	Donald Howell	School House
1961-62	Peter Martin	Choir House
1962-63	Marcus Ferrar	Creighton House
1962-63	Nigel Morrison	School House
1963-64	Robin Elt	Chappel House
1964-65	Richard Thurlow	Bright House
1965-66	William Scandrett	The Hostel
1965-66	Mike Minchin	Creighton House
1966-67	Niall Cluley	Choir House
1966-67	Guy Lawrenson	School House
1967-68	Roger Hawes	Choir House
1968-69	Aidan Walker	Chappel House
1968-69	John Weston	School House
1969-70	Stephen Tomlinson	The Hostel
1970	Jeremy Coates	Creighton House
1970-71	Norman Trapé	School House
1971-72	Charles Hamilton	School House
1972-73		
1973-74	Michael Homer	Creighton House
1974-75		
1975-76		
1976-77	Marcus Scott	Chappel House
1977-78	Richard Davis	Castle House
1978-79	Richard Dean	Wulstan House
1979-80	David Hudson	Choir House
1980-81	Andrew Hobson	The Hostel
1981-82	Chris Perks	Creighton House
1982-83	Stuart Preston	School House
1983-84	Michael Morgan	Choir House
1984-85	Rob Preston	School House
1985-86	David Mack-Smith	Chappel House
1986-87	James Cooper	School House
1987-88	Richard Owen	Chappel House
1988-89	Rupert Bader	Oswald House
1989-90	David Bull	Bright House
1990-91	Simon Patterson	Creighton House
1991-92	Keith Shindler	Oswald House
1992-93	Thomas Newitt	Chappel House
1993-94	Robert Sandford	Oswald House
1994-95	Michael Brookes	Bright House
1995-96	Abbas Kazerooni	Wulstan House
1995-96	Nick Checketts	Wulstan House
1996-97	Samuel Pearse	Choir House
1997-98	Adam Smith	Chappel House
1998-99	Jenny Pearce	Chappel House
1999-2000	Edward Smith	Chappel House
2000-01	Josh Hand	Chappel House
2001-02	Scott Rennie	Bright House
2002-03	Rachael Dawson	Creighton House
2003-04	Simon Potter	Chappel House
2004-05	Sophie James	School House
2005-06	Anna Byrne	Choir House
2006-07	Helen Jones	Kittermaster House
2007-08	Edward MacKenzie	Wulstan House
	Emma Hirons	Choir House
2008-09	Rory Johnson	Bright House
2009-10	Ilija Rasovic	Creighton House
	Emmie Le Marchand	Chappel House
2010-11	Russell Whitehouse	Oswald House
2011-12	Joe Fowles	Chappel House
2012-13	Ben Alexander	Choir House
2013-14	Corah Lewis	Choir House
2014-15	Toby Thomas	Wulstan House
2015-16	Kaushik Rai	Bright House

Appendix 11: Sports Captains

The names of sports teams captains have been collated by the Foundation Development Office, based on reports from the 'Vigornian' and other sources; some information is missing - the lists are as complete as possible.

Rugby: 1st XV

1881-82	R. W. Coats	1949-50	M. S. Lewis	1984-85	Robert Preston	2002-03	Thomas Scaife
1882-83	E. F. Wade	1950-51	A. N. George	1985-86	George Blakeway	2003-04	Simon Potter
1883-86	F. H. Coombs	1951-52	K. J. Beard	1986-87	Peter Thompson	2004-05	Joseph Newcombe
1886-88	W. H. Counsell	1952-53	G. S. W. Thomas	1987-88	Richard Bayliss		
1888-89	C. R. Davies	1953-54	J. C. B. Coles	1988-89	Nigel Richardson	2005-06	Charles Fellows
1889-91	H. H. Quilter	1954-55	J. K. Grieves	1989-90	Richard Tomlinson	2006-08	Dominic Wood
1891-92	F. H. Dutton	1955-56	I. A. M. Dickinson	1990-91	Duncan Hughes	2008-09	Liam Gwynne
1892-1923	*No Rugby played*	1956-57	P. L. Costeloe	1991-92	Anthony Thomas	2009-10	Oliver Greenhill
1922-24	W. B. Evans	1957-58	R. J. Hazeldine	1992-93	Neil Bowler	2010-12	Harrison Nuttall
1924-26	C. J. C. Molony	1958-60	J. A. C. H. Reddick	1993-95	Thomas Davies	2012-13	George Jeavons-Fellows
1926-27	C. L. Garnett	1960-61	L.G. Wadley	1995-97	Leigh Hinton		
1927-28	A. D. Arbuckle	1961-62	I. C. Barrlett	1997-99	Daniel Cullen	2013-14	William Elt
1928-29	D. A. B. Hopkin	1962-63	J. M. A. Pickup	1999-00	Richard Paul	2014-15	Ryan Kerley
1929-30	P. Beaumont	1963-64	D.A. Brodie	2000-01	Nicholas Dale Lace	2015-16	Jacob Ham
1930-31	G. N. Jackson	1964-65	C. J. P Haynes	2001-02	Ross Laidlaw		
1931-32	H. S. Clarke	1965-66	V. A. Nicholls				
1932-33	R. P. Royle	1966-67	N. B. H. Logan				
1933-34	W. J. Mercer	1967-68	R. S. Hawes				
1934-35	D. A. Hemmings	1968-69	B. J. A. Hicks				
1935-36	E. C. Luscombe	1969-70	N. J. Chinneck				
1936-37	J. F. Lavender	1970-71	A. S. Woodward				
1937-38	A. Fairgrieve	1971-72	C. R. Hamilton				
1938-39	C. M. Lavender	1972-73	M. Homer				
1939-40	D. L. Shelton	1973-74	J. Darlington				
1940-42	J. H. Coles	1975-76	P. D. Southall				
1942-43	J. M. Ansell	1976-77	Nicholas Fairlie				
1943-44	R. W. Lambert	1977-78	Richard Davis				
1944-45	P. J. Mills	1978-79	Daryl Jelinek				
1945-46	R. J. Little	1979-80	Craig Preston				
1946-47	R. C. Brown	1980-81	Nicholas Hales				
1947-48	A. R. Wiseman	1981-82	John Bracey				
1948-49	T. H. Burgess & D. N. Puddepha	1982-83	Stuart Preston				
		1983-84	Peter Robbins				

1st XV: 1946 and 1983

Hockey: 1st XI (Boys)

1951-53	D. H. Slack						
1953-54	M. J. Senter						
1954-55	A. R. Hunt						
1955-56	K. G. James						
1956-57	P. J. Randle						
1957-58	R. Hazeldine						
1958-59	J. Watkins						
1959-61	L. G. Wadley						
1961-62	C. E. Randle						
1962-63	P. M. R. Millard						
1963-64	H. S. Marshall						
1964-66	N. P. Wilson						
1966-67	N. J. Taylor						
1967-68	R. S. Hawes						
1969-70	A. Carroll						
1970-71	J.E. Hewitt						
1971-73	P. Knowles						
1975-77	R.J. Savage	1985-86	Matthew Talbot	1989-90	Timothy Johnson	1993-94	Dominic Gilhooly
1977-78	F.M.N Sutton	1986-87	Richard Roe	1990-91	William Coomber	1994-95	R. E. Haines
1979-81	Benjamin Vivian	1987-88	Timothy Randle	1991-92	Anthony Clubley	1995-96	Matthew Pearce
1981-82	Daniel Vivian	1988-89	Christopher Goodman	1992-93	Michael Gupwell & Paul Phillips		Boys' Hockey discontinued 1996
1984-85	Silas Tomlinson						

1st XI Hockey: 1963-64

Football: 1st XI

1892-94	F. T. Davies	1906-07	A. K. Beauchamp	1919-20	M. E. Webb	2005-06	Joseph Street
1894-96	A. P. Bolland	1907-08	C. H. Payton	1920-21	H. D. Tonking	2006-07	Joseph O'Connor
1896-97	T. Bates	1908-09	R. G. Hall	1921-22	V. C. Powell	2007-08	Jonathan Bird
1897-98	M. Bates	1909-10	P. R. H. Lewis	*Soccer re-introduced 1994*		2008-09	Liam Gwynne
1898-99	R. T. G. Salusbury	1910-12	P. S. Beauchamp	1994-95	Maxwell Rowan	2009-10	Jolyon Hale
1899-00	J. D. Day	1912-13	B. Kenyon-Davies	1996-97	Leigh Hinton	2010-11	Thomas Cluett
1900-01	H. D. Day	1913-15	J. G. S. Thomas	1997-98	Daniel Kendrick	2011-12	Joe Fowles
1901-03	F. L. Steward	1915-16	A. W. W. Limbrick	1998-2000	Robert Fardon	2012-13	Alistair Hunt
1903-04	G. D. Day	1916-17	C. V. Paull	2000-01	Philip Burdon	2013-14	Thomas Hutt
1904-05	B. G. Stevens	1917-18	J. C. N. Shorting	2002-03	Robert Williams	2014-15	Dan Eustace
1905-06	M. S. D. Day	1918-19	G. P. Clark	2003-04	William Woodhouse		

Hockey: 1st XI (Girls)

1986-87	Clare Holland & Kate Lumsdon	1998-99	Jennifer Howlett				
		1999-00	Olivia Borastero				
1987-88	Rebecca Nott	2000-01	Jennifer Elderkin				
1988-89	Jane Turner	2001-02	Anna Brookes				
1989-90	Samantha Hall	2002-03	Anna Brookes				
1990-91	Elizabeth Gard	2003-04	Jessica Higgs				
1991-92	Catherine Nancarrow	2004-05	Joanne Hallett				
		2005-06	Freya Marskell				
1992-93	Helen Bagshawe	2006-07	Rebecca Busher				
1993-94	Kirsten Lunn	2007-08	Lucy Senior				
1994-95	Josephine Mason	2008-09	Charlotte Mills				
1995-96	Claire Freeman	2009-10	Victoria Heath				
1996-97	Holly Gilbert	2010-11	Jessie Meikle & Lucy Scales	2012-13	Jessica Longley		
1997-98	Rebecca Jones & Rebecca Birtwhistle			2013-14	Frances Taylor		
		2011-12	Grace Caldicott	2014-15	Hannah Robinson		

1st XI, 2013, with coach Sarah Mills

Netball: 1st VII

Year	Name
1986-87	Clare O'Riordan
1987-88	Alison Mackenzie
1988-89	Joanna Cole & Helena Tarr
1989-90	Alison Wallis
1990-91	Helen Owen
1991-92	Claire Milligan
1992-93	Victoria Kite
1993-94	Ruth Tibble
1994-95	Charlotte Daniell
1995-96	Kasia Klunduk
1996-97	Zoe Skellern
1997-98	Rebecca Birtwhistle
1998-99	Dominique Laurence
1999-00	Jodie Guest
2000-01	Celia Bryant
2001-03	Frances Gwilliam
2003-04	Rebecca Gwilliam
2004-05	Emma Hayfield
2005-06	Claire Gott
2006-07	Sophie Le Marchand
2007-08	Nicola Wilkinson
2008-09	Lucy Coomer
2009-10	Isobel Anstey
2010-11	Bethany Jeavons
2011-12	Grace Caldicott
2012-13	Grace Bradley
2013-14	Charlotte Collins & Hannah Jeavons
2014-15	Anna Warburton
2015-16	Molly Evans

1st VII Netball, 1988-89, with coach Nicky Anstey

Cricket: 1st XI

Year	Name
1881	A.M. Campbell
1882	R. Baylis
1883	P.B. Wright
1884	S.B. Martin
1885-86	P.B. Wright
1887-88	W.H. Counsell
1889	C.C. Counsell
1890	H.W. Bolland
1892-93	J.T. Chamberlain
1894	F.T. Davies
1895	F. Morris
1896	A.P. Bolland
1897	A.T. Marshall
1898	H.F. Wallis
1899	A.K. Marshall
1900-01	N.M. Fergusson
1902-03	C.C. Dickson
1904-05	B.G. Stevens
1906	M.S.D. Day
1907	A.K. Chaytor
1908-09	R.G. Hall
1910	W.H. Quin
1911-12	J.M. Aldana
1913	B. Kenyon-Davies
1914	J.G.S. Turner
1915	L. Warren
1916	C.V. Paul
1917	A.K. Lewis
1918	J.D.S. Thomas
1919-20	M.E. Webb
1921-22	W.L. Shorting
1923	D. Webb
1924-25	A.G. Bain
1926-27	C.E. Porter
1928	V. Hodgson
1929	M.J. Balch
1930	F. Gale
1931	F.H.G. Bridgman
1932-33	L.M. Bailey
1934	R.E. Summer
1935	R.L. Thomas
1936	F.E.B. Mole
1937	S.N. Hackwood
1938	J.H. Trape
1939	J.H. Foley
1940	D.L. Shelton
1941	A.G. Green
1942-43	W. Davidson
1944	B.J. Mallett
1945	M.C. Winter
1946	G.W.T. Bishop
1947-48	A. Hambling
1949-50	J.H. Whitehead
1951	A.O. Jackson
1952	T.A. Brown
1953	D.H. Slack
1954	D.J. Cook
1955	J.M. Drury
1956-57	D.P.G. Westgate
1958	Hazeldine
1959-60	Goodyear
1961	T.R. Senter
1962	J. Pickup
1963	C.C. Barlow
1964-65	-
1966	A.J. Judd
1967	F.C. Barlow
1968	R.J. Harker
1969-70	N.J. Chinneck
1971	M. StJ. Pimley
1972	R.J. Bailey
1973	Mahoney
1974	D.I. Fildes
1975	S. Moseley
1976-77	R. Savage
1978	F.M.N. Sutton
1979-80	P. Wood
1981	S. Preece
1982	S. Fleming
1983	D.P.E. Rogers
1984	M. Morgan
1985	J. Mackie
1986-87	J.A. Cooper
1988	A. Underwood
1989	N. Robinson
1990	R. Tomlinson
1991	D. Hughes
1992	D. Wheeler
1993	P. Judge
1994	T. Bawden
1995	A. Fiaz
1996	S.R. Thomas
1997	T.S. Heyes
1998-99	D.A. Cullen
2000-01	Nick Dale-Lace
2002	Nick Major
2003	Osman Fiaz
2004-05	Stephen Bilboe
2006	Ben Ford
2007	Tom Longley
2008	Tom Gwynne
2009	Liam Gwynne
2010-11	Tom Bird
2012	Joe Fowles
2013	Ali Hunt
2014-15	Nick Hammond

1st XI: 1946

KSW Boat Club: Captains of Boats

1886-90	W. H. Webb	1918-19	M. E. Webb
1890-91	H. H. Quilter	1919-20	G. P. Clark
1891-92	F. H. Dutton	1920-21	M. E. Webb & A. H. Adams
1892-93	F. H. Dutton & J. T. Chamberlain	1921-22	G. H. Webb
1893-94	J. T. Chamerlain & F. C. Fuller	1922-23	R. M. Beavan
1894-95	N. G. Davies	1923-24	E. L. Fisher
1895-96	T. Bates	1924-25	W. B. Evans
1896-97	N. G. Davies	1925-26	B. H. Carter
1897-98	H. A. Lewis	1926-27	C. J. C. Molony
1898-99	M. Bates & H. A. Lewis	1927-29	D. A. B. Hopkin
1899-00	F. S. Dyke	1929-30	J. G. George
1900-01	N. M. Fergusson	1930-32	G. N. Jackson
1901-03	C. St. M. Williams	1932-33	A. P. Shrimpton
1903-05	E. V. Overell	1933-34	R. P. Royle
1905-07	H. C. B. Jollye	1934-35	W. J. Mercer
1907-09	A. K. Chaytor	1935-37	R. I. G. Brooks
1909-11	F. C. Davies	1937-38	J. F. Lavender
1911-12	J. E. Ross	1938-39	A. Fairgrieve
1912-13	J. H. Spencer	1939-40	C. M. Lavender
1913-14	W. D. Battershill	1940-41	-
1914-15	G. H. Sharpe	1941-42	S. D. Ellison
1915-16	E. J. Rees	1942-43	J. G. Morris
1916-17	M. C. Lane	1943-44	J. M. Ansell
1917-18	S. R. D. Day	1944-45	G. V. Marshall
		1945-46	R. J. Little

1946-47	G. W. Lindner	1975-77	N. A. Moss
1947-48	E. B. Wootten	1977-78	M. Mack-Smith & R. W. Hopkins
1948-50	B. T. C. Smith	1978-79	T. Curtis
1950-52	K. J. Beard	1979-80	A. J. Hobson
1952-53	J. S. Rippier	1980-81	G. Evans
1953-54	H. H. Scurfield	1981-83	S. Dobb
1954-55	N. T. Vincent	1983-84	E. J. B. Simpson
1955-57	H. G. Vaile	1984-85	R. Tallis
1957-58	R. D. F. Anderson	1985-86	S. R. M. Taylor
1958-59	C.A. Ellis	1986-87	A. J. Guy
1959-60	C. G. Hook	1987-88	A. C. Clee
1960-62	A. R. Stevens	1988-89	R. T. Bader
1962-63	P. M Martin	1989-90	P. M. Buston
1963-64	C. B. Hancock	1990-91	J. R. Newitt
1964-65	P. R. J. Burn	1991-92	T. P. E. Davies
1965-66	J. Little	1992-93	T. G. Bradshaw
1966-67	M. Minchin	1993-94	T. P. E. Davies
1967-68	M. P. Brook	1994-95	S. Godfrey
1968-69	A. S. Baker	1995-96	P. M. Beard
1969-70	S. M. Kearon	1996-97	B. D. Panter
1970-71	A. J. S. Mussett & C. H. Richardson	1997-98	L. P. Lawson-Pratt
1971-72	J. Britton	1998-99	G. A. Ludlow & K. D. Hickson
1972-73	D. G. H. Townsend	1999-00	D. S. Pearce
1973-74	N. St. J. Partington	2000-01	James Scott & Jessica Oakley
1974-75	G. J. Cox	2001-02	William Rimell & Sophie Moule
		2002-03	Myles McKinnon & Ava Goodman
		2003-04	Tom Denlegh-Maxwell & Amy Wright
		2004-05	Richard Poole & Harriet Driver
		2005-06	Harry Denlegh-Maxwell & Hayley Simmonds
		2006-07	Edward MacKenzie & Emma Hirons
		2007-08	Richard Pain & Emma Robertson
		2008-09	Nick Barnett & Katherine Rollins
		2009-10	Joshua Scholes & Zennija Clements
		2010-11	Oliver Scholes & Emily Owen
		2011-12	James Green, Rebecca Lane & Poppy Bramford
		2012-13	Ben Alexander & Cecily Nichols
		2013-14	Alex Clark, Rob Ellis & Alex Wenyon
		2014-15	Jamie MacDonald & Alex Styles
		2015-16	Theo Beever & Frances Thomas

2014-15 J16 (Fifth Form) Boys' Crew, winners of the Kingston Cup, pictured with coach Megan Glenn

Appendix 12: Presidents of the Old Vigornian Club

1889-90	Rev. J Went	
1891-92	Canon Dimont	
1893-1902	W. Holland	(1869-72)
1903-18	W. E. Bolland	(Hon OV)
1919-22	W.H Chappel	(Hon OV)
1923-31	S. Southall	(1867-72)
1932-37	A Webb	(1862-67)
1938-46	J E B Littlebury	(1875-81)
1947-51	J. B. Cavenagh	(1904-09)
1952-57	J. C. Flay	(1919-24)
1958-60	S. D. Strong	(1906-14)
1961	W. F. C. Underwood	
1962-64	H.H. Holmes	(1915-22)
1965-67	E. R. Newcomb	(1912-14)
1968-70	O.R. Craze	(School 1926-30)
1971-74	J. H Folley	(1933-39)
1975-76	L. M. Bailey	(Hostel 27-33)
1977	H. H. Trape	(School 1934-38)
1978	A.D. Bolland	(School 1932-37)
1979	S. V. Strong	(Castle 1915-18)
1980	W. G. H. Cullis	(1938-41)
1981	O.T. Storrs	(School 1921-23)
1982	T. Garden	(Creighton 1952-62)
1983	D.T. Howell	(School 1953-61)
1984	G.W. Lindner	(School 1943-46)
1985	D.G. Wright	(Creighton 1954-61)
1986	A. Hambling	(School 1943-48)
1987	D.R. Mills	(Hostel 1944-53)
1988	A.J.Wright	(Creighton 1957-65)
1989	P. C. Underwood	(Creighton 1942-47)
1990	M.R.Dudley	(Chappel 1951-59)
1991	M.R. Craze	(Hostel 1919-25)
1992	P.J. Blackham	(Chappel 1954-59)
1993	W. M. P. Child	(School 1944-48)
1994	T.E.A. Mackie	(Chappel 1947-56)
1995	B.E. Wilkes	(Chappel 1943-49)
1996	R.T. Padden	(Chappel 1946-52)
1997	R.A. Franklin	(Chappel 1943-49)
1998	J. D. Reynolds	(School 1934-39)
1999	A. L. O. Jerram	(Creighton 1950-55)
2000	D.R. Leonard	(Castle 1947-52)
2001	M.C. Joyner	(Creighton 1944-52)
2002	Michael StJ Pimley	(Hostel 1961-71)
2003	Heather [Windsor] Morgan	(College 1983-85)
2004	William Jones	(Chappel 1944-50)
2005	Richard F Underwood	(Choir 1968-79)
2006	Tony Halford	(Chappel 1952-61)
2007	Ian Smith	(Creighton 1973-78)
2008-09	Caroline [Horrigan] Krolikowski	(College 1985-87)
2010-11	Philip Mackie	(Chappel 1973-83)
2012-13	Lou Wadley	(Creighton 1953-61)
2014-16	Rob Richards	(Creighton 1979-84)

Appendix 13: Barnabas Group

The Barnabas Group was founded by Tim Keyes in 2008 as a tribute to St Barnabas, a Christian missionary and "the son of encouragement". (Acts of the Apostles Ch. 4, v.36). Members of the group are Old Vigornians who have had distinguished careers of achieved extraordinary accomplishments. Each member spent a day at King's during which he or she addressed a College Hall assembly, enjoyed a tour of the school and spoke to groups of pupils.

Members of the Barnabas Group *(up to Summer 2015)*

Zac Purchase — Chappel House 1997-2004
Rower, Olympic gold medallist (Beijing 2008)

David Bryer — The Hostel 1951-62
Former Chair, Oxfam International; Trustee, WWF, Save the Children

Nicholas Cleobury — Choir House 1958-67
Musical Director, 'Britten Sinfonia'

Richard Westley O.B.E., M.C. — Choir House 1972-81
Colonel, British Army, served in Afganistan

Sir Julian Flaux — Chappel House 1963-72
High Court Bench, specialist in commercial law

Linda Crow — College House 1988-90
Managing Director, 'Citigroup'

William Baker — Wulstan House 1985-90
Head of Palm Research, Kew

Jackie [Mills] Stevenson — College House 1984-86
Partner, 'The Brooklyn Brothers'; UK's top 100 women in media

David Edwards — Castle House 1963-73
Weston Professor of Neonatal Medicine

Lorna [Shaddick] Edwards — Choir House 1999-2004
TV news presenter, 'France 24'

David Townsend — School House 1968-73
Chairman, PEAS; Olympic rowing medallist (Moscow 1980)

Sir Stephen Tomlinson — The Hostel 1963-70
Queen's Counsel, Lord Justice of Appeal, Privy Councillor

Daryl Jelinek — Choir House 1969-79
General Manager for Coca-Cola's London 2012 team

Claire Gott — Chappel House 1997-06
New Civil Engineer of the year (2010); founder 'Cameroon Catalyst'

Edward Kemp — The Hostel 1974-83
Director, Royal Academy of Dramatic Art

Romano Subiotto — Castle House 1974-79
Queen's Counsel, expert in antitrust law

Philip Durkin — Oswald House 1985-87
Chief Etymologist, Oxford English Dictionary

Michael Pimley — The Hostel 1961-71
Former senior banker, Continental Bank (Bank of America)

Amy Donovan — College House 1991-98
Volcano specialist; Fellow of Royal Geographical Society

Kay [Seymour] Chacksfield — College House 1989-91
Consultant ENT surgeon; Honorary Clinical Lecturer, UCL

Alison Nott (Bella Merlin) — College House 1981-83
Actress, writer and professor of Acting and Directing, California

Stephen Rimmer C.B. — Creighton House 1970-80
Director General, Crime and Policing Group

Appendix 14: 2014 staff photos

Teaching Staff photograph - names and principal roles

Front row: Richard Geary - Head of Chemistry; Mark Dorsett - Chaplain, Religion and Philosophy; Mark Poole - Chemistry; Sarah Le Marchand - Head of Sixth Form, English; Steven Bain - Biology, School House Tutor; Stephan Le Marchand - Head of Careers, English; Peter Iddon - English, PE; Duncan King - Acadmic Deputy Head, Geography; Tim Keyes - Headmaster; Jon Ricketts - Senior Deputy Head, Chemistry; Russ Baum - Director of Studies, Physics; Russell Mason - Head of Economics and Business Studies; John Wheeler - Chemistry, Wulstan House Tutor; Richard Davis - English, Kittermaster House Tutor; Chris Gallantree-Smith - MFL, Tom Sharp - Lower Remove Co-ordinator, History; Vanessa Gunter - Music; Trudie Marskell - Dance and PE.

Second row: Matthew Parkin - Head of Biology; Richard James - Chemistry; Chris Atkinson - PE; Alison Hines - Head of Maths; Chris Wilson - Head of Design & Technology (D&T); Christine Battrum - Chemistry, Oswald House Tutor; Jean Vivian - Head of ICT; Jo Clark - PE; Andrew Longley - Head of Fourth Forms, Geography; Anthony Gillgrass - Head of Boys' Games, Politics; Simon Cuthbertson - Head of Geography; Chris Haywood - Art, Bright House Tutor; Simon Atkins - Head of Drama; Monica Longley - Maths, Choir House Tutor; Ian Robinson - Physics; David Haddock - Head of Physics; Andrew Maund - Head of English; Richard Ball - Head of Modern Foreign Languages [MFL].

Third row: Rosie Shearburn - MFL (Head of Spanish); Alan Deichen - D&T; Elaine Friend - Economics and Business St; Sarah Bradley - Head of Classics; Joanna Lucas - Head of Learning Skills; Anne Sansome - Cover Supervisor; Lois Haddock - Physics; Anne-Marie Simpson - Maths; Rachael Worth - Biology; Jonny Mason - Director of Sport; Lorraine Guy - English, Creighton House Tutor; Eric Lummas - D&T; Rachael Rutter - MFL, Deputy Head of Fourth Forms; Graham Gunter - Music (Head of Strings); Donna Salkeld - Maths; Mike Newby - Biology.

Fourth row: Gemma Holden - Art; Alice Briggs - English; Emma Watts - Geography; Ronan Head - Head of Religion and Philosophy, PSHE; Jules Price-Hutchinson - Drama; Claire Horacek - Art; Josh Hand - Maths, Chappel House Tutor; Katie Beever - Maths; Andrew Kerley - Maths; Adrian Ford - History; Jim Chalmers - Head of Rowing, Biology; Claire Neville - Geography; Gwyn Williams - Economics and Business St; Helen Holden - D & T; Jo Wootton - Classics; Josh Gardiner - Maths; Jenny Hewitt - Art.

Back row: Nick Rosewell - MFL; Sarah Stuart - History; William Joyce - Geography; Oliver Heydon - Maths; Nicola Sears - History; Sarah Parkinson-Mills - Head of Girls' Games; Beth Darby - Maths; Olivia Rothbury - Classics; Rhiannon Lewis - Classics; Neela Brennan - PE; Jon Sarriegui - MFL.

Missing: Peter Gwilliam - Head of History, Head of Politics; Jerry Owen - MFL (Head of French); Liz Hand - Head of Art; Fiona Short - PE; Nicole Essenhigh - Biology; Sue Stone - Physics; Lin Brighton - Maths; Lucy Walmsley - English; Jill Knipe - Learning Skills; Catherine Cantin - MFL; Rachel Stanley - MFL; Richard Mardo - Maths; Marc Roberts - Maths; Claire Brown - Biology; Rachael Graff - English; Tom Jeavons - Chemistry; Simon Taranczuk - Director of Music.

Support Staff photograph - names and principal roles

Front row: Pauline Baum - Archivist; Pete Hodson - ICT Support Manager; Danny Payne - Head of Design, Media and Reprographics; Claire Furber - Health Centre Sister; Iain Cunningham-Martin - Catering Services Manager; Christina Swainston - Headmaster's PA; Sophie Whitworth - Foundation Development Director; Galen Bartholomew - Bursar and Clerk to the Governors; Penny Hope - Deputy Bursar [Finance]; Annabel Jeffery - School Librarian; Phil Tyrell - Head Groundsman; Richard Barker - Deputy Estates Manager; Vickie Peckston - Registrar; Chris Crosswell - Technical Theatre Manager, John Moore Theatre; David Grinnell - School Transport Manager and S.S.I. (C.C.F.).

Second row: Pauline Wright - Archives Assistant; Nick Dart - Network Analyst; Sarah Key - Design, Media and Reprographics Assistant; Barry Broadley - Head Chef; Frances Mead - Deputy Heads' Secretary; Alice Brunt - Development Manager; Caroline Neil - Bursar's Secretary; Sue Hewitt - Accountant; Abigail Haywood - Assistant Librarian; Glen Collins - Groundsman; Suzanne Nevitt - Assistant Registrar and Marketing Secretary; Gemma Minton - Catering Assistant.

Third row: Sue Broadway - Hostel House Kitchen Assistant; Dan Cox - ICT Support Engineer; Julie Harrell - Pupil Supervisor; Helen Isaacs - Careers Librarian and Work Experience Coordinator; Cathryn Nesbitt - School Secretary; Annie Grove - Payroll Administrator; Maggie Roberts - Fees Clerk; Anne Westley - Biology Technician; Will Calvert - Groundsman; Terry Price and Ben Baylis - Maintenance Staff; Jacqueline McDiarmid - Catering Assistant; Tom Shepherd - C.C.F. and D of E Assistant.

Fourth row: Adam Rowberry - ICT Support Engineer; Tracey Widdows, Karen Spink, Sam Kings and Sam Green - Catering Assistants; Sian Johnson - Receptionist; Michelle Richardson - School Secretary; Oxanna Hector-Dukh - Chemistry Techician; Andrea McNeilly - Physics Technician; Julie Palmer - Design and Technology Technician; Jeni Timlin and Rosie Ellender - Art Technicians; Clive Sherwood - Maintenance Staff; Matthew Perkins - Gardener; Ryan Spink - Catering Assistant.

Cleaning Staff photograph

L-R, from back:
David Lord, Paul English, Martin Jelfs;
Craig English, Tony Skilbeck, Phil Wise, Charlie Bialy, Adam McDonald, Karen Gardener;
Sue Whiting, Jackie McDiarmid, Sylvia Zlotnik, Gemma Day, Lisa Adams, Mal Tarlington, Ryan Price, Terry Price;
Emma Shuard, Tara Shuard, Sophie Gardener, Anne Fowler, Josie Bullock;
Amy Jefferies, Jane Bennett, Carol Webster, Barbara Berry, Gillian Pugh;
Barbara Harrison;
Tracey Hundley - Deputy Cleaning Manager, Nicky MacNamee - Cleaning Manager.

The King's School, Worcester *From 1541 into the 21st Century*

Appendix 15:
The archaeology of The King's School

Mike Napthan MCIFA

The very first antiquarian interest in The King's School's site started in the early 19th century; well before the main part of the former castle premises were acquired for the school.

Demolition of the County Gaol and castle buildings

In the prosperous years of agricultural boom from the 1790s to the beginning of the 1820s Worcester was expanding rapidly, and the removal of the County Gaol from the south of the Cathedral to Salt Lane (now Castle Street) in 1814 left the former castle and gaol buildings surplus to Crown requirements. Thomas Eaton purchased the site in 1822 with a view to creating a genteel housing development along a curving road to be known as Castle Crescent. Eaton had various business interests, principally as a printer and publisher, but also had some personal antiquarian leanings.

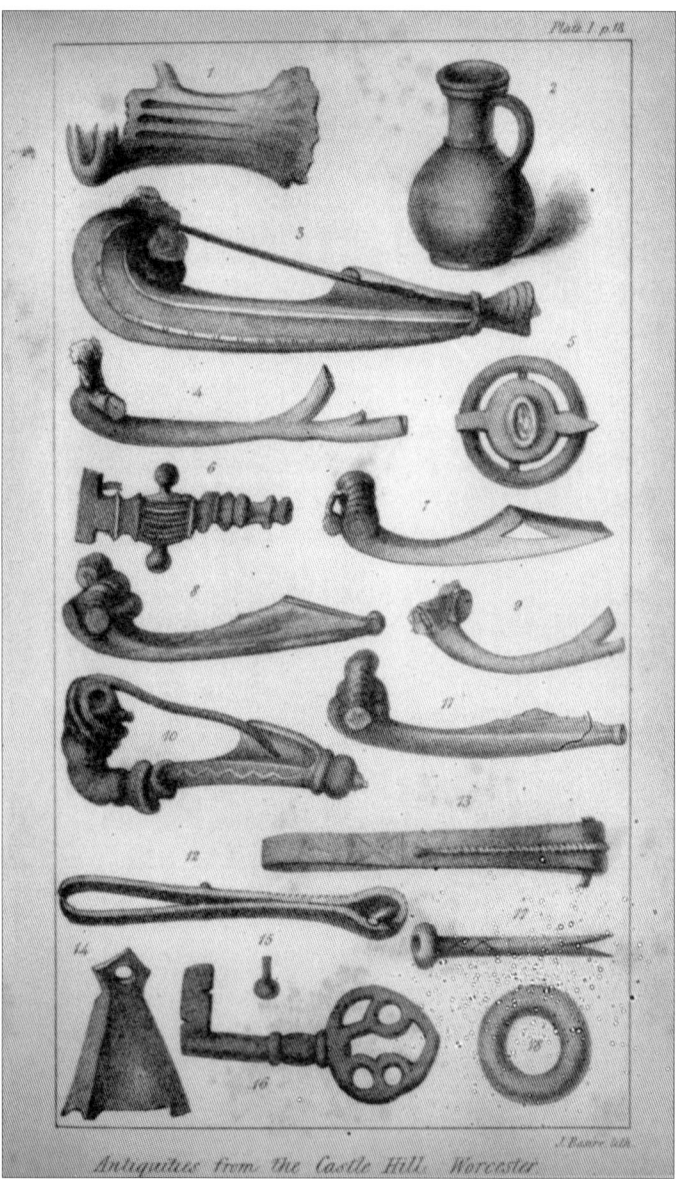

Jabez Allies' illustrations of finds at Castle Hill, published 1852

His first task on acquiring the site was to clear away the existing gaol buildings, many of which were comparatively modern having been built 1784-88; a few of the buildings had, however been retained from the Norman and medieval castle. As clearance of the buildings progressed there were a few passing references to the antiquarian interest, but frustratingly little detail was recorded. In 1829 Thomas Eaton wrote, *"There being nothing very remarkable or interesting in the buildings, they have been nearly all taken down; and soon scarce a trace will be left..."* The demolition of the castle buildings in the led to the discovery of several features - within the north side of the motte there was a well *"curiously quoined with stone, bearing marks of antiquity"*, and *"in removing the building a floor was taken up of comparatively modern construction; but underneath it another very ancient oak floor, three inches thick, was removed in which were evident marks of the effects of fire. The castle is stated to have been several times fired..."* (Eaton 1829: 54). During the removal of the castle motte Eaton instructed his workers to look out for any antiquities, but his principal purpose was to quarry the motte for the sand and gravel which were its principal constituents.

There was a visit of the British Antiquarian Association to Worcester in 1848, and this resulted in the first publication of the finds recovered from the castle site more than twenty years earlier (Wright 1848). Jabez Allies subsequently published more illustrations in 1852, pictured left, briefly raising antiquarian awareness about the site which then seems to have been largely forgotten. It had by this time been cleared of all standing buildings outside the Cathedral Precinct, and extensively quarried for salvageable masonry, sand and gravel. The projected housing scheme of the 1820s never advanced beyond the construction of the two stone faced cottages in Castle Place (of which Number 4 Castle Place survives), and for many years the site remained as vegetable gardens.

The Ordnance Survey of 1884 marked the *"Site of Castle"* and the find-spot of *"Roman Coins &c found A.D.1833"* as well as *"Site of Castle Wall"*. This restricted view of the archaeology of the site remained into the latter half of the 20th century when The King's School itself started to show an interest in its archaeology.

Archaeological discoveries

The King's School's main site occupies the southern tip of a low ridge, which at this point is flanked by the River Severn and the valley of the former Frog Brook (now the Worcester and Birmingham Canal). This promontory position, on well drained ground, strategically placed to cover the confluence of two water courses and a probable fording point across the Severn, attracted human activity from an early period. The surface geology consists of a cap of sand and gravels overlying Mercian Mudstone / Keuper Marls which form a ridge corresponding with the line of the High Street. To the south of Worcester Cathedral the cap of sand and gravel starts to diminish in thickness, and to the south of the King's St Alban's site the sandy soils are replaced by the alluvial deposits of the Frog Brook Valley.

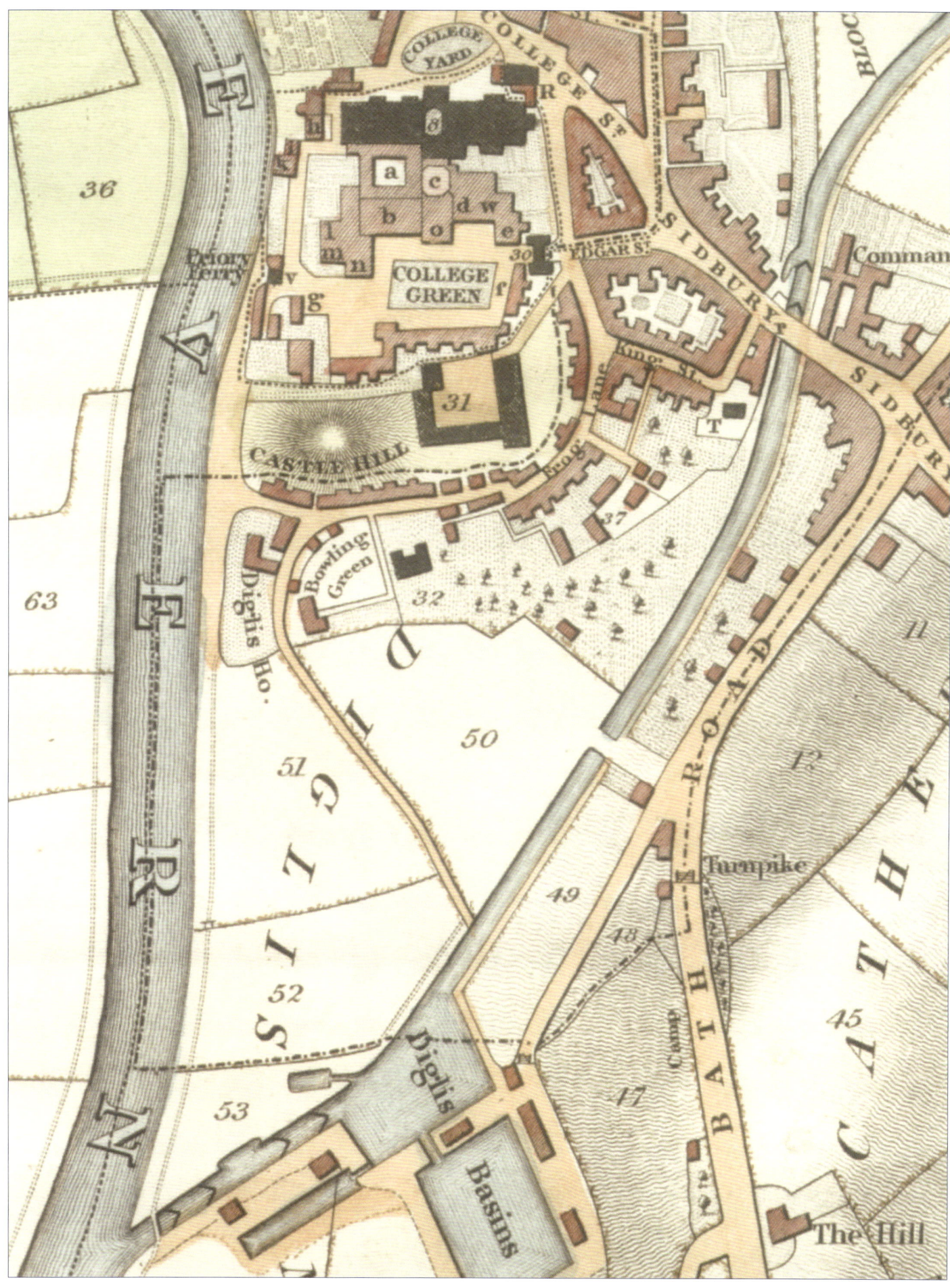

The promontory position of Castle Hill, part of the site of The King's School, is strategically set on well-drained ground adjacent to the confluence of two key waterways, the River Severn and the Frog Brook (now the Worcester and Birmingham Canal).

Archaeological works carried out at the 'SPACE' site, ahead of construction of The Keyes Building (from 2010). Discoveries included an iron age rampart as well as late-Neolithic/Bronze Age artefacts.

The Neolithic Period and Bronze Age

The earliest hints of human activity on The King's School site were found prior to the construction of The Keyes Building in Severn Street – the earliest identifiable flint flake is from the trimming of a lump of flint most characteristic of the blade orientated industries of Mesolithic or early Neolithic date. A regular blade and parallel-sided blade-like flake fragment may also derive from a blade-orientated industry. A small scatter of late Neolithic flint working debris, an asymmetrical flint arrowhead and some tiny fragments of probably late Neolithic or early Bronze Age pottery were found on the original ground surface beneath a later rampart, together with occasional fragments of stone which had been heated and cracked by rapid cooling. Such stones are frequently found in prehistoric contexts and relate to cooking activities. It is probable that there was at least seasonal occupation of the school site by the early Neolithic period – which is the earliest evidence for human activity in the vicinity of the original settlement at Worcester.

There is little certain *in situ* evidence for Bronze Age activity on the school site, but the adjacent stretch of the River Severn has produced several artefacts of Bronze Age date, including bronze axe and palstave heads. Jabez Allies illustrated what appear to be Bronze Age artefacts including *"an ancient British bronze celt"* (Allies 1852, Plate I, opp. p18) which point to local use of the river for trade and transport. Some of the very fragmentary pottery sherds and flint flakes from The Keyes Building site (referred to as 'The SPACE site' during archaeological work and construction) are also possibly of Bronze Age date, but are too small for diagnosis.

Late Neolithic asymmetrical flint arrowhead

Pottery sherd, possibly Bronze Age

There is relatively little known of the Bronze Age in Worcester – there are a few stray finds from the River Severn near the city, but contexts of this period have only been previously excavated at the Perdiswell Park and Ride site, where a circular enclosure produced a very small assemblage of Bronze Age pottery. The King's School site seems to fit comfortably amongst other sites that occupy the confluence of rivers, or alongside watercourses. The move from upland sites to river valleys occurred in the Middle Neolithic and in the Midlands the sites are generally not of the monumental scale seen elsewhere but relatively small enclosures, stone and timber circles and pit circles. Activity on The King's School site cannot presently be identified with any precision, but an enclosure overlooking the river would not be unexpected. It is possible that the site represents a riverside trading centre.

As early as the 1960s Philip Barker (whilst noting the significant lack of Middle Bronze Age and earlier material from Worcester city centre) postulated the presence of a late Bronze Age settlement followed by an Iron Age promontory fort at the southern end of the ridge of higher ground representing the Worcester Terrace (Barker 1968). Barker was relying largely on the evidence of the 1965 Lich Street excavations, which had exposed a very small area of prehistoric occupation and a prehistoric defensive ditch, both largely cut away by re-cuts of Roman date. A few years earlier Peter Gelling had exposed at Little Fish Street a major ditch (approximately 60ft wide and 14ft deep) which contained late Roman fills (Gelling 1958) and Barker, on the basis of these two observations, proposed a defensive circuit enclosing the area between Fish Street and the line between the Watergate and Edgar Tower *"without much doubt, part of the defences of a promontory fort"* (Barker 1969: 14). Little opportunity has presented itself for these theories to be further tested in the intervening decades until the school began a major programme of renewing its buildings in the late 1990s.

The Iron Age

Worked flint together with small amounts of Iron Age pottery, and a small mid-late Iron Age cut feature were encountered during excavations in advance of the construction of the Long Gallery extension to School House as part of the school library development in 2005 (Napthan and Jacobs 2006a). The pottery from this feature included an unusually large sherd of organic briquetage (a very crude and coarse grained pottery) displaying finger impressions and internal burning. In addition there were eleven sherds from a globular jar in Palaeozoic limestone tempered ware, both fabrics may date from the 5th century BC to 2nd century AD, (Napthan and Jacobs 2006a; WCM 101367; WCM 101368). The Iron Age feature was an isolated survival, truncated on all sides, but gave the first conclusive evidence of Iron Age occupation within the area of the school.

Major population growth led to political instability and territorial conflict in the Iron Age – a period which nationally saw constructions of fortifications on a totally unprecedented scale as the indigenous people fought to protect themselves from incomers, and the communities to the east sought to expand westwards. The impact on the present school site was dramatic. The site offered both good defensive potential and an ideal riverside trading position. Despite it not being a regional or tribal centre, a massive defensive enclosure was constructed overlooking the confluence of the River Severn and the Frog Brook, and the probable fording point a little above the confluence. The earthworks consisted of a ditch and rampart of monumental scale forming an enclosure centred on the present Cathedral. The King's School's main site occupies most of the southern half of this enclosure.

It is uncertain precisely when construction of the defensive circuit began, but the presence of a scatter of late Neolithic to early Bronze Age material directly beneath the first phases of the rampart does suggest that there may have been a previous earthwork enclosure which was enlarged in the Iron Age.

The rampart excavated on the site of The Keyes Building was formed by heaping earth in layers, one over another to build eventually an earthen bank at least 4 metres tall and around 12 metres wide front to back. Most of the material appears to have been quarried from a massive ditch that formed an outer line of defence. A wooden palisade of fully-grown tree-trunks set in a deep trench reinforced the front of the rampart. The palisade served both to prevent the soil from sliding back into the outer ditch and to resist mining and assault. Scientific dating of the earliest excavated line of timber posts which reinforced the front of the rampart line indicate that construction had reached an advanced level by 500-400 BC. Discoveries elsewhere in the city indicate that in total the defensive bank was around 850 metres in length (see page 235). Over time the bank was added to and the line of palisades renewed.

At The Keyes Building site it was possible only to excavate the outer part of the rampart, and small sample areas of the defensive ditch but these were sufficient to estimate the overall scale of the defences. The rampart in total appears to have contained more than 30,000 tonnes of soil, all of which must have been excavated, moved and laid in place by hand. Each timber palisade probably contained around 4,000 mature tree trunks, many of which must have been brought some distance. The entire undertaking of construction is likely to have taken several years with a full time workforce of around two hundred. Construction may however have been seasonal, in which case it might have taken a generation to complete. For many generations thereafter it stood as a very visible landmark encircling the settlement and acting both as a defence and mark of prestige.

Very little evidence of the later Iron Age has been found at The King's School, or indeed in Worcester city centre as a whole. There was occupation at this period in St John's and on a site overlooking the river just upstream from the Ketch public house, but there have been few hints of occupation within the defensive circuit. This lack of evidence may, however be attributed to the depth at which Iron Age deposits are likely to be buried in this area – in excess of 2.5 metres below ground level, and beneath the depth of most recent archaeological interventions. It is unlikely that the site was completely abandoned in the later Iron Age, but evidence of this must await future deep excavations.

Roman Era

Jabez Allies reported that the motte of the castle appeared to have been built over a layer of Roman occupational debris including pottery and glass vessels (Allies 1852: 16). Evidence of a Roman presence has also been previously identified in the wider area of The King's School and the Cathedral precincts. In 1860 the owner of the Royal Worcester Porcelain Works recorded

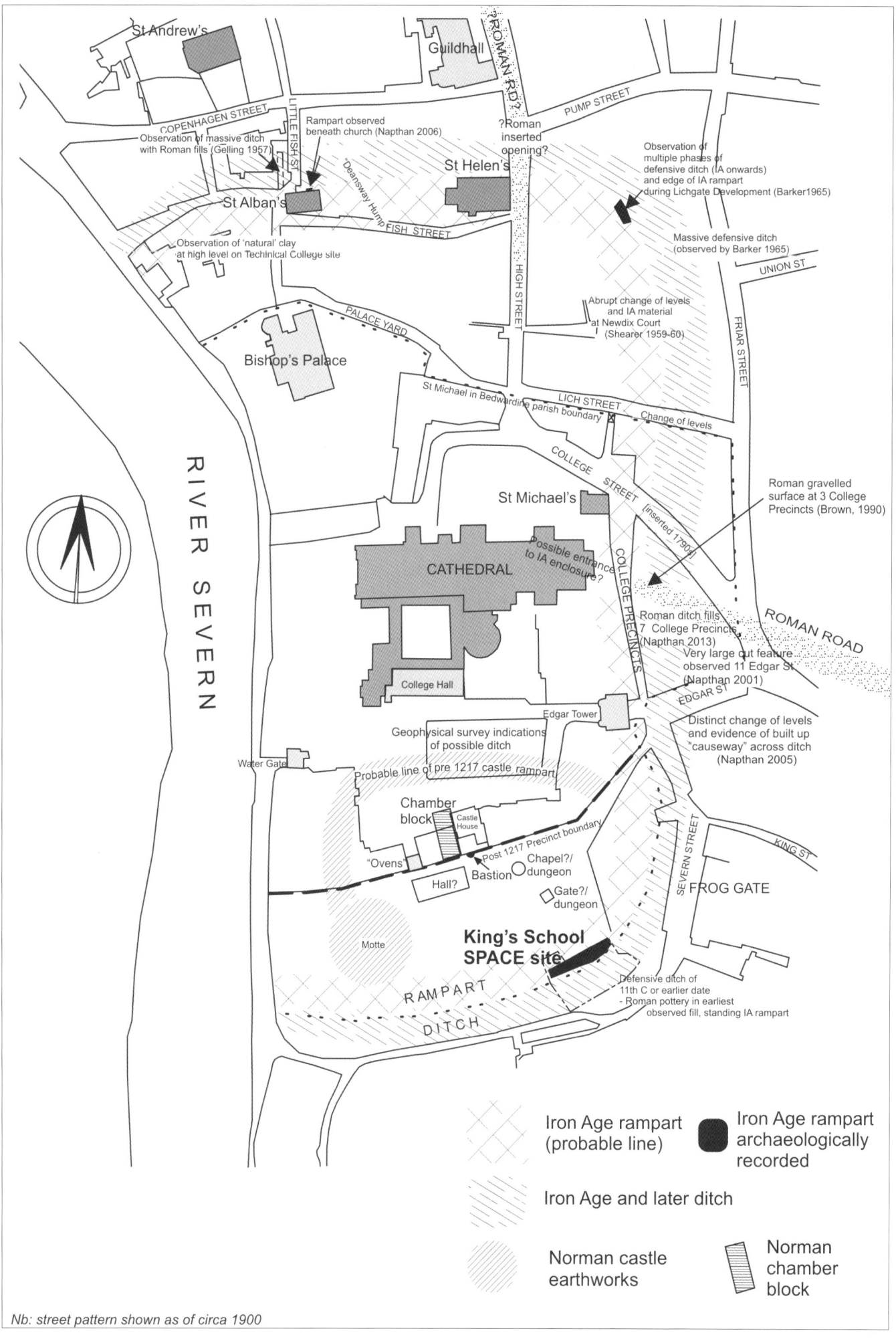

Above: Archaeological excavations ahead of groundworks for the Long Gallery addition to School House, 2005.

Right: Roman cosmetic scoop found during this work.

observations of cremations within Roman pottery vessels in the area close to King's St Alban's at the west end of Severn Street (Binns 1865: 184-6). In more recent years there have been several observations of Roman material from the area of the school, though much of the material has been residual in later contexts. Immediately to the south of Severn Street, on the King's St Alban's site, there are antiquarian references to the discovery of skeletons and a Roman inhumation cemetery was partially excavated during construction of a the 'new classroom block' (Brown & Wichbold 1991). Until recently one of the adolescent skeletons was displayed at King's St Alban's.

A range of residual Roman material has been recovered from various small interventions across the former castle site. The material is not all typical of a cemetery assemblage, and it would seem that there was possibly also some occupation in this area, though there appears to be very little building material of diagnostically Roman date. Fragments of glass vessels and a copper alloy cosmetic scoop recovered from the Long Gallery excavation (Napthan and Jacobs 2006a) and undated human remains from Castle Court (Napthan *et al* 2003; WCM 100996) do seem to confirm that the cemetery extended into the area of the castle, as was previously suggested.

The position and nature of the Roman defensive circuit at Worcester have long been subject to speculation; Valentine Green writing in 1764 suggested that *"there was a fortress of the Romans here, afterwards turned into a citadel by the Saxons"*. The presence of a defensive circuit at Worcester was not however proven until the excavations at Little Fish Street (Gelling 1958). Further observations at Lich Street (Barker 1965) fortunately corresponded with the turn of the defences towards the south and by the late 1960s it was apparent that the eastern outer edge of the defences corresponded to Friar Street. Barker proposed that the southern edge of the defences would encircle the higher ground now occupied by Worcester Cathedral, and cross the area of College Green. The plan of this circuit appears rather irregular for a Roman fortification, and (with the benefit of the observations at The Keyes Building site) we now know that the Roman settlement layout was almost certainly was dictated largely by the existing Iron Age defences. The extent to which the earlier defensive circuit was re-used by the Romans is subject to considerable uncertainty – the known areas of Roman occupation at Worcester lie principally outside the defensive circuit and there is evidence of Roman burials within the defences, contrary to normal Roman practice.

The excavated evidence for Roman occupation within the area of The King's School is entirely in the form of residual artefacts in later contexts. Roman pottery has been found in many of the smaller archaeological interventions on the site, and Roman roof-tiles are occasionally found. Interpretation of these finds is complicated by the fact that substantial amounts of material have been brought into the site from other parts of Worcester – much of the Norman motte appears to have been constructed with soil brought from the area of Roman settlement at Sidbury. No high status building materials of Roman date (e.g. mosaic tesserae) have been found within excavations at The King's School, and it seems likely that the southern half of the former defensive circuit was mainly used as a cemetery with some low level habitation. Late Roman or early Saxon inhumations were discovered under College Hall in the 1970s.

Anglo-Saxon Period

The development of the post-Roman defensive circuit at Worcester has received but scant consideration from historians. There is documentary evidence that a defensive circuit of Worcester was established between 872 and circa 904 AD, but the precise form and extent of this circuit are unknown. There are pre-Norman conquest references to the gates and wall, and of those that give locational evidence one refers to *"the haga by the south wall towards St Peter's Church"* which places it in the general vicinity of Sidbury and the modern Severn Street and King Street area. The correspondence (if any) between the putative Saxon defensive circuit and the remains of the Iron Age circuit remain unknown. Deposits seen at the Severn Street and King Street junction during gas main works in 2005 may well represent a manmade bank or rampart forming part of the Saxon defensive circuit (Napthan 2005; WCM101270). A similar deposit was observed during works by Archenfield Archaeology during evaluation work on the former Royal Worcester Porcelain Works site close to King Street, and in that case the "bank" material appeared to over-lie Roman deposits. The current evidence suggests that The King's School site lies just outside the main Saxon burgh settlement but possibly formed a distinct higher status enclosure.

Worcester Castle

The earliest mention of a 'castle' at Worcester is in a charter of Oswald dating to 989 AD *"Ego Oswaldus divina favente clementia archiepiscopus quandem particulam telluris de Monasterio Sanctae Mariae in Wiogorna castello videlicet unam mansam..."* (Kemble Codex Dipl. III 247, No. 671) This may be read as "the Monastery of St Mary within the castle of Worcester", *'castello'* in this case referring to a fortified place.

Late Saxon or early Norman activity, including evidence of metalworking, has been identified in the Mill Street area not far to the south of Severn Street (Sherlock 2004; WCM 96659). Subsequent excavations at the King's St Alban's site at Mill Street produced a small quantity of 10th - 12th century pottery, and an early medieval defensive ditch that may relate either to the castle outworks, or more probably to a counter-fort from one of several sieges during the early medieval period (Napthan 2007; WCM101533, Napthan 2008; WCM 101659, Napthan 2014; WCM 102046).

The Norman castle was founded before September 1069 by Urse (or Urso) D'Abitot (Hamilton (ed) 1870 III: 253). A stone keep was constructed before the mid twelfth century, and expenditure of £20 was recorded in 1157-8. Unusually high recorded expenditure at Worcester occurred in 1172-3 when £35.14.6 was spent (Brown 2003). Further extensive work was undertaken during the reigns of Richard I and John. In 1192 work was done on the King's hall, chamber and cellar. In 1198-9 £20.3.0 was spent. A fire in 1202 caused considerable damage: the palisade, the King's house and the treasury had to be repaired. Following the disuse of the castle for military purposes in the early thirteenth century, the site was retained as a prison, the earliest evidence for which is the documented escape of prisoners in 1221 (Hardy 1833). The buildings remained as the County Gaol until 1814, when the County prisoners were transferred to a new building in Salt Lane (later renamed Castle Street).

Evidence for the layout and form of the castle

The remains of the Norman castle have long proved elusive despite several features being shown on eighteenth and nineteenth century mapping. The earliest mapping was published not long after the Civil War (*An exact ground plot of Worcester as it stood fortified 1651* engraved by Vaughan and first published in Blount 1662). This map shows the earliest depictions of the buildings within the castle, including a gate and the gaoler's house. The plan shows and names the "Castle Gate" building in sketch elevation as of three stories with a pitched roof, there are two "towers" separated by a central roofed gateway. The measurements of a 1613 survey (quoted by Noakes

Map of the City of Worcester, 1651: the prominent position of Castle Hill is evident behind the south-western defences.

1889: 49) indicate that the *"peece of stone building"* was *"about 16 ft square"* with a dungeon; this corresponds very well with the late 18th century description by John Howard (Howard 1777) of a deep and damp dungeon *"fifteen and a half feet square"*. By the late 18th century the remnants of the castle gate were reduced to a single tower which apparently served in part as a kitchen for the Bridewell (Cathedral Library Map 69).

The dimensions and profile of the earthern motte were recorded by Samuel Mainley (Cathedral Library Drawing 89), and these reveal the steepness of the 80 ft high cone-shaped motte, the top of which was only six yards in diameter (Chambers, 1820: 242). The motte has been estimated to have amounted to some 6,200 cubic metres of material, much of it gravel (Carver 1980: 23). Fortunately the Buck brothers depicted the motte and other earthworks in The South-West Prospect of the City of Worcester (1732). The motte may also be glimpsed in two of the views published by Treadway Russell Nash in 1782 (*The North View of the City of Worcester from the Porto-Bello Henwick Hill* and *The South View of the City of Worcester from Digley Fields* both engraved by T. Sanders).

Archaeological monitoring of the excavation of large pits for trees planted in the area of Castle Court (and the later Bridewell) in 2002-3 (Napthan 2003; WCM 100996) revealed the presence of a burnt mortar floor sealed by a horizon of soil containing 11th - 14th century pottery. The limits of the floor were not apparent in the trench, but the find was significant in demonstrating the potential for localized survival of floor levels (and therefore potentially also foundations) almost certainly relating to the original castle buildings. In many of the excavated tree pits there was evidence of deep disturbance relating to the construction (and demolition) of the 1633 Bridewell building and its 1780s extensions, as well as areas of probable small scale gravel extraction/pit digging. Though there was clear potential

Works at the site of The Alma public house (demolished in 2008 to make way for The Howell Building at King's St Alban's)

for widespread survival of deposits relating to the castle the survival was however considered likely to be patchy. Amongst the material derived from the occupation of the castle excavated in 2003 was the skeleton of a female goshawk from a feature dating probably to the 13th - 14th century, but also containing much 11th - 14th century pottery. From an unstratified context there was recovered an iron window catch of 16th -17th century (or possibly earlier) date and decorated with a crown, almost certainly deriving from the castle buildings. The presence of stone roofing slabs as well as flat ceramic tile suggests that some of the earlier buildings were stone roofed (Napthan 2003).

The documented pre-1217 castle buildings in the area now occupied by The King's School are known to have included a chapel or church of St Peter the Less, a hall, chamber block and gatehouse. A gatehouse was constructed in 1204-5 (Rotuli de Liberate 1204; quoted by Noakes 1889: 46). The earliest detailed description of the castle buildings was made in 1613 (at the request of the Exchequer), at a time when few of the original structures survived in recognizable form: *"A peece of stone building called the gaole, wherein some prisoners doe lye, being about 16 footes square, having a dungeon and twoe roomes over the dungeon, one above the other, and a little cocke lofte in the same, and a paire of wooden staires without the said stone buildings to goe upp into the said upper roomes* [this is likely to have been the building marked as "Castle Gate" on the Siege plan published in Blount 1662]. *Also there is a tymber howse wherein the gaoler with his family doe dwell about 40 yards from the said gaole or stone peece of building conteyning about three bayes of building havinge in yt These roomes following, viz., a little hall, a little parlor within the said hall, two very little closets adjoyining to the same, nowe used for buttryes, a little cellor, and a store howse, all below the staires. A little chamber over the parlor, two chambers over the cellor and store howse, and twoe others over them, a little chamber over the hall, and a cocke lofte over yt above the staires"* (quoted by Noakes 1889: 49). This latter building is compatible with later plans of the Gaoler's House which stood immediately behind the present Castle House and Number 7 College Green. A letter from the Dean and Chapter dated 1815 describes this as *"the late gaoler's house, an old timber building, stands in part on our boundary wall & about 7 perches of land, and is at the extremity of the goal* [sic] *close to one of our houses"* (Cathedral Library D797a).

The location of the chapel of the castle, first mentioned in 1166, is a matter for some conjecture – the post-1217 access to the castle was via *"the lane leading to St Peter the Less"* (Dr Pat Hughes pers comm.); if the 1166 chapel may be equated with St Peter the Less this would place it firmly in the southern portion of the castle. In the later 13th century presentations to St Peter the Less were made by the Sheriff, which tends to confirm that the chapel was in that part of the castle controlled by the Sheriff. The chapel was still standing in 1408. The presence of a subterranean dungeon within this area, marked on the plans of 1784 (by George Young – Cathedral Library plan 88) and 1819 (by Henry Seward WRO BA5639 parcel 36), is suggestive of there being some re-use of an earlier cellar or undercroft. The position of this "dungeon" corresponded broadly with the present Chappel Memorial Reading Room (the naming of which is not, of course, related to the chapel). Interestingly a description of the dungeon by John Howard, the penal reformer, survives: *"near it* [the Day Room in the centre of the yard] *is a hand ventilator for airing the men felons dungeon, which is twenty-six steps underground and circular about seventeen feet in diameter with barrack bedsteads. Over it is an aperture in the court, three feet in diameter, with iron grates...there is another very damp dungeon fifteen and a half feet square, the window even with the ground"* (Howard 1777: 322). On the basis of this description it seems likely that the dungeon was a remnant of the castle buildings, and may, just possibly, have been the crypt of the chapel of St Peter the Less.

The only castle building for which there is clear surviving evidence and sufficient documentary evidence to confirm its identity is the Royal Chamber block, which survives as a two storey fragment of masonry forming the western wall of Castle House. The fact that the royal apartments lay within the portion of the Castle is expressly mentioned in the royal grant confirmed in 1217 *"...the said prior, mounks and their succesors shall for ever have and hold the said parte of the castell being on the north side of the same castell wherin our house was seated, and which is of our fee"*. The remaining fragment retains evidence of six narrow round arched head "loop" windows with vertical bars and internal shutters (on two storeys), a roll moulded string course and a flat pilaster buttress which appears to have abutted a central entrance doorway, now blocked. Below ground evidence, combined with the known dimensions of the later Schoolmaster's House suggests a building approximately 24 x 9 metres externally. This fragment of walling is deceptive as the original outer face is now within Castle House, the windows long concealed within a little used passageway until they were re-opened and identified during the re-ordering of Castle House in 2002-3. Study of the stonework details and documentary sources reveals that the building was constructed around 1170-1190. King John regularly used this building on his visits to Worcester.

It is generally the case in castles of this period that the Royal Chamber would be close to, or even adjoining, the Great Hall. Close by there would be a kitchen (most medieval kitchens were detached). In the present case we have some reason to think that the building known as 'The Ovens' in the 17th and 18th centuries may have survived as a partial relic of the castle kitchen. As this was a Royal castle there is some possibility that there was a *"privy kitchen for the king"* as at Hertford (Brown, Colvin and Taylor 1963: 680) as well as a kitchen for the humbler castle garrison. It is also likely that the castle chapel would lie close to the hall and chamber blocks. Throughout the middle ages the preferred position of the chapel was one that was easily accessible from the upper end of the hall (Thompson 1991: 133) and there may be some evidence for its location in the later position of the "dungeon". The cartographic evidence is slight, as details of the dungeon are not recorded on the late 18th / early 19th century plans, only the positions of the circular "dungeon head" and a ventilator. However, when John Howard visited the gaol circa 1777 he gave a detailed description (see above). As it is improbable that a below ground dungeon would be new built without some form of cover building it seems highly possible that each of the two separate "dungeons" represented the cellars or undercrofts of earlier buildings. The square dungeon almost certainly equates to that of almost identical dimensions beneath the stone tower described as 40 yards from the Gaoler's House in 1613. The fact that the other dungeon beneath the ventilator in the yard (marked on 18th and 19th century plans) was circular raises the previously unsuspected possibility that the chapel of the castle might have been circular like that at Ludlow Castle.

Close to the chamber block it would be expected to find the "King's Hall" and a kitchen. Whilst the site of the hall is presently unknown we have some hints as to the position of the pre-1217 kitchen in that two neighbouring buildings were known traditionally as The Ovens and Brewhouse (both identified on Collingwood's plan of 1815 as lying to the SW of Castle House; Public Record Office MPE 466 4829). The buildings are known to have been close by the Schoolmaster's House, and to the south west of the surviving fragment of chamber block. The positioning of 'The Ovens' well away from the monastic refectory and monastic kitchen (identified during demolition works in 1845 as lying to the SW of College Hall - Noake 1866: 364-366) suggests strongly that the ovens (in later years used as the melting house for the cathedral plumbers) may have been a relic of the castle kitchen. The former location of 'The Ovens' approximates to the entrance to The King's School from College Green between Number 7 and Number 9.

Little is known about the usage of the castle motte in the later medieval period, but it is highly probable that it, like the land to the south of site, was in agricultural use and had lost all visible vestiges of the tower or keep that had presumably originally surmounted it – by Leland's time (1534-43) it was *"overgrowen with brushwood"* (Toulmin-Smith 1909: 90 folio 88b). Sufficient remained of the castle buildings until the earlier sixteenth century for the County Courts to be held there, but the courts were relocated to the Guildhall in 1565 (Dyer 1973: 211) and subsequently the castle was only used for declarations and elections, which were held in the courtyard well into the 19th century. The motte was used as the basis for a small fortlet during the Civil War, with entrenchments cut around its base. It is significant that it was felt necessary to place additional ditches and earthworks to the south of Frog Lane (now Severn Street) during the Civil War as this indicates that the original ditch and rampart had declined to a point that they were no longer an impenetrable obstacle.

A very small exploratory pit was dug within the cellar of The Salmon's Leap public house (Severn Street, demolished for The Keyes Building) in 2007. This trial hole encountered the sloping outer edge of the castle ditch and a narrow, steep-sided, slot, cut parallel with the line of the ditch. This slot appeared to relate to former timber revetment of the outer edge of the ditch. The fills of the slot point to a 12th or 13th century date for the removal or decay of the revetment. Further works during the construction of The Keyes Building revealed extensive ditch fills of the 14th and 15th centuries. The basal fill of the ditch at this point was found to contain waterlogged organic remains, sampled by borehole, which were subsequently radiocarbon dated to between 902 and 1153 AD. The dating suggests that the ditch was re-cut in the late Saxon-Norman period, quite probably as part of the construction of the castle. The most recent re-cutting of the ditch appears to have occurred as part of the Civil War defences.

The programme of archaeological works at The King's School during recent years has offered tantalizing hints of the nature of the Norman Worcester Castle, and the potential for far more of its form to be determined archaeologically. The excavations at the site of The Keyes Building answered only a few questions about the castle, but the importance of the site in determining the early development of Worcester cannot be overstated.

References

Allies, J. (1852) *On the Ancient British, Roman and Saxon Antiquities and folklore of Worcestershire,* pp15-23.

Baker, N. & Holt, R. (2004) *Urban growth and the medieval church.*

Barker, P. (1968) *The Origins of Worcester.* TWAS 3S Vol 2, pp7-46.

Beardsmore, C. (1980) *Documentary evidence for the history of Worcester City Defences.* In: Carver (1980).

Brown, D. (1990) *Watching Brief at 3 College Precincts, Worcester: WCM 100158.* HWCC Internal rep SWR 17852.

Brown, D. & Wichbold, D. (1991) *Evaluation and salvage recording at King's School (St Alban's).* HWCC Archaeology Service Rep 41.

Brown, R.A., Colvin, H.M. & Taylor, A.J. (1963) *History of the Kings Works: Volume I: The Middle Ages.*

Brown, R.A. (2003) *Royal Castle-building in England 1154-1216.* In: Liddiard (2003).

Carver, M.O.H. (1980) *Medieval Worcester, an archaeological framework.* TWAS 3rd Ser Vol. 7

Cave, T. & Wilson, R.A. (Eds.) (1924) *Parliamentary Survey of the Lands of the Dean and Chapter of Worcester.* Worcester Historical Society.

Chambers, J. (1820) *A General history of Worcester.*

Cunliffe, B. (1991) *Iron Age Communities in Britain.*

Daffern, N., Keith-Lucas, F. & Vaughan, T. (2012) *Archaeological evaluation and bore-hole investigation at Zone 4, King's School SPACE, 42 Severn Street, Worcester: WCM 101909 and WCM 101943.* WAAS Internal rep 1937.

Dalwood, H. & Edwards, R.E. (2004) *Excavations at Deansway, Worcester, 1988-9: Romano British small town to late medieval city.* CBA Res Rep 139.

Douglas, D.C. & Greenaway, W. (Eds.) (1953) *Florence of Worcester.* Eng. Hist. Soc. II.

Dyer, A. (1973) *The City of Worcester in the sixteenth century.*

Edwards, R.E. (1989) *Evaluation at the King's School, Worcester: HWCM 530.* HWCC Archaeology Service Rep 33.

"Florence, A." [Lees, E.] (1828) *A strangers guide to Worcester.*

Gelling, P. (1958) *Excavations at Little Fish Street Worcester 1957.* TWAS NS Vol 35 pp 67-70.

Green, V. (1764) *A survey of the City of Worcester.*

Green, V. (1796) *The history and antiquities of the city and suburbs of Worcester.*

Goodall, J. (2011) *The English Castle.*

Hamilton, N.E.S.A. (Ed.) (1870) *Willelm Malmesburiensis monachi De gestis pontificum Anglorum. In: Chronicles and memorials of Great Britain and Ireland during the Middle Ages.* HMSO.

Hardy, T.D. (Ed.) (1833) *Rotuli Litterarum Clausarum in Turri Londinensi I (1204-1227).* London, Record Commission, 2 Vols. 1833–34.

Howard, J. (1777) *The State of Prisons of England and Wales.*

Hughes, P. (1990) *Buildings and the building trade in Worcester 1540-1650.* (Unpublished Doctoral Thesis, University of Birmingham).

Kenyon, J.R. (1990) *Medieval fortifications.*

King, D.J.C. (1983) *Castellarium Anglicanum: An Index and Bibliography of the Castles in England, Wales and the Islands. Vol I: Anglesey–Montgomery.*

Liddiard, R. (Ed.) (2003) *Anglo Norman Castles.*

Luard, H.R. (Ed.) (1854) *Annales Monastici.*

Morriss, R.K. & Sherlock, H. (2005) *Re-development of surplus land at the Royal Worcester Porcelain Factory, Worcester: The archaeology of the Portland Walk and Severn Street sites.* Archenfield Archaeology.

Meekings, C.A.F., Porter, S. & Roy, I. (Eds.) (1983) *The hearth tax collectors book for Worcester 1678-1680.* WHS NS Vol 11.

Napthan, M. (1995) *Survey at Elmley Castle.* Archaeology Service, HWCC.

Napthan, M. (2001a) *Watching brief at 11 Edgar Street, Worcester: WCM 100815.* Mike Napthan Archaeology Report.

Napthan, M. (2001b) *Watching brief at King's St Alban's Junior School Worcester: WCM100856.* Mike Napthan Archaeology Report.

Napthan, M. (2002) *Desk top assessment of the southern boundary Castle House, 6 College Green Worcester: WCM 100989.* Mike Napthan Archaeology Report.

Napthan, M., Baxter, I., Griffiths, L., Hamilton-Dyer, S. & Pearson, E.A. (2003) *Watching briefs, excavation and building recording at*

Worcester Castle site, now Kings School, Worcester 2002-3: WCM 100990, WCM 100996, WCM 100997, WCM 100998, WCM 101119, WCM 101120, WCM 101126 & WCM 101159. Mike Napthan Archaeology Report.

Napthan, M. (2005) *Archaeological watching brief during gas main replacement works at College Street, Edgar Street and Severn Street, Worcester: WCM 101270.* Mike Napthan Archaeology Report.

Napthan, M. & Jacobs, A. (2006a) *Archaeological works at School House, King's School Worcester: WCM 101378 & WCM 101408.* Mike Napthan Archaeology Report.

Napthan, M., Jacobs, A., Pearson, E. & Warman, S. (2006b) *Archaeological watching brief during re-pavement works, Worcester High Street 2004-5: WCM 101275.* Mike Napthan Archaeology Report.

Napthan, M. (2006c) *Archaeological watching brief at King's School, new Art block, Severn Street, Worcester: WCM 101460 & WCM 101499.* Mike Napthan Archaeology Report.

Napthan, M. (2007a) *Former Alma PH, 35 Mill Street, Worcester - building assessment and archaeological field evaluation: WCM101532 & WCM101533.* Mike Napthan Archaeology Report.

Napthan, M. (2007b) *Archaeological evaluation at King's School: former Salmon's Leap PH, Severn Street, Worcester: WCM 101573.* Mike Napthan Archaeology Report.

Napthan, M. (2008) *Site of former Alma PH, 35 Mill Street, Worcester: archaeological excavation and watching brief: WCM 101659.* Mike Napthan Archaeology Report.

Napthan, M. (2010a) *King's School boathouse, Severn Street, Worcester – archaeological field evaluation and recording of retaining wall: WCM101800 & WCM101808.* Mike Napthan Archaeology Report.

Napthan, M. (2010b) *King's School boathouse, Severn Street, Worcester - excavation of a trial pit: WCM 101800.* Mike Napthan Archaeology Report.

Napthan, M. (2012) *Archaeological works at the proposed King's School "SPACE" sports hall site, Severn Street, Worcester: WCM 101746, WCM 101735 & WCM 101762.* Mike Napthan Archaeology Report.

Napthan, M. et al (2014) *Worcester Castle site: an update on the Origins of Worcester.* TWAS 3rd Ser Vol 24 1-48.

Napthan, M. (2014) *Watching brief during construction of extension to King's School, Howell Building, Willow Street, Worcester: WCM 102046.* Mike Napthan Archaeology Report.

Noake, J. (1866) *The monastery and cathedral of Worcester*, pp346-378.

Noake, J. (1889) *Worcestershire Nuggets by an old digger*, pp45-52.

RCAHMW (1925) *An inventory of the Ancient Monuments of Pembrokeshire.* HMSO: p. 407 no. 1150.

Sherlock, H. (2004) *13-15 Mill Street, a report on an archaeological evaluation.*

Toulmin Smith, L. (Ed.) (1909) *The Itinerary of John Leland in or about the years 1535-1543.*

Wallis, S. & Colls, D. (2006) *Portland Works, Royal Worcester Porcelain, Portland Walk, Diglis, Worcester; An Archaeological Evaluation.* Thames Valley Archaeological Services report 04/65.

Webster, J., Crawford, A., Daffen, N., Robson Glyde, S. & Wilkinson, K. (2011) *Archaeological Investigations at the Michael Baker Boathouse, The King's School, Severn Street, Worcester.* WHEAS P3580 Rep 1841.

Webster, J., Vaughan, T., Griffin, L. & Pearson, E.A. (2014) *Archive Report Archaeological works at King's School SPACE, Severn Street, Worcester P4065.* Report reference: 2027. HER reference: WCM 101973 & 101975. WAAS.

Wright, T. (1848) 'Antiquities of the site of Worcester Castle'. In: *Journal of British Antiquarian Association*, pp34-40.

Mike Napthan MCIFA

Mike Napthan is a Member of the Chartered Institute for Archaeologists with nearly 30 years of professional experience; Mike has worked in Worcestershire for much of the past 24 years, where his specialist archaeological contracting business is based.

Mike has been involved in more than a hundred archaeological digs, with discoveries and assessments ranging from the prehistoric era to the Second World War. His speciality is historic building assessments, recording buildings for planning purposes. Having worked for Worcestershire County Council and Worcester City Council, among other public and commercial clients, Mike first worked on a project at The King's School, Worcester in 2001 - the Wilf Thomas Library at King's St Alban's - and has maintained a close working relationship with the school ever since. Mike is responsible for the archaeological work and discoveries made at Castle House, School House, The Michael Baker Boathouse, The Keyes Building and at King's St Alban's.

Appendix 16: A photographic miscellany

During construction of The Keyes Building, a large red crane dominated the skyline. At the end of its work on site, an even larger crane arrived in Severn Street to dismantle it!

Left:
RIBA Regional Architecture Award for the transformation of the lower floors of School House, awarded in 2008.

Below:
Nick and Heather Witherick, responsible for catering at King's since the 1970s until the early 2000s.

College Hall set up ready for an assembly. The photograph is undated but the scene would be recognisable to generations of pupils.

'Out with the old...' - 2000s entrance sign replaced by a modern counterpart (2011)

MUSIC DEPARTMENT - HONOURS BOARD

1960	John Langdon	Organ Scholarship, Kings, Cambridge
1966	Stephen Cleobury	Organ Studentship, St. John's, Cambridge
1967	Nicholas Cleobury	Organ Scholarship, Worcester, Oxford
1967	Roger Parkes	Organ Scholarship, Corpus Christi, Cambridge
1968	Christopher Tolley	Organ Scholarship, New College, Oxford
1970	Stephen Darlington	Organ Scholarship, Christ Church, Oxford
1970	Andrew Millington	Organ Scholarship, Downing, Cambridge
1971	Simon Judd	Choral Exhibition, Gonville & Caius, Cambridge
1973	Adrian Leang	Organ Scholarship, Christ's, Cambridge
1973	John Penny	Organ Scholarship, Pembroke, Oxford
1976	Timothy Minton	Choral Scholarship, St. John's, Cambridge
1977	Adrian Partington	Organ Scholarship, King's, Cambridge
1977	Geoffrey Webber	Organ Scholarship, New College, Oxford
1978	Martin Holmes	Instrument Scholarship, Worcester, Oxford
1979	John Davies	Choral Scholarship, St. John's, Cambridge
1980	Nicholas Kok	Organ Scholarship, New College, Oxford
1980	Steven Kings	Music Exhibition, St. John's, Cambridge
1980	Paul Renney	Choral Exhibition, Trinity, Cambridge
1980	Jonathan Nott	Choral Scholarship, St. John's, Cambridge
1983	Robert Millner	Choral Exhibition, Trinity, Cambridge
1984	Andrew Lawson	Organ Scholarship, Girton, Cambridge
1984	Christopher Dyer	Choral Exhibition, Jesus, Cambridge
1984	Joyce Renney	Choral Exhibition, Trinity, Cambridge
1987	John Bowley	Choral Exhibition, King's, Cambridge
1987	Philip Glenister	Choral Scholarship, Clare, Cambridge
1989	John Harris	Organ Scholarship, Trinity, Oxford
1989	Clare LeFort	Choral Exhibition, Emmanuel, Cambridge
1990	Philip Glenister	Exhibition, Royal College of Music
1993	Marie-Claire Brookshaw	Choral Scholarship, Trinity, Cambridge
1994	William Carslake	Organ Scholarship, Pembroke, Cambridge
1994	Giles Gasper	Choral Bursary, Exeter, Oxford
1996	Tom Blunt	Organ Scholarship, Trinity, Cambridge
1998	Alastair Brookshaw	Choral Scholarship, Trinity, Cambridge
1998	Robert Webb	Choral Scholarship, Christ's, Cambridge
1999	Jennifer Howlett	Music Scholarship, Swansea University
2000	Allan Clayton	Choral Scholarship, St. John's, Cambridge
2000	Tom Dupernex	Choral Scholarship, Trinity, Cambridge
2001	Sam Bayliss	Organ Scholarship, Somerville, Oxford
2001	Julia Guy	Choral Scholarship, Trinity, Cambridge
2003	Helena Culliney	Choral Scholarship, Gonville & Caius, Cambridge
2004	David Newsholme	Organ Scholarship, New College, Oxford
2004	Shulah Oliver	Scholarship, Royal Academy of Music
2004	Allan Clayton	Sir Elton John Scholarship, Royal Academy of Music
2004	Alastair Brookshaw	Dame Judi Dench Scholarship, Mountview Academy
2005	Andrew Furniss	Organ Scholarship, Oriel College, Oxford
2005	James McCreath	Nettleship Instrumental Exhibition, Balliol, Oxford
2006	Adrian Uren	Scholarship, Guildhall School of Music & Drama
2006	Alan Uren	Cork Scholarship, Royal Academy of Music
2006	Anna Byrne	Choral Scholarship, St. Peter's, Oxford
2007	Allan Clayton	Queen's Commendation for Excellence
2008	George Austin-Cliff	Choral Scholarship, St. Catherine's, Cambridge
2008	Jolyon Loy	Choral Scholarship, Magdalen, Oxford
2008	Heather Uren	Joan Conway Music Scholarship, ChristChurch, Oxford
2009	James Greenwood	Choral Scholarship, Trinity, Cambridge
2009	Elizabeth Grew	Instrumental Exhibition, ChristChurch, Oxford
2009	Peter Holder	Scholarship, Royal Academy of Music
2009	Hannah Lucas	Choral Scholarship, Royal Holloway, London
2010	Gareth Ceredig	Scholarship, Guildhall of Music and Drama
2011	Sam Harris	Anna Haxworth Music Prize, St. Hugh's, Oxford
2012	Edoardo Toso	Choral Scholarship, Warwick University
2013	Rebecca Hardwick	Scholarship, Royal College of Music
2013	Peter Shepherd	Organ Scholarship, Merton, Oxford

Music Department Honours Board, Music School (2015)
Inset: William Davey (School House 1915-22), whose cap (pictured) is the oldest item of uniform held in the School Archive's collection.

College Hall set up for summer examinations, May 2014: a scene of terror for many over a number of decades, while many others will have learned the names on the scholars' boards by heart! The opening of The Keyes Building heralded the end of College Hall's function as the main examination centre, with most exams due to be taken in the new sports hall from 2016.

Before the days of trailers for boats, a roof rack on a minibus had to suffice.
Notice the solid wooden doors on the Fourth Form Building in the background.

Jonathon Hartwright and Tom Wall at Severnside Printers for the printing of the second edition of The King's School, Worcester and a history of its site, 1998.

Sabrina, Roman goddess of the River Severn, atop the fountain in the Creighton Memorial Gardens

The imposing front door of College House: not for the use of pupils!

Index

1541 Society	189
Academic subjects, Departments:	
Art	32-33, 86, 104, 110, 124, 183, 194, 196
Biology	64-65, 108, 110, 126, 181
Chemistry	64, 108, 123-124, 126, 160
Classics	32, 33, 40, 56, 59, 70, 86, 92, 119, 168, 182
Design and Technology (D&T, C.D.T.)	123, **124-125**, 194
Drama	12, 14-15, 36, 90, 92, 104-106, 130, 138, **163-165**, 168, 181, 199, 206, 215-217
Economics	70, 137, 181
English	9, 18, 32, 59, 60, 70, 92, 182, 227-228
Geography	30, 36, 93, 106, 110, 186, 194, 206
History	32, 37, 70, 92
Mathematics	92, 104, 183
Modern Foreign Languages	40, 68, 92, 123, 166, 186, 194, 203
Music	**10-17**, 23, 25, 48, 50, 63, 76, 90, 104-105, 109, 126, 130, 137, 159, 183, 264
Physics	64-65, 108, 160
Religious Studies, Divinity	67, 92, 194
Alice Ottley School	14, 75, 89, 104, 107, 207, 221
Almonry, Almonry School - see 'St Mary's Priory'	
Archaeology	25, 95, 146, 182, **252-262**
Architects:	
Christian, Ewan	23, 24, 51, 60, 64, 66
Christophers, John (Associated Architects)	61, 157, 182, 186, 192, 204, 212, 215, 225, 263
Hill Parker, Alfred	65, 76, 141
Bishop Perowne Church of England College	174, 180, 187, 202, 222-223
Boarding, Boarders	36, 40, 48, 58-62, 66-67, 71-72, 76, 85, 93, 143-144, 146, 158, 171, 180
Buildings:	
1899 Classrooms - see '7 College Green'	
1925 Classrooms	32, 88, 90, 93, 97, 106, 110, 123, 159, 161, 186
Annett Building (New Block)	117, **118-119**, 183, 238
Art School	196
Chappel Memorial Reading Room	88, **90-91**, 158-159, 186
Dining Hall	106, 123, 126, 159, 186, 199
Fishermen's Cottages	12, 88, 116, 239
Fives Courts	40, 50, 61, 85, 175, 183
John Moore Theatre	160, **163-165**, 183
The Keyes Building	125, 136, 178-179, 186-187, 189, 191, 210, **215-217**, 222, 254-255, 257, 263
Michael Baker Boathouse	44, 95-96, 178-179, 187, **204-205**, 210, 271
Sports Hall	122-123, 174
Winslow Building	108, 159, 183, 194
Wolfson Building	123, **124-125**, 183
Bursar, Bursary	61, 115, 116, 135
Bartholomew, Galen	115, 147, 151, 154-157, 170-171, 180-182, 204, 209, 211, **212**, 213-214, 225, 269, 270
Cadets	78-81
Combined Cadet Force (C.C.F.)	**79-81**, 106, 130-131
Officer Training Corps (O.T.C.)	12, 40, 60, 76, **78-79**, 82, 88-89, 92, 97, 102-103
Careers Department	68, 70, 195
Castle Court	183, 186, 257
Castle Hill - see 'Worcester Castle'	
Castle Place	94, 97, 116, 121, 183
Cathedral Choir, Choristers	5, 7, 10-11, 15, 17-18, 26, 40, 105, 141, 143, 226
Cathedral Ferry	106
Chaplain, Chaplaincy	70, 92, 127, 147, 180, 199-201, 214, 223
Charity work	206, 218, 222
Charnel House, Carnary Chapel	8, 27-28
Choir School	11, 48, 56, 76, 86, 105, **140-141**, 238, 240
Co-education	70-72, 81, 128, 132, 135, 146, 158, 160, 167-168, 174, 180
College Green	30, 34-35, 38, 56-57, 76, 83, 86, 183
Edgar Tower	iv, **31-33**, 56, 86, 88, 98, 122, 183-184, 192-193
2 College Green	56
3 College Green - see 'Choir House'	
4 College Green	32, 36, 60, 75-76
5 College Green - see 'Hostel House'	
6 College Green - see 'Castle House'	
7 College Green	50-51, 54-55, 64, 69, 75, 183
8 College Green - see 'School House'	
9 College Green	1, 34, 54, 69, 86
10 / 10a College Green	48, 50, 69-70
11 College Green	35, 70
12 College Green	70-71, 137, 186, 239
13/14 College Green	12, 49, 71, 75, 105, 109
15 College Green - see 'College House'	
Schoolmaster's House	34, 36, 39, 41, 45, 71
College Hall	8, 13, 15, **20-25**, 26-28, 37, 45-48, 74-75, 86, 88, 102, 134, 263, 265
Comenius Project	180, 195, 202-203, 222-223
Common Room	61, 72, 75, 208
Common Table	8, 9, 21, 26
Creighton Memorial Gardens	88, **94-96**, 103, 190, 204, 265
Criccieth	12, 24, 79, 98, **100-102**
Curriculum, Examinations	9, 18, 30, 36-37, 39, 52-53, 76, 92, 102, 158, 181-182, 194-195, 227-228
Dean and Chapter	7, 23, 26-27, 34-35, 37, 39-40, 45, 50, 72, 74, 226
Discipline	62, 77, 120, 132, 137, 144, 197
Duke of Edinburgh's Award	201-202
Ecclesiastical Commission	23, 40-41, 45, 77

Evacuation - see 'Criccieth'	
Extra-curricular activities	77, 82, 104, 106, 113, 130-131, 169, 184, 199-203, 206
Floreat Schola Vigorniensis - see 'School songs'	
Foundation Development Office	61, 84, 136, 183-184, 187, 188-189, 210, 215, 223, 225
Fourth Forms, Middle School	98, 199
Government grants, Assisted Places	85-86, 88, 90, 92-93, 105, 129, 137, 158, 210
Governors, Governing Body	50, 74, 85, 138, 154-155, 207, 209, 211-212
Howell, Donald	67, 148-150, 155, 170, 182, **209**, 210, 212, 220, 225, 243, 248
Hawford Lodge - see 'King's Hawford'	
Headmasters, Schoolmasters (Masters)	236
Annett, David	13, 23, 59, 111-114, 119, 132, 236
Armstrong, Matthew	1, 69, 225, 236
Bolland, William	11, 48, 52, 55, 66, 68, 134, 193, 236, 238
Bradshaw, Thomas	19, 21, 26, 236
Bright, Henry	10, 21, 26-28, 236
Chappel, William	66, 74, 77, 82, 84, 236, 238
Creighton, Cuthbert	85-86, 88, 93-95, 99, 101-103, 236, 238
Day, Maurice	21, 40-41, 45, 236
Griffin, John	23, 36, 236
Helm, William	39, 172, 236
Keyes, Timothy	9, 69, 180, 182, 188, 215, 223, 225, 236
Kittermaster, Ronald	12, 66, 104, 106, 11, 236, 238
Milne, Andrew	15, 69-70, 137-139, 146, 236
Moore, John	59, 69, 146, 158, 170, 236
Pether, John	4, 7-8, 19, 236
Toy, John	10, 28, 30, 236
Wilding, Longworth	97-98, 100-101, 236, 238
Health Centre, Sanatorium	59, 62, 71, 75, 138, 182-183, 214
Houses	76, 97, 103, 109, 113-114, 118, 159, 161, 170-171, 182-183, 199
Bright House	59, 114, 239
Castle House	16, 55, 62, 76, 86, 94, 98, 100, 104, 109, 126, 238
Chappel House	59, 238
Choir House	56, 58-59, 63, 105, 140-141, 182, 239
College House	72-73, 126, 128, 167, 171, 180, 239, 265
Creighton House	59, 62, 68-69, 238
Eliot House	70, 158, 239
The Hostel, Hostel House	34, 60, 75-76, 86, 100, 104, 126, 181-182, 238
Kittermaster House	59, 67 ,239
Natland	93, 238
Oswald House	68, 239
School House	16, 51-52, 64, 66-69, 75-76, 86-88, 94, 100-101, 103-104, 109, 126, 159, 161, 192-193, 238
Tredennyke	105, 142, 239-240
Wulstan House	67, 114, 239
Information Technology, Computing	108, 127, 130, 159, 169, 183, 194, 220, 225
King's Day, Speech Day	1, 25, 55, 86, 88, 97, 104, 133
King's Hawford	105, 147, **150-157**, 240
The King's Herald	166, 169, 203
King's Scholars, Queen's Scholars	7, 18, 30, 35-37, 39, 41, 77, 88, 197
King's School Parents' Committee (KSPC)	183, 190, **207**, 223
King's School Worcester Development Trust	122, **210**
King's St Alban's	11, 59, 105, 109, **142-149**, 238, 240, 257
KSW Boat Club	40-41, **42-44**, 55, 106, 110, 114, 130, 172-174, 178, 202, 204-205, 247
Leach, Arthur	4, 75
Letters Patent - see 'Statutes'	
Library	32-33, 51, 68, 90, 122-123, 183, **192-193**
Long Gallery	68, 190, 192-193, 257
Majestas	1, 19-21, 26, 40, 45
Marketing	220-221, 234-235, 269
Masters (Assistant Masters), Teachers:	
Allum, Robert	62, 70, 180, 238, 239
Bailey, Bill	59, 79-80, 107, 109, 114, 130, 142-143, 239-240, 248
Bentley, Arthur	62, 78, 92, 98-99, 101, 109, 238
Bramma, Harry	12-15, 23, 117, 130
Bridges, Keith	13, 16, 60-61, 90, 108, 128, 160, 208, 238

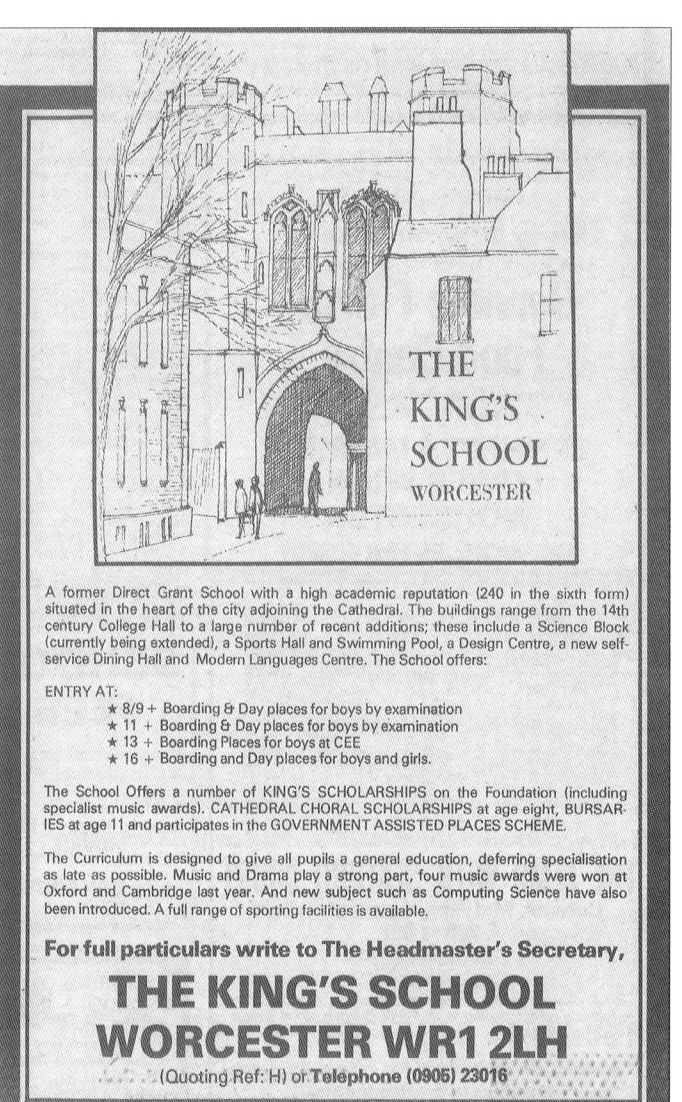

Brookshaw, David	14-17, 50, 164, 241	Howell, Donald - see 'Governors, Governing Body'	
Brown, Ian	58-59, 239	Somers, Lord (John)	29
Campbell, Myfanwy	32-33, 77, 86, 98, 104, 107	Tomkins, Thomas	10, 34, 54, 69
Castley, Reginald	60, 76-77, 88, 98, 238	Wall, John	35
Cattermole, Paul	113, 130, 274	Winslow, Edward	26, 28, 108
Curle, Peter	59, 174, 187, 239	Vaughn, Sir John	29
Day, Edgar	12-13, 89, 92, 101	Pipe organ	13, 23, 130
Diamond, Peter	14-15, 127-128, 130, 163, 166, 239, 242	Playground	40, 76, 88, 93-94, 173
Drummond, Malcolm	14-16	Playing fields	40, 86, 88, 1005, 122, 172-173, 224
Franklin, Arthur	12, 23, 60, 89-90, 92, 99, 101, 238	Royal Grammar School (RGS)	5, 26, 40, 53-54, 100, 103-104, 154, 173, 176, 207, 221
Griffiths, Brian	14-15, 70, 127, 143, 163, 169, 195, 238, 240	School Archive	32, 68, 84, 127, **184-185**, 264
Gwilliam, Peter	70, 181, 184	School day	9, 18, 24, 35, 38, 74, 198
Iddon, Peter	46, 59, 61, 171, 180, 208, 238, 239	School Fete	106, 108, 117, 121, 169, 274
Knight, Richard	43-44, 60, 114, 130, 238	School gates	69, 183
Le Marchand, Sarah	72, 167, 180-181, 239	School motto	i, 46, 192, 240
Le Marchand, Stephan	14, 72, 163, 181, 195, 238	School prizes	38, 242
Longland, Paul	12, 58, 60, 104, 238, 240	School shield / insignia	235
McTurk, Dan	66-68, 79-80, 107, 109, 111, 114, 192-193, 238	School songs	11, 50, 240
Macdonald, Alec	12, 92-93, 99, 101, 103-104, 108, 110, 274	Scouting	77, 82, 92, 97, 130
Mason, Russell	59, 70, 181, 220, 239	Senior Management Team	181, 211-212, 237
Rammell, Thomas	53, 55, 62, 76-77, 86, 88, 130, 134, 173, 237, 238	The SPACE Campaign - see 'The Keyes Building'	
Roberts, Marc	66-67, 127, 174, 213, 218, 238, 239	Sport, Physical Education	38, 40, 42-44, 55, 66, 76-77, 83, 86, 88-89, 101, 103, 106, 116, 130, 135, 167, **172-179**, 187, 202, 244-247
Roslington, Caroline	6, 32, 36, 72, 81, 126-128, 160-161, 166, 184, 208, 239, 269, 274	St Alban's, St Alban's House - see 'King's St Alban's'	
Roslington, John	46, 72, 126-128, 166, 169, 174, 181, 203, 208, 220, 239	St Mary's Priory	4-5, 20-21, 26, 31
Sheppard, Stuart	62, 79-80, 106, 109, 114, 131, 238	St Oswald	4, 20-21, 32-33, 239
Stacey, Alan	66-67, 81, 110, 238	St Wulstan	5, 14, 20-21, 24, 32-33, 239
Strong, Sam	12, 42, 62, 78, 92, 98, 101-102, 238, 248	Statutes	4, 7, 9, 18-19, 21, 30, **226-228**
Thomas, Frank	60, 66, 97, 101, 103-104, 238	Swimming Pool	116, 122, 137, 174
Thomas, Wilfred	79, 120, 143, 147, 238, 240	Three Choirs Festival	10, 16, 25, 36
Thompson, Paul	127, 161, 165, 168	University of Worcester	177, 194-195, 222-223, 225
Turner, John	127, 128, 131, 169, 237, 238	Ushers, Second Masters, Deputy Heads	7-8, 18, 30, 36, 38, 63, 109-110, 160, 211-212, 237
Wilson, Lester	58-59, 109, 142-143, 238, 240	Baxter, Thomas	38-40, 45, 237
Meeke Scholarships	30, 41, 49	Hickson, Tim	64, 90, 121, 127, 159, **160**, 167, 181, 208, 210, 212, 237
Memorials	24, 76, 83-87, 102, 106	Hincks, Sue	63, **198**
Monarchs:		Moule, Henry	10, 26-28, 237
King Edward VI	19, 21	Stevens, Patricia	**167**, 181, 237
King George III	25	*The Vigornian*	40, **46-47**, 74, 82, 221
King George V	82	Wilson, Canon James	32, 71, 74, **75**, 76-77
King George VI	97	Worcester Castle	38, 50, 62, 88, **94-95**, 252-253, 255, 258-260
King Henry VIII	4, 6-8, 18, 193	Worcester Cathedral	7, 18, 27, 30, 45, 75, 226-228, 235
Queen Elizabeth I	26	Young Enterprise	203
Queen Elizabeth II	166		
Queen Mary I	19		
New Scheme	9, 23-24, 40, 49-50, 53-54, 64, 66, 74, 77, 209, 236-237		
Old Chapel	**111-113**, 130, 202		
Old Vigornians:			
Old Vigornian Club, OV Reunions	54-55, 86, 95, 106-107, **134-136**, 186, 188, 248		
Barnabas Group	184, 188, 249		
Craze, Michael	88-89, 274		
Eckersley, Basil	62, 98-99, 210		

Acknowledgements

The idea of updating the history of The King's School, Worcester for the school's 475th anniversary had been discussed for a number of years, and, to this end, Caroline Roslington (Staff 1977-2011, School Archivist 1998-2011) gathered a body of material, mainly through interviews with staff, Governors and Old Vigornians; much of this material has been used in the writing of this new history.

I am grateful to Tim Keyes, Headmaster from 1998 to 2014, for his confidence in my ability to produce this book and to Galen Bartholomew, Bursar and Clerk to the Governors since 1996, who has shown similar confidence and support. Galen has contributed much to this project, including valuable information about College Hall, King's Hawford and the recent development of the school's facilities.

Substantial contributions to this book have been made by James Bartholomew (Creighton House 1996-2007). Other key contributors include Megan Glenn (Boathouse Manager 2012-present) and Stephan Le Marchand (Hon OV 1983-present). I am grateful to each of them and to all the other contributors to this book. My thanks especially to Mike Napthan who has written a fascinating summary of the archaeological work carried out around the school site since 1990 especially for this book. A number of contributions, mostly included in the 'King's Remembered' series, are drawn from The King's School, Worcester - and a history of its site (Roslington (ed.), 1998). Thank you to Nick Dart (Hon OV 1991-present) for photographs taken in 2015 which illustrate recent campus developments, and to Chris Wilson (Hon OV 2001-present) for the up-to-date aerial photography.

Pauline Baum (School Archivist 2009-14) proved to be a great source of information and a useful sounding board for ideas, for which she has my thanks. Donald Howell, OV and Chairman of Governors from 1986 to 2009, generously produced summaries of Governors' papers from this period, and has given permission for these to be used in writing the later chapters of this book. In a similar way, Douglas Garrad has shared a wealth of information about Hawford Lodge, for which I am grateful. I have also drawn from numerous articles published in The Vigornian magazine, from 1882 to the present day.

I would like to thank everyone else who has contributed to this history of the school - Old Vigornians, staff and governors - which is as accurate and up-to-date as I have been able to make it. Thank you also to all those who have kindly and patiently answered my questions, especially Alice Brunt in the Foundation Development Office, Sarah Key in Design, Media and Reprographics for a great deal of help with scanning and printing the numerous draft copies of the book, Harriet Fisher in the School Archive and to James and Galen Bartholomew and PC Thompson for proof-reading and error checking. Any remaining errors are mine.

Thank you to Mike Fardon for his professional support in getting this book to publication, and to Malcolm Payne for his patience and support.

My personal dedication for this book is to a wonderful teacher: John Arthurs (Creighton House 1944-48), who passed away in 2009. John was my inspiration to become a primary school teacher, the first to give me a love of history at St George's RC Primary School, and the person who encouraged me to sit the entrance exam for King's in 1991. Thank you, Mr Arthurs.

Danny Payne
Henwick Grove, Worcester
September 2015

Danny Payne

Editor

Daniel David John Payne is an Old Vigornian (Daniel Hankins, School House 1992-99) who enjoyed much of his time at King's and especially the Sixth Form in which he was a member of the first Drama Exchange with Notre Dame Academy (Worcester, Massachusetts), Editor of 'The King's Herald', Director of a Young Enterprise company and Head of School House - even despite a remarkable lack of sporting prowess!

Danny returned to work at The King's School, Worcester in 2001, initially in the ICT Department and later as Head of Design, Media and Reprographics. It was in this role that he became involved in the project to produce an updated history of the school ahead of the 475th anniversary celebrations, allowing him to indulge his keen interest in the history of King's and the school archive. Danny left King's for the second time in 2014 to pursue a degree in Primary Education at the University of Worcester. He maintains regular contact with The King's School as a member of the Old Vigornian Club Committee and 1541 Society.

Contributors

Matthew Armstrong (Headmaster 2014-present)	Foreword
James Bartholomew (Creighton House 1996-2007)	Co-author of Chapter 1 and Chapter 2
Galen Bartholomew (Bursar 1996-2016)	Co-author of 'College Hall'
Megan Glenn (Boathouse Manager 2012-present)	'KSW Boat Club'
James Bartholomew (Creighton House 1996-2007)	'Cadets at King's'
D.M. Forrest (School House 1919-22)	King's Remembered*
Michael Craze (The Hostel 1919-25)	King's Remembered*
Basil Eckersley MBE (Castle 1930-37)	King's Remembered*
Cyril Havard FRCS (Castle 1938-41)	'King's during the Second World War'*
Peter Oades (School 1938-41)	'King's during the Second World War'*
Alec Mackie (Choir House 1947-56)	King's Remembered
David Gillard (Castle House 1947-54)	King's Remembered*
David Annett (Headmaster 1959-79)	'Old Chapel' *Written for the School Archive, 2002*
Derek Griffiths (Chappel 1956-67)	King's Remembered*
Barbara Cookson (The Hostel 1971-73)	King's Remembered*
Gillian Hunt (Castle House 1975-77)	King's Remembered *Written for the School Archive, 2011*
Mike Fardon (St Alban's 1959-62)	King's Remembered
Galen Bartholomew (Bursar 1996-present)	Co-author of Chapter 7
Leanne Sheen (King's Hawford 1993-99)	King's Remembered
Stephan Le Marchand (Staff 1983-present)	'The John Moore Theatre and Drama at King's' and 'Patricia Stevens'
Lauren Pruden-Lawson (Chappel 1991-98)	King's Remembered
Jessica Page (Chappel 1994-99)	King's Remembered
James Bartholomew (Creighton House 1996-2007)	'Music at King's'
Tim Keyes (Headmaster 1998-2014)	'Sue Hincks'
Galen Bartholomew (Bursar 1996-2016)	'The competitive scene in Worcester'
Galen Bartholomew (Bursar 1996-2016)	'Parents' Committee'
Tim Keyes (Headmaster 1998-2014)	'Donald Howell' *From his farewell speech for Donald's retirement, 2010*
Sophie Whitworth (FDO Director 2008-present)	'The King's School Worcester Development Trust'
Donald Howell (Chairman of Governors 1986-2010)	'Galen Bartholomew'
Rory Johnson (Bright House 2003-09)	King's Remembered
James Bartholomew (Creighton House 1996-2007)	Appendix 7: School motto
Mike Napthan (Mike Napthan Archaeology)	Appendix 15: The archaeology of The King's School

* Taken or adapted from *The King's School, Worcester - and a history of its site*

James Bartholomew

Contributor: Chapters 1 and 2, 'Music at King's', 'Cadets at King's' and Appendix 7

While at King's, James Bartholomew (Creighton House 1996–07) was a King's Scholar, Monitor, journalist and double bass player. After a year's specialist double bass tuition at Birmingham Conservatoire, he studied at London University: Law with French at UCL, and Linguistics at SOAS. He then moved to Hong Kong, employed by the Tricor Group as an editor and language consultant. James has also worked in music administration, and is now studying for a postgraduate degree in Speech and Language Processing at Edinburgh University, with a view to developing a career in language technology.

Galen Bartholomew

Contributor: Chapter 7, 'College Hall' and 'The competitive scene in Worcester'

Galen Bartholomew was appointed Bursar and Clerk to the Governors at King's in 1996, after three years as Bursar of St Clement Danes School. He had previously worked in the contracting industry, latterly in a senior management position with the Costain Group, where he gained experience in the strategic and financial management of large companies and contracts in many parts of the world. Born and brought up in Worcestershire, he has been actively involved with the Three Choirs Festival for many years, and is a Governor of St Richard's Hospice. Galen is due to retire from King's in 2016 after 20 years' service.

Picture Credits

Unless listed below, all images used in this book are owned or held by The King's School, Worcester and are either photographs, graphics or other imagery created by King's School staff or photographs sourced from the School Archive, many of which have been donated by Old Vigornians and their families. Many of the photographs have been taken or supplied by the Editor. All images used in *Appendix 15: The archaeology of The King's School* were supplied by Mike Napthan. Images in the public domain are used under *Creative Commons* licences.

Image	Credit	Location
Aerial photograph, senior school campus, 2015	Chris Wilson	Front Cover
Edgar Tower, 2013	Chris Ham Photography	Title Page
Bust of King Henry VIII, School House, 2007	Associated Architects	Page ii
Matthew Armstrong, 2015	Beth Martyn Smith Photography	Page 1
Number 9 College Green, 2015	Nicholas Dart	Page 1
Detail of ancient doorhandle and keyhole, College Hall, 2014	Nick Stephens (Bright House 1979-84)	Page 3
Conjectural painting of St Mary's Priory c. 1500 by Dr. Pat Hughes	Clive R Haynes	Page 4
Portrait of King Henry VIII by Joos van Cleve, The Royal Collection	luminarium.org (Creative Commons)	Page 6
Cabaret, Theatre, 1990	Tom Bader Photography	Page 14
Les Miserables School Edition, John Moore Theatre, 2012	Joe Singh Photography	Page 14
Elgar Room, Castle House, 2015	Robin Booth	Page 16
Cathedral Choristers, Worcester Cathedral, 2015	Julian Marment Photography	Page 17
Portrait of King Henry VIII by Hans Holbein the Younger, c. 1537	(Creative Commons)	Page 18
Portrait of Thomas Cranmer by Gerlach Flicke, 1545	(Creative Commons)	Page 19
Graham Sutherland's 'Christ in Majesty', Coventry Cathedral, 2012	Jim Linwood (Creative Commons)	Page 19
Western end of College Hall, 2015	Nicholas Dart	Page 24
Entrance to College Hall, 2013	Chris Ham Photography	Page 25
Miniature of Queen Elizabeth by Nicolas Hilliard, c. 1575	(Creative Commons)	Page 26
Portait of Edward Winslow, 1651	(Creative Commons)	Page 28
Art Room in Edgar Tower, c. 1930, Postcard	Marshall, Keene and Co., Sussex	Page 33
Library in Edgar Tower, c. 1990	Tom Bader Photography	Page 33
Norman arches, Edgar Tower, 2014	Nicholas Dart	Page 33
Edgar Tower statuary, 2015	Nicholas Dart	Page 33
'The run of the Cloth or A College Walk' by Maria Caroline Temple, 1870	Trustees of the British Museum	Page 34
Rev. W E Bolland, 1890	Elliott and Fry	Page 48
School House, from the north-west, 1889	Worcester Herald	Page 51
Headmaster's residence, School House, 2015	Nicholas Dart	Page 55
College Green, 1948	Brendan Kerney, Worcester	Page 56
Numbers 2 and 3 College Green, c.1910, Postcard	Walter Scott, Bradford	Page 56
Number 2 College Green from Cathedral tower, 2014	Megan Glenn	Page 56
College Green as seen from the Cathedral tower, 2009	Chris Dobbs	Page 57
Choir House with Ian Brown, 1988	Tom Bader Photography	Page 58
'Three Headmasters' - Opening of Choir House, 2001	Tom Bader Photography	Page 59
The Sixth Form Reading Room, Postcard, c.1920	Marshall, Keene and Co., Sussex	Page 60
The Hostel with Keith Bridges, 1978	Tom Bader Photography	Page 61
Castle House, southern aspect, 2014	Chris Ham Photography	Page 62
Castle House, 2015	Nicholas Dart	Page 63
1899 Classrooms (Biology Block), 2013	Chris Ham Photography	Page 64
Physics Laboratory, 1948	Brendan Kerney, Worcester	Page 65
School House, 1989	Tom Bader Photography	Page 66
School House, from the playground, 1889	Worcester Herald	Page 66
School House, western aspect, 2015	Julian Marment Photography	Page 67
School House, eastern aspect with Long Gallery, 2015	Julian Marment Photography	Page 68
Numbers 10 and 10a College Green, 2015	Nicholas Dart	Page 70
Eliot House, 1986	Tom Bader Photography	Page 70
Number 12 College Green, 2015	Nicholas Dart	Page 71
Number 14 College Green, aerial photograph, 1978	Clive and Malcolm Haynes	Page 71
College House, 1985	Tom Bader Photography	Page 72
Number 15 College Green, from above, 2013	Megan Glenn	Page 73
First World War memorial board, College Hall	John Roslington	Page 83
Great War memorial plaque, St George's Church, Ypres (Belgium), 2014	Adrian Ford	Page 84
Chappel Memorial Room, 2015	Nicholas Dart	Page 91
Creighton Memorial Gardens, aerial photograph, 2015	Chris Wilson	Page 96
Creighton Memorial Gardens, 2015	Nicholas Dart	Page 96
View into Fourth Form Playground, 2015	Nicholas Dart	Page 96
Second World War memorial board, College Hall	John Roslington	Page 102
'The Last Betty', Cathedral Ferry, 1958	H.W. Gwilliam	Page 106
Alec Mackie, C.C.F. cadet, 1951	Alec Mackie	Page 107
Winslow Science Block and Wolfson Building site, 1972	Ian Parkin	Page 123
'Art and CDT Building' concept sketch, 1971	Philip Bedwin, I.D.C. (Special Works)	Page 124

Wolfson Building, 2015	Nicholas Dart	Page 125
Tim Keyes address, King's Day 2014	JDA Media	Page 133
First girls at St Alban's, 1991	Neil Gardner	Page 146
Opening of new building at St Alban's, 1991	Evening News	Page 146
St Alban's playground and rear extension, 1990	Neil Gardner	Page 146
Children in the Pre-Prep Department, King's St Alban's, 2010 (3 images)	Redwing Interactive	Page 148
Hawford Lodge School, 1955	Douglas Garrad	Page 151
Leanne Sheen, King's Hawford, 1990s	Leanne Sheen	Page 152
King's Hawford, aerial photograph, facing south, 2015	Chris Wilson	Page 156
King's Hawford, aerial photograph, facing east, 2015	Chris Wilson	Page 156
Bartholomew Barn at King's Hawford, concept visual, 2014	Associated Architects	Page 157
Aerial photograph, centred on School House, 1985	Andrew Underwood	Page 159
Aerial photograph, centred on Monitors' Lawn, 1985	Andrew Underwood	Page 162
Aerial photograph, centred on Edgar Tower, 1985	Andrew Underwood	Page 162
John Moore Theatre auditorium, 2014	Chris Crosswell	Page 163
Tess of the d'Urbervilles, Theatre, 1998	David Thurlby	Page 163
Les Miserables School Edition, John Moore Theatre, 2003	Chris Crosswell	Page 164
Cinderella, John Moore Theatre, 2004	Roger Plant	Page 165
Jessica Page in *Oliver!*, Theatre, 1996	David Thurlby	Page 168
The Hostel, 1992	Tom Bader Photography	Page 171
Swimming pool 'bubble', 1990	Neil Gardner	Page 176
Girls' IV 1995-1999, 1999	Tom Bader Photography	Page 177
Swimming Pool, 2015	Nicholas Dart	Page 178
Sports Hall, The Keyes Building, 2015	Nicholas Dart	Page 178
1st XV and 1st VII, 2012	Beth Martyn Smith Photography	Page 179
Training in the Michael Baker Boathouse, 2012	Associated Architects	Page 179
Numbers 4, 5 and 6 Castle Place, 2015	Nicholas Dart	Page 183
School Archive exhibition room, Edgar Tower, 2013	Chris Ham Photography	Page 185
Castle Court, 2015	Nicholas Dart	Page 186
The Weston Centre, 2015	Beth Martyn Smith Photography	Page 189
Fourth Form Playground, 2015	Nicholas Dart	Page 190
Library Square, 2015	Nicholas Dart	Page 190
Aerial photographs, senior school campus, 2015	Chris Wilson	Page 191
Entrance to Library from Long Gallery, School House, 2006	Associated Architects	Page 192
Library, School House, 2006	Associated Architects	Page 192
Art School, 2008	Associated Architects	Page 196
King's and Queen's Scholars, 2005	Tom Bader Photography	Page 197
Rev. Dr. Mark Dorsett, King's Day, 2014	JDA Media	Page 199
School Photograph, 2014	Tempest Photography	Page 200
CCF Cadets, 2007	Worcester News	Page 202
Baker family at opening of Michael Baker Boathouse, 2012	Beth Martyn Smith Photography	Page 204
Michael Baker Boathouse, 2012	Associated Architects	Page 205
Teaching Staff, 2014	Tempest Photography	Page 208
Senior Management Team and Governors, 2014	Beth Martyn Smith Photography	Page 211
Support Staff, 2014	Beth Martyn Smith Photography	Page 211
Galen, Irene and James Bartholomew, Hong Kong, 2003	James Bartholomew	Page 212
Senior Management Team 2002-2007, 2007	Tom Bader Photography	Page 212
Health Centre, Choir House courtyard, 2015	Nicholas Dart	Page 214
The Keyes Building, from Severn Street, 2015	Nicholas Dart	Page 215
Original concept image for 'SPACE', 2009	Associated Architects	Page 215
The Weston Centre, The Keyes Building, exterior, 2015	Nicholas Dart	Page 217
Crow Dance Studio, The Keyes Building, 2015	Nicholas Dart	Page 217
Wightman Drama Studio, The Keyes Building, 2015	Beth Martyn Smith Photography	Page 217
Vigornian Room, The Keyes Building, 2015	Nicholas Dart	Page 217
The Weston Centre, The Keyes Building, 2015	Nicholas Dart	Page 217
King's advertisement banner displayed at David Lloyd Worcester, 2014	Clive Yeomans	Page 220
Aerial photograph, senior school campus, 2015	Chris Wilson	Page 224
Aerial photograph, playing fields, 2015	Chris Wilson	Page 224
Matthew Armstrong, 2014	Beth Martyn Smith Photography	Page 225
Southern aspect of Worcester Cathedral, 2015	Julian Marment Photography	Page 228
Headmasters' board, College Hall, 2015	Nicholas Dart	Page 236
Detail of Edgar Tower gates, 2014	Nick Stephens (Bright House 1979-84)	Page 239
Spiral staircase, Edgar Tower, 2014	Nick Stephens (Bright House 1979-84)	Page 240
Detail of Headmaster's chair, College Hall, 2014	Nick Stephens (Bright House 1979-84)	Page 242
Masonry shield above the door of the Chappel Memorial Room, 2014	Nick Stephens (Bright House 1979-84)	Page 249
College Hall as examination room, 2014	Russ Baum	Page 265
Sabrina, Creighton Memorial Gardens, 2014	Nick Stephens (Bright House 1979-84)	Page 265
The Michael Baker Boathouse, 2012	Associated Architects	Page 271
Bust of King Henry VIII, School House, 2007	Associated Architects	Rear Cover

References

Barker, P. & Romain, C. (2001)	*Worcester Cathedral - A Short History*	Herefordshire, Logaston Press.
Bawden, C. (ed.) (2012)	*The King's School Worcester Boat Club Anecdotes and Memoirs*	Worcester, The King's School, Worcester.
Cattermole, P. (1970)	*The Old Chapel Grwynefechan*	Worcester, The King's School, Worcester.
Craze, M. (1972)	*King's School Worcester 1541 - 1971*	Worcester, Ebenezer Baylis and Son.
Craze, M. (1981)	*College Hall Worcester*	Worcester, Printcraft.
Dyer, Alan D (1973)	*The City of Worcester in the sixteenth century*	Leicester, Leicester University Press.
Follett, F. (1951)	*A History of the Worcester Royal Grammar School*	Worcester, Ebenezer Baylis.
Goodge, M. (ed.) (2014)	*British Listed Buildings*	[Available online: **www.britishlistedbuildings.co.uk**. Accessed April 2014].
Gwilliam, H. (1982)	*Severn Ferries and Fords in Worcestershire*	Worcester, N. Milne.
Leach, A. (ed.) (1913)	*Documents Illustrating Early Education in Worcester 685 to 1700*	London, Mitchell Hughes and Clarke.
Macdonald, A. (1936)	*A History of the King's School Worcester*	London, Ernest Benn Limited.
Roslington, C. (ed.) (1998)	*The King's School, Worcester - and a history of its site* (2nd ed.)	Worcester, The King's School, Worcester.
Roslington, C. (ed.) (2009)	*100 Years of the Cadet Corps*	Worcester, The King's School, Worcester.
Roslington, J. (2011)	*A Transcription of the King's School Honours Boards of College Hall, Worcester*	Worcester, J.M. Roslington.
Wheeler, A. (1990)	*Royal Grammar School Worcester 1950 to 1991*	Worcester, Billing & Sons.
University of London (2014)	*British History Online*	[Available online: **www.british-history.ac.uk**. Accessed April 2014].
Unknown (c. 1950-59)	*Worcester Cathedral: Its History, Its Architecture, Its Library Its School*	The British Publishing Company

Bibliography

Berry, A. (ed.) (2012)	*Belmont Abbey - Celebrating 150 Years*	Leominster, Gracewing.
Doyle, R. (ed.) (1995-2009)	*The Order of Saint Benedict*	[Available online: **www.osb.org**. Accessed August 2014].
Dyer, A. (1973)	*The City of Worcester in the sixteenth century*	Leicester, Leicester University Press.
Follett, F. (1951)	*A History of the Worcester Royal Grammar School*	Worcester, Ebenezer Baylis.
Goodge, M. (ed.) (2014)	*British Listed Buildings*	[Available online: **www.britishlistedbuildings.co.uk**. Accessed April 2014].
Griffith, G. (1852)	*The Free Schools of Worcestershire*	London, Charles Gilpin.
Haynes, C. (1996)	*Worcester Within the Walls*	Worcester, Osborne Books.
Hughes, P. & Leech, A. (2011)	*The Story of Worcester*	Herefordshire, Logaston Press.
Knight, K. (ed.) (2012)	*Catholic Encyclopaedia*	[Available online: **www.newadvent.org**. Accessed August 2014].
Leicester, H. (1970)	*Forgotten Worcester*	Worcester, S. R. Publishers.
Leicester, H. (1935)	*Worcester Remembered*	Worcester, Ebenezer Baylis.
Lewis, A. (ed.) (2014)	*Worcester Branch of the Birmingham & Midlands Society for Genealogy and Heraldry*	[Available online: **www.worcesterbmsgh.co.uk**. Accessed August 2014].
Meekings et al (eds.) (1983)	*The Hearth Tax Collectors' Book for Worcester 1678-1680*	Worcester, Worcestershire Historical Society
Plowden, A. (1976)	*The House of Tudor*	London, Weidenfeld & Nicolson
Whitehead, D. (1976)	*The Book of Worcester*	London, Barracuda Books
University of London (2014)	*British History Online*	[Available online: **www.british-history.ac.uk**. Accessed April 2014].
Unknown (c. 1950-59)	*Worcester Cathedral: Its History, Its Architecture, Its Library Its School*	The British Publishing Company